TIME IS OF THE ESSENCE

SUNY series, Studies in the Long Nineteenth Century
Pamela K. Gilbert, editor

TIME IS OF THE ESSENCE

Temporality, Gender, and the New Woman

Patricia Murphy

State University of New York Press

Published by
State University of New York Press, Albany

© 2001 State University of New York

All rights reserved.

Printed in the United States of America

No part of this book may be used or reproduced in any manner whatsoever without written permission. No part of this book may be stored in a retrieval system or transmitted in any form or by any means, including electronic, electrostatic, magnetic tape, mechanical, photocopying, recording, or otherwise without the prior permission in writing of the publisher.

For information, address State University of New York Press, 90 State Street, Suite 700, Albany, NY, 12207

Production by Christine L. Hamel
Marketing by Michael Campochiaro

Library of Congress Cataloging-in-Publication Data

Murphy, Patricia.
    Time is of the essence: temporality, gender, and the New Woman / Patricia Murphy.
       p. cm. — (SUNY series, studies in the long nineteenth century)
       Includes bibliographical references and index.
       ISBN 0-7914-5109-7 — ISBN 0-7914-5110-0 (pbk.)
       1. English fiction—19th century—History and criticism. 2. Feminism and literature—Great Britain—History—19th century. 3. Women and literature—Great Britain—History—19th century. 4. Schreiner, Olive, 1855-1920. Story of an African farm. 5. Hardy, Thomas, 1840-1928. Tess of the d'Urbervilles. 6. Haggard, H. Rider (Henry Rider), 1856-1925. She. 7. Feminist fiction, English—History and criticism. 8. Grand, Sarah—Criticism and interpretation. 9. Caird, Mona. Daughters of Danaus. 10. Sex role in literature. 11. Women in literature. 12. Time in literature. I. Title. II. Series

PR878.F45 M87 2001
823'.809352042—dc21
                                          00-054731
                                          CIP

10 9 8 7 6 5 4 3 2 1

To my parents, for everything,

and to K. Schoenbrod, for ever-wise counsel

Contents

Acknowledgments ix

Chapter 1
Introduction: Victorian Temporality and the New Woman 1

Chapter 2
Buttressing the Binary: Temporal Dichotomies in *She* 31

Chapter 3
Trapping the Female in Time: History and Aesthetics
in *Tess of the d'Urbervilles* 71

Chapter 4
Reinterpreting Evolutionary Development: Feminine
Psychology in *The Beth Book* and *The Heavenly Twins* 109

Chapter 5
Controlling Women's Time: Regulatory Days and
Historical Determinism in *The Daughters of Danaus* 151

Chapter 6
Dissolving the Boundaries: Temporal Subversion in
The Story of an African Farm 189

Afterword: Pointing the Way to Modernist Time 227

Notes 233

Works Cited 259

Index 285

Acknowledgments

The formative stages of this book extend back in time several years to my work on a dissertation. I especially wish to thank Garrett Stewart for his invaluable suggestions, comments, and advice on this project and on the related endeavors it generated. Equally appreciated were his encouragement and enthusiasm, which made the experience enjoyable as well as instructive. I additionally want to thank Florence Boos and Teresa Mangum for their time and energy in reading and responding to versions of the chapters, as well as readers Mary Lou Emery, Sabine Golz, and Kristin Brandser.

I also owe an enormous debt of thanks to two other readers—Heidi Johnson and Dal Liddle—for their careful analysis, insightful feedback, and wonderful suggestions. I cannot thank them enough for the hours they spent in reading each chapter and sharing their ideas. To Heidi I wish to add a special thanks for years of reading, listening, supporting, and amusing.

My thanks go, too, to the anonymous readers of the journals to which I had sent earlier and shorter versions of some chapters and also to the anonymous readers of the State University of New York Press. I am grateful to all for their helpful advice, ideas, and commentary on my efforts. I also wish to thank the journals that published a version of my work—*Victorian Literature and Culture, Studies in English Literature*, and *Style*—and appreciate their allowing me to share it here.

Finally, I want to thank my parents, Sue and Jim Murphy, for their unflagging moral support. To my parents, saying thanks can only begin to show my appreciation for always encouraging me to pursue my interests. I also wish to thank my brother, Jim Murphy, and sister, Sue Roche, for their unfaltering encouragement. To K. Schoenbrod I will be eternally grateful for unfailingly wise advice.

Chapter 1

Introduction:
Victorian Temporality and the New Woman

> [M]an lives in Time, has his whole earthly being, endeavor and destiny shaped for him by Time.
> —Thomas Carlyle, *Sartor Resartus*

> We see nothing of these slow changes in progress [of natural selection], until the hand of time has marked the lapse of ages.
> —Charles Darwin, *On the Origin of Species*

> Is man's time more valuable than woman's?
> —Florence Nightingale, *Cassandra*

> "If you knew Time as well as I do," said the Hatter, "you wouldn't talk about wasting *it*. It's *him*."
> —Lewis Carroll, *Alice's Adventures in Wonderland*

The notion that Victorians were obsessed by both time and gender is not a revolutionary assertion, for the writings of the period unambiguously reveal a fascination with these issues. Yet the existence of a pronounced and vital interrelationship between the two concerns is, perhaps, an unexpected claim to introduce into critical commentary. Feminist critics have turned unprecedented attention in recent years onto the plight of nineteenth-century women, and other scholars have frequently remarked upon the Victorian fascination with time, but the intricate connections between time and gender have remained virtually unexplored. It is my contention, however, that late-century novels responding to the cultural and literary figure of the New Woman import temporal discourses, in subtle but revelatory ways, to illuminate the heightened gender anxieties wrought by this rebellious anomaly. The *fin de siècle* novels that I investigate in the following chapters foreground a latent, but marked, discursive intersection, revealing temporality as a vehicle for reifying a patriarchal order that depended upon rigid gender boundaries to ensure its stability and viability. In effect, time became a covert but potent means of naturalizing repressive definitions of female subjectivity in response to the threatening New Woman. Temporality thus offers not only an enlightening but a crucial approach for examining the formation, inscription, and problematization of gender boundaries in the century's waning decades.

Appearing in an era aptly termed the early modernist period, these "chronocentric" New Woman novels occupied a transitional literary moment, one that both continued the Victorian attentiveness to temporal forces[1] and presaged the modernist disillusionment with an inherited temporal burden. Modernists are often credited with "discovering" time and defamiliarizing it as a cultural construct, but that project began long before D. H. Lawrence, James Joyce, or Virginia Woolf took pen to paper. The novelists responding to the New Woman were the true literary pioneers in probing time's ideological allegiances, specifically through a gendered lens.

Although interrelationships between gender and temporality appear throughout the corpus of New Women novels, I have chosen five writers, avidly read in the *fin de siècle*, whose texts are particularly rich in demonstrating these correspondences. As the following chapters reveal, H. Rider Haggard's novels sensitize us to the ways in which the values associated with time perpetuated the dominant culture and marginalized women. Thomas Hardy's oeuvre reveals history and art as controlling temporal forces through which women were reductively perceived in terms of the body. Sarah Grand's fiction demonstrates the complicity of temporal discourses in naturalizing sex-based presumptions of superiority and inferiority. Mona Caird's prose decries the despotism that time exercised over women in their individual lives and throughout the course of history. Finally, Olive Schreiner's narrative and linguistic experimentation represents an early assault on a masculinized linear form and language. Though all of these novels about the New Woman certainly chart the avenues that modernism would follow, they deserve recognition as far more than mere transitional texts, for they are equally important in their own right as are the iconoclastic novels of the next era.

Even though time and gender individually were prominent subjects of cultural discussion before the end of the nineteenth century, as evidenced in numerous examples of both fictional and nonfictional prose, the two strains of thought tended to converge in early texts only obliquely or infrequently if at all. The insistent intermingling of gender and temporal discourses in *fin de siècle* writings is unique both to the historical moment and the novelistic form, an appropriate confluence when viewed against the absorptions and turbulence of the period. Late-century developments in time-based physical and social sciences, a profound esteem for history and progress, and the expansion of schedule-conscious railways fueled Victorians' temporal acuity, while burgeoning discontent, social upheaval, and sexual uneasiness focused interest on increasingly unstable delineations of femininity.

The widespread nervousness over the Woman Question that had characterized the century thus intensified at its end, primarily through a clash of perspectives on separate spheres, degeneracy, immorality, and feminism. Indeed, as essayist A. G. P. Sykes noted in 1895, "It is not possible to ride by road or rail, to read a review, a magazine or a newspaper, without being continually reminded of . . . the Woman Question" (396). The New Woman was a primary cause of this discursive maelstrom, for she provided a readily identifiable and conveniently localized site for the Victorian discussion about gender roles. Opponents maligned the New Woman for initiating the downfall of civilization; proponents lauded her for attacks on the restraints that kept women from achieving occupational, educational, and behavioral parity with men. The New Woman was perennially steeped in controversy, but she was never ignored. As Olive Schreiner commented in her 1911 feminist treatise *Woman and Labor*, "On every hand she is examined, praised, blamed, . . . ridiculed or deified—but nowhere can it be said, that the phenomenon of her existence is overlooked" (266).

In protesting the female's subordinate position within Victorian society, New Woman advocates implicitly sought to undermine what I term a veritable "natural order of time." Based on prevalent and positive views of history, progress, Christianity, and evolution, this temporal order was constructed by Victorians to cope with the relentless and unnerving pace of change brought by myriad scientific, technological, material, and philosophical developments throughout the century. The boundaries between the four elements of this "natural" order were blurred in the Victorian mind, as each factor influenced the others and gave rise to a seemingly monolithic ideology of time that carried its own set of values. Prominent among them were a sense of modernity, a feeling of superiority over earlier cultures, a confidence in Victorian thought, and an adulation of science as the savior of civilization, as well as a belief in human perfection and the assumption that it had reached its apotheosis in nineteenth-century Britain.

Central to the "natural order of time" was an unspoken but undeniable assumption: the temporal construct was shaped and reinforced by a masculinist perspective. The values associated with this temporal order were all weighted in favor of the males who determined their direction and interpretation, proceeding from a presumption of female inferiority, which, in practical terms, precluded substantive change in women's prospects. Underlying the temporal mythology was the kind of gendered binary that Julia Kristeva articulates in the seminal essay, "Women's Time," a term used to distinguish between a valorized masculine time and a marginalized feminine time. As we shall see, it is in masculine time that history, progress, Christianity, and evolution unfold, contributing to the advance of civilization across the centuries. Seemingly invisible and therefore incontestable to the dominant culture, this masculine temporal order instead was both defamiliarized and attacked by New Woman advocates who sought to identify its complicity, question its reliability, and negate its authority in prescribing a restrictive female role.

The New Woman Debate

The controversy over the New Woman erupted in the periodical press and book-length studies, as well as fiction, with opponents stridently arguing that this revolutionary feminist confused and undermined the natural distinctions between the sexes.[2] These writings, penned by both the abundantly familiar and the utterly obscure, appeared primarily during the 1890s, after the bulk of the New Woman novels themselves had been published. Building on conventional presumptions that women were more emotional, affectionate, sympathetic, and spiritual than men, many antagonists strove to reassert traditional gender roles that relegated women to the domestic sphere. Positivist Frederic Harrison's 1891 musings on the subject typify the dominant view of gender positions:

> We come back to this—that in body, in mind, in feeling, in character, women are by Nature designed to play a different part from men. And all these differences combine to point to a part personal not general, domestic not public, working by direct contact not by remote suggestion, through the imagination more than through the reason, by the heart more than by the head.... That is to say, the sphere in which women act at their highest is the Family, and the side where they are strongest is Affection. The sphere where men act at their highest is in public, in industry, in the service of the State; and the side where men are the strongest, is Activity. Intelligence is common to both, capable in men of more sustained strain, apt in women for more delicate and mobile service. That is to say, the normal and natural work of women is by personal influence within the Home. (447)

Although the New Woman certainly had her defenders in the periodical press, Victorian journals tended to catalog her failings rather than her virtues. One vitriolic critic, novelist and essayist Eliza Lynn Linton, identified this "Wild Woman" as simply "a social insurgent preach[ing] the 'lesson of liberty' broadened into lawlessness and licence" ("Wild Women" 596). Linton excoriated wild women as "[a]ggressive, disturbing, officious, unquiet, rebellious to authority and tyrannous to those whom they can subdue" and claimed they represented "about the most unlovely specimens the sex has yet produced" (604). New Woman advocates, Linton argued, "are doing their best to bring about one of the greatest social and national disasters that could befall us" ("Partisans" 455).

Other Victorian observers echoed Linton's unflattering descriptions of the New Woman. The *Saturday Review* lamented that "the rage now is for women to appear manly and to copy men in all things; and a great mistake it is" ("Manly Women" 757). In the curiously titled *Revolted Woman,* Charles G. Harper contended that the modern female sought to "crucify the male sex" and "aspire to rule him" even though "she has no efficient control over her own hysterical being" (ix). Popular novelist Ouida adopted a similar tone in castigating the New Woman's "fierce vanity, her undigested knowledge, [and] her over-weening estimate of her own value" and in noting that "when the New Woman splutters blistering wrath on mankind she is merely odious and baneful" (615). Sexologist Havelock Ellis remarked that the women's movement would bring massive social changes that "many people would look with dread upon" and consider "as nothing less than a new irruption of barbarians" (*New Spirit* 9).

Many of the New Woman's opponents believed that she was ignoring physiological truths in refusing to accept the "natural" limits on her intellectual development. Darwinian writings, both general and scientific, had argued in the 1870s that women lagged behind men in intellectual development and were destined to remain in their wake, perennially occupying a lower position in evolutionary progression. Anthropologists, sociologists, psychologists, biologists, and physicians all contributed such "objective" findings. Although some of the New Woman's critics adhered to the belief that the female was mentally inferior, others argued in an ostensibly less judgmental way that the sexes simply had different mental traits and reproductive duties, which meant that certain intellectual activities were inappropriate for women to pursue.

In contesting her ordained gender role, detractors claimed, the New Woman not only imperiled the stability of Victorian society, but the future development of the human species. Arguing that women were relegated to their traditional cultural position through physiological and evolutionary determinism, opponents asserted that the New Woman's agenda countered the natural progression of civilization and hampered the female's primary reproductive function. New Women were not devoting the proper attention to their childbearing duties, according to conventional wisdom. Ouida, for example, observed that "[t]he elegant epithet of Cow-woman implies the contempt with which maternity is viewed by the New Woman" (616). Harper ominously wrote of the consequences of such an attitude in an often-quoted remark: "nature, which never contemplated the production of a learned or a muscular woman, will be revenged upon her offspring," he pontificated; New Women ignored "the prospect of peopling the world with stunted and hydrocephalic children" and "the degradation and ultimate extinction of the race" (27).

Educational reform in particular came under fire, as opponents voiced dire predictions about the effects of intensive intellectual work on reproduction, fearing that generations of enfeebled offspring would be the result. As eugenicist Karl Pearson cautioned: "The higher education of women may connote a general intellectual progress for the community, or, on the other hand, a physical degradation of the race, owing to prolonged study having ill effects on woman's child-bearing efficiency" (355). He feared that "in the future the best women will be too highly developed to submit to child-bearing," which boded ill for "the continuation of the species" (374). Biologist and fiction writer Grant Allen mused that women's "training and education should fit them above everything else" for reproduction, "their main function in life" ("Plain Words" 451–

52). Psychologist George Romanes argued that female education should not "run straight athwart [of] the mental differences of the sexes," for attempts to alter women's "complementary" distinctions would "make of woman an unnatural copy of men" and were "certain to fail" (671). Physician Henry Maudsley had helped to establish the negative attitude several years earlier in railing against equality of education, characterizing as "the plain statement of a physiological fact" that women "cannot rebel successfully against the tyranny of their organization" (468). Maudsley addressed his audience in alarmed tones:

> Each sex must develop after its kind; and if education in its fundamental meaning be the external cause to which evolution is the internal answer, if it be the drawing out of the internal qualities of the individual into their highest perfection by the influence of the most fitting external conditions, there must be a difference in the method of education of the two sexes answering to differences in their physical and mental natures.... There is sex in mind and there should be sex in education.
>
> ... [A] proper regard to the physical nature of women means attention given, in their training, to their peculiar functions and to their foreordained work as mothers and nurses of children. Whatever aspirations of an intellectual kind they may have, they cannot be relieved from the performance of those offices so long as it is thought necessary that mankind should continue on earth. (471)

Although Maudsley was both immediately and subsequently criticized— physician Elizabeth Garrett Anderson, for example, noted in the same year of 1874 that a significant aspect of his argument was based on "a *non sequitur*" (584)—Maudsley's reactionary stance offers insight into the presumably scientific assumptions that preceded and informed the *fin de siècle*.

The New Woman's critics also dreaded the effects of her modern ideas upon the institution of marriage. Pearson, though claiming merely to be raising vital issues rather than judging their merits, nevertheless opined that "it is difficult to conceive" that the educated woman would "be prepared to limit her sphere of activity to marriage, or her function in life to child-bearing" (367). Presuming that traditional views of marriage would be "questioned and remoulded by the woman's movement," Pearson added that "there can be little doubt that the cultivated woman of the future will find herself compelled to reject its doctrines" (370). In an article unambiguously titled "The Anti-Marriage League," Margaret

Oliphant castigated novels like Thomas Hardy's *Jude the Obscure* for "displac[ing] love altogether" in their brutal attacks on marriage (144). Janet E. Hogarth analogously decried the "wearisome iteration" with which women writers viewed marriage as "the head and front of society's offending" behavior against them (591).

Part of the reason that the New Woman's critics feared her deleterious effects on marriage was the widespread perception that she was highly sexualized, eager to experiment outside the bonds of wedlock to satisfy unwomanly needs—despite the celibacy of many New Woman characters. The fiction was lambasted for its unflinching treatment of sexuality in countless reviews and essays bemoaning the decay of literary standards. Oliphant, for example, worried that the success of New Woman novels would encourage other writers "to believe that the Shock *quand même* is enough to sell the most trumpery of productions" (145). Edmund Gosse, though paradoxically commenting that "we do not object to the intentions of these revolting women," characterized their work as "giv[ing] us the discomfort which we feel in the presence of loud ill-bred people" (118). Hugh E. M. Stutfield vilified New Woman writers for "literary scavaging" in "refuse-heaps," warning that their "squalid stories" should not be "encouraged" and that their popularity "is not a healthy sign" ("Psychology" 115). "Emancipated woman," he contended, have caused "all the prating of passion, animalism, 'the natural workings of sex,' and so forth, with which we are nauseated" ("Tommyrotics" 836). Hogarth could only express the hope that "sex mania in art and literature can be but a passing phase" (592).

On the other side of the New Woman issue, proponents argued that broad social changes were both indispensable and inevitable to correct a host of inequities. Mona Caird echoed John Stuart Mill in pointing to the enslavement of women in marriage and urged that "marriage and domestic life [be] brought up to the tide-line of general progress" ("Emancipation" 37). Like the New Woman's detractors, Caird and other advocates turned to Darwinian verbiage to link their arguments to evolutionary progression.[3] The human species would suffer, Caird stressed, if women were not allowed to develop intellectually and vocationally, for natural selection would be thwarted ("Phases" 1:42). Sarah Grand insisted that women would continue to lead evolutionary progression through cultivation of their finer instincts, since "[w]omen are farther advanced morally than men, less sunk in sensuality, more ready to respond to ennobling influences" (*Modern Man* 31). Improving the marital state represented a critical phase in human advancement, Grand said, for "it is upon the perfecting of the marriage relation that the upward progress of mankind depends" (29). As A. Amy Bulley declared, women's evolution has "hardly begun"; the woman's movement, she maintained, "can rightly be viewed only as the advance of a wing of the great human army, and therefore intimately related to the movement of the other sections" (1).

To many defenders, the New Woman's agenda for social reform represented an admirable cause, dedicated to improving the lives of both sexes. Rhetoric that presented the New Woman as "a presentment of simulated mannishness," "a monstrosity to be condemned and defeated," "an absurdity to be laughed at," and "an interloper into matters beyond and outside her stereotyped 'sphere'" was simply the creation of "the bigoted and the superficial," insisted Nat Arling (576). For "[t]hose who have an intimate acquaintance with the real new woman," he answered her critics, "she is known as the woman who ... longs to strengthen the cause of right and justice, to make head against evil, to help the fallen, to raise her own sex to the highest level it can attain, and the other to a nobler ideal." Juliette Adam similarly remarked that "it has become a matter of necessity that the activity, the faculties, the influence, the powers of woman should be brought to bear upon the proper adjustment of the social equilibrium" and observed that "[w]oman nowadays is a force, and as a force must find her suitable employ" (526–27). New Women's motives, argued H. E. Harvey, are unfairly questioned, for "those women who dare to make complaint of existing social institutions are told that they wish to overthrow morality and order, and introduce a state of chaos" (196). More rightly, Harvey indicated, since "women have, on the whole, obediently conformed to the character which was required of them for six thousand years or so," they are owed, "at the very least, a fair hearing" of their opinions. In the century's final year, Herbert Jamieson advised Victorians that "the time is only now ripe for a just and cool-headed survey of the situation" (571) and predicted that the New Woman "has only ... to be understood properly, and her admirers will be legion" (572).

Building on conventional views that women's primary duty was to bear and nurture children, many New Woman advocates argued that improving the female condition would better prepare her for this function. As Emma Churchman Hewitt put it, "The 'new' woman with her independence, her clearly defined ideas of right and wrong, her knowledge of the world, and her superior education, is far better fitted to be the mother of noble men" in contrast to "the 'old' woman with her narrow environments and her knowledge, which went little beyond household lore" (337). Grand believed that maintaining "the most perfect ignorance of everything connected with [marriage]" interfered with the maternal education of children, and she condemned as "foolishness" the common notion that "women indiscriminately should undertake the duties of motherhood" ("Modern Girl" 706). Caird similarly pointed to "the tremendous rigor with which maternal duties are pressed upon a woman" ("Emancipation" 33) and claimed that more equitable marital relations would bring the more positive situation of "all children [being] the children of mothers who bore them willingly" (35). Arling voiced the position of many proponents in stressing that "women must and will continue to assert their right to freedom of thought and conduct and they may be trusted" to "do nothing that will ruin their motherliness" (583).

The New Women themselves were as varied as the fictional treatments that charted characters' successes and failures in the more than one-hundred novels published in the 1880s and 1890s.[4] Despite attempts of some Victorian writers to do so, New Women cannot be unproblematically defined in broad terms, even though they did share many concerns and qualities.[5] As recent scholarship has noted, New Women were primarily members of the middle class, yet they differed in assigning priorities and energies to the overall agenda of better educational programs, greater marital rights, and unimpeded entrance into masculine professions. Many New Woman proponents accepted the essentialist designation of masculine or feminine traits, eliding biological sex and gender, but a minority questioned any presumptions of physiologically driven behavioral or intellectual differences. The female characters I discuss in the following chapters demonstrate both the general similarities and particular differences that the term "New Woman" implies.

The Preoccupation with Time

Victorian engrossment in temporality stemmed from a veritable revolution in the way time was theorized during the century, following a plethora of scientific and technological developments that began in the 1830s.[6] Before then, time had been represented as a relatively stable continuum, based on Christian theories of creationism described in the biblical book of Genesis. Under that scenario, the six-day creation of the world culminated in the ultimate event, the birth of humanity in God's own image. In the seventeenth century, one cleric, Bishop Ussher, even attached a date to the beginning of creation, claiming that the process began in 4004 B.C., while another clergyman further clarified that creation started on October 23 at 9:00 a.m. (Altick 98–99). As the *Westminster Review* remarked, "That the 'Creation of the World' took place 4004 years before the Christian era, used to be taught in our schoolboy days as a fact not less certain than that the Norman Conquest took place 1066 years after it" ("Antiquity" 517). Not until Charles Lyell's influential revelations in *Principles of Geology* (1830–33) did geological evidence begin to gain broad acceptance as confirmation that the Earth had originated hundreds of thousands of years before previous estimates. Comparing the immensity of time to that of space, Lyell commented: "We are prepared to find that in *time* also, the confines of the universe lie beyond the reach of mortal ken" (qtd. in Buckley 27).

By the 1850s, Lyell's premise of an enormous span of natural history characterized scientific thought, but the subject took on a particularly startling dimension when archaeological discoveries late in the decade unearthed evidence that dated human origins far earlier than ever imagined. Until these archaeological findings of ancient tools found proof of human presence at the time of long-extinct animals, Lyell could confidently proclaim that human life was of relatively modern origin. As one archaeologist informed the Society of Antiquaries in 1859, however, these striking artifacts pushed back the origins of humanity "remote beyond any [period] of which we have hitherto found traces" (Buckley 28–29). Though some scientists continued to adhere to biblical estimations of a much more recent debut of humanity, Lyell's 1863 publication of the avidly read *Antiquity of Man* converted many Victorians to his view that humans had populated the earth for a hundred thousand years—and some radical thinkers even placed the date considerably earlier (Van Riper 144–56). As the *Saturday Review* opined in evaluating Lyell's book, "[T]he searcher after primaeval Man is as one using an inverted telescope which lengthens as he seeks, and throws the object of his investigation ever farther and farther off" (312). Indeed, the *Westminster Review* said, Lyell's book "can leave no doubt in the mind of any competent and unprejudiced inquirer, that the Human Race must be accredited with an antiquity far higher than is usually admitted" (519). The tool and fossil findings, coupled with Lyell's pronouncements on human antiquity, gave dramatic impetus to the nascent time-based science of anthropology and its constituent branches of archaeology and ethnography, all of which captured the popular as well as the scientific imagination and pervaded cultural discourse.[7]

The virtually coterminous publication of Charles Darwin's explosive *On the Origin of Species* brought additional proof of a vast temporal span, since the workings of natural selection proceeded slowly over millennia. The *Origin,* of course, initiated decades of vituperative debate about the application of natural selection to human development, even though Darwin merely alluded to the connection in his 1859 treatise. Whether advocating or vilifying Darwin's contentions, however, Victorians were perpetually reminded of the workings of time.

Also contributing to the profound interest in temporality was the mid-century discovery of the second law of thermodynamics, which problematized the future rather than the past. The law augured a finite but unidentifiable endpoint of human life, as usable energy was consumed and human time literally came to a stop. Other scientific developments during the century intensified the fascination with time's passage that Lyell and Darwin had initiated. The vital role that time played in geology and evolutionary biology was also identified throughout the physical sciences; astronomy, physics, and mathematics, for instance, emphasized the importance of temporal laws and principles to comprehend the workings of the universe (Buckley 6). Even the new social sciences that arose in the Victorian era and were to gain prominence in coming decades analyzed the effects of time (6).

In raising the prospects of an immeasurable past, uncertain future, and incessant change, scientific findings generated vexing questions about humanity's origins and possibilities that left Victorians uncertain as to their placement within a dizzying temporal span. As Richard D. Altick describes the effect, "The human imagination had to adjust itself to staggering new concepts of time," which "profoundly affected the Victorians' view of their own place in the cosmic sequence" (99). With the biblical version of creationism no longer providing the solace of a stable temporal continuum, Victorians instead sensed that time was a controlling but uncontrollable force. Humans were merely another form of animal life governed by the relentless and unsympathetic process of evolution and the vagaries of change found elsewhere in the physical world.

Along with the scientific advances that accentuated Victorians' consciousness of time were the technological developments—improved machinery to hasten industrial and agricultural production, for example— that shortened the hours needed to perform various tasks. Most significant to an altered perception of temporality, however, was the rapid expansion of the railways with their revolutionary approach to tracking time's passage. In the past, as the British journal *Nature* noted in 1886, time measurement had been a casual affair, with each village setting its own time without considering that a minute hand—if there even was one—could vary substantially in the next hamlet, often by a half-hour or longer (522). As an 1892 *Nature* article explained, "[I]n pre-railway days every town, and every garden large enough to boast a sun-dial, set itself by its own local time" (175). In those days of horse-drawn transportation, the 1886 *Nature* article observed, "minutes were of little importance" (521). Yet any inconsistency in time measurement could cause confusion in a world increasingly dependent on the movements of the train, as an 1841 timetable suggests: "London time . . . is about 4 minutes earlier than Reading time; 5–1/2 minutes before Steventon time; 7–1/2 minutes before Cirencester time; 8 minutes before Chippenham time; and 14 minutes before Bridgewater time" (qtd. in Lawrence Wright 145).

The railways responded to such temporal confusion by attempting to standardize time so that arrivals and departures could be precisely coordinated—a goal that often met with stiff resistance from the populace. Recalcitrant localities deplored "railway-time aggression" (Landes 287), and a certain rail official, fearing that punctuality would become compulsory, even declined a request to furnish information for schedules (Wright 143). Nevertheless, the movement toward uniformity progressed, even leading to the introduction of double-dial watches that kept both local and railway time to accommodate the growing influence of the latter. Midway through the spurt of railway growth between the 1830s and 1850s, rail companies individually standardized time for their own trains, but that simply created a series of uncoordinated railway times (Schivelbusch 43). Eventually, the companies agreed that their own lines would follow Greenwich time—and, indeed, the fact that this English burg offered the universal standard by which the world would set its clocks itself attests to the influence that time was exerting on Victorian life. Resistance to standardized time continued, however. *Nature* captured such sentiments in 1883 by observing that "ordinary business everywhere must for ever be conducted on local . . . time," arguing that "people at large do not care to know by what time-system any railroad manages its trains" and "the best system" would be that uniform time be known only to railway officials (70).

Yet the push for uniformity had much broader effects than simply regulating the trains. Railway timetables indirectly but dramatically altered individual lives by suddenly subjecting once-unregulated events to the clock. As David S. Landes comments in *Revolution in Time*, "Train schedules opened new possibilities for appointments, for work done within time limits, for long-distance comings and goings, hence for ordering of movement and multiplication of activity"; rail riders "found their entire consciousness of time altered by the requirements and opportunities of a railway world" (285). As *Nature* noted in 1892, "Railways have made the uniformity of time within narrow belts of longitude a necessity, and so largely does the railway affect modern civilized life that railway time soon comes to regulate all affairs" (175).

Throughout the century, the growing consciousness of time spurred by the railways and other developments was reflected in a Victorian fascination with timekeeping devices, which was apparent on both a public and individual scale.[8] The 1851 Great Exhibition, for example, "was loud with clocks," as Lawrence Wright observes in *Clockwork Man* (150). Among the horological marvels showcased at this paean to technological development were a half-ton timepiece, which required adjustment in merely 130-year intervals, and the "Alarum Bedstead," which would fling a sleeper who refused to heed the alarm onto the floor by tilting the mattress from which the bedding had first been mechanically stripped (150). Big Ben debuted soon thereafter, symbolizing the public's growing consciousness of time, which was mirrored on a personal level by the proliferation of the affordable pocket watch.[9] Despite their questionable accuracy, watches became a kind of status symbol (Landes 282), sported not only by the wealthy but by a broad cross-section of the populace. Within the British household, the clock became "as much the focus of family life as the hearth itself," Wright asserts, and "a symbol of domestic law and order" (151).

Even the most fundamental activities came under the rule of the clock, causing one twentieth-century historian, Lewis Mumford, to identify it as the "key-machine of the modern industrial age" (14). New importance was placed on the careful measurement of time, and attention was focused on its tiniest units rather than the broad diurnal or even seasonal intervals that previous civilizations had been content to mark. Small wonder, then, that Victorians sensed that time was moving more rapidly as the century progressed, leading Thomas Carlyle to remark in an 1867 essay that "the series of events comes swifter and swifter, at a strange rate; and hastens unexpectedly" ("Shooting Niagara" 300). As Robin Gilmour describes the prevalent mind set, Victorians "were fascinated by time because they were conscious of being its victims" (25). The century, Gilmour explains, became "the age of the memento, the keepsake, the curl of hair cherished in the brooch, the photograph in the locket—all those sentimental stays against the quickening pace of time's erosion."

The "Natural Order of Time"

I turn now to a discussion of the four elements of the "natural order of time"—history, Christianity, progress, and evolutionary theory—to examine their importance, influence, and interrelationship. Perceptions of history offer a logical starting point for this endeavor, since Victorians' new consciousness of history offered a means to impose at least the illusion of control over temporal fluctuation, bewildering change, and troubling questions about humanity's place in the vast reaches of time. Assaults on the biblical version of creation generated by the findings of Lyell, Darwin, and others implied that the universe was governed by chance rather than a beneficent divinity and that humanity held no special role in the relentless process of evolution and natural selection. The Victorian view of history provided an alternative to that bleak scenario in returning humanity to a position of importance over the course of the centuries. Instead of being powerless victims of incessant flux, individuals could view themselves as integral parts of a meaningful historical continuum. As Peter Bowler comments, Victorians were "desperately hoping that history itself might supply the reassurance that could no longer be derived from ancient beliefs" (3).

In effect, nineteenth-century thinkers constructed history as a secularized religion—a "substitute for theology" (3), as Modris Eksteins puts it—that replicated the sense of order, purpose, and meaning in Christian teachings. G. W. F. Hegel, for instance, perceived human history as an ongoing process of spiritual and moral development, governed by reason and following a divine pattern: "the History of the World," he said, thus involved "the carrying out of [God's] plan" (36). In his 1836 lectures on history, as Hans Meyerhoff notes, Hegel suggested that reason could replace faith in interpreting the significance of events (*Philosophy* 7). Carlyle similarly proffered history as religion in the 1841 *On Heroes and Hero Worship* through the cult of the "great men" whom Victorians were urged to venerate.

Not only did the Victorian sense of history confer a measure of stability, but it offered a way to discover eternal "truths." Thomas Arnold, for example, commented early in the century that history is "simply a search where . . . truth seems to be forever more within your grasp" (qtd. in Chapman 19–20), while late-century historian James Froude contended that through history one can understand "moral law" (28). Other prominent writers also suggested that the revelations and lessons of the past provided valuable tools for understanding the nineteenth century. In his 1830 essay "On History," Carlyle urged his contemporaries to "search more and more into the Past . . . as the true fountain of knowledge," through which "the Present and the Future can be interpreted" (89). Thomas Babington Macaulay likewise observed that "we [cannot] fully comprehend any one of these memorable events unless we look at it in connection with those which preceded, and with those which followed it" ("Sir James Mackintosh" 104).

The pivotal role that the Victorian view of history played in shaping the culture has been stressed repeatedly by modern scholars,[10] who have linked the Victorian fascination with the past to a host of trends. The Pre-Raphaelite revival of medievalism, the passion for tracing origins in science and in individual lives, the popularity of historical fiction, and the resurgence of classical, Gothic, and Renaissance styles in art and architecture are but a few examples. Indeed, Victorian historian George Grote mused that "this *historical sense* [is] now so deeply rooted in the modern mind that we find a difficulty in conceiving any people to be without it" (*A History of Greece* 385). An additional sign of the Victorian valuation of the past is that the nineteenth century saw the study of history become an academic and empirical discipline for the first time. Historian H. T. Buckle even blended science with history, for which he is credited by fellow historian J. B. Bury with gaining acceptance for the view that general laws could be applied to the operations of history (311).

For many Victorians, the perception of history as a kind of religion stemmed in large part from questions about the biblical version of time raised by the scientists, rather than about Christianity's basic tenets. Though a few intellectuals rejected religion altogether, other Victorians could valorize history not so much as an alternative to Christianity but as a complement to it, since humanity played a crucial role in both. Furthermore, while many observers called the scientific findings blasphemous, others sought to contextualize geologic or evolutionary theories of time's origins within a Christian framework.[11] Lyell, for example, punctuated his comments about the immensity of time and space in arguing that, regardless of the "direction we pursue our researches, . . . we discover everywhere the clear proofs of a Creative Intelligence, and of His foresight, wisdom, and power" (qtd. in Buckley 27). Even Darwin attempted to dilute the religious implications of the *Origin* in asserting that "I see no good reason why the views given in this volume should shock the religious feelings of any one" (452). As support, he quoted a letter sent to him by a "celebrated author and divine":

> [H]e has gradually learnt to see that it is just as noble a conception
> of the Deity to believe that He created a few original forms capable
> of self-development into other and needful forms, as to believe that
> He required a fresh act of creation to supply the voids caused by
> the action of His laws. (452)

Moreover, the basic model of history that Victorians tended to embrace—the belief that history followed a linear path rather than the cyclical pattern that previous cultures had posited—was itself derived from the Christian theorization of divine history. The Christian view, in turn, represented a dramatic intellectual shift from the beliefs of pagan civilizations, thereby signifying modernity and advanced thought. To understand the implications of the pagan and Christian models, which play an important role in subsequent chapters, a brief chronology of the models' own histories is first necessary.

Classical pagan civilizations, as the writings of both Plato and Aristotle reveal, had assumed that time moved in a perpetual series of repetitions. In *Timaeus*, for example, Plato called time "'a moving image of eternity' [that] incorporates the metaphor of the circularity of motion," while Aristotle similarly argued that time was circular (Patrides 3). Christianity, however, followed a different path, as scholars have noted. Rather than the cyclical model embraced by the ancients, Christianity was predicated on the idea that events are unique and follow a one-way progression through time. Building upon the six-day creation of the world, the Fall, the Incarnation, and the Crucifixion as unrepeatable occurrences, Christian time posited a movement toward a distinct conclusion, the Last Judgment. As Francis C. Haber observes in *The Age of the World,* Christianity's rejection of the ahistorical presumption of a perpetual return was one of its most "revolutionary aspects" (12).[12] Augustine's writings in particular articulated and disseminated this belief in the linear movement of time and history—the "sound doctrine of a rectilinear course" rather than a "false cycle discovered by false and deceitful sages" (qtd. in Whitrow 6)—through which the divine plan unfolded. Unlike pagan creeds, then, Christianity represented a historical religion with its definitive beginning and eventual endpoint.

Yet Christianity itself carried temporal intricacies that late-Victorian fiction often elided. Although Christianity presumes time's unidirectional movement, it also blends into this model a very different conception of time through the importance placed on eternity.[13] As we shall discover, however, *fin de siècle* fiction tended to make definitive distinctions that connected Christianity to linear time and paganism to a more eternalized view of time. In an influential modern study that offers an intriguing perspective for our understanding of late-Victorian novels, Mircea Eliade views the archetypal repetitions of ancient cultures as suggesting attempts to enact an "eternal return" to a privileged mythic time. The societies sought to regenerate themselves through this process, endlessly attempting to bring forth "a new Creation" (52). In so doing, Eliade suggests, pagan cultures could be seen as also seeking to deny history by refusing to accept that events were unique and time was irreversible. These civilizations "regenerated[d] themselves periodically through the annulment of time," evidencing an "antihistorical intent" in the desire to exist in an eternal present (85–86). In *fin de siècle* texts, Christianity—specifically, Protestantism—is virtually equated with historicity and paganism with ahistoricity. Ignored is the contradictory evidence of the ancients' own sense of history in even theorizing cyclical models, in recording the events of the past as early Roman historians did, or in considering the broad spectrum of ancient societies that included cultures incorporating a progressive view of history into their cyclical approaches.

Contributing to this novelistic binarism was the fact that the nineteenth century saw the linear model dominating cultural conceptions of secular history as well as religious thought. Until then, cyclical theories held great influence, particularly before and through the medieval era.[14] As scholarship has also shown, though, perceptions slowly began to change in the Renaissance, spurred in part by Galileo's representation of time as a straight line. Renaissance thinkers would build upon the Christian theorization of history as a sequential movement that conveyed a sense of continuity. Nevertheless, in the sixteenth and seventeenth centuries, as Haber observes, "cyclical ideology survive[d] side by side with the new conceptions of linear progress professed by a Francis Bacon or a Pascal" (*The Study of Time* 395–96). The "scientific revolution of the seventeenth century," however, gave impetus to the linear view, according to G. J. Whitrow in *The Study of Time*; scientific developments shifted "attention away from the past, with its cyclical assumptions, to the future, with its prospect of linear advancement" (10). Yet the cyclical view of time continued to hold sway into the next century. G. B. Vico's 1725 theorization in *New Science* gave resurgence to that model in asserting that the rise and fall of civilizations tended to follow a distinct circular pattern marked by specific phases (Russell 72). Later in the century, though, Enlightenment philosophers encouraged the view that history was progressive rather than repetitive, and the nineteenth century inherited both perceptions.

Robin Gilmour sees the schism reflected in the approaches of the era's two most prominent historians, Carlyle and Macaulay. Carlyle's 1837 *History of the French Revolution*, Gilmour notes, promulgates "a vision of history that is apocalyptic and cyclical," while Macaulay's mid-century *History of England* "is linear and progressive" (32). Although few Victorians adhered to a strict belief in the cyclical model, as Bowler explains, the two views were often synthesized. In that way, civilizations were seen to follow general trends in "growth, maturity and decline" that were "superimposed on the overall ascent of civilization" (11). Nonetheless, a growing confidence that the history of humanity was the history of progress tended to tip the cultural scale in favor of the linear model.

That presumption of progress was, in a sense, another inheritance of Christian thought. In Christian doctrine, progress is manifested by humanity's movement toward eternal spiritual life (Haber, *Age* 11); in the secularized religion of history, progress represents a continual movement toward a more civilized and idyllic state. This belief in progress was a peculiarly modern phenomenon (Buckley 38) that in the Victorian period became widespread. Like the Victorians' new consciousness of history, this confidence can be interpreted as a response to the unsettling changes witnessed during the century.[15] One way for Victorians to come to terms with change was to assume that it portended a general movement toward a better human condition, thereby generating a spirit of optimism rather than despair.

The correlation between change and progress was borne out on a number of fronts. Many Victorians had seen vast improvements in the general living conditions of the populace, despite the social ills produced by an increasingly industrialized culture. As Altick points out, scientific and technological developments implied that humanity was conquering the vagaries of nature and that a host of material advances could be enjoyed in the future. The sense of progress extended to social and moral issues, for Victorians assumed that humanity was moving toward a more perfect state ethically and spiritually as well as materially (107–108). Colonial and imperialist ventures contributed to the faith in progress, since, as Raymond Chapman reminds us, Victorians saw the British empire continually expand in power and territory across the globe (3).

Macaulay's mid-century encomiums did much to foster the belief that Britain was proceeding along a path of prosperity, for he characterized "[t]he history of England [as] emphatically the history of progress" ("Sir

James Mackintosh" 102). He commented, for example, that "great progress goes on" in a "race [that] has hitherto been almost constantly advancing in knowledge" (97); over "the course of seven centuries, the wretched and degraded race have [sic] become the greatest and most highly civilized people that ever the world saw" (103); and "in the course of ages," the British have "become, not only a wiser, but also a kinder people" (*History* 383). Whig perceptions of British history echoed Macaulay's views, stressing a linear pattern of progress from generation to generation. The 1851 Great Exhibition, itself a monument to British advancement, was credited in the official catalog with "seiz[ing] the living scroll of human progress, inscribed with every successive conquest of man's intellect" (562). In a speech marking the event, Prince Albert reinforced this optimistic belief when he noted the "great end, to which, indeed, all history points" (110) as humanity nears the "fulfillment of the great and sacred mission" (111) it must undertake. In the 1851 *Social Statics*, Herbert Spencer similarly argued that "[a]lways towards perfection is the mighty movement—towards a complete development and a more unmixed good" (qtd. in Bury 340), and in an 1857 essay he even proclaimed a law underlying all forms of progress, the "evolution of the simple into the complex" ("Progress" 10).

Moreover, continental philosophy wafted over the English Channel and corroborated the connection between history and progress. Hegel's theorization of history presupposed a teleological pattern, through which the dialectical workings of history brought constant improvements in the moral condition of humanity. Positivist Auguste Comte, whose British sympathizers included John Stuart Mill and Frederic Harrison, viewed history in terms of a three-phase process that proceeded through theological, metaphysical, and scientific stages, each of which represented a progressively higher level of civilization. Defining progress in terms of the intellectual and social developments he assigned to each stage, Comte perceived the movement of history as ultimately leading to a more perfect version of humanity.

Not all nineteenth-century thinkers, of course, viewed progress in the same way that many British optimists did; though the Whig version of history that Macaulay popularized made Britain and progress virtually interchangeable terms, the stirrings of the socialist movement relegated capitalist England to merely an intermediate player on the broad stage of world history. Karl Marx took Hegelian dialectics to a new level in articulating a materialist view of history based on the modes of production—"the basis of all social structure," as Friedrich Engels put it (362)—

whereby capitalism was doomed through inevitable class conflict. Considering capitalism as "the closing chapter of the prehistoric stage of human society" (*A Contribution* 380), Marx, in effect, saw true history commencing only through the abolition of the very system that undergirded the British sense of accomplishment and optimism. In Marxist terms, British society was not only anachronistic but anti-progressive.

Despite dissenting voices like Marx's that rejected the Macaulayan version of progress, this roseate view nevertheless continued to hold sway as the decades passed, surviving relatively unscathed into the 1880s. Even Darwin contributed to the British mythos of advancement, since natural selection implied that life forms "tend to progress towards perfection," according to the conclusion of *The Origin of Species* (459). As Bowler points out, however, the governing principle of Darwin's theory actually undermined the linear pattern of progress that Victorians assumed, for Darwin's approach involved "not a ladder of development but a branching tree" (12). Bowler credits the popularization of natural selection with Darwin's ability to downplay the concept of brachial development in favor of the idea that "a main line of progress" underlay evolutionary changes (135). Instead of suggesting random and disconcerting change ungoverned by a benevolent divinity, natural selection could be interpreted by Darwinians as bringing humanity to a greater state of perfection. The presumption of earlier Victorians that human history followed a teleological path thus was simply updated, not discarded, as evolutionary discourses were shaped by Darwin and his followers to coincide with the dominant faith in progress (135). In George Levine's words, Darwinism could "easily . . . be assimilated to traditional teleology and to its new form, progressivism" (7). Indeed, Darwinism found some teleological analogies in Christianity, notwithstanding critiques of the *Origin* by outraged clergy. As S. G. F. Brandon discusses, the Christian belief that humanity was progressing toward salvation was secularized by Darwinian thinkers (184).

Though Darwin, as Johannes Fabian stresses, "reject[ed] tendencies to read some sort of inner necessity or meaning into the temporal dimension of evolution" (14)—that is, a kind of temporal law governing the evolutionary process—Darwin did underscore the importance of time in allowing the process to unfold:

> The mere lapse of time by itself does nothing, either for or against natural selection. . . . [I]t has been erroneously asserted that the element of time has been assumed by me to play an all-

important part in modifying species, as if all the forms of life were necessarily undergoing change through some innate law. Lapse of time is only so far important, and its importance in this respect is great, that it gives a better chance of beneficial variations arising and of their being selected, accumulated, and fixed. (*Origin* 108)

Darwin's followers, however, seemed to assume that a temporal law was indeed at work, through which the passage of time necessarily brought advancements in civilizations as well as individuals.

As my discussion of these varied aspects of evolution, history, and progress has suggested, Christianity provided a vital underpinning to and unifying philosophy for the elements of the natural order of time. Indeed, the notion that the passage of time could and should be measured stemmed in large part from Christian influence, when monks' need to mark the appropriate moments for prayer led in the medieval period to the invention of the mechanical clock (Whitrow 2), a primitive invention that did not evolve into a truly accurate timepiece until the mid-seventeenth century with the introduction of the pendulum clock (8). Christianity's ubiquitous role in the construction of Victorian temporality is not unexpected, of course, when we consider the overwhelming influence that religious thought carried in the nineteenth century, particularly in the decades preceding the *fin de siècle*. Despite the dissenting voices that challenged the dominant Anglican doctrine during Victoria's reign and contributed to the fragmentation of the Church begun generations earlier, Protestant Christianity in its broadest sense continued to exert extraordinary power over the culture at large. The religious conservatism of the age reinforced the traditional values that the middle class had long embraced, among them the valorized components of the "natural" temporal order.

The positive connotations of Christian teleology, evolutionary theory, history, and progress that we have traced thus far began to diminish as the nineteenth century came to its final decades, however. Confidence in history as a source of guidance for the current generation began to ebb in the late century as Friedrich Nietzsche and others characterized an absorption in the past as unhealthy and anti-progressive. Veneration of history, Nietzsche argued, inhibited necessary and radical changes that would allow individuals and cultures to chart new directions. The belief that England would continue its progress was countered by a gradual recognition that massive poverty, social upheaval, and unrest at home and across the empire equally signaled the possibility of decline. The "motif of doubt," comments Eksteins, "if not dominant, was still strong" (8) in the *fin de siècle*. More and more, Victorians realized that "progress" included, as J. Edward Chamberlin stresses, "a pathology of decay" along with "a logic of growth" (263). T. H. Huxley and his followers warned that natural selection could bring devolution as well as evolution, claiming that it was "an error to imagine that evolution signifies a constant tendency to increased perfection" (199). Biologist E. Ray Lankester cautioned that the "tacit assumption of progress" was "an unreasoning optimism" (15). Max Nordau's *Degeneration* further questioned the notion that humanity was proceeding along a ladder to perfection. These pessimistic views persistently gained supporters, becoming a significant aspect of cultural discourse as the century drew to a close. As my forthcoming chapters will suggest, some of the most intriguing manifestations of those negative perceptions would appear in novels about the New Woman.

Gendered Time

The preceding review of the four components of the natural order of time leads to the important observation I alluded to in my opening remarks: the Victorian temporal order carried not only the prevalent positive, and dissenting negative, connotations examined thus far, but crucial gender-charged valuations as well. Victorian perceptions of the natural order of time inconspicuously but emphatically stemmed from intrinsic masculinist biases that served to bolster inflexible gender boundaries.[16] In British culture, for example, it was the male who was perceived to determine the course of history and whose accomplishments furthered the cause of progress.[17] In Christianity it was the male who served as prophet, priest, and typological precursor of Christ. In Darwinian theory it was the male, specifically the white European male, who represented the most advanced specimen in the human developmental chain. Class- and race-specific as well as masculinist, the Victorian construction of temporality represented the time that governed the social order, the time that tracked the men who dominated the system, the time that influenced standards in the political, religious, scientific, and literary arenas. Those individuals who were not members of the British power base were, in effect, disassociated from its time.[18] The irony, of course, is that this view of the masculine temporal order prevailed in a century dominated by a queen, yet perhaps we can explain this oddity in light of the British ruling structure being firmly controlled by its male ministers and parliamentarians.

In the following chapters, I argue that a gendered binary shapes Victorian appraisals of temporality in the *fin de siècle* fiction I analyze, with the privileged element of the dyad denoting those aspects identified with the British male.[19] Although these novels hint at the complexity of Victorian perceptions of time that threaded through the broader cultural discourse, the texts tend to proceed from a rather reductive stance in adopting a more unproblematic binary economy as a means of reinforcing or undermining gender roles. The rich network that formed the cultural construction of time—with its nuances, intricacies, and inconsistencies—thus is manipulated and often simplified in late-Victorian fiction to conform to the texts' ideological matrixes. As a result, we see the novels attempting to inscribe or erase binarisms that, for example, align the male with history and the female with ahistoricity; the male with intellectual acuity and the female with mental deficiency, based on Darwinian presumptions; the male with progressive civilization and the female with stultifying primitivism; or the male with Christianity and the female with paganism.

Among these gendered pairings, that of Christianity and paganism necessitates further comment here to inform my analysis in subsequent chapters. This dyad stems, to some extent, from the perceived biblical justification for the marginalization of women that is both applauded and challenged in the fiction. In effect, Christianity becomes a marker of a character's participation in patriarchy, whereas paganism becomes a sign of one's Otherness to it. We see this strategy operating especially in the novels of H. Rider Haggard and Thomas Hardy, which attempt to demarcate an impermeable boundary between male Christianity and female paganism; conversely, in Olive Schreiner's fiction, that boundary is immediately problematized, as the text's central male character reveals an ambivalent relationship to Christianity and the patriarchal order it represents.

The gendered opposition between Christianity and paganism further translates into a novelistic distinction between a privileged linear model and an unprivileged cyclical model of history. A male character's association with linear time becomes a marker of progress, civilization, and modernity, whereas a female character's connection to cyclical time represents stasis, chaos, and anachronism. Male characters are identified with an acute historical consciousness, and female characters are positioned as virtually oblivious to and removed from history—in effect, the fiction suggests, ahistorical. As Christina Crosby asserts, "nineteenth century 'history' is produced as man's truth, ... which in turn requires that 'women' be outside history"—that is, "'[w]omen' are the unhistorical other of history" (1). I adopt the terms "historical" and "ahistorical" in my discussion rather than, say, "synchronicity" and "asynchronicity," because the former pair of terms conveys a more severe judgment on female characters that the texts strive to make; females are not simply presented as slightly at odds with the rhythms of history but utterly insignificant and Other to them.

There were, of course, dissents to the view that history implied a masculinized teleology, most notably in the anthropological arena. An early theorist, J. J. Bachofen, in the 1860s posited the existence of a matriarchal era antecedent to patriarchy. In this formulation, as Elizabeth Fee notes, "the female fertility principle had been glorified," although women were associated with materiality and men with spirituality (27). Matriarchy, however, was viewed by Bachofen as an interim phase in social evolution, replaced by a patriarchal structure characterized by what Fee terms "more abstract 'masculine' values" as opposed to "concrete 'feminine' ones" (28). Despite such qualifications, Bachofen's theory tended to be a minority view with, as Fee remarks, its "obvious absurdities given what every Victorian knew about the eternal nature of woman," such as the notion of women exercising complete control over offspring (27-28). Another anthropologist, Fee points out, "cleansed Bachofen's theory of the unseemly notion of matriarchal power" (30), and the discipline emphasized that "patriarchalism was . . . inextricably linked with the progress of civilization" (38). As Rosalind Coward explains in *Patriarchal Precedents*, the latter part of the century saw intense controversy over such issues as the power dynamics inherent in matriarchal and patriarchal societies, which she links to the emergence of feminism (9–10). Because theories like Bachofen's implied not simply matrilineal descent but also female authority, later anthropologists labored to separate the two issues, which enabled these theorists to argue that men enjoyed political dominance even in matrilineal societies (53). By the *fin de siècle*, then, the notion of a female authority and influence on historical progression had been widely discredited, and the course of history could be viewed more comfortably as directed by males rather than females. We will return to this matter in examining H. Rider Haggard's *She*, for it builds upon late-century views that saw matriarchal societies as primitive stages in the evolutionary process.

Along with the assumptions about societal progression to patriarchal culture, the issue of individual evolution took on significant gender overtones in this Darwinian age. Darwin's theories in the 1871 *Descent of Man and Selection in Relation to Sex* lent credence to the belief that women were primitive manifestations of an ongoing process that reached its apotheosis in the white male. Women would perennially evidence the stunted mental powers of children, "the lower races" (587), and barbaric civilizations rather than the advanced cognitive capabilities demonstrated by white males. Asserting that "[m]an is more powerful in body and mind than woman" (620), Darwin identified numerous characteristics that set the sexes apart. Males are "more courageous, pugnacious, and energetic," while they demonstrate "more inventive genius" than females (580). Women, in contrast, reveal the lesser faculties of "intuition, of rapid perception, and perhaps of imitation" (587). As will become apparent in my chapter on Sarah Grand's fiction, Darwin's perceptions of sex-based differences in evolutionary development carried enormous repercussions for the New Woman struggling to overturn widespread cultural presumptions of female inferiority.

In drawing their discrete categories of gendered time, the late-century novels remind us of the similar distinctions articulated in Julia Kristeva's essay, "Women's Time." Building from Friedrich Nietzsche's theorization of cursive time, which she designates as "the time of linear history," and monumental time, which "englobes these supranatural, sociocultural ensembles within even larger entities" (14), Kristeva confers essentialist designations on these temporal modes. In Kristeva's formulation, masculine temporality signifies the linear, advanced, and orderly, while feminine temporality suggests the cyclic and chaotic. Linear time represents "time as project, teleology, . . . and prospective unfolding"; it is "time as departure, progression, and arrival—in other words, the time of history," which "is inherent in the logical and ontological values of any given civilization" (17). Since linear time is associated with the course of history, traditionally determined by males in Western culture, this temporal dimension is "readily labeled masculine" (18). As Alice Jardine explains in her introduction to Kristeva's essay, "History is linked to the *cogito*, to the paternal function, representation, meaning, denotation, sign, syntax, narration, and so forth" (8).

In contrast, Kristeva argues, feminine time seems to be inextricable from female subjectivity, which "retains *repetition* and *eternity* from among the multiple modalities of time" known through the centuries (16). The term "women's time" involves two components: the cyclical time that conforms to nature through gestation, regularity, and biological rhythms; and the monumental time that evokes infinity through its affiliation with myth, mysticism, and the cosmos.

> On the one hand, there are cycles, gestation, the eternal recurrence of a biological rhythm which conforms to that of nature and imposes a temporality whose stereotyping may shock, but whose regularity and unison with what is experienced as extrasubjective time, cosmic time, occasion vertiginous visions and unnameable *jouissance*. On the other hand, and perhaps as a consequence, there is the massive presence of a monumental temporality, without cleavage or escape, which has so little to do with linear time (which passes) that the very word "temporality" hardly fits: All encompassing and infinite like imaginary space. (16)

The presumption of masculine and feminine time may seem hopelessly essentialist to us as modern critics accustomed to distinguishing between biological sex and gender, but it is important to consider temporality as late-Victorian novels constructed it. Thus, my project is to explore, not endorse, this temporal ideology. I invoke Kristeva's assessments of masculine and feminine time repeatedly in subsequent chapters because her theory offers such a helpful starting point for investigating the gendered underpinnings and implications of the novels' temporal maneuvers. Kristeva's approach does not seamlessly apply in every particular to the late-century fiction I address, of course, but the model does offer a fascinating and remarkably useful perspective for evaluating the temporal undertones of Victorian gender roles.

Although it may appear, at first glance, curiously paradoxical to draw upon an essentialist theoretical paradigm in a study that foregrounds the social construction of gender, the novels are responding to a discursive cultural framework that was itself based upon essentialist presumptions. Whether supporting or disputing those assumptions, the texts necessarily must address them. Because Victorian culture tended to elide sex and gender, a theoretical approach that calls attention to essentialist preconceptions offers, in my view, a valuable means of assessing gender construction in the *fin de siècle*. For that reason I also turn to other theoretical models, particularly those of Luce Irigaray and Hélène Cixous, that similarly inform both the essentialist and deconstructive aspects of the novels' thematic, linguistic, and structural moves.

In light of the fulsome attention given to gender in Victorian thought, it is perhaps a reasonable assumption that the novelists I address could be said to view femininity and masculinity in accordance with their own gender status. We would expect, then, that male authors would reinforce conventional gender roles and female novelists would assail them. Yet we also see complications in making such a sweeping generalization. For instance, the fiction of H. Rider Haggard destabilizes gender boundaries even as it struggles to inscribe them, Sarah Grand's novels are predicated on a troubling essentialism, and Thomas Hardy's fiction reveals a measure of ambivalence about gender roles. Nevertheless, a correspondence between authorial gender and attitudes about femininity and masculinity does, to a large extent, obtain in the novels I analyze, which perhaps seems a logical bias when we consider the particular and distinct perspectives that an author's own life experiences as a Victorian male or female would provide. This is not to say, of course, that male authors cannot proceed from a feminist stance in their writings or female authors from an antifeminist position, as some Victorian writers did.

Even though I characterize the Victorian temporal construct as a specifically masculine order, I view gender in the broad sense that modern critics favor in claiming, as Anne McClintock does, that gender is inextricably connected to categories of class and race. The marginalization of Victorian women parallels a similar strategy operating on the racial or working-class Other, whether male or female. Perceptions of time provided a useful vehicle for furthering this project. As Fabian argues in describing time as an ideological tool, "there is no knowledge of the Other which is not also a temporal, [as well as a] historical, a political act" (1). In effect, a culture's construction of time offers a means of demonstrating difference, whether measured by sex, socioeconomic status, or racial origin. Time thus becomes an "instrument of power" in Fabian's terms and underscores the distance between an individual identified with modernity and a lesser "mirror image" associated with archaism (144). In Victorian culture, as McClintock similarly asserts, a gendered "national time" shaped views of women, working classes, and colonized races; "[w]omen were not seen as inhabiting history proper" but instead "a permanently anterior time," in contrast to "[w]hite, middle-class men" who seemed "to embody the forward-thrusting agency of national progress" (359–60).[20] Though I certainly agree with critics who stress that gender, class, and race are closely linked in any discussion of Victorian ideology, my aim in this study is to cull those aspects of the construction of time that most tellingly affect women in general and the New Woman in particular.

My rationale for addressing issues of class and race only briefly as they inform gender concerns stems from two pertinent factors about the New Woman. First, in regard to class status, these females, as noted earlier, tended to come from the same rank—that is, the middle class. Even those New Women who enjoyed upper-class status, such as Sarah Grand's Angelica in *The Heavenly Twins*, shared the gender-based anxieties and experiences of their middle-class counterparts. Though Thomas Hardy's Tess, the central figure in my chapter on his fiction, is undoubtedly a lower-class character, she represents not a New Woman but a lesson, in effect, for rebellious females. Like Grand's aristocratic heroine, Tess serves as a warning that women, regardless of class status, are always already perceived in terms of an enduring female essence that limits their potentialities.

Second, my reasoning for limiting my study in terms of race again devolves from the particular background of the New Woman—the white Englishwoman, or in Olive Schreiner's case, the white South African woman. Although the racial Other experienced similar forms of disempowerment and disdain as the New Woman, there was an important difference seen between them. As Antoinette Burton explains in her discussion of Victorian female activists, these individuals frequently sought to separate themselves from and elevate themselves above the stereotypical female colonial of the British empire. In so doing, Burton comments, British women endeavored to craft a self-construction that allied them with the masculine projects of empire and nationhood, employing "contrasting evidence of their own cultural superiority and female agency" (8) to distance themselves from the colonial female Other. For that reason, I see fiction responding to the New Woman as worthy of study as a distinct entity, rather than unproblematically grouping her among other oppressed women across the empire.

I begin my analysis of New Woman novels in the second chapter with Haggard's 1887 *She*, a best-selling quest romance that persistently attempts to use time to solidify gender binaries by adopting all four main components of the natural order of time. In so doing, the text serves as a useful foil for later examinations of novels that aim to interrogate those gender divisions. The third chapter focuses on Hardy's 1891 *Tess of the d'Urbervilles,* the clearest and most important example of time's gender ramifications in the ongoing master narrative about time that characterizes his work as a whole. The next chapter explores Sarah Grand's popular novels, *The Beth Book* and *The Heavenly Twins*, which contest the Darwinian psychologists' most basic assumptions to position women within an evolutionary vanguard rather than rearguard. Mona Caird's 1894 *The Daughters of Danaus* offers us a way in the fifth chapter to assess both the broad theoretical implications of time and its minutely practical applications. Olive Schreiner's 1883 *The Story of an African Farm* concludes my discussion of the novels with its intriguing approach for unsettling gendered notions of time both narratologically and linguistically. In each chapter, I also address other texts in the writer's late-century oeuvre to elucidate further the temporal strategies at work in the fiction that is my central concern. Let us turn, then, to the fiction itself.

Chapter 2

Buttressing the Binary: Temporal Dichotomies in *She*

> Good and evil, love and hate, night and day, sweet and bitter, man and woman, heaven above and the earth beneath—all these things are necessary, one to the other.
> —Haggard, *She*

This epigraph provides a succinct summary of a crucial strategy at work in H. Rider Haggard's 1887 best-seller *She:* the construction of gendered binarisms that position women in general and the New Woman in particular as not only the lesser term in the opposition, but a disturbingly sinister one as well.[1] Though other male quest romances follow a similar approach in establishing a binary framework through which a nineteenth-century male is privileged at the expense of a female counterpart, *She* locates this dyad in an especially complex register by means of an intricate series of temporally based oppositions. Through these temporal moves, *She* aligns its British male travelers with a valorized model of a masculinized linear time and simultaneously maligns She-who-must-be-obeyed by associating her with the negative connotations of a feminized monumental and cyclical time. In so doing, *She* unmasks its avatar of the New Woman as an adulterating female essence who threatens the integrity of gender roles and the stability of Victorian culture.[2]

Even though the term "New Woman" did not enter the British lexicon until the mid-1890s, it is nevertheless an appropriate one to adopt in assessing Haggard's text, for the appellation reflects the heightened debate over the Woman Question and burgeoning anxieties over gender roles that characterized the 1880s as well as the following decade. Like its generic followers, *She* captures the discursive strains prevalent in late-century Britain, revealing an uneasiness with and rehearsing the rhetoric against the transgressive female who so vocally contested the inflexible gender roles characteristic of the period. Although critics have argued that *She*, like other male quest romances, denounces the New Woman while pursuing the primary goal of furthering imperialist initiatives,[3] the central role performed by temporal discourses in this misogynistic project has remained unexplored. *She* derives much of its ideological force, however, by manipulating cultural conceptions of time to articulate its nervousness over the potential slippage between gender roles that the New Woman so ominously portended.[4]

The text's positioning of linear time as a signifier of "the good" conforms to the gendered "natural order of time" theorized in my opening chapter. Through this temporal construct, as we saw, linear time connotes the positive masculinist values of history, progress, Christianity, and evolutionary advancement, all of which *She* marshals to conduct its ideological work. Monumental and cyclical time, by contrast, evoke the ahistoric, mythic, pagan, and devolutionary traits associated with female subjectivity and immutable essence. Through these temporal conceptions, *She* offers a deceptive proposition: the civilizing projects of linear time are the exclusive, superior, and predestined province of the male; procreative and nurturant functions are biological and temperamental markers of the lesser female. Inferentially, any woman who attempts to appropriate the temporal prerogatives of the male violates a natural division of the sexes.

The essentialist portrait of Woman in *She* also gains texture from the strokes used to create similar pictures of racial Otherness. Postcolonial theorists have frequently noted the similarity between gender and racial discourses, and *She* imports the latter in part to reinforce its binary structure. As Abdul R. JanMohamed argues in observing the multiform alterity that colonialist fiction displaced onto depictions of non-Europeans, such narratives "fetishize a nondialectical, fixed opposition between the self and the native" (65). Seeking "naïve solutions" that tend to conclude with the textual expulsion of the bothersome Other, these narratives "substitut[e] natural or generic categories for those that are socially or ideologically determined" and thereby transform "all specificity and difference into a magical essence" (67). The Manichaean relationship that JanMohamed identifies is especially pertinent to *She*, since the text follows a similar approach with gender, manipulating colonialist discourses to solidify the sex-based binary. If, as Toril Moi argues, a patriarchal perception of women as marginal situates them on a "frontier between man and chaos," the repercussions of a transgression of gender boundaries become alarmingly clear: because women "seem to recede into and merge with the chaos of the outside" (167), they obscure the boundaries that separate not only the sexes but classes and races as well.

As poststructural and postcolonial theorists have reminded us, however, narratives like *She* that vaunt the ideology of the dominant culture evidence their own discursive fissures even as they seek to occlude such weaknesses. The epigraph to this chapter suggests such an intrinsic gender instability in including among its chain of opposed terms—good and evil, love and hate, sweet and bitter, man and woman, heaven and earth—a signifying pair that reverses the privileging of the first and otherwise masculine element of the binaries. Rather than designating the anomalous coupling as "day and night," the text transposes the order of the terms, hinting at the impossibility of attempts to obviate the pressures working against a prevalent discourse. Though suppressed, contradictory discourses are as unavoidably present in Haggard's textual microcosm as in the culture at large. Nevertheless, *She* attempts to conceal its ideological rifts through diligent efforts to establish layers of interlocking binarisms designed to naturalize and reinforce the gender assumptions the text validates. Even though the novel reveals the fragility and periodic collapse of those oppositions, *She* attempts to deny such inconsistencies by ultimately annihilating its potent anti-heroine and applauding the restoration of order that such a tidy closure represents.

The authorial choice of a quest romance helps to further *She*'s overall project of eliding gender instabilities in favor of strict demarcations between masculinity and femininity. Unlike the novels we will encounter in subsequent chapters, which could be broadly characterized as realist New Woman texts, Haggard's *fin de siècle* fiction depends upon the conventions of romance to pursue its agenda. As Northrop Frye has noted, romance offers a means of escape from the nettlesome complexities of everyday life, simplifying troubling ambiguities by recasting them into reductive confrontations between good and evil (195). Haggard's own definition of romance in his autobiography suggests that the goal of such fiction is to produce an uncomplicated picture of the world in which, "[a]bove all, no obscurity should be allowed" (*Days* 2:92). Quest romances allow readers to participate in the kind of "wish-fulfilment dream" that Frye attributes to the genre through a "search for some kind of imaginative golden age" (186).

Frye's definition of romance further offers a useful formulation for our analysis of *She* in that "all the reader's values are bound up with the hero" (187). In *She*, the dual heroes of the English adventurers take on the larger cultural role of the New Woman's opponents, and their presumed values—courage, adventurousness, Christian virtues, determination, perseverance, and the like—are all mustered to confront and undermine the threatening She. The "ideological plasticity" that Wendy R. Katz attributes to the quest romance's perceptions of empire thus extends to the genre's treatment of gender as well, for the form in this respect can likewise "be controlled and manipulated so easily that it can be made to do the romancer's ideological bidding" (44–45)—in *She*'s case, employing temporal binarisms as part of the novel's overall strategy of condemning the New Woman.

Valorized and Masculinized History

The novel begins to construct its binary layers in the initial paragraph by juxtaposing history and ahistoricity, the main binarism operating in *She*. In the introductory statement tracing the genesis of the manuscript he has been asked to publish, the "editor" opens the novel with a remark laced with telling clues to *She*'s determined efforts to align history with masculinity, credibility, and consequentiality:

> In giving to the world the record of what, looked at as an adventure only, is I suppose one of the most wonderful and mysterious experiences ever undergone by mortal men, I feel it incumbent on me to explain what my exact connection with it is. And so I may as well say at once that I am not the narrator but only the editor of this extraordinary history, and then go on to tell how it found its way into my hands. (1)

Though the use of a frame narrative to establish a story's verisimilitude is not an unusual approach, *She*'s version is immediately remarkable for its extreme concern with believability. Of special interest in the quoted passage are the multiple insinuative signifiers of authenticity and authority that position the forthcoming account as an "extraordinary history"—resonating with the novel's subtitle as a "History of Adventure"—rather than merely an entertaining yarn. As a "record" of events "giv[en] to the world," the manuscript assumes the status of a historical document, presumably entitling it to be included among the reams of British archives. The narrator's explanation of the manuscript's origins establishes a provenance of sorts that can attest to the document's validity and the veracity of the story to unfold. Included in the passage are insistent reminders of the editor's attentiveness to detail, as if such precision is itself evidence of the reliability of the history he will present. The opening passage of the novel serves, then, as both a prehistory and a classificatory gesture, positioning a narrative that could be considered a fanciful tale as a true report analogous to other factual records that would be evoked in the mind of the implied reader: a male consumer of the quest romance, as critics have noted, who is immersed in a culture marked by an acute historical consciousness and a fascination with origins.

The tale's status as history is not merely signaled but accentuated when the narrative focus shifts to the letter that accompanies the manuscript sent by its pseudonymous author, L. Horace Holly. Repeatedly invoking the word "history" to describe his narrative and urging the editor to maintain its *"bona fides"* (4), Holly both emphasizes the truthfulness of this "real African adventure" (3) and elevates his text to the status of a document, as did its editor. Holly, however, enhances the manuscript's significance by claiming that the account properly belongs in the public sphere rather than in the private, where he would have preferred it remain unknown until his death. Indeed, Holly remarks that "it has become a question whether we are justified in withholding [the manuscript] from the world . . . merely because our private life is involved" (4). The manuscript undergoes a subtle but decisive change in import through this statement, for its publication is no longer a matter of preference but duty; refusal to share it becomes tantamount to denying the world a crucial chapter of history.

As in the editor's opening remarks, Holly's letter stresses the manuscript's accuracy and consequence, particularly in the missive's concluding paragraphs:

> "And now what am I to say further? I really do not know beyond once more repeating that everything is described in the accompanying manuscript exactly as it happened.
> . . . "[Y]ou will, we believe, have the credit of presenting to the world the most wonderful history, as distinguished from romance, that its records can show. Read the manuscript (which I have

copied out fairly for your benefit)...
"Believe me." (4)

The reiterations of authenticity have become compulsive in this passage. There is, for example, nothing "to say further" because the sole point to be conveyed is the document's truthfulness; Holly's "history" is again firmly distinguished from "romance" through "its records"; and the admonition to "believe me" is the parting phrase. A less overt indication of credibility emerges in the penultimate sentence with Holly's remark that he has "copied out [the manuscript] fairly," for his adverb suggests exact transcription and conjures the image of a medieval scribe meticulously replicating the annals of history for future generations.

The final evidentiary claim presented in the frame narrative to underscore the manuscript's status as a historical record comes as the editor returns to his introductory remarks. Again, the editor focuses on the believability of the account, but he seemingly elevates the document to a biblical standard of truth in advising the proper readerly perspective. In his autobiography, Haggard views the Bible as a historical account to be accepted literally, implicitly arguing against allegorical interpretation since the events it chronicles "took place substantially as they are recorded" (2:240). Similarly, the editor suggests that Holly's narrative be read as history rather than allegory:

> At first I was inclined to believe that this history of a woman on whom, clothed in the majesty of her almost endless years, the shadow of Eternity itself lay like the dark wing of Night, was some gigantic allegory of which I could not catch the meaning. Then I thought that it might be a bold attempt to portray the possible results of practical immortality.... But as I went on I abandoned that idea also. To me the story seems to bear the stamp of truth upon its face. (5)

Appropriately, the novel truly commences after the frame narrative with Leo Vincey's twenty-fifth birthday, the "date this strange... history really begins" (22). In marking a coming of age, the birthday represents Leo's symbolic entrance into the patriarchal order and thus provides a logical narrative origin because of the gender valence of history as the record of men's actions through time. Leo's suitability as a participant in that structure is ratified by his extensive patrilineal heritage, detailed by his dying father as he arranges for Holly to become the young Leo's surrogate father. Leo's assumption of the Vincey legacy two decades later thus adds yet another link in an ancestral chain traced through male descendants, with only an occasional reference to a wife.[5] In the catalog of forebears Leo's father tracks across some sixty-five generations to Kallikrates, a priest of the Egyptian goddess Isis, the paternal figures seem to generate and preserve the line virtually unaided; women are mentioned only in fleeting allusions to Kallikrates's wife, Amenartas, and to Leo's unnamed mother. Yet even those maternal roles are minimized. Amenartas serves as a vehicle for "bearing a child" to safety (11), a choice of phrasing that signals her primary function as a maternal receptacle, while incidentally invoking the historical authority of Aristotle, with his similar supposition; moreover, Leo's mother has apparently died in childbirth, leaving Vincey to arrange for his son's upbringing without female interference. The male attentiveness to the linear time of history imparted in Vincey's detailed recapitulation of ancestry—reminiscent of the genealogical emphasis of the Bible, the ultimate patriarchal narrative—is conveyed in more immediate terms as well: the ailing Vincey punctuates his request that Holly adopt Leo with the repeated phrase, "I have no time" (12).

To reinforce the masculine affiliations of history in Vincey's monologue, the novel relegates the task of recuperating the past exclusively to male interpreters. In a chapter that incessantly calls attention to the linear movement of history and its shaping through the actions of men—suggestively titled "The Years Roll By"—the significance of Leo's heritage is gleaned from layers of ancient texts secreted in a silver "casket," a noun choice that connotes death to serve as an additional reminder of linear time. Further suggesting the masculine tenor of history are Vincey's connections to the linear time that underlies it: he informs Holly of his imminent death "in a few hours," with "the journey done, the little game played out" (14); he speaks to his son "from the unutterable silence of the grave" (27); and he intends to "put a period" to his sufferings through suicide, tacitly reiterating the connection between masculinity and textuality. Transmitting the Word of the Father through a letter accompanying the array of documents, Vincey ensures that influence over the family history is paternally determined through his appropriation of the word of the original mother. The legend inscribed on an ancient potsherd by Amenartas, calling for vengeance upon Ayesha by future generations, is translated by Vincey; his words therefore direct the interpretation and shade the nuances of her text, one that presumably has been firmly in male control since it was passed to him by his own father. Texts, and the family history they delineate, thus are effectually male-authored; Vincey can influence both the reading of the past and the direction of the future course of that history by instructing the next generation "through this link of pen and paper" (27).

These texts—Vincey's letter and the potsherd it "rewrites"—are but two of the documents found in the opening chapters that confer a gender designation on history and establish the written word as a male province. Accompanying the textual package Leo inherits are the official male-inscribed documents that properly consign it to him: a circumlocutory Dickensian letter whose "utter unintelligibility" guarantees its legality (18), a duly executed will drawn up by Vincey's lawyers, and a doctor's certificate attesting to Vincey's death. The effect of these documents, like Holly's earlier request to the editor urging publication of his manuscript, is to move private life into the public sphere so that male personal experience becomes the basis of historical record.

This supposition is borne out by the many documents contained within the casket that translate the sherd into several languages and record Vincey responses spanning two millennia to the call for vengeance against She. Representing each major period in Western culture, as critics have remarked,[6] these texts blend personal and public history, for Vincey males take part in major events of each era through the family's residence in ancient Egypt, a migration to early Rome, a journey with Charlemagne, and service in the Crusades. The private literally melds with the public in these entries, since several of the signatories are names Holly recognizes from "history and other records" (37). Written in a host of classical learned languages—uncial and cursive Greek, medieval black-letter Latin, and Old English, all of which are graphically reproduced in the pages of *She* itself—the Vincey history is exclusionary not only because it is limited to the actions of its prominent men, but also because the languages that preserve it would be accessible only to an educated man. As a result, Vincey history belongs solely to its male descendants, who alone would have the education and expertise to inscribe and translate family records over the centuries. Even Holly—a surrogate Vincey, as Leo's adoptive father—holds such credentials; a Cambridge fellow immersed in a community of overwhelmingly male scholars in this notable seat of Western learning, Holly is uniquely poised to analyze the historical record Vincey bequeaths to his son.[7]

The inference to be drawn, of course, is that all significant events in Western culture proceed from the male, reminding us of Hélène Cixous's claim that "[h]istory has never produced or recorded anything else [than phallocentrism]" ("Sorties" 83). Even the scarab that accompanies the casket of documents suggests the masculine tone of history with its symbol of Ra, the sun god, and the repetition of this homonym for "son" in the scarab's translation, which identifies its owner as "the Royal Son of Ra or the Sun" (26). A woman's tangential participation in that history places her in a double bind, as Amenartas's fate reveals, for she is either a vessel whose words are expropriated and reinterpreted or a potentially disruptive source of inaccuracy. As Vincey equivocates in his letter, Amenartas's story is "the greatest mystery in the world" or "an idle fable, originating in the first place in a woman's disordered brain" (29).

The preoccupation with historicity and historiography that marks the novel's early chapters seems even more pronounced when measured against authorial preparations and cultural responses. Haggard's desire for historical verisimilitude is evidenced by his exhaustive efforts to demonstrate a scholarly attention to detail and authenticity. The Greek translation of the sherd was penned by Haggard's former master, whom he identifies as "one of the best Greek scholars of the day" (*Days* 1:251); the black-letter Latin and Old English transcriptions were produced by "a very great authority on monkish Latin and mediaeval English" (252); and "an elaborate sherd" copied from "a genuine antique" by Haggard and his sister-in-law to illustrate the six-shilling Longmans version of the novel was so effectively reproduced, Haggard boasts, that "a great expert" could remark only that "it might *possibly* have been forged" (248).[8]

Not surprisingly, several parodic treatments of *She* respond to the novel's excessive interest in historiographic paraphernalia and scholarly trappings. Andrew Lang's 1887 *He* includes mock footnotes that identify absurd historical, textual, etymological, and orthographical references. The author, for instance, glosses the comment that "no woman can curse with a daric" with the conjecture that use of the word "daric" means a certain ancestor "lived under the Persian Empire. There or thereabouts" (23). With comparable aplomb, the editor responds to the publisher's skepticism that a pharaoh's daughter settled in Ireland with the claim that "it is in all the Irish histories," instructing him to "[s]ee Lady Wilde's *Ancient Legends of Ireland*, if you don't believe me" (16).[9] Advising the reader to refer to *"The Mark of Cain* [Arrowsmith]," which he recommends as an "excellent shillingsworth," the unabashedly commercial editor causes the publisher to complain, "Is this not 'log rolling'?" (12). Replying to the publisher's query about the accuracy of "walri" as a plural form, the editor grumbles that he "can't find walrus in the Latin dictionary nor anything else beginning with W somehow, but it *seems* all right" (42-

43). Asked if the story refers to "the quivering footsteps" of the "Dawn" rather than the "Don," the editor querulously counters that "[e]very Oxford man knows what I mean" (32).

Throughout the parody, the editor and publisher acridly but hilariously debate whether the text's elaborate descriptions and references are overwrought. In one heated exchange, for instance, the publisher questions whether the lengthy discussion of hieroglyphics is not "a little steep" (16) or "a little dull," since "[t]he public don't care about dead languages" (15). Despite the editor's claim that the "[s]tory can't possibly get on without" these additions, since "[y]ou *must* have something of this sort in a romance" (15), the publisher interjects such admonitions as, "Don't keep hammer hammering [sic] away at Greek! This is a boy's book, not a holiday task, this is!" (34). The parody similarly targets the self-conscious scholarship of *She* with an absurd reproduction of an ancient sherd rendered in typographical gibberish, the discussion of which rapidly disintegrates into a pun on pi, a term designating a jumble of printing types, and the Leo character's claim that "pie or no pie, I love it like pie, and I've broken the crust" (20).

Such a frivolous tone, however, can be attributed to the parody's transposition of gender designations in converting Leo and Holly into Leonora and Polly; thus, it is the notion of female scholarship that becomes the object of ridicule, not the interest in historiography itself. That interpretation gains credence when other popular parodic versions, such as John De Morgan's 1887 *He* and G. F. Forrest's 1905 *Misfits* chapter on "The Deathless Queen," are examined, since neither mocks the scholarly approach of Haggard's text. Although such restraint is not maintained in other parodies, the attention accorded to Haggard's academic accouterments in all cases foregrounds *She*'s emphasis on representing itself as a historical and verifiable record.

Short parodies, such as *Punch*'s amusing version by "Walter Weird" (5 Dec. 1889), tended to go for the quick laugh, and *She*'s historical baggage offered an easy target. The *Punch* version—one of several that the publication produced—features "Unredd," a writer, and "Spoylpaperos," a sketcher, who find an odd scroll filled with a hodgepodge of languages, including a fragment "that might be antediluvian Irish." Even a voice speaks in hieroglyphics, which Unredd deciphers as "You be blowed?"—a correct assumption, since the utterer "gravely inclined its head." An earlier *Punch* effort (26 Feb. 1887) made much of Vincey's narrative of ancestry, which the parody describes as "a long incoherent story" told by an inebriated "Winkle," who is either the "sixty-sixth or six hundred and sixty-sixth" descendant (100). His tale originates with "Killikrankie," identified as a "[c]hap at Isis—hic!—priest, you know," who apparently "quarrel[ed] with a lady of theatrical tastes." Among his descendants is one who traveled with "Champagne," which perhaps inspired another descendant to "ma[k]e a fortune in beer," a product that Winkle apparently has enjoyed greatly. The textual version of Winkle's story, written on a "pot of pomatum," or pomade, is dismissed as merely "the same incoherent story that poor Winkle had tried to tell me with his head resting in the coal-scuttle." As in the other parodies, the mere fact that *Punch* satirizes *She* so excessively for its historiography points to the novel's obsessive interest in the workings, implications, and consciousness of history, as well as the text's efforts to construct history.

She as Ahistorical Woman

Returning to *She* brings us from the absurdity of the parodies to the solemnity that Haggard accorded to history, even in regard to Ayesha, the bizarre She. In stark contrast to the overdetermined connection between masculinity and historicity established in the opening chapter, however, She is remarkable for a dearth of historical acuity. As a self-described "very woman" (199)—merely "an intensified woman," according to the *Saturday Review* (44)—She is emblematic of all women in her obliviousness to and distance from historical developments. Though Ayesha is aware of events in the long-distant past, the novel chooses to ignore this aspect of historical consciousness; instead, the text equates historicity with a recognition of the progression of Western civilization—knowledge that Ayesha lacks, since she is unaware of critical events marking Western history. In contrast, she has insulated herself in a static world where the passage from the classical societies of Egypt and Greece to the dawn of Christianity is unknown, as an interrogation of Holly intimates:

> "[A]nd there is yet an Egypt? And what Pharaoh sits upon the throne? . . .
> . . . [I]s there still a Greece?
> . . . The Hebrews, are they yet at Jerusalem? And does the Temple that the wise king built stand, and if so, what God do they worship therein? Is their Messiah come, of whom they preached so

> much and prophesied so loudly, and doth He rule the earth?
> ... Ah, thou canst speak the Latin tongue, too! ... It hath a strange ring in my ears after all these days, and it seems to me that thy accent does not fall as the Romans put it. ... Knowest thou Greek also?"
> "Yes, oh queen, and something of Hebrew, but not to speak them well. They are all dead languages now." (146–48)

Posing her queries in an archaic phraseology whose form is as revealing of ahistoricity as its content, She aligns herself with the remote past through her facility with the tongues that Holly, as an avatar of modernity, designates as "dead languages now." Despite an acquaintance with such ancient languages, Holly nevertheless evidences a telling distinction from the more fluent She in not "speak[ing] them well" and in betraying the semantic alterations occurring through the centuries that confer upon his replies an unfamiliar accent. As the linguistic distinction between the two speakers reveals, only Holly is identified with the diachronic movement of history.

Parodic interest in this passage, specifically in Lang's *He*, suggests that the distinction drawn in *She* between historicity and ahistoricity represented a cultural touchstone. In Lang's version, the disembodied voice of "He-who-was-mummied"—another amusing gender switch that illustrates a carnivalesque world in which women are the explorers and men the explored—asks such absurd questions as, "Who sitteth on the throne of Hokey, Pokey, Winky Wum, the Monarch of the Anthropophagi?" (63). These questions, which reveal that He "had been for a considerable time out of the range of the daily papers," baffle his servant, "Pellmelli," and can be answered only by Polly. The reference to the "daily papers," although a humorous aside, nevertheless associates an attentiveness to history with modernity, a significant connection in the Victorian mind.

Both *She* and the parody incorporate a culturally formed binarism through which historicity signified a civilized superiority opposed to a primitive inferiority. Ignorance of history served as a kind of *prima facie* evidence that one also denied history and instead sought to return to the notion of cyclical temporality discredited by many nineteenth-century theorists. As Mircea Eliade explains in another context that illuminates *She*'s ideological leanings, refusal to accept oneself as a historical entity perpetuates the illusion that one exists in an eternal present; acceptance of oneself as "a historical man" represents the marker of "modern man," one "who consciously and voluntarily creates history" (141).[10] Ayesha thus becomes a mere anachronism, bound to the outmoded thought processes of the ancients with their advocation of a cyclical model of history, whereas the British adventurers perceive the linear progression of the past from the appropriate perspective of the present.

The gender overtones that *She* brings to the binarism emerge in a telling passage:

> How was it possible that I, a rational man, not unacquainted with the leading scientific facts of our history, and hitherto an absolute and utter disbeliever in all the hocus-pocus that in Europe goes by the name of the supernatural, could believe that I had within the last few minutes been engaged in conversation with a woman two thousand and odd years old? ... It must be a hoax, and yet, if it were a hoax, what was I to make of it? What, too, was to be said ... of the woman's extraordinary acquaintance with the remote past, and her ignorance, or apparent ignorance, of any subsequent history? What, too, of her wonderful and awful loveliness? This, at any rate, was a patent fact, and beyond the experience of the world. (158)

In the opening sentence, masculinity is linked to reason, history, and knowledge in a tight metonymic chain as Holly attempts to apply logistic tools to derive a plausible explanation for "hocus-pocus," a particularly loaded noun in this context. Besides denoting trickery and magical incantation, the term carries a connotative hint of Otherness, since in Europe the concept would be labeled by the less judgmental word "supernatural." Situating Holly as the subject dubiously pondering an indecipherable object elevates him above an Other allied with phantasm, nescience, and exoticism. As a trafficker in "patent fact," Holly in his self-addressed queries foregrounds She's resistance to classification—the late-Victorian scientific technique that could illuminate her "extraordinary acquaintance" with an occlusive past by precisely locating her within a historical continuum.

Ayesha is also consigned to a devalued eternal present through her paradoxical "awful loveliness." The phrase yokes the wondrous yet disturbing implications of her immunity from the somatic markers of time, distinguishing her from the male protagonists who bear such traces throughout the text. Elsewhere depicted and indicted as an unchanging essence who manifests, for example, a "beauty [that] endures even as I endure," Ayesha belies the supposition that "woman's loveliness . . . passes like a flower" (154). In contrast, Leo experiences temporal alterations, since "[t]he child grew into the boy, and the boy into the young man, as one by one the remorseless years flew by" (20); his father's countenance, once "a beautiful face," displays the ravages of time, since "disease had wrecked it" (14); and Holly's appearance, though only slightly transformed during a quarter-century, nevertheless reflects "some modification" (8). Ayesha's unmarked body thus serves as damning evidence as much as enviable immutability: it exposes her imperviousness to the linear time that ushers in the changes determining the course of history.

Further condemning the ahistoric Ayesha is her affiliation with "degenerate" non-European cultures. In identifying her Arabian background, *She* connects Ayesha to the racial Other constructed through the Victorian conception of Orientalism. Edward Said has pointed to Orientalism's binary underpinnings, with its presumption of Western superiority fortified by the specular image of Eastern inferiority, which created a widely accepted matrix for interpreting and homogenizing cultural differences.[11] Defining Orientalism as "a style of thought based upon an ontological and epistemological distinction" that assumed an unbridgeable chasm between East and West (2), Said credits it with creating "one of [the] deepest and most recurring images of the Other" (1)—a perspective especially in evidence in *She*.

Most pertinent to my discussion, however, is the assumption of Oriental immutability. Theorized as an isolated psychic and physical terrain, the Orient represented a "static system of 'synchronic essentialism'" (240) that stood in striking contrast to the putatively progressive movement of British life. In *She*, the Oriental separation from history is transposed onto ancient Kôr's unchangeability across centuries. She's first glimpse of it two thousand years earlier, for example, revealed it "even as it is now" (179). In effect, the novel situates She and her subjects in the kind of eternal present that Johannes Fabian theorizes with anthropology's temporal construction of the Other. Under that model, the "savage . . . lives in another Time" (27), through which this "referent" is "removed from the present of the speaking/writing subject" (143). In that way, Other societies become the "negative mirror images" (144) that oppose stasis to progress.

She's ahistoricity is also informed by the careful distinction Orientalists drew between contemporary and classic non-European civilizations, appraising the former as an inferior manifestation of the latter. As mapped onto *She*, the dichotomy emerges through the substantive difference in the relationships that Ayesha and Leo hold to ancient cultures. Ayesha is allied with the vitiated and isolated descendants of once-noble Arabic societies through her rule over the Amahagger, despite a recognition of her subjects' barbarism. The Amahagger have regressed to the cannibalistic and other primitive practices of earlier civilizations, which is mirrored in a linguistic deterioration: Ayesha laments that the Amahagger have "debased and defiled" the "purity" of the ancient language once her "own dear tongue," compelling her to converse "in what is to me another tongue" (146). Leo, however, is doubly linked with the advanced civilizations that initiated Western history as the descendant of an Egyptian priest of Greek extraction living in the time of the pharaohs—authorial choices of ethnicity that build upon the Victorian veneration of the classical world.[12] As monarch of Kôr, which chronologically and developmentally predated the civilization of Leo's Egyptian forefather, Ayesha represents a culture that not only has fallen into ruins but lacks any pretensions to historical pedigree, since its Amahagger descendants are merely "a bastard brood of the mighty sons of Kôr" (181).[13] If, as Darwinian social theorists postulated, civilizations progressed along an evolutionary continuum, then the Amahagger apparently followed a separate and doomed path from the Egyptian cousins who shared their Kôr ancestors, thus holding only a tenuous connection with Kallikrates's historically vital culture. Ayesha's association with the Amahagger separates this emblem of Woman even further from the shaping of Western history—indeed, the Amahagger do not even speak of their origins (89)—and relegates her to the margins of that process.

Though Ayesha's ahistoricity separates her from linear time, she is further divorced from it through an essentialist connection with motherhood. Identified with cyclical time through the processes of nature and with monumental time through the perpetuation of life across the centuries, motherhood is twice removed from linear temporality. Motherhood presented a vexing double bind for the New Woman: adherence to this proper Victorian role relegated her to the stifling private sphere, while a resistance to or reinterpretation of that role transformed her into a disruptive anomaly. *She* responds to the latter choice, arguing that the New Woman's venturesome departures from her appointed function make her unfit for motherhood and jeopardize the continuation of the human species—frequent charges leveled against feminist proponents at the *fin de siècle*, as I discussed in my opening chapter.

Most indicative of the New Woman's perversion of the maternal role are Ayesha's eugenic experiments upon her hapless attendants, whom she selectively breeds as mutes to propagate "the safest of servants" (154). Particularly disquieting is her decidedly unmaternal Darwinian detachment from her creations, for she views them with the disinterested eye of a scientist observing natural selection in process:

> I bred them so—it hath taken many centuries and much trouble; but at last I have triumphed. Once I succeeded before, but the race was too ugly, so I let it die away; but now, as thou seest, they are otherwise. Once, too, I reared a race of giants, but after a while Nature would no more of it, and it died away. (154)

Absent from Ayesha's reflections is any nurturant or protective sentiment that the normative Victorian mother would display. Moreover, as the passage implies, Ayesha's experimentation is a violation not only of woman's "nature," but also of the force of nature itself.

The relationship with nature evidences a degree of ideological pliancy in the novel, serving as a slippery signifier of both female essence and unseemly power. In the first regard, *She* builds upon nature's traditional and judgmental designation as female Otherness. Margaret Homans's appraisal of Wordsworthian influence is especially germane here, since she identifies "feminization of nature [as] the most obvious example of sexual polarization in the literary tradition" (13). Of particular significance is the notion that nature, as Cixous has argued in her Derridean rupture of sex-based binarisms, is specifically opposed to history in a gender economy. The nature/history dichotomy mirrors the "dualist and hierarchical" divisions of gender that Cixous similarly locates in other pairings, since this opposition juxtaposes "immobility/inertia to the march of progress, terrain trod by the masculine footstep" ("Castration" 44). Nature, then, provides an ideal foil for the historically attuned explorers in *She*, building upon the gendered distinction the text has elsewhere drawn between historicity and ahistoricity.

In the second regard, however, Ayesha reveals an unsettling bond with and manipulation of nature, designating herself as one "who know[s] the secrets of the earth and its riches, and can turn all things to my uses" (150). That capability is given a decidedly adverse connotation when her denial of its likeness with the sinister practice of magic instead becomes a virtual syntactic equation: "there is no such thing as magic, though there is such a thing as understanding and applying the forces which are in Nature" (194). Lang's parody of *She* similarly suggests that Ayesha's disclaimer is a distinction without a difference. Though insisting that there is "no magic," but merely "a little knowledge" of nature's secrets, He-who-was-mummied paradoxically proceeds to attempt a magic trick (73). Moreover, Lang's *He* suggests that the exercise of such power is an explicitly male prerogative, since this "stately Magician" (70) who reads *Modern Magic* (68) practiced centuries earlier at the Court of Ptolemy Patriarchus (93).

Also consigning nature to a negative register is the distinction Haggard himself draws in his autobiography between natural and divine law, which offers a clarifying perspective on nature's role in *She*:

> [T]he laws of Nature differ from the laws of God as these are revealed to us (and we must follow the higher Light)—a fact from which I am sometimes tempted to argue that Nature, "red in tooth and claw," is not begotten of God alone. Surely the powers called Satan and Death have had a hand in its makings. (2:255–56)

Not only does nature take on satanic overtones in *She* as Ayesha manipulates its forces, but it also works against late-century theories of nature as changeable and vibrant. When ideologically useful, *She* suspends its Darwinian allegiances and resurrects the Hegelian conception of nature prevalent earlier in the century to further the novel's indictment of the New Woman. In his theorization of history, Hegel opposed the endless reproduction of nature to the non-repetitive quality of history, applauding the latter for its novelty and emancipation from a return of the same (Eliade 90). Applied to *She*, the Hegelian binary reinforces the valorization of linear time, since the shiftings of history suggest a purposeful dialectic contributing to human advancement in contrast to nature's unproductive iterations of a stagnant past.

An intertextual aside further points to Haggard's ideological manipulation of nature, in this instance conflating it with motherhood in demonstrating the New Woman's menacing iconoclasm. Initially, nature and maternity are approvingly blended in the 1889 *Cleopatra* through the characterization of Isis as "the Divine Mother of whom all nature is" (27), a "[h]oly" (23) and "Universal Mother" (29). Soon, however, Isis takes on the qualities associated with the "bold harlot" Cleopatra (34), a New Woman figure described as "Woman the Destroyer" (8). In fact, the difference between the two puissant females becomes virtually indistinguishable when Cleopatra identifies herself as "Isis come to earth" (57). Satanic resonances position Isis as a false god who—much like the New Woman—has exceeded her appropriate role, evidenced by her periodic switches between meek female and diabolic presence. Descending to her altar from a dark cloud, for instance, Isis reveals herself as a "fiery serpent" (29) whose "forky tongue" metamorphoses into a "sweet" feminine voice (30). Temporal and biblical references further come into play to stress that Isis has usurped the Christian divinity's role. Like God, Isis is a "Measurer of Time" who was "born of Nothingness" and thus a "Creatrix uncreated" (29); a "Vessel of Life, from whom all Life is, to whom it again is gathered" (29); and an imitator of "heavenly accents" (30) who speaks from a cloud in a disembodied voice, as did the Old Testament God addressing his faithful subjects. Like the New Woman, such references insist, she has overstepped her boundaries.

Paganism Versus Christianity

Ayesha's multiple manifestations of womanhood—her ahistoricity as well as her affiliations with motherhood and nature, however problematic—lead us to a related and crucial opposition permeating the text. That binarism situates She as the "essence of Paganism," in the words of *Murray's Magazine*, in condemnatory contrast to the British explorers as Christian faithful. The temporal connection emerges from the dichotomy we have just explored: the ancient pagans' presumed lack of historical consciousness and their belief that events recurred in a cyclical pattern differed dramatically from the Christian concept of history and the presumption that experience can be mapped onto an irreversible teleological path. In opposing She to Christianity, the text further separates her from the linear temporality underlying the broader natural order of time theorized in my first chapter, since religion, like historicity, is one of this order's integral components. Ayesha is set in opposition to that temporal order with each heathen tenet she imparts, each sacrilegious action she performs, and each proof of virtual immortality she conveys.

In marked contrast to the recreant Ayesha, frequent allusions to religious dogma and pertinent biblical quotations associate Leo and Holly with a Victorian version of the true faith, as does their connection with the linear time underlying Christian teleology that Holly specifically notes:

> [T]he mind wearies easily when it strives to grapple with the Infinite, and to trace the footsteps of the Almighty as he strides from sphere to sphere, or deduce His purpose from His works. ... Here the lot of man born of the flesh is but to endure midst toil and tribulation ... and when the tragedy is played out, and his hour comes to perish, to pass humbly whither he knows not. (117–18)

Signifiers of linearity punctuate the passage to differentiate human mortality from divine infinitude. The human "tragedy" that "is played out" invokes the customary dramatic form in which sequential emplotment expires in a definitive conclusion. Humanity is "born of the flesh," a noun choice that stresses the finite limits on somatic endurance. The reference to the "hour" in which one "comes to perish" not only directs attention to a discrete unit of linear time, but also hints of a progressive movement toward death and willing participation in, rather than defiant resistance to, the divine plan.

As a "practically immortal" being (120), however, Ayesha inhabits the cosmic time of the Christian divinity. Like Him, she can "see without eyes and hear without ears" (84). Yet the difference between them, as references to the Christian God elsewhere reveal, is one of good versus evil. Religiosity intersects with gender in this Manichaean relationship through Christianity's traditional designation as a male-ruled province. In conflating woman with heathenism, *She* builds upon an extant religious discourse that maintains Christianity as an exclusionary patriarchal institution, perpetuating the misogynistic perspective traceable to biblical writings. Ayesha, as the representation of all women, thus can claim no right to power. In effect, She becomes a female Lucifer figure—even Job, the Englishmen's ignorant servant, perceives Ayesha's resemblance to "the old gentleman," a euphemism for Satan (245)—whose hubris will bring retribution from a righteous and vengeful God.[14]

The text's many depictions of Ayesha in satanic terms support this interpretation. Like Lucifer, the bringer of light, She emits "a supernatural radiance" that distinguishes her from any "merely mortal woman" (158); yet her "almost angelic rapture" is superficial, since it can rapidly dissolve into "the very reverse of angelic" (201). With her resemblance to a serpent—indeed, at one point she "half hissed, throwing back her head like a snake about to strike" (156)—Ayesha is exposed as a deviant divinity in this common late-century metaphor for the New Woman:[15]

> [M]y eyes travelled up her form, . . . instinct with a life that was more than life, and with a certain serpent-like grace that was more than human. . . . About the waist her white kirtle was fastened by a double-headed snake of solid gold. . . . I have heard of the beauty of celestial beings, now I saw it; only this beauty, with all its awful loveliness and purity, was *evil*. . . . Never before had I guessed what beauty made sublime could be—and yet, the sublimity was a dark one—the glory was not all of heaven—though none the less was it glorious. (155)

The passage is saturated with overdetermined yet paradoxical references to She's diabolism to mirror Lucifer's twin qualities of magnificence and maleficence. The yoking of "serpent-like" and "grace" defiles the latter as the currency of salvation; not merely a snake—a long-standing trope of demonized female sexuality—but a "double-headed" one forms She's belt, crafted of the lustrous metal traditionally chosen for sacred vessels and symbols; and the modifier "awful," with its medieval meaning of "dreadful" undercutting the word's other connotation of "majestic," imposes a sinister cast upon terms ("loveliness and purity") frequently employed to depict saintly or Marian figures.

The coupling of beauty with sublimity complicates the Burkean distinction between the two conditions, uneasily blending the splendor and harmony attributed to the beautiful to the overpowering emotion and vague terror indicative of the sublime. Contributing to the tension emanating from opposition is the troubling quality of Ayesha's "glory," a term conventionally accompanying references to the Christian divinity in a host of biblical passages and devotional supplications; indeed, the "glory of God" constitutes a lengthy *OED* listing under the common noun. Ayesha's "glory," however, defies exegesis, for it can be defined only by negation as a "glory [that] was not all of heaven." The passage's play between light and dark, created through such images as the coruscant gold of Ayesha's kirtle and the dark sublimity of her beauty, produces an unsettling chiaroscuro that blurs the binary to present She as the locus of both desire and disdain.

Such examples typify the abundant religious inversions that construct She as a female antichrist. Like William Morris's late-century "Hill of Venus" in *The Earthly Paradise* and Algernon Charles Swinburne's "Anactoria," for example, *She* adopts the medieval literary practice of twisting religious references into blasphemous revisions, using the trope to demonize obstreperous female figures. Female potency, such inversions imply, reverses the natural order that rightly relegates women to a posture of submission. As a practitioner of "unholy rites" (164), She appropriates and profanes Christian liturgy, most revealingly in her adaptation of the baptismal ceremony. Although mimetic of an ecclesiastical chamber, the curtained alcove in which She has placed her version of a baptismal font is tainted by Oriental sensuality, as Holly's description reveals:

> I entered, shuddering. This woman was very terrible. Within the curtains was a recess, about twelve feet by ten, and in the recess

was a couch and a table whereon stood fruit and sparkling water. By it, at its end, was a vessel like a font cut in carved stone, also full of pure water.... The place was softly lit with lamps... and the air and curtains were laden with a subtle perfume. Perfume too seemed to emanate from the glorious hair and white-clinging vestments of *She* herself. (145–46)

The setting resembles a seraglio with its concealing curtains, inviting couch, luxurious fruit, and provocative scent. Numerology contributes to the blasphemous picture, since the alcove's dimensions coincide with the Christian measurements of perfection (twelve, indicative of the dimensions of heaven) and obedience (ten, the number of the Commandments). Sacerdotally but sacrilegiously garbed in erotic "white-clinging vestments," She assumes the role of the priest for which she is trebly unsuited as a pagan, a woman, and a sensualist. Ayesha sullies the baptismal apparatus not only in placing its simulacrum in such an unseemly chamber, but also in employing it to gain inappropriate knowledge, raising unearthly visions upon the vessel's pure surface. In effect, She appropriates both the Law and the Word of the Father in her assumption of omnipotence.

Similarly, She's self-immersion in fire to attain virtual immortality defiles the baptismal purpose of entering into a purified state. Designated as "the place of Life" (250), with its telling capitalization suggesting the honorific form accorded references to divinity, the fire resembles the sacred font in which nascent Christians entered a "living bath" (290): Ayesha lifts the fire "as though it were water" to "pour it over her head" (292). Yet her baptismal ritual is intended not as a means to serve God but instead to become God, for from the fire one "come[s] forth glorified, as no man ever was before" (250). Ayesha wields the quasi-divine power she attained in ancient times through this blasphemous baptism conducted in imitation and defiance of the Christian God with a control over life and death, as evidenced by her resurrectional effect upon Leo (199), and by her conveyance of the mummified Kallikrates from "[d]ust to dust" (240). Like a deviant example of religious iconography, She's "awesome power seemed to visibly shine about her like a halo, or rather the glow from some unseen light" (174). Ayesha becomes a sacrilegious idol who not only establishes herself as a false god, but in so doing, tempts a faithful Christian into damnation: an overwhelmed Holly later asserts that he would risk his "immortal soul" to remain with the creature whom he "worshipped... as never woman was worshipped" (190).

A brief discussion of Haggard's 1895 *Elissa; or The Doom of Zimbabwe* informs the rigid binarism that *She* creates in its treatment of Christianity and paganism. Although written after *She*, *Elissa* forms part of Haggard's misogynistic master narrative, retrospectively illuminating the gender dichotomies traced in the 1887 novel. A virtually unknown Haggard text, *Elissa* has escaped nearly all critical and bibliographic attention. Set in southeast Africa a thousand years before the birth of Christ, the novel offers an entirely Old Testament twist on *She*. Though similarly counterpoising a heathen female and devout males, *Elissa* depends upon this opposition even more insistently through the centrality of idolatrous resonances to the workings of the plot.

The title character is a priestess of the "she-devil" Baaltis, a deity so perfidious that adherence to her "abominable creed" was deemed "a scandal... even in the ancient world" (55). Her very name, an echo of the pagan god Baal, recalls the biblical condemnation of the semitic deity's worshippers (Judges 2:13–20). As in *She*, numerous essentialist links bind female divinity to evil and the unknown. Only women, for example, can be Baaltis's votaries, while male priests attend the benevolent El; an effigy depicts Baaltis with a hundred breasts, a mockery of the maternal function, since she also demands human sacrifices; and she personifies the moon as "the emblem of fertility" (12), two traditional markers of mysterious womanhood. Elissa is similarly tainted as a sorceress through both her heathenism and her sex, requiring no "witcheries... beyond those lips and form and eyes" (111) to lead the Israelite Prince Aziel, a "worshipper of the true and only God" (55), to "the unpardonable sin of his apostasy" (193).

Maligned by Aziel's mentor, Issachar, as a "fair idolater" who will "sap" Aziel's faith and "cause him to cast away his soul" (111–12), Elissa begins to exert a disturbing influence on this representative of the "Chosen People" (55). Aziel himself succumbs to idolatry, for he admits that "from the moment" he glimpsed Elissa, "she became life of my life, and soul of my soul" (155). Despite Issachar's portentous warnings that Aziel's ardor is merely "the wile of Beelzebub waiting to snatch your soul" (46), Aziel proclaims his undying devotion. Informing Issachar that he will convert Elissa to his faith, Aziel seemingly wards off the threat to his soul when Elissa renounces her paganism in favor of Aziel's creed. Against her wishes, however, Elissa is named Baaltis's primary priestess, but she is threatened by death unless Aziel recants his own faith and agrees to assume the joint position of dutiful spouse and pagan priest. Though Aziel recognizes that this clerical role would require him to "abjure his faith at the price of his own soul," he agrees to marriage (187).

As in *She*, the boundaries between womanhood and heathenism collapse, for Aziel's religious transgression stems from his exposure to the former. Compelled to commit "the greatest of sins . . . for the sake of a woman" (191), Aziel errs solely because he has been "caught by the bait of the beauty of a priestess of Baaltis" and "seduced by her distress to deny and reject Him" (194). Both novels, then, equate women with evil to suggest that female essence always already signifies temptation, corruption, and damnation. Redemption is possible only through the annihilation of the females who cause righteous men to stray from the path to salvation. In positioning both Ayesha and Elissa as idols who blasphemously inspire male protagonists to worship them, the novels accord the female characters the strongest possible condemnation under Christian doctrine: they have caused devouts to ignore the divine prohibition against setting up false gods.

Immortality and Temporal Reversal

These intertextual and intratextual examples all attest to Haggard's ongoing preoccupation with validating a gender binarism that gains its force through temporal distinctions. Ayesha's immortality contributes to this project not only through her diabolical divinity but also through identifications with mythic and Gothic figures. All of the mythic characters whom She resembles—Eve, Circe, Aphrodite, Venus, and Galatea— were infamous for their injurious influence upon men and bring a gender valence to the *fin de siècle* theories of myth that they invoke. Those theories, offered in multiple permutations, presumed that mythic figures were emblematic of enduring human traits.[16] John Ruskin, for example, advised that "the right reading of myths" is predicated on the recognition that "all true vision" presupposes "constant laws common to all human nature" and identified "things which are for all ages true" (31). Walter Pater, summarizing the "three successive phases" of mythic development, noted that ancient figures "are realised as abstract symbols, because intensely characteristic examples, of moral or spiritual conditions" (91). Victorian historians likewise distinguished myth from history. In midcentury writings, for instance, the well-known George Grote argued that "mythus differs essentially from accurate and well-ascertained history" (*Grecian Legends* 81–82). *She* builds upon such discourses in specifically attributing mythic immutability and inherent unreliability to Woman, situating the sex in an eternal present. The characterization of Ayesha weaves these discursive threads even more tightly by suggesting that the New Woman is merely another manifestation of Everywoman, one whose dangerous effects upon men replicate those of her mythic counterparts.

Yet that threat, the mythic resonances hint, is containable. Rather than signaling a revolutionary change in which women wrest power from their rightful male masters, *She* suggests that Woman's ahistoricity may ultimately preclude her from participating in and redirecting the course of history. We are reminded of Rachel Blau DuPlessis's feminist reading of myth, which she identifies as a frequently "hostile" response to the historical underpinnings of gender roles (106). Displacing mythic qualities onto women confers "universal, humanistic, natural, or even archetypal status" that divorces them from history and the possibility of change in their role across generations. Like the mythic narratives that DuPlessis describes, *She* participates in "the solidification, consolidation, and affirmation of a hegemony" (107) in which patriarchal figures ultimately prevail. In *She*, that project unfolds through the eventual disempowerment of the virago. The New Woman threat can be dispelled, the text implies, by exposing her as a mere woman who eventually can be controlled as any other can.

Spanning the centuries figuratively as a perpetual object of Vincey narratives and literally as a somatic anomaly, She has a dual claim to mythic immortality. Through her defiance of death, however, She enacts a monstrous transgression of temporal boundaries, mirroring the New Woman's refusal to remain within her sex's sphere. *She* imports Gothic tropes to convey the horrific implications of that uncontainability, structurally evidencing many of the trappings that Eve Kosofsky Sedgwick identifies as intrinsic to the genre: tales embedded in tales, sinister landscapes, a feudal structure, unfathomable writings, and dreams, for example (9–10). Indeed, *She* internalizes the conventions within the corpse-like Ayesha herself, as Holly's first glimpse of her reveals:

> [T]he curtain was drawn, and a tall figure stood before us. I say a figure, for not only the body, but also the face was wrapped up in soft white, gauzy material in such a way as at first sight to remind me most forcibly of a corpse in its grave-clothes. . . . I felt more frightened than ever at this ghost-like apparition, and my hair began to rise upon my head as the feeling crept over me that I was in the presence of something that was not canny. I could, however, clearly distinguish that the swathed mummy-like form before me

was that of a tall and lovely woman, instinct with beauty in every part, and also with a certain snake-like grace which I had never seen anything to equal before. . . . [H]er entire frame seemed to undulate. (142)

Implied in the passage are several other elements that Sedgwick designates as typically Gothic—live burial, doubleness, the unspeakable, a blurring of inside/outside boundaries, and a metaphor of depth—which are joined explicitly to She to portray her as a virtual embodiment of the Gothic. She's immortality, the most significant and disturbing of her qualities, is the nexus of these characteristics and the locus of power. The metaphor of depth in Sedgwick's catalog is therefore of most interest here, since in *She* it becomes less a spatial dimension than a temporal one under which all of the novel's other Gothic tropes are subsumed. The bewildering layers of centuries incorporated within She create a suffocating and disorienting effect that stymies efforts to affix her within a temporal span. Through this confusion, Ayesha resembles the transgressive Gothic character who elides the distinctions between the rational and the irrational, the apparent and the actual, the self and the Other.

In effect, Ayesha becomes a kind of Gothic sublime—an oddly pleasurable source of fear who embodies not only centuries-old qualms about enigmatic Woman, but heightens the effect by linking them to the specific threat of female empowerment in the late nineteenth century. In so doing, *She* suggests that its Gothic female endangers not only the male protagonists she encounters, but the fate of Western civilization as well. If, as Rosemary Jackson contends, early Gothic novels represented a reaction to historical events that revealed a longing for an idealized social order (97), then *She* demonstrates the perils to that order posed by the New Woman.

She not only points to Ayesha's antithetical relationship with linear time but also casts her as a devolutionary figure who seemingly reverses and subverts it. As noted in my introductory chapter, *She* responds to and builds upon prevalent evolutionary and anthropological discourses of the late Victorian period, which, as Elizabeth Fee observes, "all worked toward a similar end: the construction of a refurbished, scientific patriarchalism" (29). These theories, Fee adds, bolstered a concept of human history in which matriarchal cultures represented a primitive social form that, through evolution, advanced to the apex of patriarchal civilization (38). In *She*, Ayesha's reign over the Amahagger therefore serves not as a signifier of female advancement but of cultural decline, since a matriarchy represents a step backward in time: not only female rule, but the brutal, ritualistic, and cannibalistic practices of the Amahagger identify them as an early strain in human development. In reducing matriarchal society to the kind of "prehistory" that Luce Irigaray identifies as a "partial, reductive, and fruitless conception of History," *She* gives credence to the notion that patriarchy is "the only History possible" (*Je, Tu, Nous* 24)—a point abundantly underscored by the repeated attempts to align the Englishmen with history in *She*'s opening chapters.

To an extent, the gendered relationship to prehistory crafted in *She* reminds us of the anthropophagic perspective that modern critics have proffered in analyzing responses to the Other. As Maggie Kilgour suggests in opposing the privileged term of the "inside" to the inferior yet menacing term of the "outside," the latter must be absorbed into the former "to maintain a situation of centripetal control" and ensure that "there is no category of alien outsideness left to threaten the inner stability" (5). Such a maneuver, Kilgour remarks, represents "a nostalgia for a state of total incorporation" upon which much Western belief is founded. As bell hooks says, "It is by eating the Other ... that one asserts power and privilege" (36), which both "displaces the Other" and "denies the significance of that Other's history" (31). We can see this type of "incorporation," to borrow Kilgour's term, at work in the Western response to non-Western history. The Other's history is virtually "swallowed" and assimilated as the West appropriates it as a form of its own prehistory. In *She,* both Orientalist and gendered forms of historical marginalization are blended in this cannibalistic scenario—an ironic twist in which the human-eating Amahagger themselves become figuratively eaten—since Ayesha and her Amahagger subjects represent both barbarism and matriarchy. Indeed, *She*'s readers could find contemporary "proof" of their twinned prehistory in Darwin's *Descent of Man*: the 1871 text equates the physiological markers of women's presumed inferiority with those of "the lower races," themselves deemed evidence of "a past and lower state of civilization" (587) through which Victorians could see living examples of their own precursors—and, in effect, absorb the Other into their own history.

Since the Other is prone to absorption, then Woman's Darwinian reversion, on some level, poses a threat to the progress brought by the masculine projects of linear temporality. Ayesha's destruction at the novel's end reinforces the images of regression in a scene that has drawn much critical commentary for its devolutionary implications:[17]

> "Look!—look!—look! she's shrivelling up! she's turning into a monkey!"
>
> ... [S]maller and smaller she grew; her skin changed colour, and in place of the perfect whiteness of its lustre it turned dirty brown and yellow, like an old piece of withered parchment. She felt at her head: the delicate hand was nothing but a claw now, a human talon. . . . [S]he shrieked—ah, she shrieked!—she rolled upon the floor and shrieked!
>
> Smaller she grew, and smaller yet, till she was no larger than a baboon. Now the skin was puckered into a million wrinkles, and on the shapeless face was the stamp of unutterable age. . . . [N]obody ever saw anything like the frightful age that was graven on that fearful countenance, no bigger now than that of a two-months' child, though the skull remained the same size, or nearly so, and let all men pray to God they never may, if they wish to keep their reason. (293–94)

The return to the primitive, the diction suggests, is almost unbearably hideous. Significantly, though, the novel links devolution to women in general and the New Woman in particular, for iterations of the verb "shrieked" resemble both an animalistic cry and a virago's hysteria.[18] Equally unsettling is a curious conjunction of temporal opposites within She herself, creating a disorienting effect that mirrors her disruption of an orderly world; by simultaneously incorporating age and youth in her wrinkled yet childlike countenance, She initiates a vertiginous blending of times. Elaborating on She's horrific transformation, "too hideous for words," Holly alludes to its temporal upheaval in sputtering, "And yet, think of this—at that very moment I thought of it—it was the *same* woman!" (294).

In effect, Ayesha's physical devolution serves as a further confirmation of female primitivism that *fin de siècle* anthropologists constructed in their rewriting of Bachofen. *She* contributes to the cultural discourse in confining devolution to women and those subject to their will, avoiding in the quoted passage any pointed racial or ethnic references that would broaden the category of Otherness. The text thus suggests that Woman does not merely signify an earlier step on the evolutionary ladder but specifically embodies the regressive tendencies so feared by late-century Victorians. In aligning Ayesha with the New Woman, *She* conveys that this emergent figure represents not an evolutionary progression, but a return to chaotic primitivism.

The Blended Binary

Despite the novel's many feverish efforts to marshal temporal discourses in support of distinct gender roles, the border between masculine and feminine cannot be indelibly marked or practicably policed in *She*. As emblematized by She, the female evinces a disquieting tendency to exceed the boundaries set to contain her and compromise the unfortunate males she encounters. By undermining the men's attempts to resist female contamination, Ayesha foregrounds the feminine traits they have left unacknowledged within themselves, particularly in regard to Leo. In thus problematizing the distinction between masculinity and femininity, She *is* the quintessential New Woman.

If, as Irigaray asserts, Western culture seeks "the murder of the mother" (*Irigaray Reader* 47) on a primal level to nullify female power, then part of *She*'s project to align the male characters so emphatically with irreversible time represents a movement away from this ultimate symbol of female Otherness. That movement, in Kristevan terms, suggests a desire for abjection to enact the process of separation in the mirror stage. By confusing the division between self and Other, the mother represents both an external and an internal threat to the integrity of the autonomous male subject. Abjection of the mother is an attempt to solidify that border, to remove "what disturbs identity, system, order"—that is, "[t]he in-between, the ambiguous, the composite" (*Powers* 4). Yet the effort to expel any vestigial traces of the mother and the female principle she represents is thwarted in *She*, as suggested by the mere fact that the novel is itself centered upon the Englishmen's search for this problematic mother.[19]

As Sandra Gilbert and Susan Gubar have compellingly argued, the explorers travel across a progressively feminized terrain of "vaporous marshes and stagnant canals"[20] in their "symbolic return to the womb."[21] The feminine quality of the landscape is indeed startling: "miles of quagmires" (116) connote a devouring sexuality, a rich meadowland forms a uterine space in a volcanic crater (79), and the marshy terrain can be penetrated only with a knowledge of its "secret paths" (91). The Englishmen's voyage mimics the passage through the birth canal, these critics maintain, since the men eventually reach the womb-like "vast cup of earth" that She inhabits. Although I agree with this reading, I suggest that the significance of that journey also rests in its temporal implications. Through their figurative return to the womb, the travelers are moving back in time and retracing linear progress. Instead of proceeding through the

Father's linear time, the Englishmen become trapped in the mother's time, thereby confusing the separation of self and Other. Rather than expel the mother in a discrete and unrepeatable phase of the maturational journey that brings them into the Law of the Father, then, the travelers re-enter the prohibited maternal body.

The resultant loss of self within the mother is conveyed in part by the men's passage through the feminized terrain that leads to Kôr:

> [W]e proceeded to the edge of the swamp, and looked over it. It was apparently boundless, and vast flocks of every sort of waterfowl came flying from its recesses, till it was sometimes difficult to see the sky. Now that the sun was getting high it drew thin sickly looking clouds of poisonous vapour from the surface of the marsh and from the scummy pools of stagnant water. (63)

Of special significance in this topographical portrait is the vast swamp, part of the "Freudianly female *paysage moralisé*" that Gilbert and Gubar identify (13). The marsh suggests an engulfing female Otherness that threatens to extend endlessly and poses a multitude of hazards to the male trespassers. At the same time, the swamp paradoxically creates a claustrophobic atmosphere: masses of waterfowl conceal the sky, implying that the marsh represents a form of imprisonment or suffocation. Among the swamp's perils is its connection with disease—the marsh is "poisonous," "sickly," "scummy," and "stagnant"—in another gesture toward the adulterated mother. Indeed, as Irigaray asserts, Western culture associates the mother with "contagion, contamination, . . . madness and death" (*Irigaray Reader* 40). The misty exhalations from the swamp spread contagion both across and above the landscape, leaving no safe space wherein one can escape the harmful vapor. The link between the mother and contamination is fused more firmly when Holly later remarks that the "stench" from the bog was "too awful," leading the men "instantly to swallow precautionary doses of quinine" (65).[22] Left unprotected within the figurative maternal body, the Englishmen face destruction from asphyxiation, drowning, or disease.

One telling indication that She as primeval mother has indeed contaminated the Englishmen is her effect upon their facility with language. Communicating in an archaic tongue distinguished by its awkward syntax—remarking, for example, "Wot ye why I have brought you here to-night, my Holly?" (262)—Ayesha has an insidious influence upon the Englishmen's speech. Leo, for instance, utters an uncharacteristic "thou" in addressing She at one point (228), but more significant are the anachronisms that begin punctuating the speech of the comparatively articulate and voluble Holly. The effect is to obfuscate his formerly unambiguous language, which tended to follow an uncomplicated linear sequence proceeding from subject to predicate to object. Through She's influence, Holly's speech occasionally becomes antiquated and circuitous, suggesting a twofold inference. The alterations in language represent a movement backward in time to the syntactic oddities of She's ancient culture and also identify Holly with the verbal chaos traditionally attributed to the maternal body.

More significant, however, is that She's influence tends to deprive Holly of linguistic aptitude altogether. Once embarked upon the voyage to She's land, Holly demonstrates for the first time an inability to voice his experiences. Although the scene unfolding before him leads to "heartbreaking excitement," it is one he "cannot hope to describe" (54). Such disclaimers appear with increasing frequency as Holly travels closer to She's womb-like home. Once ensconced there, Holly comments on nearly a dozen occasions about his incapacity to capture a moment in words. He notes, for example, that "I wish that it lay within the power of my pen to give some idea of the grandeur of the sight that then met our view" (259); "here again my pen fails me" (263); and "no words of mine can tell how sweet she looked" (291). Holly's linguistic failings underscore that his journey to She as the primeval mother is simultaneously a passage backward through the symbolic order—a temporal regression from the Word of the Father to the prelinguistic state of the maternal body. Indeed, the temporal implications are manifold, as Kristevan theory suggests, for Holly's movement away from the symbolic order represents a movement outside of time itself. Since the symbolic, in Kristevan terms, is "the order of verbal communication, the paternal order of genealogy," it is a "temporal order" ("About Chinese Women" 152); because "there is no time without speech," Julia Kristeva argues, "there is no time without the father" (153).

Further confusing the border between masculinity and femininity in *She* is the fusion of times—past and present—that results when Leo encounters his doppelgänger, Kallikrates. Such temporal blending separates Leo as actor and Holly as witness from unidirectional linear time and places them within the vertiginous realm of monumental time:

> [H]ave no fear, Kallikrates, when thou—living, and but lately born—shalt look upon thine own departed self, who breathed and died so long ago.

> ... [T]he sight was an uncanny one. ... For there, stretched upon the stone bier before us, robed in white and perfectly preserved, was what appeared to be the body of Leo Vincey. I stared from Leo, standing *there* alive, to Leo lying *there* dead, and could see no difference; except, perhaps, that the body on the bier looked older. Feature for feature they were the same, even down to the crop of little golden curls, which was Leo's most uncommon beauty.... I can only sum up the closeness of the resemblance by saying that I never saw twins so exactly similar as that dead and living pair.
>
> I turned to see what effect was produced upon Leo by this sight of his dead self and found it to be one of partial stupefaction. He stood for two or three minutes staring and said nothing, and when at last he spoke it was only to ejaculate—
>
> "Cover it up and take me away."
>
> "Nay, wait, Kallikrates," said Ayesha.
>
> ... "Do thou, oh Holly, open the garment on the breast of the dead Kallikrates, for perchance my lord may fear to touch himself." (237–38)

Temporal confusion results from the difficulty in differentiating between death and life, since the boundary between a deceased Leo represented by the ancient Kallikrates and a living Leo figured as contemporary Englishman periodically collapses and reappears. Holly comments, for example, that he could see no difference between the living and dead versions of Leo. Although Holly immediately qualifies the remark with his uncertain statement that the dead body "perhaps" appeared older, this seeming differentiation between the two Leos cannot hold either. The age of the corpse suggests linear time, but the mere fact that the two Leos are virtually indistinguishable evokes the unbounded quality of monumental time, making it impossible to draw a sharp line between the two forms of temporality. Leo remains a kind of "undead," poised between oppositions.

In severing the Englishmen's temporal moorings, the text calls into question their complacent perceptions of themselves as unified subjects and thus problematizes the whole notion of identity and the gender assumptions from which it proceeds. The temporal amalgamation further hints at an inability to expel the female from the male subject, which in psychoanalytic terms should have happened within the oedipal journey from the mother's realm to the father's. The inseparability of the female component from male subjectivity is made manifest in the feminization of Leo/Kallikrates that occurs in the above passage. Leo is distinguished by "curling hair . . . of the ruddiest gold" (297), his "most remarkable personal beauty" (212)—traditionally considered a feminine attribute, as are She's splendid tresses. Although this comparison between Leo and She seems to signify an opposition rather than a conflation, since Leo's hair is blond and She's is raven, that boundary cannot be sustained either; the two characters are linked at the novel's end when Leo takes a lock from the head of the dead Ayesha. Leo is additionally feminized through the identical garb of Ayesha and Kallikrates, whose white robes present them as pagan priestly figures but also resemble flowing Victorian gowns.

The interchangeability of Leo and Kallikrates suggests the very impossibility of defining oneself as an autonomous subject with a discrete and impervious identity. Particularly illustrative of the unstable border between self and Other is Leo's verbal reaction to the sight of his deceased double, urging She to "cover it up and take me away." The statement is fraught with ambiguity through the unstable signifier, "me." We can read the remark either as Leo's wish to be removed from Kallikrates's presence or as a desire for his dead self to be covered and taken away. The difficulty in differentiating between selves is likewise complicated when She implores Leo to observe "thine own departed self," addresses him as Kallikrates, and comments on his "fear to touch himself."

Such a confusion of self and Other, wrought by the analogous uncertainty between present and past, problematizes the gender binarism that elsewhere also comes under assault. Holly, for example, is repeatedly described in simian terms that suggest a Darwinian devolution as unsettling as Ayesha's in her final moments. Unusually hirsute, with hair growing "right down on his forehead" (2), Holly is characterized by the "editor" in the frame narrative as "a gorilla" (2), and Holly himself refers to his countenance as offering proof of "the monkey theory" (8), albeit in a devolutionary form. In the explorers' passage to the pillar of flame that presumably will bring immortality, Holly, like Leo, "found it necessary to go down on my hands and knees and crawl" like a primate; Ayesha, however, "never condescended to this" (272).

Temporal confusion emerges in other respects as well, especially when the amorphous temporality that the text associates with She also absorbs the male characters, most revealingly with Holly. He periodically becomes dislocated in time, viewing the past with the immediacy of the present to imply that, like She, he is suspended in an eternal present in which linear time holds little meaning. Prone to disturbing dream states, Holly is frequently unable to distinguish between past and present. In one typical daydream, for instance, Holly is transported to ancient Kôr, where he "could almost for a moment think that I had triumphed o'er the Past, and that my spirit's eyes had pierced the mystery of Time" (185). Quotidian events themselves tend to mimic the incomprehensibility of dream states so that the line between fantasy and reality becomes less and less distinct. Holly remarks at one point, for example, that "I know not how long we remained thus," opining "[m]any hours, I suppose" (294), and even argues that time should be interpreted subjectively in commenting that "[t]ruly time should be measured by events, and not by the lapse of hours" (315). The explicit temporal units that Holly characteristically includes in his narrative to tick off the passage of a precise number of hours or days are jarringly omitted on occasion as Holly loses all sense of time. Indeed, after She's demise, Holly and Leo "had no watch left that would go" (301).

In addition, the very distinction between linear and cyclical temporality sometimes becomes confused in *She*, as the following representative examples reveal. Leo's father, who, as we saw, was seemingly bound tightly to linear time, nevertheless tells Holly that "[t]here is no such thing as death" but "only a change" (14), a biblical allusion that Ayesha virtually repeats in explaining the cyclical rhythms of death and reincarnation (149). Holly, despite an insistent "distaste for prolongation of [his] mortal span" (297), is overcome by a desire to share She's immortality—and, once under She's influence, displays no skepticism about the likelihood that immortality and reincarnation can occur. Both Englishmen accept the idea that Leo himself appears to be a reincarnated version of Kallikrates, and both increasingly participate in She's ritualistic and primitive culture.

The gendered binary between self and Other also becomes problematized in complicating the conventional association of women with nature, intellectual dullness, and materiality. Although Ayesha is unflatteringly allied with nature, Holly unexpectedly comments that he "dr[e]w comfort from [nature's] breast, and hers only" (8). Although women were judged to be mentally inferior to men by many Victorian scientists, Ayesha earns Holly's praise for intellectual acumen when he notes the "majestic sentences" she utters with "a grandeur" that Holly laments he is "quite unable to reproduce" (238). Ayesha is even praised by the "editor" for "the splendour of her mind" that he directly opposes to Leo's lesser intellectual capabilities, a contrast so remarkable that the editor wonders whether "extremes meet" in attempting to explain Ayesha's "worship at the shrine of matter" (6). Finally, although Ayesha is frequently allied with the body in the text's descriptions, Leo is similarly presented as an enviable "beauty" whose physical charms rival She's own.

Resolution of the New Woman Threat

In response to She's disconcerting tendency to foreground the blended binary, the novel attempts to expel this transgressive figure and reinforce the gender divisions she has disturbed. Condemned to an appalling death in a pillar of flame, She is appropriately punished for her hubris through this Luciferian fate. Like She's female Amahagger subjects, who are ritualistically murdered by males every second generation, Ayesha's demise translates into a patriarchal desire to demonstrate that "we are the strongest," as one male Amahagger remarks (114). Through her death, She is forced to submit to and be conquered by linear time and, inferentially, the men who determine its course through their control over human history. Indeed, as She herself had earlier remarked, "to the tomb ... must we all come at last! Ay, even I who live so long" (186). Though temporarily a disruptive presence, She ultimately is contained and her threat dispelled—an apposite end, as the text implies simply by choosing this form of closure, for her New Woman counterparts as well.

She's resolution thus elides the troubling questions the text had raised about the viability and stability of gender roles. In annihilating She and returning the travelers to the comforting environs of Cambridge—an event, incidentally, described in precise temporal terms as occurring "exactly two years from the date of our departure upon our wild and seemingly ridiculous quest" (316)—the novel concludes with the restoration of order. Even the hint that She will reappear, conveyed by Holly's prescient supposition that "the end of this history ... is not reached yet" (316), serves not so much as a warning as a prediction that She will succumb to divine will and natural law. Presumably, She's eventual "obedience to a fate that never swerves and a purpose that cannot be altered" (317) will be a repetition of the same. That is, She as embodiment of the New Woman will be brought under control by a Providence that will reinscribe the natural separation between the sexes.

John de Morgan's 1887 parody, *He*, hints that such a destiny for the New Woman is appropriate. In this version, the troubling powers of Haggard's She instead are wielded by Kallikrates as He, a gender switch that avoids the problematic issue of the New Woman by firmly establishing patriarchal authority. Haggard's Ayesha is split into two properly gendered characters, thereby according power to a dominant He and feminine beauty to a submissive She. Even the landscape descriptions have changed to signal the shift in power relations, depicting a "transcendently beautiful" Eden (48) that connotes a taming of a feminized nature in lieu of a voracious female Otherness. Instead of posing a threat, de Morgan's Alethea is contained and controlled. To protect men from her beauty and feminine wiles, Alethea turns to stone "at once" whenever they approach her dwelling (36), reviving only "when [H]e wills it" (59). As a marble statue, Alethea becomes an object of art and the gaze; unlike Haggard's Ayesha with her penetrating look, this She closes her eyes whenever men look upon her (80). The matriarchal society of the earlier novel is converted to a patriarchal one in which women are ordered around by "the Father" and serve men silently and erotically, wearing belts "luxuriantly" draped with grapes that the men take at will (53–54). "[A]bsolutely spotless in mind and body" (198), Alethea displays none of the sexuality characteristic of She. Instead, Alethea has "retained her virgin purity for two thousand years," saving herself for the Leo character (199). To him, Alethea is "a perfect woman" who is "[p]atient and gentle as a nurse" (198).

The defusing of the New Woman also emerges as Haggard's aim in his "conclusion" to *She*, the 1904 *Ayesha* that charts She's return, only to disempower and, more explicitly, convert her to Victorian ideology.[23] *Ayesha* resumes the story two decades after Holly and Leo's journey to Kôr and chronicles the Englishmen's further adventures as they search for a reborn She in Asia. Their travels include a five-year visit to Tibetan monasteries, where they study the laws and traditions of the lamas, and a harrowing interlude in Kaloon. Ruled by the passionate and despotic Khania, a reincarnated version of Amenartas, Kaloon is a Kôr-like kingdom whose New Woman monarch entertains lascivious designs on Leo. After a narrow escape from Kaloon, the Englishmen return to their quest for She, traveling across a frozen landscape before reaching the mountain home where she presides as priestess of Isis. Heavily veiled to conceal the hideous appearance she had assumed during the final moments of *She*, Ayesha regains her unearthly beauty through Leo's kiss. The 1904 Ayesha is even more ambitious than the 1887 version; she does not seek merely to invade England as planned in the earlier novel, but she instead intends to destroy civilization by bankrupting the West's monetary exchanges and then establish Leo as king of the earth. Through Leo's intercession, however, Ayesha eventually relinquishes her plan of world domination. Accepting his plea to "forget they greatness and be a woman and—my wife" (178), Ayesha gives him a passionate, but fatal, kiss. As she gathers Leo's corpse to her and claims that their souls are now joined, Ayesha disappears into the heavens, presumably to await Leo's next incarnation. Holly, sensing that his own end is near, retraces his journey and returns to England to die.[24]

To a certain extent, *Ayesha* duplicates the structural and thematic maneuvers characteristic of *She*. Launched by a frame narrative that compulsively positions Holly's "conclusion" to the earlier tale as another historical document, *Ayesha* further dignifies the account through its capitalization as the Record. Like other historical papers whose authenticity is self-evident, "the Record must speak for itself" (2). To assuage any lingering doubts of the manuscript's veracity, Holly sends with his text "the only piece of evidence that is left to me of the [document's] literal truth," the scepter that She wielded as "the rod of her power"—a "token of verity," as the *Dial*'s reviewer approvingly noted. As in its predecessor, *Ayesha* establishes a provenance for this carefully designated "history" through Holly's cover letter requesting its publication, the editor's introduction tracing the manuscript's journey to him, and an official letter by the doctor who attended Holly shortly before the scholar-adventurer's death. Private experience again provides the basis of public history, since Holly's narrative opens with the comment that "[d]estiny kept my breath in me, perhaps that a record might remain" (6).

As in *She*, Ayesha is depicted as a contaminatory and idolatrous influence who causes men to err. At the lamasery, for example, a monk in his fiftieth incarnation laments not only that she "lit a fire in my heart which will not burn out" but asserts in emphatic italics that "*she made me worship her!*" (17). In describing "this priestess of a false faith" (23), the monk recalls She's blasphemous demand to "kneel you down and do me homage" (18). Other idolatrous references abound. Ayesha was a "divinity" whom Holly "was doomed to worship from afar" (6); Ayesha visits Leo in a prophetic "vision" pointedly distinguished from a less religiously laden "dream" (9); and She inhabits the "Promised Land" for her English seekers, who view her "mystic Mount" (27)—a "sacred" and "inviolable" dominion (83)—from a distant mountaintop, like Spenser's Red Cross Knight observing the New Jerusalem. As in the 1887 novel, Ayesha resembles the Christian divinity as a disembodied voice who "speaks from the fire," a "spirit no man has ever seen or shall see" (83). Satanic allusions likewise reinforce She's untoward divinity, especially through a description of her garb. In unveiling, She reveals a "hooded asp" as well as her customary belt formed from a double-headed snake (130). Ayesha's repeated desire to immortalize Leo, though a prospect he dreads as "a thing unholy, and . . . not permitted by [his] faith," nevertheless briefly tempts him to "inherit [immortality] for [her] dear sake" (147). Mimicking the true God in wielding apocalyptic destruction with a terrifying storm she looses in the novel's final pages, Ayesha demonstrates yet another manifestation of the "superhuman powers" that seem "unrestrained by any responsibility to God or man" (151).

The corpse-like demeanor of *Ayesha*'s veiled She also merges the temporal states of life and death. The confusion initiated by She affects the Englishmen's perceptions of time in *Ayesha* as it did in *She*, evidenced by Holly's repeated lapses into a vague subjective temporality that refuses to correspond to precise linear units. Holly, for example, notes that an incident that occupied "only two hours, or perhaps less," instead "seemed a score of centuries" (76); standing before She's "black altar," Holly recalls that "[h]ours, years, ages, eons seemed to flow over us"; and "a while" that passes "may have been a minute or an hour" (122). Again the Englishmen's journey to Ayesha's domain replicates a move backward in time to the mother, for she inhabits a "great cup" entered through a "natural gateway" (97).

Yet *Ayesha* is a repetition of *She* with a difference. In her latter incarnation, She progresses from the demon of the temple to the angel in the house.[25] Her eventual transformation is heralded through her capacity as priestess to Isis, "the universal Mother" (114) whose statue conforms with Victorian expectations of the maternal role. As Holly contemplates this "lovely thing" that he specifically identifies as a "study of motherhood," he comments favorably on its "unchanging tenderness" and suggestion of "strength to shelter [a child] from every harm" (98). Unlike the aggressive gaze that characterized the 1887 She with her eyes "more deadly than any Basilisk's" (189), the statue looks out with "great, calm eyes"; indeed, "[a]ll love seemed to be concentrated in the brooding figure, so human, yet so celestial" (98–99). If any Victorian readers missed the significance of the statue, Holly sets them straight in commenting that "its interpretation [was] made clear even to the dullest by the simple symbolism of some genius—Humanity rescued by the Divine" (99).

That Ayesha has indeed been "rescued" is reinforced by her response to Leo after his transformative kiss. The ideological focus shifts slightly in this scene, for the text positions Leo not only as the eventual conqueror of the New Woman's will, but also as a Christ figure through whom She can attain salvation. Resembling a Christian devout in bowing her head and "meekly" remarking that "[t]hy will is mine," Ayesha acknowledges that Leo "hast a right to thine own faith, which doubtless is mine also" (134). "[D]oomed to suffer" for the "great sin" that "befouled her immortal state," She ponders the possibility that Leo's love would be "permitted to redeem her" (141). Like Christ taking upon himself the burden of humanity's transgressions, Leo proclaims, "Let they sin, great or little . . . be my sin also'" (136). Flinging herself at his feet like a Victorian Mary Magdalene, Ayesha clings to Leo's garments until he stoops to lift her. Although in *She* Ayesha similarly bows down before Leo and addresses him as her lord (284), the 1904 version makes much more of her submissive pose and gives it a decidedly Christian resonance. Through Leo's Messianic act in assuming her sins, She asserts that "I am regenerate in thee" and "may hope again for some true life beyond" (136). Leo's death becomes for Ayesha a kind of penance that she must endure until his resurrection in another time and place.

The potent She of the 1887 version thus becomes, in *Ayesha*, a chastened and submissive handmaiden who transfers agency to both her secular savior and his earthly "father," Holly, in announcing that she "will obey thy words and his" (117). She's metamorphosis from castrating virago to dutiful spouse and upholder of motherhood is "the most . . . thrilling of her many changes" (178) that ushers in a newfound passivity, delicacy, and superficiality. In the repudiation of unseemly masculine ambitions and acceptance of the "natural" role as caring wife and loving mother, Ayesha's conversion suggests the desired and destined fate for the New Woman:

> Ayesha grew human; I could see her heart beat beneath her robes, and hear her breath come in soft, sweet sobs, while o'er her upturned face and in her alluring eyes there spread itself that look which is born of love alone. Radiant and more radiant did she seem to grow, sweeter and more sweet, no longer . . . the Oracle of the Sanctuary, no longer the Valkyrie of the battleplain, but only the loveliest and most happy bride that ever gladdened a husband's eye.
>
>   She spoke, and it was of little things, for thus she proclaimed the conquest of herself. (179)

In considering *Ayesha* as a conclusion rather than a sequel to *She*, as Haggard did, we see that the solution to the New Woman problem is twofold: the goal is not simply to conquer but to enlighten her. Only by internalizing and validating Victorian ideology can the New Woman truly be tamed, *Ayesha* suggests, and the gender binarism buttressing the doctrine of separate spheres firmly reinforced. In effect, both the 1887 and 1904 novels intimate, Ayesha is ultimately controlled by the natural order of time that she so persistently attempted to defy. Her affiliations with ahistoricity, paganism, myth, and devolution, as well as the many permutations of these elements that we have observed, serve not to empower but to destroy her as a threat to cultural stability. Haggard leaves his readers, then, with a message that comforts the reactionary and troubles the visionary: the New Woman cannot prevail against the potent force of the natural order of time.

Chapter 3

Trapping the Female in Time: History and Aesthetics in *Tess of the d'Urbervilles*

> Time was chanting his satiric psalm at her.
> —Hardy, *Tess of the d'Urbervilles*

Authorial constructions of hegemonic time seemingly reach an apogee of intensity in Thomas Hardy's *fin de siècle* fiction, particularly the 1891 *Tess of the d'Urbervilles*. Although many Hardy texts reflect a temporal obsession—beginning with the juvenilia and extending into the mature poetic works, one of which was even titled "Time's Laughingstocks"[1]—*Tess* offers the most compelling example in Hardy's massive canon of the multifarious gender ramifications posed by time. *Tess* heightens and fuses the temporal concerns that surface throughout Hardy's oeuvre to demonstrate the monolithic power of the natural order of time and, as the epigraph to this chapter suggests, the futility of attempts to evade its control.

Emphatically capitalized and assigned the masculine pronoun, "Time" takes on a definitive personality in Hardy's works. Time contracts and expands, displays treachery, exacts revenge, and ultimately triumphs. The young Hardy's first extant verse addressed time, contrasting a languid pastoral past with the frenzied concerns of the modern age; in adolescence Hardy copied a poem about a cottage clock and affixed it to his grandfather's own timepiece; and his first published work focused on the fate of a publicly displayed clock (Osborne 543). Beginning with the 1871 *Desperate Remedies*, 1872 *Under the Greenwood Tree*, and 1873 *A Pair of Blue Eyes*, Hardy brought his temporal fascination to the novel, presented most intriguingly in the early fiction with the 1878 *Return of the Native*'s Darwinian twists. It is in Hardy's later novels, however, that time becomes an especially ubiquitous and omnipotent presence ordering characters' lives, emphasized overtly through recurrent images that appear in several texts.

Watches and clocks provide the most obvious examples, frequently encountered in the *fin de siècle* fiction as characters proceed through their typical days. *Jude the Obscure*'s protagonist wears a watch chain, consults his watch, forgets to set his alarm, times eggs, and hangs his watch above him before dying.[2] Jude hears church clocks chiming in the distance, observes clocks while working and strolling, fraternizes with bar patrons who look at their watches, and calls his child Father Time. Similarly, *The Well-Beloved*'s protagonist wears a watch and eyes it regularly; clocks are wound and inexplicably stop in *The Woodlanders*; parsons and bishops check their watches in *Two on a Tower*; and a shiny new clock replaces an ancient one relegated to a cellar in *A Laodicean*. The railway, with its strict time schedules, is likewise an ever-present symbol in Hardy's 1880s and 1890s novels. Jude and Sue regularly take trains, miss trains, and order their lives by trains. *The Well-Beloved*'s inconstant hero decamps with a new lover by train and visits other lovers by rail. *A Laodicean*'s female protagonist inherits a paternal fortune gained by building a third of the nation's railways. Like railway tracks, ruins dot Hardy's Wessex landscape and accentuate the contrast between past and present. Significant events in *The Mayor of Casterbridge* occur in the crumbled settings of Roman roads and edifices; Jude's cherished Christminster is distinguished by its medieval buildings; the primary locale of *Two on a Tower* is a decrepit column erected more than a century earlier; and a New Woman prototype resides in the dusty confines of a feudal castle in *A Laodicean*.

Tess, however, rarely employs such material images to convey the text's similar assessment of time as an inescapable force. Instead, *Tess* brings more subtle strategies to bear in its examination of temporal influences, focusing on a thematic issue treated only tangentially in the other late-century novels: the particular and peculiar gender ramifications that the workings of time entail. In so doing, *Tess* serves as a cautionary tale for the New Woman. That Tess is a member of the lower class rather than the middle class of the New Woman is immaterial; the novel foregrounds the ways a woman, regardless of class status, is reductively appraised as merely a specimen of the sex in a culture that always defines women in broad biological terms rather than attend to individual characteristics or concerns. Although generally classified as a New Woman novel because of its frank treatment of female sexuality, *Tess* features a protagonist who is wholly an Old Woman, seemingly so dissimilar from a Sue Bridehead that any attempts to trace correspondences between Tess and her modern-minded counterparts would appear strained at best.[3] Yet *Tess* conveys an apposite message by suggesting that women are always judged by physiology, enmeshed within cultural conceptions that perpetuate the notion of an unchanging female essence across the ages and negate the possibility of substantive improvement in women's status.

As will become apparent, Hardy's characterization of Tess reveals a curious ambivalence about essentialism, for she is both deemed an immutable female type and shown as resistant to such a narrow representation. Yet the overall thrust of *Tess* more convincingly demonstrates that Hardy assumed that a definable female essence existed, despite the sympathies he conveyed for his character's inability to escape such a constrictive position. Support for this assessment comes from Hardy's expressed views in life as well as fiction, as a glance at his late-century letters reveals. Even though Hardy proclaims in one letter that the "doll of English fiction must be demolished" (250) and asserts that fiction does not do women justice—a point he never clarifies—Hardy perpetuates the stereotypes he ostensibly condemns. He presumes, for example, that an identifiable female type endures when he critiques women who attempt to stray from that standard. "[W]omen are quite worthy enough in nature to satisfy any reasonable being," he remarks, even though some "do not exhibit that nature truly & simply" (33) because of inappropriate actions. As a result, "the nature is condemned . . . when the form of its manifestation only is in fault." That Tess herself serves as an exemplar of this female "nature" is hinted through Hardy's suggestive characterization of her in another letter as "Tess the Woman" (249)—and indeed, the novel's subtitle reiterates Hardy's estimation of Tess as essence by designating her even more explicitly as a "pure woman."

It is the construction of "Tess the Woman" achieved specifically through the novel's temporal resonances that this chapter will address, examining both the broad structural inferences and the precise textual references that inform Tess's positioning within the natural order of time. Although numerous scholars have discussed *Tess*'s elaborate treatment of time,[4] the gender implications of this temporal attentiveness have received relatively little attention. My analysis focuses specifically on the intricate relationship between Tess and gendered time, which situates her in an inescapable double bind: she is controlled within the masculinized linear time of history and the feminized monumental time of art. In both cases, Tess is temporally defined through the materiality of the female body. In the first instance, Tess is inserted within patriarchal history as a somatic pawn who can participate in that history only marginally, always figured as an Other to the course of civilization.[5] In the second instance, Tess is wholly divorced from history, transformed into an aesthetic object frozen in time to become simply another exemplar of unchanging female essence.

Masculinized History

In a strategy reminiscent of *She, Tess* commences with the protagonist's entrance into history, signaling the prominent role that historical forces will play in the novel. As with Leo Vincey, Tess's particular positioning within history serves as the point of origin and impetus for the narrative; as in *She*, however, history is figured as a masculine province. In *Tess*'s opening paragraphs, it is her father's history that we are given, not her own, hinting that Tess is always already incorporated within a historical determinism over which she has no control. As Parson Tringham, an "antiquary," apprises John Durbeyfield of his familial past to initiate the narrative, the gendered component of history becomes increasingly evident:

> "Don't you really know, Durbeyfield, that you are the lineal representative of the ancient and knightly family of the d'Urbervilles, who derive their descent from Sir Pagan d'Urberville, that renowned knight who came from Normandy with William the Conqueror, as appears by Battle Abbey Roll?
> . . . "Yes, that's the d'Urberville nose and chin—a little debased.... Branches of your family held manors over all this part of England; their names appear in the Pipe Rolls in the time of King Stephen. In the reign of King John one of them was rich enough to give a manor to the Knights Hospitallers; and in Edward the Second's time your forefather Brian was summoned to Westminster to attend the great Council there. You declined a little in Oliver Cromwell's time, but to no serious extent, and in Charles the Second's reign you were made Knights of the Royal

Oak for your loyalty. Aye, there have been generations of Sir Johns among you. (43–44)

The startling parallels to *She* in this passage derive from a similar tracing of the course of Western civilization through the male line. In *Tess* the exclusively masculinist derivation of history is even more pronounced, since women are wholly absent from the chronicle, not even serving as vessels to carry the family from one generation to its successor.[6] As in *She*, male private history underlies public history, since the family's fortunes coincide with the pivotal events of Britain's illustrious past recorded in ancient annals. Sir Pagan's exploits are inscribed in the Battle Abbey Roll, a catalog of William the Conqueror's followers who accompanied him to England, and d'Urberville ancestors appear in the Pipe Rolls, the Exchequer documents detailing county events.[7] Linear references suffuse the passage to equate the progress of civilization with masculine linear time: John Durbeyfield is a "lineal representative" of Sir Pagan; Parson Tringham traces the "descent" of the family; and the recitation of ancestry proceeds methodically and sequentially from one historical period to the next. Indeed, the d'Urberville lineage reminds us of Hélène Cixous's designation of history as phallocentric repetition—"[t]he same masters" shape history throughout time, "inscribing on it the marks of their appropriating economy" in a substantively iterative pattern ("Sorties" 79). The connection between history and the natural order of time is further solidified with the choice of Parson Tringham as chronicler of the past.[8] As a representative of Christianity and an antiquary, Tringham embodies both the historical and religious discourses that buttress masculine temporality.

The gendered component of history also emerges through the marked ahistoricity of the female side of the family, represented by Joan Durbeyfield.[9] Joan herself draws the distinction in commenting that "I was never of no family" (67), a point the narrator stresses in citing her "unknightly, unhistorical" background (58). Instead, Joan evokes a sense of prehistory through her affinity for paganism, orality, and superstition. Her "people"—a telling noun that contrasts with her husband's "family" and the history implied by the latter term—reside near Stonehenge, perhaps the ultimate symbol of heathenism (484). Allied with the primitive past through her "lumber of superstitions, folk-lore, dialect, and orally transmitted ballads" (61), Joan can claim only a scant acquaintance with written texts, the emblems of civilization and progress. Her limited reading centers on *The Compleat Fortune-Teller*, a kind of pagan alternative to the Bible that she regularly consults, and she evinces a "curious fetichistic" compulsion connoting the ritualism of pagan cultures (61). With her "feminine voice," Joan keeps her own version of time as she rocks a cradle and sings a "favourite ditty" to her child (56). Other references to her propensity for song and musicality abound in the text, intermittently reinforcing her connection to the oral tradition of a prehistorical past.

Tess similarly displays the pagan inclinations and affiliations that mark her mother, as numerous references to Tess's distance from Christianity attest. The reader first encounters Tess, for instance, as she participates in the heathen ceremony of the May-Dance with the "votive sisterhood" who "uphold the local Cerealia" (49). Though subsequently identified as one "well grounded in the Holy Scriptures" (143), Tess prefers to indulge in "the half-unconscious rhapsody [that] was a Fetichistic utterance in a Monotheistic setting," revealing "far more of the Pagan fantasy" than of "systematized religion" (158). Not even aware if her sparse religious background conforms to "High, Low, or Broad" church practices, Tess's "confused beliefs," though "Tractarian as to phraseology," are "Pantheistic as to essence" (234). Tess's paganism thus separates her from the natural order of time both by distancing her from Christianity, with its grounding in linear time, and by linking her to the cyclical perception of time indicative of ancient cultures.[10]

The connection between women and paganism conveyed by these varied references is forged even more solidly when we consider its intertextual reappearance in the 1895 *Jude the Obscure*. Like the Durbeyfield women, Sue Bridehead displays heathen propensities that separate her from masculine time, especially when contrasted to Jude's absorption in Christian studies as "a parson in embryo" (278) striving to realize his theological vocation in the aptly named Christminster. In one of the text's most overdetermined scenes, Sue purchases two pagan statues at a stand significantly placed "almost in a line between herself and the church towers of the city" (140) to highlight through physical position her preference for paganism over Christianity. As she clutches the naked statues of Venus and Apollo, importantly "the largest figures on the tray" (141), Sue "entered with her heathen load into the most Christian city in the country" and selected "an obscure street running parallel to the main one" to reinforce geographically her intellectual displacement from Christian ideology. Sue's enshrinement of the pagan deities becomes a mockery of religious ritual: she puts them upon the altar-like surface of a bureau, bracketed by candles to imitate the reverent attention accorded icons within an ecclesiastical setting. Moreover, she selects a volume of Gibbon to read while she periodically observes the statues and turns to one of its most heterodox passages, a chapter on Julian the Apostate. As she registers the contrast between her statues and a "Calvary print hanging between them" in its Gothic frame, Sue consults yet another heathen text, the "familiar" Swinburne "Hymn to Proserpine" (143), and "read[s] to the end" its blasphemous lament over the rise of Christianity. Subsequently, Sue even offers to construct for Jude her own version of the New Testament by excising the original text and rearranging it like one she had devised for herself, a prospect to which Jude reacts "with a sense of sacrilege" (206) as he calls her "quite Voltairean!"(207).

Like *Tess*, *Jude* blends heathenism with ahistoricity to accentuate women's alienation from masculine temporality. Although Sue's fascination with classical cultures could connote a historical acuity, there is no past outside "the masculine" to which a female can retreat; to separate Sue from masculine history, the text instead foregrounds the ancients' pagan origins and affiliations. Indeed, Sue denies Jude's contention that she is "a creature of civilization," deeming his surmise "very odd" (201), an assessment with which Jude will come to agree when he associates her with the periods he studied in his "bygone, wasted, classical days" rather than consider her "a denizen of a mere Christian country" (337). When the pair attends an exhibition of a miniaturized ancient city, Sue asserts that "I fancy we have had enough of Jerusalem"—a site linked to Christianity—and insists "[t]here was nothing first-rate about the place, or people, after all" in contrast to "Athens, Rome, Alexandria"—early centers of paganism (156).[11]

Sue's displacement from masculine history becomes more pronounced through her reactions to Christminster, doubly associated with masculine time as an "ancient kingdom" (124) where "the past is deeply graven" (132) and as an "ecclesiastical romance in stone" (76). To Sue, however, Christminster history is meaningless; when Jude asks her "[h]ow can you do otherwise than cling to a city" so steeped in history, she answers, "What a funny reason for caring to stay! I should never have thought of it" (151). She dislikes ruins—a prominent feature of the city—and outspokenly "hate[s] Gothic" (189), Christminster's distinctive architectural style and the physical evidence of its past. Emphasizing that she has "no respect for Christminster whatever" (204), Sue characterizes it as an "ignorant place" inhabited by "fetichists and ghost-seers" (205).

Even Sue's own history is elided in the text; the minimal clues imparted about her life before meeting her cousin Jude are invariably filtered through his story. Sue's background garners only a passing comment in the narrative's lengthy recitation of Jude's own familial and personal past. Their aunt, for instance, remarks upon Jude's voracious consumption of books, noting, "It runs in our family," but merely adds the offhand comment that "[h]is cousin Sue is just the same—so I've heard" (52).[12] Sue's experiences thereafter are always mediated by a male character, presented in terms of their effects upon Jude or her sometime husband Phillotson. Like *Tess,* then, *Jude* persistently demonstrates that women—whether New or Old—can claim only a marginal connection with the masculinist workings of history.

That Hardy strove to make that point abundantly clear in *Tess* gains further support if we briefly consider a novel published a decade earlier, the 1881 *A Laodicean.* The text follows the fortunes of Paula Power, the heiress of a railway tycoon, who purchases the castle of the once-illustrious De Stancy family. Like Sue and the Durbeyfield women, Paula holds a perfunctory and problematic relationship with history, gaining access to it only through proximity as the inhabitant of the castle's ancient expanse. Seemingly entrenched within modernity as a New Woman figure who articulates advanced views on religion and education and installs a telegraph in the decrepit castle, Paula instead cannot truly locate herself within a historical continuum. "A mixed young lady" (39), Paula is poised between eras, as intimated by her eclectic bedchamber in which Victorian papers and prints are "ensconced amid so much of the old and hoary," seeming "as if a stray hour from the nineteenth century had wandered like a butterfly into the thirteenth, and lost itself there" (40). Further evidence of Paula's confused placement within history comes through her odd plans for restoring the castle in an array of historical styles, combining her fondness for classical architecture with the edifice's original medieval form that she has already adulterated with her modern alterations. Paula, along with her Hardy sisters, is out of step with the rhythms of history and Other to its time.

Problematized Relationships to History

As John Durbeyfield's "debased" facial profile has hinted, however, *Tess* does not construct history in the unequivocally positive terms we encountered in *She.* Instead, *Tess* incorporates the antithetical strains of Victorian discourse theorizing the workings of history. The prevalent view saw history as progressive, building on Thomas Babington Macaulay's influential mid-century essays that were echoed in later decades by Darwinians who equated evolution with advancement; the contrary position anxiously pointed to the devolutionary ramifications of Darwinism through which the decline of humanity seemed as plausible as its progress. As John Ruskin framed the dichotomy, "'progress and decline' were 'strangely mixed in the modern mind'" (qtd. in Siegel 199), for the continual changes of the nineteenth century evoked the intertwined processes of development and decay (Chamberlin 263).[13]

Negative connotations of history permeate *Tess* to mirror the anxieties about degeneration and extinction that emerged with increasing frequency in the *fin de siècle* and to counter the positive associations generated by the d'Urberville chronicle. Images of materiality, for example, convey a physical erosion that reflects the diminishment of Tess's family over time and add a disquieting element to the seemingly progressive course of history. The d'Urberville name is "worn away to Durbeyfield" (80), the familial inheritance has been reduced to an "old seal and spoon" (156), and an ancestral estate has deteriorated into an inn where the lower-class Tess spends her wedding night (283). In effect, the family is reduced to an abstruse text, a page in a dusty tome in the British Museum itemizing "extinct, half-extinct, obscured, and ruined families" (78) that can be readily appropriated and reinscribed by Alec Stoke, the counterfeit d'Urberville. So dissipated is the family line that it seemingly has "gone round the circle and become a new one" (184); so disempowered is familial authority that "[t]he little finger of the sham d'Urberville can do more ... than the whole dynasty of the real underneath" (449).

Jude the Obscure and *A Laodicean* provide instructive parallels for *Tess*'s ambivalent view of history. *Jude,* for example, figures Christminster as a site of present decay as well as past progress to convey the twin aspects of historical movement. The vibrant qualities of Christminster that Jude unfailingly praises are undercut by degenerative images, such as the "decrepit" chambers of the colleges (125), one of which appropriately carries the name of Sarcophagus College; their "wounded, broken" buildings reflect "something barbaric" and resemble "family vaults" (130). Indeed, "[t]he spirits of the great men had disappeared," leaving as their only trace the "rottenness" of the "historical documents" the buildings contain. Rather than embodying the primitive energy that Victorians applauded, medievalism in *Jude* is "as dead as a fern-leaf in a lump of coal," left behind by "other developments" fashioning a world "in which Gothic architecture and its associations had no place" (131). Other historical references in the text similarly trace the forces of deterioration and replacement. Throughout Jude's childhood village of Marygreen, for instance, modern edifices or alterations appear where ancient churches, temples, and relics once stood. Even the landscape itself bears telling marks, for "fresh harrow-lines seemed to stretch like... new corduroy," obliterating "all history beyond that of the few recent months" and silencing the historical echoes of "every clod and stone" (53).

Like *Tess*, *A Laodicean* narrows history to specific familial terms rather than the broad scope of *Jude* in focusing on the faded De Stancy line, whose current representatives are all severed from their own past. The patriarch Sir William has steeped himself in modern concerns, attuned to fluctuations in currency and foreign stocks but oblivious to De Stancy history. His daughter Charlotte, Paula's close acquaintance, echoes her father's lack of interest in ancestry and "cares nothing about those things" (103). The younger William, eventual heir to the baronetcy and frustrated suitor of Paula, displays only a fleeting concern with the De Stancy lineage as a means of winning his beloved. Throughout the text come intimations that the family will continue its decline. Now impoverished, the family can hope to improve its fortunes only through the advantageous marriage that the younger William envisions with Paula, but the union never comes to fruition. Neither son nor daughter will continue the De Stancy bloodline by providing a legitimate child, literally or figuratively—in fact, the sole offspring is the future baronet's bastard son, who barely avoids the imprisonment that his deceitful maneuverings deserve. Ultimately, the De Stancy castle burns into ashes, annihilating all vestiges of the family's illustrious past and auguring the line's fated destruction.

Yet the deterioration of the De Stancy line, like its d'Urberville counterpart, comes only after centuries of family progress. In *Tess* the reminders of familial glory are encapsulated in the sir-name and surname of Sir Pagan d'Urberville himself: the family evolved from the heathen origins incorporated in his given name to become influential figures shaping British culture. In a sense, family history follows the process of natural selection, moving toward virtual extinction only after generations of flourishing growth. Darwinian associations in Parson Tringham's chronicle reinforce that connection; the family has "quite died out of knowledge" (44) to become "extinct—as a county family," one that can hold only the minimal interest of "the local historian and genealogist" (45). Though Tringham advises John Durbeyfield that he can do "nothing, nothing" to reverse the familial fortunes other than "chasten yourself with the thought of 'how are the mighty fallen,'" John can at least take consolation in musing upon ancient d'Urberville achievements. To an extent, the d'Urbervilles controlled their own destiny, for at each stage in their progress, the forefathers actively directed the course of family history—aiding in conquests, presiding over estates, and participating in political deliberations. Though the precipitative cause of the d'Urberville decline remains untold, the suggestive verb that Tringham repeats in noting that the family is "extinct in the male line—that is, gone down—gone under" conveys a modicum of agency on the part of the patriarchs. Since John is a representative of the male line, it is extinct only in a figurative sense, presumably disempowered through the patriarchs' misguided actions or imprudent decisions.

For the female, however, no such agency ever exists. Tess' seduction/rape, for example, represents her unwitting and passive incorporation into family history, as she is punished for "the sins of [her] fathers" (119). Tess becomes a temporally displaced victim, in a sense, converted into a modern analogue of the peasants "ruthlessly" raped by her "mailed ancestors"—an apt pun that accentuates the masculine control over history (119). A female's participation in history involves only a predestined role, such as Tess's fated re-experiencing of ancient rape, or a supportive role, such as the one performed by her mother. This ancillary function is best exemplified by Joan Durbeyfield's careful schemes for Tess to claim kinship with the parvenu d'Urbervilles and wed the son after the Durbeyfield connection to the noble line is revealed. Despite the "energy" of her own "unexpended family" (158), Joan links her daughter's destiny to the dissipated d'Urberville side, intimating that a mother's family—regardless of its comparative vitality—is immaterial. The fate of her immediate family, Joan's machinations suggest, rests exclusively on its relationship to the male line. Through her sex, Joan is figured as an Other to history; if we apply Cixous's useful terms, d'Urberville history proceeds through an appropriation of the Other, an "alterity that does settle down" to become incorporated within the dialectical process that enables history to unfold ("Sorties" 71).

Further support for this interpretation comes in Hardy's treatment of d'Urberville history in a dramatic version of *Tess* he penned in 1894–95 under the same title.[14] With logistic and temporal constraints, a theatrical presentation allows only the crucial thematic elements of a story to be culled and told—and Hardy's drama reflects the focal importance that the novel accords to male history. The five-act play immediately directs attention to that history in its opening lines, which relate Joan Durbeyfield's conversation with a young acquaintance:

> *Sarah*: Has this notion of Tess's going away anything to do with your husband finding out that he is descended from the old ancient family of D'Urberville?
> *Joan*: Why yes! As soon as Pa'son Tringham the antiqueerian told us that my husband is Sir John D'Urberville by right I thought of the rich lady and her son of that name, living out at Trantridge, and I packed off Tess to claim kin. (3)

As this exchange discloses, the drama takes both its narrative impetus and subsequent direction from the influence and workings of male history. Tess's story—launched by her "going away"—is initiated solely by her relationship to the d'Urberville line and her mother's efforts to promote Tess's connection with its presumed modern descendant.

The obsessive concern with history that suffuses Hardy's novel correspondingly pervades his drama, with frequent references to the d'Urberville past highlighting both the family's ancient pedigree— "We've been here ever since the Conqueror's day"—and its degeneration, signaled by John Durbeyfield's linguistic failings as he notes the family's survival "all through Oliver Grumble's time" and the "skillentons" in the family vault (20). Unlike the novel, however, the drama overtly conveys Joan's discontent with the subordinate role she is obliged to perform in furthering Tess's fortunes through the male line. Following the recitation of the family's exploits that her husband has just verbally mangled, Joan responds, "Hang your old family blood! 'Tis what shall we do to keep our heads above water now this has happened to Tess" (20). Moreover, she silences her spouse after he advises Tess to "stand out for your family" with the rejoinder, "Shut up—you stupid,—with your family!" (28). When her husband inquires, "Who's that a-mentioning my family name?" Joan chooses the ambiguous pronoun in the contraction "'tis" to begin her reply, which paradoxically nullifies the value of the cognomen: "'Tis nothing, Sir John" (24).

Joan's pointed remarks in the drama concerning the d'Urberville line offer insights into the novel's latent hints of her similar discontent with the female relationship to history. As Joan's musings and plottings for Tess's future imply, a masculinist view of history constructs the female role merely in terms of the body; a woman's tenuous link to history is limited to the materiality of an eroticized form.[15] A casual interjection in the dramatized *Tess* accentuates this connection, as Joan prefaces a remark to her daughter about gentlemen always "tak[ing] notice of 'ee'" with the suggestive phrase, "Upon my body!" (27). Like the drama, the novel identifies the female's contribution to history as the perpetuation of her body into the next generation. The "personal charms" that distinguish Tess are "in main part her mother's gift" (58); demonstrating a similar propensity for song, earlier associated with the female body as Joan sang her lullaby to the child she rocked, Tess reveals an "innate love of melody ... inherited from her ballad-singing mother" (133); and noting that she carries "as much of mother as father in me," Tess comments that "[a]ll my prettiness comes from her" (156). As her father unwittingly recognizes in promoting Tess's introduction to Alec d'Urberville, Tess's effect upon family history is confined to her status as "such a comely sample of his own blood" (91).

An exchange between the Durbeyfield elders corroborates the notion that, within a masculinized historical perspective, the female is always defined in terms of the body. In the scene, Tess's parents debate the wisdom of allowing her to leave the family cottage for the d'Urberville estate:

> Joan Durbeyfield always managed to find consolation somewhere: "Well, as one of the genuine stock, she ought to make her way with 'en, if she plays her trump card aright. And if he don't marry her afore he will after. For that he's all afire wi' love for her any eye can see."
> "What's her trump card? Her d'Urberville blood, you mean?"
> "No, stupid; her face—as 'twas mine." (93)

In Joan's construction of events, Tess's appearance, not her ancient blood, will determine her future history with Alec d'Urberville and enable her to repeat an experiential pattern initiated by a tempting visage. The body becomes a marker of female trickery, as insinuated by the reference to the "trump" card, an adjective that connotes deceit and conquest. Tess's body will serve as the vehicle for entrapping the wealthy cousin, since pregnancy presumably will force a marriage if mere attraction fails; only through the market of female bodies that marriage can be considered to represent could Tess achieve social mobility and alter her history.

The correlation between female history and the female body is reinforced by the personal calendar that Tess later constructs. To Tess, all of history can be related to somatic experience:

> She philosophically noted dates as they came past in the revolution of the year; the disastrous night of her undoing at Trantridge with its dark background of The Chase; also the dates of the baby's birth and death; also her own birthday; and every other day

> individualized by incidents in which she had taken some share. She suddenly thought one afternoon, when looking in the glass at her fairness, that there was yet another date, of greater importance to her than those; that of her own death, when all these charms would have disappeared. (149)

Tess reveals through this egocentric chronology her distance from the broader workings of history as recorded in a public calendar. Nearly all of the dates identified by Tess relate to the eroticized body: the night of her seduction/rape, the resulting birth of a baby, and the eventual death she ponders while examining her corporeal attractions in a mirror. Death, to Tess, represents not so much the cessation of life as the moment "when all these charms would have disappeared." Indeed, as a later reference underscores, "[u]pon her sensations the whole world depended to Tess" (214).

As her relationship with Angel Clare further demonstrates, the definition of history for Tess invariably translates into the history of her body. Tess fears, for instance, that the banns for her marriage will be challenged on "the ground of her history" (271). She repeatedly expresses a desire to tell Angel of her past—exclaiming, for example, "But my history. I want you to know it" (252)—yet shrinks from the revelation, substituting family lineage for somatic history. Tess longs to present "her whole history" (373) to Angel's mother, who in turn wonders if Tess is "a young woman whose history will bear investigation" (337). Significantly, admonishments to conceal the past come from Joan Durbeyfield, writing in her anachronistic, "wandering last-century hand" (256), based on her recognition that female history and destiny are irrevocably tied to the body.

The force of that connection within the natural order of time is compounded when Tess coincidentally encounters an itinerant sign-painter. Writing in a lurid vermilion, the painter seemingly directs his biblical admonition specifically to Tess, shouting his message through the capitals and commas that emphasize each word of the phrase, "Thy, damnation, slumbereth, not" (128). An eroticized reference to the phrase's "enter[ing] Tess with accusatory horror" suggests that Tess equates damnation with sexuality, since the painter writes as if he "had known her recent history" despite being "a total stranger." With its warning that damnation never slumbers, the phrase implicitly links perdition to the body itself, as if Tess's damnation is preordained merely through corporeality. Attesting to the general sexualization of the female, the painter responds to Tess's query whether he "believe[s] what you paint" in unequivocal terms: "Believe that tex [*sic*]? Do I believe in my own existence!" The painter strengthens the sexual link in musing that he will inscribe another message "for dangerous young females like yerself to heed"—the command not to commit adultery.

Tess's recognition that female history is defined by and equated with the body leads to discontent with the workings of history itself. In one signal scene, Tess rejects the offer of Angel, "a student of history" (183), to teach her about the subject and "help you to anything in the way of history" (182):

> [W]hat's the use of learning that I am one of a long row only—finding out that there is set down in some old book somebody just like me, and to know that I shall only act her part; making me sad, that's all. The best is not to remember that your nature and your past doings have been just like thousands' and thousands', and that your coming life and doings 'll be like thousands' and thousands'. (182)

Juxtaposed in the passage are contrasting definitions of masculine and feminine history. The linear progression and dynamism underlying Victorian conceptions of historical movement, which could be attributed to the "long row" that Tess identifies, are immediately countered by the notion of a static female history, regardless of a woman's class status, in which Tess will simply repeat the "part" enacted by all other women. In yoking "nature" and "past doings," Tess makes the terms analogous; female nature determines her history, a pattern repeated endlessly without substantive variation. Furthermore, a later reference rearticulates the distance from history conveyed in this passage. When Angel asks Tess if she is not "interested yourself in being one of that well-known line," Tess replies with an emphatic negative as she appraises her d'Urberville affiliation as "sad" (253).

The exhausted and repetitive tone that history carries in these passages reflects a persistent concern surfacing in Hardy's canon, particularly in two poems that retrospectively provide a context for reading *Tess*'s historically troubling scenes. Hardy's 1916 "The Pedigree" captures the sense of despair that *Tess* similarly imparts through the representation of personal history as numbing repetition. With its central image of a mirror, the poem depicts history as a kind of *mis-en-abîme*, an infinite sequence of iterative acts through which subjects can only reflect their predecessors. In effect, history initiates its own mirror stage through which subjectivity is fashioned exclusively in response to the past. The second poem, titled "Tess' Lament" and included in the 1901 collection "Poems of the Past and Present," narrows the thematic valences to gender terms. Again the persona equates history with repetition, but in this poem the feeling of enervation is far more pronounced, as if history imposes an especially heavy burden on women. The poem conveys a weariness that collapses into an unbearable despair and sense of entrapment escapable only by a nullification of the subject.

The novel *Tess* offers the same message of history as a constrictive and ensnaring force early in the narrative to focus our reading of the text through this perspective. As Tess drives the family wagon to the marketplace, she seemingly strives to loosen the bonds of historical determinism by transcending time itself. While the cart moves hypnotically, Tess lapses into a reverie and mentally elides temporal states as she immerses herself in the ambient natural phenomena. Suggesting the traditional dichotomy between temporal history and eternal nature, the scene fuses the two to disrupt time as an ordering principle controlling Tess's existence:

> The mute procession past her shoulders of trees and hedges became attached to fantastic scenes outside reality, and the occasional heave of the wind became the sigh of some immense sad soul, conterminous with the universe in space, and with history in time.
>
> Then, examining the mesh of events in her own life, she seemed to see the vanity of her father's pride; the gentlemanly suitor awaiting herself in her mother's fancy. . . . Everything grew more and more extravagant, and she no longer knew how time passed. (70)

In the passage's opening sentence, the markers of the present—the trees and hedges of Tess's surroundings—collapse into the "fantastic scenes outside reality" that confuse a temporal grounding. Contributing to this vertiginous blending is the juxtaposition of space and time as a disembodied soul occupies both the amorphous time of the cosmos ("the universe in space") and the linear time of history. Yet the atemporal state that Tess has cognitively created dissolves immediately, for in the sentence following this passage, "[a] sudden jerk" awakens her to the present. Appropriately, the disturbance occurs when the wagon collides with a mailcart, a multivalent signifier of linear time. Conforming to tight schedules, a mailcart transmits the written texts that record lived history; yet it privileges a masculine version of history, as the mailcart's homonymic pun, like Tess's "mailed ancestors," connotes. Even the movement of the mailcart replicates the unidirectional progression of linear time, "speeding along these lanes like an arrow, as it always did" (71). Tess's effort to escape time, the scene hints, is not simply ineffectual but also punishable. The mailcart kills the horse that has economically sustained the Durbeyfields, creating overwhelming guilt in Tess and leading her to accede to her parents' wish that she meet the sham d'Urbervilles.

On a broad thematic level, the mailcart incident is critical for examining Tess's ongoing resistance to history and perpetual struggle to elude its control, evidenced in part by her attempts to separate herself from her origins through language. She responds, for instance, to Alec's distinction between his surname and the humble Durbeyfield with the comment, "I wish for no better" (82), and in indirect voice she rejects her noble ancestors as "useless" (156). More compellingly, the novel translates Tess's discontent with history into a series of attempted physical dislocations from the past. In effect, Tess labors to escape time through space, both by geographically distancing herself from her origins and, as we shall later see, by diminishing her own corporeality.[16]

Tess's desire to separate herself physically from her history manifests itself in her periodic wanderings across the Wessex landscape. As J. Hillis Miller observes in *Distance and Desire*, such travels represent the transformation of time into space, for Tess's "temporal passage" is reconfigured as a sequential pattern of movement across the terrain (200). To Miller, this transformation underscores the determinism shaping Tess's life; "[s]pace fatalizes" (200) by implying that Tess's temporal path is already marked out, as she proceeds from a past to a predetermined future demarcated within a spatial grid (202). In *Fiction and Repetition,* Miller elaborates on the point by identifying a "linear sequentiality" to Tess's life path that adheres to a preordained pattern of "repetition with a difference" (128–29). Tess's journeys represent not only a temporal or spatial continuum governed by repetition, however, but a series of inadvertent returns to the past that stress the impossibility of an escape from history—and, indeed, ultimately bring her to the very origins of history in the penultimate scene at Stonehenge.

Each segment of Tess's travels entails a return to the family history she seeks to transcend, as a brief recapitulation of her movements makes evident. The pivotal seduction/rape scene occurs in The Chase, the primordial setting where Tess's "mailed ancestors" once roamed (119).

The Talbothays dairy to which she flees after the death of her illegitimate child lies near the former d'Urberville estates and family vaults (151). The marital journey to Wellbridge follows an acquaintance's recognition of Tess and her resulting desire to "go away, a very long distance, hundreds of miles from these parts," where "no ghost of the past [can] reach" (274); yet the Wellbridge lodgings—nearby, not distant—where she and Angel retire were once a d'Urberville manor, complete with a gallery of disturbing family portraits (283). Tess's flight to Flintcomb-Ash, begun as a means of "disconnecting herself by littles from her eventful past at every step, obliterating her identity" (349), merely returns her to Alec's unwanted attentions and incessant reminders of the past. The family relocation to Kingsbere after her father's death places her at the vaults of the d'Urberville ancestors, where her mother decides to reside temporarily until "the place of your ancestors finds us a roof" (447). The Sandbourne watering place to which Tess accompanies Alec is distinguished by a "prehistoric" soil (463) that again suggests the omnipresence of Tess's own history. Tess's concluding journey to Stonehenge represents both the furthermost return to the past and provides an ancient tableau upon which Tess's personal history will wind to its close. Throughout Tess's journeys come references to the "roundabout railway" (123) that "engirdled this interior tract of country" (155), delineating an enclosed space from which efforts to escape are futile.

Of these many returns, those that herald a critical change in Tess's fortunes incorporate another equally meaningful return—a retracing of her steps to her mother. Tess's seduction/rape, failed marriage, and fateful reunion with Alec that leads to murder and her own death are all connected with a retreat to the Durbeyfield home. Coupled with the multiple returns to the d'Urberville past, these visits remind us of Tess's double enmeshment in history: she is both a patrilineal pawn, as we have seen, and an embodiment of an enduring female nature informing a masculinist construction of history.

Tess's returns to the family cottage reinscribe her status as female essence, because the home is multiply identified as a female space in both geographic and individualistic terms. On a large scale, the home is located in a "fertile and sheltered tract of country" (48), metonymically associated with female fecundity and maternal protection. On a more localized scale, the village of Marlott in which stands the Durbeyfield residence evokes the essentialized Victorian diptych of woman as virgin or whore: the town's first syllable, "Mar," visually conveys a Marian resonance that is countered by the rhyme with "harlot" that the full name carries. The initial description of the cottage itself is replete with definitive feminine images. Long before Tess enters the home in the novel's opening pages, "rhythmic sounds" become audible as Joan rocks the thumping cradle and sings to her child (56). Within the house, Joan's children surround her while she does the weekly wash as part of her domestic routine (57). Joan's propensity for speaking dialect and her fondness for *The Compleat Fortune-Teller*—linguistic and paganistic signifiers of the female, as I have discussed—first emerge within the confines of the home. In contrast, the text distances Joan's husband from the domestic realm: he is absent from the house in this first glimpse of its interior; he is a "shiftless husband" frequently away from the home (60) who contributes nothing to the family's survival, ignoring even the cultivation of a vegetable plot; and he learns of his ancestral past during one such absence, encountering Parson Tringham in the outskirts of Marlott. The periodic visits to the Durbeyfield cottage that punctuate Tess's movement across the countryside serve, then, to throw into relief Tess's association with the body through an affiliation with her mother and also initiate her numerous attempts to dissociate herself from the female form.

Female Essence

The critical role that the body will play in the novel as the signifier of female essence is presaged not only by Tess's resemblance and returns to her mother, but also by the array of religious and mythological references that bind Tess to timeless female subject positions and establish a foundation for a subsequent reading of Tess as an aesthetic form. Among the most arresting parallels drawn between Tess and archetypal women are the frequent comparisons to Eve. For example, in one particularly significant passage, in which Angel observes his beloved, Tess becomes an "Eve at her second waking" (232):

> She was yawning, and he saw the red interior of her mouth as if it had been a snake's. She had stretched one arm so high above her coiled-up cable of hair that he could see its satin delicacy.... The brimfulness of her nature breathed from her. It was a moment when a woman's soul is more incarnate than at any other time: when the most spiritual beauty bespeaks itself flesh; and sex takes the outside place in the presentation. (231)

The sole positive reference in this passage, attesting to Tess's "spiritual beauty," is undercut by abundant suggestions of sexuality and danger. In "bespeak[ing] itself" as "flesh," the spiritual component immediately collapses into the conventional designation of the female as an unclean body, implied by the resonance of "incarnate" with carnality. Tess's serpentine mouth and coiled hair convert her into a satanic figure who is further condemned by the sexual undertones of devourment ("yawning") and Medusan menace. Such attributes, the passage hints, are manifestations of an inherent female core, for they represent "[t]he brimfulness" of a "nature" that "breathed from her." As such, the body, "the outside place in the presentation," is the marker of an inner and integral corruption. Other textual references reinforce Tess's connection with Eve: she is specifically addressed by that name, for example, soon after the fateful reunion with Alec precipitating his Adam-like lapse into temptation (431); and during an early encounter with Angel the two reenact the prelapsarian scene as "the first persons up of all the world," like "Adam and Eve" (186).

Mythological allusions expand Tess's affiliation to an immutable female type, beginning with the May-Dance honoring Ceres, an emblem of female fertility and nature (49). In another telling passage, Tess herself assumes the essentialized qualities of pagan divinities—one representing chastity, the other fecundity—again through Angel's perspective:

> She was no longer the milkmaid, but a visionary essence of woman—a whole sex condensed into one typical form. He called her Artemis, Demeter, and other fanciful names half teasingly, which she did not like because she did not understand them.
> "Call me Tess," she would say askance. (187)

Despite Tess's unfamiliarity with the goddesses to whom she is compared, the text assumes that an innate female intuitiveness warns Tess that such designations deny individual difference. In urging Angel to "[c]all me Tess," she resists such reductive attempts to position her as the quintessential female.

Other male-conferred names for Tess similarly evoke conventional categorizations of women that reduce her to an eroticized body linked to temptation, cunning, and peril. To Alec, for example, Tess is "my Beauty" (79), a "witch of Babylon" (402), and an "artful hussy" (97); to Angel, Tess is an "interesting specimen of womankind" (186) and a "bewitching milkmaid" (259). As with Medusa, a careless glance alone can bring disaster. Gazing upon Tess "might be dangerous" (388) to Alec, a presumption borne out by the rekindling of his lust once he observes "those eyes and that mouth again," before which he had been as "firm as a man could be" (402). Indeed, Tess internalizes an ongoing cultural presumption that "she was somehow doing wrong" merely by "inhabiting the fleshy tabernacle with which nature had endowed her" (388).

The preceding examples lead us to the text's most complex and consequential representation of female essence: the figuration of Tess as an aesthetic object. As Terry Eagleton asserts, aesthetics illuminates "a range of wider social, political and ethical issues" (*Ideology* 1) that carry gender ramifications as well as the class implications he specifically addresses. If, as Eagleton comments, views of "the aesthetic artefact" are bound to "[t]he construction of the dominant ideological forms of modern class-society" (3), then aesthetic judgments are equally embedded in the gender constructions that undergird the social order. As Kathy Alexis Psomiades observes, "representations of femininity . . . play an integral part in the cultural work aestheticism does" (2). Through the artistic process, I argue in my reading of *Tess,* one woman becomes emblematic of Everywoman, a distillation of an essence perpetuated across time through the depiction of the female body.

Art thus serves a dehistoricizing function, converting a discrete moment within linear time into eternity by presenting seemingly immutable truths divorced from the vagaries of history. Julia Kristeva's theorization of "woman's time" illuminates this gendered relationship between art and history. In effect, aesthetic representation transforms the living woman into an immortal woman frozen within monumental time—an infinitude, Kristeva observes, traditionally associated with female subjectivity through women's reproductive power and the continuation of humanity across generations. Mapped onto the aesthetic process, Kristeva's paradigm situates the artist within linear temporality, located at a precise historical point and contributing to the course of civilization through his work. An aestheticized woman, however, transcends her historical grounding as his model to become a symbol of womanhood that spans the centuries through the eternalizing quality of art itself.

Although primarily attentive to the implications of visual art, *Tess* constructs its protagonist as a polysemic aesthetic symbol: she is a blank canvas to be worked, a landscape figure to be rendered, and a portrait to be gazed upon, as well as a malleable substance to be sculpted. In aestheticizing Tess, the novel echoes and extends a Victorian literary tradition, most pronounced in poetry, that accords to art an explicitly masculinist perspective of female essence. In so doing, *Tess* participates in the commodification and victimization that such figurations of women entail. As in Robert Browning's ironic "My Last Duchess," for instance, the metaphoric portraiture of Tess enables a male observer to mold her subjectivity within a narrow construct of womanhood. As in Elizabeth Barrett Browning's "A Musical Instrument," *Tess* hints that the creative perspective is attained through female pain. As in Dante Gabriel Rossetti's *House of Life* sonnet sequence, Tess as female body is reduced to a collection of fetish objects. And as in Christina Rossetti's "In an Artist's Studio," the masculine aesthetic vision conveyed in *Tess* is self-referential, depicting the female merely as an idealized conception of the artist.

Penned during the height of Paterian influence, *Tess*, like Hardy's other *fin de siècle* novels—particularly *The Well-Beloved* and, to a lesser extent, *The Woodlanders*, *Jude the Obscure*, and *The Mayor of Casterbridge*—brings the dominant tenets of late-century aestheticism to bear upon fiction. Those principles reveal an ethical elasticity that allows an artist to manipulate "reality" in the service of "truth." In *The Renaissance*, for example, Walter Pater denied art's "responsibilities to its subject or material" (108), intimating a certain amorality underlying the creative process. In the essay, "The English Renaissance of Art," Oscar Wilde similarly presupposed "a separate realm for the artist, a consciousness of the absolute difference between the world of art and the world of real fact" (130); in the prefatory aesthetic manifesto of *The Picture of Dorian Gray*, Wilde asserts that "[t]here is no such thing as a moral or an immoral book" (21). In a disquisition on nineteenth-century painting, Arthur Symons admired the artistic ability to proceed "through outward things to their essence, that is, to their essential reality" (227). Hardy himself articulates these views in commenting that "[a]rt is a changing of the actual proportions and order of things, so as to bring out more forcibly ... that feature in them which appeals most strongly to the idiosyncracy of the artist" (*Life* 228). In distinguishing art from "realism," Hardy further asserts: "Art is a disproportioning—(i.e. distorting, throwing out of proportion)—of realities, to show more clearly the features that matter in those realities, which, if merely copied or reported inventorially, might possibly be observed, but would more probably be overlooked" (229). The same principles apply to the novel reader, Hardy advises in the 1888 "Profitable Reading of Fiction": one who reads "for something more than amusement" must distinguish a text's "eternal" truths (145).

The blending of visual and narrative art achieved in Hardy's fiction through aesthetic descriptions of women doubly serves to suggest the validity of the "eternal truths" that the texts, particularly *Tess*, strive to present. Yet through the narrative voice, *Tess* hints at authorial uneasiness about art's role in reflecting and reifying essentialist ideology. In its overwrought descriptions of the comely Tess, the masculine narrative voice evinces not only a fondness for such representations, but also the realization that they imprison their objects. Nevertheless, the narrator joins with the text's male characters in objectifying Tess. In proffering biased descriptions of Tess as objective narratorial omniscience, the narrator assimilates the reader into such reductive assessments as well. By ignoring the individual woman in favor of a standard, aesthetic representations of Tess suggest that all women can be apprised and defined by immutable "truths."

The workings of aestheticism in *Tess* reflect the thematic valences of a subsequent Hardy text, *The Well-Beloved*, which traces in expansive strokes the view of art that emerges more covertly in the 1891 novel. Simply by designating its protagonist as an artist, the 1892 *Well-Beloved* foregrounds the complicity of aesthetic tradition in perpetuating the fallacious conception of an essential femaleness. With its primary focus on the masculine aesthetic vision, *The Well-Beloved* thus provides a useful companion text for examining the relationship between art and essence that similarly informs *Tess*.

Intriguingly titled "Time Against Two" in an early manuscript, *The Well-Beloved* traces the quest of Jocelyn Pierston—a sculptor of humble origins who gradually gains prominence and becomes a Royal Academician—for the elusive "Well-Beloved" of his imagination. The Beloved encapsulates Jocelyn's estimation of ideal womanhood, an essence that drifts from female to female during the course of his life:

> To his Well-Beloved he had always been faithful; but she had had many embodiments. Each individuality known as Lucy, Jane, Flora, Evangeline, or whatnot, had been merely a transient condition of her. . . . Essentially she was perhaps of no tangible substance; a spirit, a dream, a frenzy, a conception, an aroma, an epitomized sex, a light of the eye, a parting of the lips. (16)

As this passage reveals, the Well-Beloved transcends the current form in which it takes residence, a point reiterated in epigraphs, chapter titles, and the invariable capitalization of the Beloved's nominal designations. In the novel's initial epigraph, for example, the male persona of a brief verse asserts that he will end his search for "Her," the woman who accords with his version of ideality, once he finds "Her that dares be / What these lines wish to see" (8). Chapter titles herald a "Suppositious Presentment of Her," proclaim "The Incarnation is Assumed to Be True," and catalog "Her Earlier Incarnations." Inhabiting a broad array of physical types and social classes, the Well-Beloved moves rapidly and unexpectedly, a "Protean dream-creature" (88) independent of Jocelyn's will:

> For months he would find her on the stage of a theatre.... She would reappear, it might be, in an at first unnoticed lady, met at some fashionable evening-party, exhibition, bazaar, or dinner; to flit from her, in turn, after a few months, and stand as a graceful shop-girl.
> ... She was a blonde, a brunette, tall, petite, svelte, straight-featured, full, curvilinear. Only one quality remained unalterable: her instability of tenure. (51-52)

Not only is the specific woman in whom the Beloved temporarily resides insignificant, but once Jocelyn gains even a slight familiarity with an individual, the Beloved soon departs. As Jocelyn explains the phenomenon to an acquaintance, "[a]s flesh she dies daily"; once he "grapple[s] with the reality she's no longer in it" (52). The women in whom the Beloved appears function merely as vessels for the essence, a series of interchangeable domiciles—a "human shell" (13), "tenement" (36), "abode" (37), "lodgings" (64), and "fleshly tabernacle" (17). In contrast, the Beloved endures as "a subjective phenomenon" (16) whose transcendence of time is underscored through mythic associations that identify the Beloved as a "deity" (35), "Aphrodite," "capricious Divinity" (85), "nymph," and "mystic magnet" (85).

Jocelyn can arrest the migratory Beloved only through his art, capturing his perception of female essence through a variety of sculptural manifestations. Indeed, his artistic fame rests on such portrayals, accommodating and influencing public interest through "all these dreams he translated into plaster" (52). So pervasively does the Beloved inform his aesthetic sense that he works upon these statues to the exclusion of all others, becoming "a one-part man—a presenter of her only" (63). Yet Jocelyn's sculptures suggest a curious slippage between the real and the ideal, for the aesthetic vision that shapes his work is grafted onto and made inseparable from lived experience. Jocelyn can become enamored of an individual woman only when he figuratively transforms her into an aesthetic form, a sentient representation of the essence captured in marble.

This blurring of art and reality is especially pronounced in Jocelyn's relationship with Avice Caro, his first fiancée, and her daughter and granddaughter. In all three cases, Jocelyn converts the woman into his conception of Woman, each indistinguishable from the others.

Jocelyn's infatuation with Avice Caro develops years after her death, decades after he had ignored his betrothal promise because he feared that the Beloved did not inhabit Avice's form. Only when he chances upon a photograph of the young Avice does Jocelyn realize that the Beloved had indeed existed in her, but that recognition comes only after she has been converted into the quasi-aesthetic form of photographic representation, enabling him to love "the woman dead and inaccessible as he had never loved her in life" (72). Avice is translated into an essentialized woman; once "[t]he flesh was absent altogether," Jocelyn can experience "love rarefied and refined to its highest attar"—having "felt nothing like it before" (73) because no other woman in his past had been similarly aestheticized.[17]

Jocelyn subsequently transfers his aesthetic vision to Avice's daughter, whom he insists on calling Avice rather than her given name of Ann. To Jocelyn, Avice the Second, as he terms her, becomes merely a rendering of Avice the First—that is, an aesthetic object that captures the essence of the original. Abundant references to her mimetic status characterize Jocelyn's appraisal of the daughter: she resembles "her prototype" (92) as "the present embodiment" (84) of a "resuscitated" (87) and "revitalized" (96) Avice; and he depersonalizes her as "the copy" (95) whose "individual character" (90) Jocelyn neither can nor cares to read because of her similitude to her mother.[18] Like Avice in her photographic form, Ann Caro has been transformed into the eternal woman, "the epitome of a whole sex" (107).

The pattern repeats with Avice the Second's own daughter, whom Jocelyn demands be given the name of her grandmother. Twenty years later Jocelyn becomes infatuated with the third Avice, a "modernized" version of the other two (146) whom Jocelyn again reduces to an aesthetic copy in musing, "It was the very she, in all essential particulars" (147), an "extraordinary reproduction of the original" (150). Despite his desire to wed the third Avice, Jocelyn asserts that "I do not require to learn her," for "she was learnt by me in her previous existences" (154). As interchangeable manifestations of the Beloved, "the three Avices were interpenetrated with her essence" (149), continuing the chain of essential womanhood that Jocelyn accepts as unconditional truth.[19]

The ambivalence about essentialism that appears in Hardy's treatment of Tess surfaces in *The Well-Beloved*, but in different terms. In the novel's closing scenes a raging fever inexplicably causes Jocelyn to lose interest in the Beloved, which precipitates his loss of aesthetic vision, suggesting both a movement toward maturity and a death of subjectivity. In the first regard, Jocelyn's Dorian Gray-like visage ages rapidly, and he chooses a companionate spouse, an elderly woman who lacks any trace of the Beloved. In the second regard, the tone of the narrative implies that in losing his sense of female essence as a verifiable truth, Jocelyn begins an irreversible deterioration as both man and artist. Though Jocelyn claims no regret for the demise of "a faculty which has, after all, brought me my greatest sorrows" (201), he descends into mediocrity, capable of appreciating only "utilitarian matters" (198).

As Proust noted, *The Well-Beloved* is a reversal of the 1873 *A Pair of Blue Eyes*,[20] in which the female protagonist, Elfride Swancourt, views male suitors in analogous interchangeable terms. The key difference in the texts, I suggest, is that *A Pair of Blue Eyes* presents both male and female characters as aesthetic objects. Although Elfride is variously described as a Raphael madonna, a slim Rubens model, and a characteristic example of Correggio's female faces (52), she also views her lovers in similar artistic terms. In one scene, for instance, Elfride observes her suitor, Henry Knight, at a church service:

> The sun streamed across from the dilapidated west window, and lighted all the assembled worshippers with a golden glow, Knight as he read being illuminated by the same mellow lustre. Elfride at the organ regarded him ... [and turned] her face for a moment to catch the glory of the dying sun as it fell on his form. (236)

By the *fin de siècle* novels, however, Hardy reserves such depictions exclusively for his female characters. In Hardy's 1887 *The Woodlanders*, for example, women are observed either by the narrator or a male character through an artist's perspective, often framed by a window, doorway, or mirror.[21] Early in the novel, a passerby watches a peasant girl through an opened door, transforming her into an impressionistic painting:

> In her present beholder's mind the scene formed by the girlish spar-maker composed itself into an impression-picture of extremest type, wherein the girl's hair alone, as the focus of observation, was depicted with intensity and distinctness, while her face, shoulders, hands, and figure in general were a blurred mass of unimportant detail lost in haze and obscurity. (48)

Throughout *The Woodlanders* women are persistently portrayed in such aesthetic terms. The female protagonist, for instance, becomes "a piece of live statuary" to her eventual husband (178) and is repeatedly seen through the frame of a window. His illicit lover bears the "almond eyes ... so common to the angelic legions of early Italian art" (101)—the "frightened eyes" evocative of a "replica of the Sudarium of St. Veronica" (327).

Similar artistic descriptions appear in the 1890s texts that follow *Tess*, although only perfunctorily. In *The Mayor of Casterbridge*, the eponymous character's wife is highlighted by "the rays of the strongly coloured sun, which made transparencies of her eyelids and nostrils and set fire on her lips" (70). The mayor's subsequent lover at one point "arranged herself picturesquely in the chair" to find the most compelling aesthetic position, moving "this way, then that ... so that the light fell over her head" (227). In *Jude the Obscure,* the hapless protagonist first becomes infatuated with Sue as he studies her photograph—which freezes Sue in time— irradiated "like the rays of a halo" (124). Once he obtains possession of the photograph, he sets it upon the mantelpiece as if it were a work of fine art, comforted by the suggestion that Sue "seemed to look down and preside over his tea" (132). This ongoing preoccupation with women as aesthetic presences that permeates Hardy's *fin de siècle* fiction is nowhere more insistently or pervasively manifested as it is in *Tess*, however.

Tess as Aesthetic Object

It has become a prominent theme of Hardy criticism that *Tess* constructs its heroine as an aesthetic symbol. Tess, for example, represents a canvas for her mother, who observes her enhancements to Tess's appearance by moving "back, like a painter from his easel," to "survey her work as a whole" (90). Tess's body represents a more eroticized canvas in The Chase as "beautiful feminine tissue" that was "practically blank as snow" (119), to be transformed by Alec as painter. The diamond necklace that Angel confers as his marital gift transforms Tess into another version of the ancestral paintings of d'Urberville women that hang in the honeymoon lodging (305). Sculptural allusions elsewhere convert Tess into a piece of plastic art: her profile appears as "a cameo" detached from a "dun background" (208), her arms resemble "wet marble" (250), and she assumes a pose of "sculptural severity" in one encounter with Alec (103).

It is not my intention here to catalog the myriad examples of the text's aestheticizing of Tess but instead to examine their ideological import. In transmuting Tess into visual art, the text further enmeshes her within the natural order of time, subjecting her to a masculinist aesthetic perspective that displaces her from history by presuming an immutable female essence.[22] As we have seen, the impossibility of transcending this temporal order is signaled in the novel's initial pages in which Tess's story begins with her interpellation within the family history. Yet the text's early chapters situate Tess within art as well, implying that she is always confined within both temporal frames, as demonstrated in the May-Day scene honoring Ceres. Depictions of this ritualized event are infused with the language of aesthetics, as the verbal portrait resembles a visual one drawn from the perspective of a male observer:

> [The women and girls] were all dressed in white gowns. . . . Their first exhibition of themselves was in a processional march of two and two round the parish. Ideal and real clashed slightly as the sun lit up their figures against the green hedges and creeper-laced house-fronts; for, though the whole troop wore white garments, no two whites were alike among them. Some approached pure blanching; some had a bluish pallor; some worn by the older characters . . . inclined to a cadaverous tint, and to a Georgian style.
>
> In addition to the distinction of a white frock, every woman and girl carried in her right hand a peeled willow wand, and in her left a bunch of white flowers. (49–50)

With its precise attention to detail, the passage conveys a picture so elaborately crafted as to differentiate between multiple but subtle hues of whiteness. Despite the slight variations in color, however, the verbal portrait presents the group as a homogenous mass through its distinction from the verdant background. As one of the "picturesque country girl[s]" (52), Tess becomes the focal point of the canvas as the sole possessor of a red ribbon that contrasts with the white blur of the garments. Her "mobile peony mouth" (51), a "pouted-up deep red mouth" (52), likewise arrests an observer's eye by repeating the coloration of the ribbon, while her compelling eyes bring "eloquence to colour and shape" (51). Yet, in wearing the white gown of her companions, Tess still forms part of the amorphous group, merely one woman singled out to represent Woman.[23]

Critics have commented extensively on this scene, most pertinently for my purposes in Kaja Silverman's analysis of a fluctuating figure/ground relationship. Silverman argues that Tess is periodically distinguished as the dominant figure of a narrative tableau who attracts an observer's eye and conversely blends into the background as part of an undifferentiated mass. This continual shift between figure and ground is initiated, Silverman contends, by the presence or absence of a male gaze. In making Tess an accessible image only when she comes under male observation, Silverman asserts, the text constructs her "interiority" along with her body (23), replicating the "cultural structuration" of female subjectivity (27). Yet the fluidity of the figure/ground relationship enables Tess to "ruin representation" (26) in "retreating *out of*, rather than *into* corporeality," merging into the landscape to avoid scopic attention (27). In so doing, Silverman implies, Tess achieves a measure of freedom from a constricting male gaze, "slip[ping] constantly out of focus" through this "oscillating" pattern (12). I suggest, however, that Tess never escapes masculinist representation by this technique, despite repeated attempts to do so, but only shifts the terms by which she is appropriated.[24]

To examine Tess's response to these representations, we must first distinguish between her initial and subsequent reactions. Let us return briefly to the scene in which Joan Durbeyfield views Tess as a canvas to be worked upon, as the mother explains her intentions to the daughter:

> [I]t will be wiser of 'ee to put your best side outward. . . .
> "Very well; I suppose you know best," replied Tess with calm abandonment.
> And to please her parent, the girl put herself quite in Joan's hands, saying serenely—"Do what you like with me, mother."
> (89)

Most notable about the short exchange are the multiple references to Tess's passivity as she transfers all agency to her parent. As we have observed, Joan's relationship to and absorption with her husband's ancestral past positions her as a kind of lesser male who promotes Tess's involvement in that history. In the present scene, Joan continues this subordinate function, anticipating the repeated appropriations of Tess into an object of art that male characters and the narrator himself will enact. Moreover, Joan encourages Tess to internalize her role as an aesthetic commodity, urging after completing her ministrations that "[y]ou must zee [*sic*] yourself!" (90). Not content with a looking glass that would reveal only "a very small portion of Tess's person at one time," Joan fashions a makeshift mirror by arranging a black cloak so that Tess can view her entire reflection in the window panes. Joan's contrivance underscores the impossibility of escape from representation; Tess is mirrored in the panes entirely, not simply in discrete body segments that could suggest a degree of evasion.

In early encounters with the two primary male characters, Tess displays a similar passivity to their aestheticizing gazes. Soon after her sexual initiation, she informs Alec:

> "See how you've mastered me!"
> She thereupon turned round and lifted her face to his, and remained like a marble term while he imprinted a kiss upon her cheek. . . . Her eyes vaguely rested upon the remotest trees in the lane while the kiss was given, as though she were nearly unconscious of what he did.
> "Now the other side, for old acquaintance' sake."
> She turned her head in the same passive way, as one might turn at the request of a sketcher. (126)

Again, Tess languidly accepts her status as an aesthetic medium fashioned by an artist: she "remained like a marble term," a phrase connoting through its adjective a sculptural immobility and through the accompanying noun the twin denotations of definition and delimitation, both spatially and temporally; she allows herself to be "imprinted" without resistance; and she directs her few bodily movements to conform to both the unstated and articulated desires of her artist.

Similarly, Tess becomes a doubly drawn aesthetic object as a sculptural and landscape figure while observed by Angel at the Talbothays dairy:

> She was milking Old Pretty thus, and the sun chancing to be on the milking-side it shone flat upon her pink-gowned form and her white curtain-bonnet, and upon her profile, rendering it keen as a cameo cut from the dun background of the cow.
> She did not know that Clare had followed her round, and that he sat under his cow watching her. The stillness of her head and features was remarkable: she might have been in a trance. . . . Nothing in the picture moved but Old Pretty's tail and Tess's pink hands, the latter so gently as to be a rhythmic pulsation only, as if they were obeying a reflex stimulus, like a beating heart. (208)

The passage accentuates the virtual absence of agency on Tess's part. She is shone upon by the sun, gendered masculine throughout the text;[25] her body is remarkable for its "stillness"; and she performs her duties mechanically, as if hypnotized. With only her hands in seemingly involuntary motion, Tess is virtually frozen into an artistic rendering. Once Tess realizes that she is being watched, she again displays the passivity that marked her response to Alec: "She then became conscious that he was observing her; but she would not show it by any change of position, though the curious dream-like fixity disappeared, and a close eye might easily have discerned that the rosiness of her face deepened" (209). Though the scene appears to be a mere repetition of Tess's response to Alec, it evidences an important distinction. Despite remaining in a static position as Angel observes her, Tess sheds the "dream-like fixity" that characterized the encounter with Alec, responding to Angel's gaze with a blush.

This reaction to Angel's aesthetic appraisal presages a shift in Tess's behavior in which she increasingly struggles against similar appropriations of her form, seeking to efface or diminish her own corporeality. In so doing, Tess pursues the same objective I earlier identified as instigating her movements across the Wessex countryside to distance herself from history. By manipulating space, Tess attempts to escape her entrapment in the monumental time of art with its perpetuation of female essence through the body, simultaneously striving to elude the determinism of linear time that inserted her within familial history. Yet such efforts to retreat from monumental temporality, Hardy suggests, allow no more slippage than did her attempts to evade the past, for Tess is always confined within a representational frame, even though the contours may alter slightly.

Tess's most successful attempt to retreat from corporeality comes during her journey to Flintcomb-Ash following her infant's death:

> Tess resolved to run no further risks from her appearance.... [She] took from her basket one of the oldest field-gowns, which she had never put on even at the dairy.... She also, by a felicitous thought, took a handkerchief from her bundle and tied it round her face under her bonnet, covering her chin and half her cheeks and temples, as if she were suffering from toothache. Then with her little scissors, by the aid of a pocket looking-glass, she mercilessly nipped her eyebrows off, and thus insured against aggressive admiration she went on her uneven way. (354)

Tess employs a tripartite strategy to minimize the body. The old field-gown serves as a form of disguise by which she can blend into the background, the handkerchief figuratively reduces the space of the body itself in removing part of her visage from observation, and the clipping of eyebrows literally lessens corporeality. Yet the passage portends that Tess's ministrations will fail to isolate her from representation, for the looking-glass that she consults reminds us of her reflection in Joan Durbeyfield's makeshift mirror and the aestheticizing of the body.

Tess's actions initially appear effective, since she becomes "a figure which is part of the landscape; a fieldwoman pure and simple" (355). That phrasing, however, intrinsically undercuts her ostensible success in retreating from representation. Silverman's notion of a figure/ground relationship can be reconceptualized here in the aesthetic terms of portraiture and landscape to interpret the failure of Tess's strategy. The protagonist's efforts to diminish corporeality suggest a desire to avoid the invasive attention that portraiture entails, in which the eye is immediately drawn to the contours of the face and upper body. Though she recedes into the landscape, Tess nevertheless remains within representation; the limited relief she obtains from a meandering scopic interest is illusory, since a landscape painting, like the d'Urberville history, inserts her into a prewritten story. In effect, a landscape painting forms a kind of narrative, a segment of life thrown into relief.[26]

A subsequent passage in which Tess works with another woman in the dreary Flintcomb-Ash fields emphasizes the futility of her attempts to evade representation:

> [T]heir movements showed a mechanical regularity; their forms standing enshrouded in Hessian "wroppers"—sleeved brown pinafores . . . —scant skirts revealing boots that reached high up the ankles, and yellow sheepskin gloves with gauntlets. The pensive character which the curtained hood lent to their bent heads would have reminded the observer of some early Italian conception of the two Marys. (360–61)

The description of the workers' clothing stresses homogeneity and anonymity; both even display the same expression with their "pensive character." Yet the uniformity of the pair does not liberate Tess from the delimiting effects of representation. Although not singled out as the subject of a portrait, Tess is again inserted into a narrative painting and subsumed within an ongoing narrative of Mariolatry previously captured in art through "some early Italian conception."

Moreover, Tess's recision into the landscape connects her even more tightly to the cyclical time that Kristeva reminds us has been traditionally allied with female essence. In merging into the pastoral background, Tess becomes a part of nature, participating in the cyclical rhythms that evoke female subjectivity through the analogous bodily cadences of fertility and procreation.[27] The gender implications of Tess's absorption into the landscape in this scene build upon the similar associations of an earlier passage that differentiates male from female workers as they bind sheaves of corn:

> But those of the other sex were the most interesting of this company of binders, by reason of the charm which is acquired by woman when she becomes part and parcel of outdoor nature, and is not merely an object set down therein as at ordinary times. A field-man is a personality afield; a field-woman is a portion of the field; she has somehow lost her own margin, imbibed the essence of her surrounding, and assimilated herself with it. (137–38)

References to an essential female nature permeate the passage, beginning with the use of the term "woman" in the opening sentence to encompass the entire sex rather than refer to individual specificity. A field-man is distinguished from the landscape as a particular personality, whereas a field-woman is incorporated within it, losing "her own margin" through an affinity to "the essence of her surrounding." Presumably, a woman is "assimilated" within nature because she is innately part of it. Subsequent references reinforce Tess's connection to nature: to Angel, for example, Tess initially represents "a fresh and virginal daughter of Nature" (176) and "a new-sprung child of nature" (302). These seemingly positive appellations take on a decidedly unfavorable and sexualized cast, however, through the narrator's further musings upon the "vulpine slyness of Dame Nature" (314).

Even when Tess appears to have triumphed over her own corporeality, she remains an aesthetic form. Finding Tess after she has been reunited with Alec, living with him as a wife, Angel is struck by Tess's emotional distance from her own body: "[H]e had a vague consciousness of one thing, though it was not clear to him till later; that his original Tess had spiritually ceased to recognize the body before him as hers—allowing it to drift, like a corpse upon the current, in a direction dissociated from its living will" (467). As a preceding passage describing her newly acquired garb has stressed, Tess continues to be defined by her body. The sumptuous garments provided by Alec accentuate her connection to an essential womanhood by putting her beauty into relief, through which she resembles a statue of Greek divinity whose drapery calls attention to the contours it graces:

> Her great natural beauty was, if not heightened, rendered more obvious by her attire. She was loosely wrapped in a cashmere dressing-gown of gray-white, embroidered in half-mourning tints, and she wore slippers of the same hue. Her neck rose out of a frill of down, and her well-remembered cable of dark-brown hair was partially coiled up in a mass. (465)

These two passages hint that Tess has not escaped the body, as Angel had contemplated, but instead has wholly lost control over its representation. In the first excerpt, the body once defined by Angel—"his original Tess"—has ceased to exist. As Tess's earlier manifestations of ardor for him implied, Tess has internalized his perceptions of her subjectivity, accepting his definition of her in accepting his hand. The corpse-like demeanor of the present Tess merely attests to the substitution of Alec's representation for Angel's, foreshadowed during Tess's wedding night as a somnambulant Angel—repeatedly muttering "Dead! dead! dead!" (317)—deposited his bride in a coffin (320). As the second passage implies, the "dead" Tess has been resurrected in another form, as envisaged by Alec and realized through the luxurious garb with which he clothes her. The seeming separation from corporeality that Angel attributes to Tess simply reflects her sense of alienation from the new representation, viewing her body as "dissociated from its living will."

Both of these passages help to illuminate an ongoing thematic concern: Tess's representations conform to differing expectations of female essence as seen through male eyes.[28] To borrow the terms Luce Irigaray employs to theorize female specularization, Tess serves as "an image of and for man" deprived of "specific qualities of her own" and becomes a "value-invested form" only through male inscriptions of her body (*This Sex* 187). To Angel, Tess emblematizes either the virginal child of nature or a besmirched practitioner of sexual arts; to Alec, Tess is simply a reincarnation of Eve, an eroticized temptress who corrupts men against their will. Tess's eventual demise, through which she is transformed from a vibrant body to a black flag, indicates not an ultimate triumph over corporeality but a continuation of the typological chain of womanhood. In losing her body, Tess is literally reduced to a conception of the essential female that will be reinserted within the similar corporeal form of her sister 'Liza-Lu, a "spiritualized image of Tess" (488)—that is, a further distillation of female essence into its purest form. Tess's attempts to elude time through space thus collapse into a reinvigorated version of her own body, again defined within an aesthetic framework: walking hand in hand with Angel, as a clock strikes in the background, 'Liza-Lu resembles a figure from "Giotto's 'Two Apostles,'" inserted into the fresco's own underlying narrative.[29]

Seeking a State of Atemporality

Tess's attempts to escape both the monumental time of art and the linear determinism of history suggest that she strives to attain, in effect, a state outside of time.[30] The rare instances when she displays contentment with her fate come in the brief moments that seem divorced from time, as in her Edenic encounters with Angel at Talbothays:

> [T]hey seemed to themselves the first persons up of all the world. In these early days of her residence here Tess did not skim, but went out of doors at once after rising, where he was generally awaiting her. The spectral, half-compounded, aqueous light which pervaded the open mead, impressed them with a feeling of isolation, as if they were Adam and Eve. (186)

In actively precipitating her meetings with Angel, Tess seeks to return to the "non-human hours" (187) that replicate the prelapsarian condition in which time does not exist.[31] The original parents predated time, existing in an eternal present; time did not begin its linear movement until Eve succumbed to temptation. Through her encounters with Angel, Tess continually relives the fluid temporal state before the Fall—before Eve became the emblem of essential womanhood that will define Tess and every other female, and before Tess will be enmeshed within her father's familial history.[32]

The desire to inhabit an eternal present is manifested in Tess's reluctance to set a wedding date, preferring to extend her brief period of happiness indefinitely by delaying the revelation of the past that she would otherwise feel compelled to share with Angel:

> This penitential mood kept her from naming the wedding-day. The beginning of November found its date still in abeyance, though he asked her at the most tempting times. But Tess's desire seemed to be for a perpetual betrothal in which everything should remain as it was then. (266)

Similarly, Tess cherishes the interludes in which she transcends both time and space through a kind of transmigration of the soul:

> "I don't know about ghosts," she was saying; "but I do know that our souls can be made to go outside our bodies when we are alive."
> ... "A very easy way to feel 'em go," continued Tess, "is to lie on the grass at night and look straight up at some big bright star; and, by fixing your mind upon it, you will soon find that you are hundreds and hundreds o' miles away from your body, which you don't seem to want at all." (175)

Appropriately, the impossibility of eluding one's immersion within time is stressed in the text's most temporally overdetermined passages. At each of these three significant moments Tess's destiny takes a decided turn as her inscriptions within both history and essential womanhood coalesce. In the first incident, as I have discussed, Tess's sexual initiation looms while she is enveloped in a primordial fog in The Chase, reduced to a primeval body that will be marked by Alec's lust and the re-enactment of ancestral history. In the second pivotal incident, Tess's separation from her new husband is prefigured by her reaction to the d'Urberville portraits hanging at the humbled ancestral estate where they spend their wedding night:

> "What's the matter?" said he.
> "Those horrid women!" she answered, with a smile. "How they frightened me." He looked up, and perceived two life-size portraits. . . . [T]hese paintings represent women of middle age, of a date some two hundred years ago, whose lineaments once seen can never be forgotten. The long pointed features, narrow eye, and smirk of the one, so suggestive of merciless treachery; the billhook, nose, large teeth, and bold eye of the other, suggesting arrogance to the point of ferocity, haunt the beholder afterwards in his dreams. (283–84)

The linear time of history and monumental time of art have been fused in the d'Urberville portraits. That Tess is entrapped within both temporalities becomes particularly apparent minutes later when she dons pieces of heirloom jewelry, becoming a sculptural replica of the d'Urberville women from whom she has inherited traces of the family's distinctive facial features. Indeed, at that instant, Angel recognizes that "[h]e had never till now estimated the artistic excellence" of his wife's form (288).

The incident precedes Angel's temporally suggestive rejection of Tess because of her own history, coupled with his mental transformation of Tess from virginal to sexual essence of womanhood.

The third and most charged example of temporal overdetermination comes in the climatic scene at Stonehenge shortly before Tess's death.[33] At Stonehenge, historical and mythic temporalities come together, blurring the distinctions between them. Stonehenge is both inserted within history and separated from it, for the ancient locale is "older than the d'Urbervilles" and "[o]lder than the centuries" (484).[34] As a "heathen temple," Stonehenge evokes the pagan divinities whose names Angel had earlier applied to Tess, a mythic affiliation amplified through Tess's recognition that her mother's kin came from the surrounding area. Placing herself on a sacrificial altar, Tess is absorbed into her mythic origins as she rehearses the conclusion that her personal past will necessitate. In uttering "I am at home," Tess resignedly accepts her constrictive temporal placement—fixed both in the linear time shaping history and the monumental time connoting female essence.

In selecting this form of closure, Hardy leaves us with a troubling message: the constructions of womanhood that support the natural order of time are absolute. Even the circular structure of the novel reinforces the point, for the conclusion, in effect, returns us to the beginning. Immediately inscribed within the masculine temporal order through the opening chronicle of the d'Urberville past and introduced into the novel as an aestheticized form participating in the Cerealian May-Dance, Tess similarly departs the novel within the pictorial setting of ancient Stonehenge. By enmeshing its protagonist so inextricably within a historical determinism and aesthetic representation that shape female subjectivity, Hardy leaves readers with his conviction that the Victorian woman—whether Old or New—cannot avoid reduction to an essentialized female body within the natural order of time. Trapped within the linear time of history and the monumental time of art, Tess unwittingly suggests that we should accord a specifically temporal reading to her defining lament, "Once victim, always victim—that's the law!" (411).

Chapter 4

Reinterpreting Evolutionary Development: Feminine Psychology in *The Beth Book* and *The Heavenly Twins*

> *Differences in the Mental Powers of the Two Sexes.—* With respect to differences of this nature between man and woman, it is probable that sexual selection has played a highly important part.... The chief distinction in the intellectual powers of the two sexes is shown by man's attaining to a higher eminence, in whatever he takes up, than can woman.... [I]f men are capable of a decided pre-eminence over women in many subjects, the average of mental power in man must be above that of woman.
> —Charles Darwin

The figure of Darwin hovered like a specter over the *fin de siècle,* not only through the explosive 1859 *Origin of Species* that redirected evolutionary thinking, but also through the 1871 *Descent of Man and Selection in Relation to Sex* from which this epigraph was taken—less heralded, but generating equally significant repercussions with its pronouncements on the intellectual capacities of the sexes.[1] In linking a perceived mental inferiority of women to the mechanism of evolution, Darwin purportedly brought scientific proof to a cultural truism. In so doing, Darwin reinforced Victorian strictures that maintained women in a subservient state, which now could be justified on the basis of biological determinism. Yet,

Sarah Grand's two popular 1890s novels, *The Beth Book* and *The Heavenly Twins,* contest the Darwinian verities, questioning scientists' specious conclusions about sex-linked traits and identifying culture as an equally significant force determining the mental dispositions of the sexes.

I focus specifically on Darwinism in my analysis of Grand's texts because it represents such an important component of the "natural order of time": through evolutionary theory, female inferiority could be inscribed as a natural and necessary condition ordained by the workings of time across the centuries. Even though Darwin had denied that a temporal law was at work in evolution, as I noted in my introductory chapter, there was among his followers an implicit supposition to the contrary. In effect, Darwinians saw the passage of time through the evolutionary process as determining certain mental traits in men and women that were immutable to cultural effects. As Patrick Geddes and J. Arthur Thomson, authors of the popular 1889 *Evolution of Sex,* noted in describing the mental differences between the sexes, "to obliterate them it would be necessary to have all the evolution over again on a new basis. What was decided among the prehistoric Protozoa cannot be annulled by Act of Parliament" (267). Evolutionary psychology, a nascent but influential discipline at the *fin de siècle,* reinforced the notion that the passage of time ordained significant mental differences between the sexes, particularly through the scientists' initial preoccupation with the supposed inferiority of women's intellect.

Grounded on the belief that the male—specifically a white, upper-class, European man—represented the pinnacle of the evolutionary process, Darwinian theory held that the female represented a lesser developmental stage through which the male passed in his progression to maturity. Women, Darwinians argued, resembled both the child and the "savage" in their incomplete development and could never pretend to mental equality with their male superiors. This model of "recapitulation" always already placed women on a lower rung of the evolutionary ladder, for a female could never hope to achieve developmental equality with a male, despite the amount of time that passed. As she reached each increasingly advanced stage of intellectual power, he would attain a yet higher one. All advancements to the human race, these theorists contended, thus were initiated via the male line through secondary sexual characteristics; women's role was merely to serve as a vehicle for the transmission of these characteristics to the next generation. As Geddes and Thomson characterized the distinction between the sexes that earlier thinkers had drawn: "In short, Darwin's man is as it were an evolved woman, and Spencer's woman an arrested man" (37).

My primary concern in this chapter is to investigate the Darwinian underpinnings of evolutionary psychology, which held daunting implications for the New Woman.[2] In perpetuating the notion that women's mental difference was an indisputable physiological fact, Darwin's disciples could characterize efforts to alter women's status as violations of nature that would threaten the advancement of the entire human species. If women were biologically ill-advised to strive for mental parity with men, as Darwinists claimed, then the New Woman's agenda seeking widespread changes in marital, educational, and vocational opportunities that would accord women equal cultural status was both anti-evolutionary and unnatural. Sarah Grand's novels, however, refute conservative psychologists' most basic assumptions, offering recuperative explanations to position women within an evolutionary vanguard.

I use the term "evolutionary psychology" in my discussion of Grand's texts to address the specifically Darwinian valences of the discipline, to group the divergent backgrounds—medicine, anthropology, sociology, and biology, among others—that these theorists brought to the study of the sexes.[3] Despite its claim to be an objective and empirical practice, however, psychology could realistically presume to neither distinction, as Cynthia Eagle Russett has demonstrated in examining the field's Victorian origins.[4] "Heavily reliant on casual observation, anecdote, and folk wisdom," Russett observes, psychology was "all but bereft" of "figures and facts," a failing that few practitioners admitted (45). Indeed, as Susan Sleeth Mosedale relates in her discussion of the gender biases underlying nineteenth-century science, evolutionists clung to any evidence that could bolster the separate spheres, distorting "any fact, or alleged fact" in their strained postulations of causal relationships (3). Through assertion rather than evidence, the cultural capital of science was mustered for the conservative side of the Woman Question, undercutting New Women's attempts to alter the status quo.

Central to evolutionary psychology was the concept that the sexes were so dissimilar in their mental powers that they actually represented two distinct psychological species, ostensibly proved by the peculiarities of the female's specialized physiology. To Geddes and Thomson, for example, the "anabolic" female was distinguished by her greater passivity, conservatism, and altruism, in contrast to the more active, intelligent, and original "katabolic" male (270–71). To Herbert Spencer, the very idea that the sexes were mentally similar was "as untrue" as their being "alike bodily" ("Psychology" 31). To psychologist Harry Campbell, natural selection differentiated the sexes' mental capacities in numerous ways, conferring on the female, for example, a greater "rapidity" of perception to compensate for her "inferior intellectual power" (52). To many scientists, the different mental capacities of women were directly attributable to the demands of reproduction, identified as woman's primary function.

Considered a male complement in physiological terms, the female was granted certain attributes to balance the male's intellectual gifts: emotionality, sensitivity, and sympathy were among the traits deemed to have been assigned specifically to women by natural selection, along with a pronounced moral sensibility. Conforming seamlessly with cultural views that had endured across the centuries, evolutionary theory likewise accorded women the responsibility of transmitting moral principles to successive generations through the careful nurturing of offspring. In physiological as well as cultural terms, motherhood thus stood as the highest vocation a woman could attain; any distractions from this function—pursuing an advanced education or seeking to join the professions, for example—would endanger the viability of the human species. Such contentions were widely disseminated not only in the scientific texts of Darwinians that were devoured by a fascinated public, but also by the plethora of articles in popular journals that circulated on both sides of the Atlantic.[5]

Dissenting voices that questioned the evolutionary foundation of the separate spheres, though insistent, were barely heard. David G. Ritchie, one of the few male critics of evolutionary philosophy, castigated the widespread tendency to claim scientific support for social policy in his 1889 *Darwinism and Politics*. Noting that there is "no doubt that the formulae of Evolution do supply an apparent justification . . . to the champions . . . of existing inequalities of race, class and sex" (12), Ritchie argued that the "alleged difference" in mental qualities (81) stemmed from scientists' desires to continue "what they happen to have grown accustomed to" (79). Feminist critics of evolutionary theory both echoed and anticipated Ritchie's contentions, building on John Stuart Mill's arguments in the 1869 *Subjection of Women* that similarly distinguished between culture and biology. Shifting the focus from physiology to pedagogy, feminist evolutionists blamed educational deficiencies for the dearth of female contributions to the intellectual advancement of humanity that Darwinians linked to biological deficiency. Antoinette Brown Blackwell, for example, denied in her 1875 *The Sexes Throughout Nature* that any discrepancy in the sexes' capacities for abstract thinking existed when educational opportunities were identical. "Roy Devereux" (Margaret Pember-Devereux), lamenting the "burden of [woman's] madonnaship" in her 1896 *Ascent of Woman,* also contended that education held the key to awakening women's intellect (19). Eliza Burt Gamble, maintaining in the 1894 *Evolution of Woman* that the "female organization is in no wise inferior to that of the male" (v), disputed the evolutionists' presumption that men represented the superior sex. Instead, Gamble claimed, evolution "furnishes much evidence" that women occupy a "higher stage of development" (v), a point that Darwin ignored in "certain facts which he himself adduced" (viii).

It is this latter contention that Grand argues in *The Beth Book* and *The Heavenly Twins*.[6] Grand's familiarity with evolutionary theory is undeniable, not only because of its prominence in cultural discourse, but also through references to Darwin and other evolutionists that appear sporadically in her texts.[7] Like many feminist thinkers writing on evolution, Grand tended to accept that certain traits—moral superiority, compassion, and gentleness, for example—were sex-linked characteristics more fully developed in women. Yet she offered a vastly different interpretation from conservative male evolutionists of the significance of such qualities, viewing them not as evidence of inferiority but as markers of human advancement.[8] Educational restrictions, marital inequities, and vocational limitations affecting women worked against—rather than for—the continued progress of humanity, Grand asserted, both in her novels and in numerous essays.[9] Unlike reactionary scientists, Grand assigned a critical role to cultural vectors in characterizing the intellectual differences between the sexes, implicitly interrogating the soundness of psychological doctrines purportedly derived from an objective analysis of physiological data.

The final years of the century did evidence a shift in thinking about women's mental capacities, however, in that the experience of previous decades had demonstrated women's ability to compete intellectually with men; women had distinguished themselves in academic work and other intellectual pursuits, which tended to belie many presumptions of their presumed mental inferiority.[10] Nevertheless, the belief persisted that the sexes' mental traits and reasoning abilities were dissimilar and that strenuous intellectual endeavor would impair women's reproductive capacities and thus imperil future generations. In her fiction, though, Sarah Grand takes issue both with evolutionary psychologists who adhered to the belief in women's mental inferiority as well as scientists who distanced themselves from that claim and instead pointed to the dangers of a robust educational program for Victorian females. Grand argues against both perspectives in asserting that the recognition and nurturance of women's particular mental talents was imperative if humanity was to continue to evolve.

One reason I have selected Grand's noncanonical texts as the basis for this chapter is their cultural prominence, both in England and the United States. *The Heavenly Twins* was a best-seller, while *The Beth Book*, though less successful, nevertheless benefited from its predecessor's impact on the reading public and Grand's well-established reputation as a feminist.[11] My project is to locate the key intersections of Grand's novels with evolutionary psychology, identifying the moments when the texts contest, undermine, or reinterpret the discipline's foundational principles. Although published in 1897, four years after *The Heavenly Twins* appeared, I begin with *The Beth Book* because of its extensive exploration of childhood and the development of subjectivity, turning to the earlier text thereafter to discuss its detailed treatment of the cultural forces at work during adolescence. I focus on these phases of individual development, supposedly prescribed by the workings of time, because they reveal so dramatically the terms on which Grand is contesting the tenets of evolutionary psychology. In *The Beth Book*, Grand challenges scientists' subjective valuation of presumably sex-linked traits; in *The Heavenly Twins*, she emphasizes the importance of nurture as opposed to nature, interrogating assumptions of biological determinism and stressing the significance of environmental influences.

The Beth Book's Reassessment of Darwin

Although *The Beth Book* recognizes and emphasizes culture's role in shaping female subjectivity, the novel more compellingly queries the Darwinian bases of the psychological discipline itself. To do so, the text follows a thread of Darwin's theory that was generally left ignored by social scientists because it problematized notions of a teleological sequence underlying human development and an implicit justification for the doctrine of separate spheres. In his conclusion to the *Origin of Species*, Darwin had bolstered the Victorian belief in progress by indicating that the mechanism of natural selection could be viewed as "tend[ing] to progress towards perfection" (459).[12] Rather than validating a linear model of human evolutionary movement, however, *The Beth Book* builds upon another observation that evolution more insistently suggests a brachial pattern that allows for multiple models. By assuming that the evolutionary course could follow more than one path, *The Beth Book* recuperates the female developmental process, assessing it as a variant but not lesser version of the male experience. The very qualities associated with female inferiority—an identification with the body over the mind, a preference for reading nature over the printed page, and a facility with the uttered over the penned word, for example—become in *The Beth Book* signs of an equal if not superior route to adulthood. In urging a reevaluation of such essentialized traits, while still maintaining their validity as evidence of gendered propensities, *The Beth Book* reverses the terms of the psychologists' equation by positing the female as the culmination of the evolutionary process; the seemingly optimum endpoint of male maturation merely becomes an interim developmental step and thus offers a radically different way of interpreting the Darwinian concept of recapitulation.

Identifying the novelistic project as the study of "a woman of genius," the text's subtitle represents an oxymoron in terms of evolutionary psychology. Through this specific reference to the protagonist's sex, though, the subtitle hints at both the novel's rejection of scientific truisms and its approbation of the denigrated feminine qualities that the eponymous protagonist cultivates to become a renowned feminist orator. The novel privileges an expressionistic acquisition of language over a sequential, logical, and rational process; it designates the body as the preferred type of text to be read and represented, revealing performative and expressive lexicons to be deciphered; and it validates the oral tradition over the inscriptive, as the linguistic tools of the master are borrowed to proceed past written competency to verbal fluency. As salient passages reveal, *The Beth Book* seemingly conforms initially to authoritative psychological precepts but then reinterprets them to figure female inferiority as superiority.

The Beth Book appropriates the form of the *Bildungsroman* to provide its alternate model of development, but this New Woman novel shifts generic conventions to a decidedly feminine register in its triadic treatment of childhood, marriage, and vocation. The novel traces the experiences of the unconventional Beth Caldwell, focusing particularly on her early years growing up in seaside Irish villages and in rural England where the family moves after her father's premature death. Living on the dubious charity of a wealthy uncle, James Patten, who has cheated Mrs. Caldwell of her rightful inheritance, the family struggles in poverty in a small dwelling on the outskirts of his estate, along with Beth's great-aunt whom Patten banishes from the main house when he discovers that her investments have failed. After Beth's mother discovers that she has kissed a visiting physician, Dr. Dan Maclure, Beth is compelled to marry in early adolescence and spends several unhappy years in the isolated English countryside. A sensualist who attempts to sully Beth's moral sensibilities and even invites his paramour to live with the couple under the guise of a paying patient, Maclure secretly operates a Lock hospital and covertly conducts vivisection experiments at home. Disgusted by her husband's behavior, Beth flees to the anonymity of London and the pursuit of the writing career she had begun, to her husband's dismay, during their strained marriage. Despite a resounding success with her first published book, Beth abandons writing in favor of feminist oratory, discovering her true vocation accidentally when she is inspired to speak before a gathering of New Woman advocates. When the doubtful investments bequeathed by her great-aunt turn highly profitable, Beth can devote her energies exclusively to her oratorical career and gains even greater prominence as a speaker than as a writer.

Opening moments before Beth's birth, the novel immediately draws the connections among gender, class, and racial attributes that triply position the infant Beth at the low end of the evolutionary continuum. As a member of an impecunious family headed by a shabbily genteel Englishwoman and an unexceptional military officer serving in Ireland, Beth holds an ambiguous class position despite her middle-class status. Denigrated by proximity, though not by birth, to the Irish—a primitive race by nineteenth-century English standards—Beth is considered their unenviable equal by her snobbish uncle. Coupled with the contaminatory influence of the Irish is the uncertain racial background that Beth inherits through the paternal line, carrying the "dark drop, . . . probably African," that her father revealed through his complexion and curly hair (4). Although the novel concentrates particularly on gender, it implicitly extends its critique across the entire spectrum of an evolutionary theory built on the supremacy of the white male holding an appropriate class status, positioning Beth as a universal symbol of marginality.

The Beth Book anticipates Freud's proclamations on the critical role of childhood in shaping subjectivity, devoting more than half of its pages to Beth's formative years.[13] Like other Victorian *Bildungsromane*, *The Beth Book* introduces its protagonist by cataloging the sensory experiences of the young child. The descriptions of nascent development, such as the following passage, seemingly could be transferred into any prototypical *Bildungsroman* of a Victorian child with the ungendered and universal responses they depict:[14]

> It was the sunshine really that first called her into conscious existence, the blessed heat and light; up to the moment that she recognised these with a certain acknowledgment of them, and consequently of things in general outside herself, she had been as unconscious as a white grub without legs. But that moment roused her, calling forth from her senses their first response in the thrill of warmth and well-being to which she awoke, and quickening her intellect at the same time with the stimulating effort to discover from whence her comfort came. She could remember no circumstance in connection with this earliest awakening. All she knew of it was the feeling of warmth and brightness. (10)

As in similar passages in the novel describing sensory impressions, this depiction conforms to prevalent late-century psychological theories in identifying sensation as the initial stage of human development. William James, for example, asserted in his widely read 1890 *Principles of Psychology* that "[o]ur earliest thoughts are almost exclusively sensational" (2:3) and "first make us acquainted with innumerable things" (6). Like Spencer and other evolutionary psychologists, James distinguished sensation from perception, viewing the former as a preliminary step that differed from the latter "in the extreme simplicity of its object or content" (2). For these theorists, the mental progression from crude sensation to the more complex thought processes of perception—formed through multiple sensations and the cognitive act of determining their interrelationships—marked a pivotal stage in human development that led to the far more advanced faculties of judgment and analysis.

The transition from raw perception to sophisticated cognition carried significant gender implications in psychological theory, for a propensity toward perceptual ability separated the less developed female from the more intellectual male. In an 1887 article titled "Mental Differences Between Man and Woman," psychologist and physiologist George J. Romanes assumed that "with regard to judgment, I think there can be no real question that the female mind stands considerably below the male"— a deficiency that "has been a matter of universal recognition from the earliest times" (656). In compensation, a woman evidences a "higher evolution of sense-organs" and a "rapidity of perception" that enable her to detect in a moment such signal observations as the fashion intricacies of another female passing in a carriage at high speed. Psychologist Harry Campbell similarly denigrated this trait in his lengthy 1891 treatise on the differences in the sexes' nervous organization, dismissing perception as "a characteristic of the lower races" (52).

Grand's text, however, deems sense experience as a determining factor in shaping Beth's genius. Like feminist evolutionist Eliza Burt Gamble, Grand accepted the notion that perception, along with intuition, was a peculiarly feminine trait whose importance, as Gamble contended, Darwin "overlooked" in "his zeal to prove the superiority of man" (65). The novel's early chapters repeatedly stress the impact of sense impressions, intimating that they represent the inchoate material of Beth's later brilliance. Thus, the unidentified narrator remarks, "[a]ll of Beth that was not eyes at this time was ears, and her brain was as busy as a squirrel in the autumn, storing observations and registering impressions" (18). "[K]eenly susceptible" to the environment, Beth amasses in her memory "impressions which were afterwards of inestimable value to her" (22). Indeed, her sensory acuity—particularly a "fine faculty of observation"—increasingly develops through each stage of childhood so that "nothing she noticed now was ever forgotten" (63). Like a "photographic apparatus," Beth's maturing mind registers "[e]very incident . . . somewhere in her consciousness for future use," a "hoard" upon which Beth "drew eventually with such astonishing effect" (119). Rather than relegating sensation and perception to an early maturational stage, as did the psychologists—William James's *Principles of Psychology,* for instance, argued that "[p]ure sensations can only be realized in the earliest days of life" and that it was "all but impossible" for adults to recapture such impressions (7)—*The Beth Book* emphasizes the validity and importance of sensory experience throughout the protagonist's lifetime. Beth's propensity for responding to the sensory qualities of nature in later years initiates her most productive creative moments, revealing that "[t]he senses have their uses" as "the first stage of fine thought" (416) in adulthood as well as childhood.

To justify the text's extensive discussion of Beth's sensory experiences, the narrator stresses that early influences hold the key to understanding the mature individual:

> Each incident that she remembered is apparently trifling in itself, but who can say of what significance as an indication? . . . [T]hese earliest impressions are more interesting than much that occurred to her in after life, and I have carefully collected them in the hope of finding some clue in them to what followed. In several instances it seems to me that the impression left by some chance observation or incident on her baby mind, made it possible for her to do many things in after life which she certainly never would have done but for those early influences. (11)

According to the evolutionists, however, the female's susceptibility to such sensory impressions served merely as damning evidence testifying to a stunted nervous system and impaired reasoning power. To Spencer, "those having well-developed nervous systems"—that is, the "larger brained races" or "the civilized man"—revealed "a greater tendency" to suspend and modify judgments; the "smaller brained races" and women were "prone to premature conclusions" (*Principles of Psychology* 581) and displayed a "relatively impulsive" emotional nature (583). To Campbell, the female's "far more unstable nervous system" (91) sharply contrasted with the "more vigorous and stable" male nervous system honed through "[i]ntensive combativeness and courage" (84). To physician and nervous-disorder specialist Henry Maudsley, women's "nerve-centers" existed in "a state of greater instability" because of the peculiarities of their "reproductive functions," making them "the more easily and the more seriously deranged" than men (197). *The Beth Book* similarly suggests that the female nervous system evinces a more pronounced receptivity to impressions—indeed, Beth's "sensitive nervous system received too many vivid impressions at once" (85). Yet her characteristic spontaneous reactions serve not as symptoms of arrested development but as markers of intellectual acuity, for "works of genius," the narrator argues, "are the outcome of an irresistible impulse, a craving to express something for its own sake ... with no thought of anything beyond" (233).

Language and Mimicry

In the conventional *Bildungsroman,* the transition from sensory impression to linguistic competence signals a seminal stage of development. *The Beth Book,* though, departs from the pattern of presenting a character's entrance into and increasing facility with language as the sign of maturation. Instead, the text contests the notion that an unproblematic interpellation within language is even desirable for a female subject. In chronicling the events of Beth's childhood, the novel foregrounds her resistance to language—specifically her disdain for acquiring reading and writing skills—and the cultural norms that language inherently promotes and perpetuates. A continued reliance on sensory impression, primarily achieved through an immersion in the traditionally feminine world of nature, is valued over linguistic facility during Beth's formative years.

A dichotomy between feminized nature and masculinized language emerges repeatedly in the novel's opening chapters to suggest a certain reluctance rather than an inherent tendency for a female to assume her designated cultural role. Nature and language are yoked periodically in uneasy juxtaposition within the same sentence to posit an intrinsic opposition: Beth, for example, "took no interest in the alphabet in those days, and hunted black-beetles with the bellows instead of learning it" (17). In other passages, the distinction between emancipatory sense experience and constrictive linguistic order is conveyed by Beth's forceful rejection of the latter:

> Books she flung away impatiently; but the woods and streams, and the wild flowers, the rooks returning to roost in the trees at sunset, the horses playing in the paddocks, the cows dawdling back from their pastures, all sweet country scents and cheerful country sounds she became alive to and began to love. (102)

The inference to be drawn in these and analogous passages is that the conventional path toward maturation through the acquisition of language forecloses development while seemingly fostering it, channeling a subject into restrictive modes of cognition and behavior. In privileging nature over language, *The Beth Book* intimates that the presumed markers of female inferiority—impulsive responses to the environment, displays of emotional fervor, and a slowness to acquire the power of ratiocination—are integral facets of the maturational process, as the following passage reveals:

> Her big eyes looked out of an impassive face solemnly; no one suspected the phenomenal receptivity which that stolid mask concealed, and because the alphabet did not interest her, they formed a poor opinion of her intellect. The truth was that she had no use for letters or figures. The books of nature and of life were spread out before her, and she was conning their contents to more purpose than any one else could have interpreted them to her in those days. (19)

Counterpoised against the sequential acquisition of knowledge that retards intellectual breadth is a more spontaneous and fruitful creativity. Beth rejects the restraints implicit in the well-trodden cognitive paths of Western culture by charting her own alternate routes. Rather than proceeding through a discrete progression of thoughts and words by which ideas are honed and ordered according to logical patterns, Beth relies upon expressionistic responses that capture the imaginative faculty without constricting it—an early manifestation of stream-of-consciousness utterance based on sensation. As she attempts to describe the workings of her consciousness to a curious interlocutor, Beth comments: "I'm not thinking exactly.... Things come into my mind, but I don't think them, and I can't say them. They don't come in words. It's more like seeing them, you know, only you don't see them with your eyes, but with something inside yourself" (178). Continuing her explanation, Beth describes a visceral response to nature to differentiate between careful meditation and involuntary apprehension. In a lyrical depiction of the sea's movements, Beth indirectly credits an immersion in natural phenomena for her creative aptitude: "at last you seem to be the sea, or the sea seems to be you—it's all one; but you don't think it."[15]

Renowned among her small social circle for her talent of inventing complex verse, Beth again contrasts systematic cognition and reflexive reaction. She replies affirmatively to a suspicious listener who questions her authorship of a poem in asking whether she "made that up" before she clarifies, "I didn't make it up, it just came to me" (178). In effect, Beth's imaginative acts are the manifestations of intuition, identified by evolutionary psychologists as analogous to perception and thus another sign of female mediocrity. Campbell, for instance, remarked that "woman's intuitions essentially pertain to human actions: she is peculiarly quick in learning character, and in divining her husband's varying moods" (52). He hastened to add that "[t]he rapidity of the feminine perception ... harmonises with the inferior intellectual power commonly attributed to her." William James similarly noted that while the "masculine brain deals with new and complex matter" efficiently, the "feminine method of direct intuition"—though operating "admirably ... within its limits"—could only "vainly hope to cope with" intellectual challenges (2:369). *The Beth Book* inverts such judgments not only by associating Beth's creativity with intuition, but by designating it as a more reliable faculty than masculine reasoning. Pondering a youth's question as to "what makes you think such queer things," Beth answers: "I don't think them ... I know them. The things I think are generally all wrong; but the things I know about—that come to me like this—are right. Only I can't command them. One comes to me now and again like a flash" (240–41). Intuition is privileged over the ability to "command," a verb choice that further distinguishes feminine creativity from a presumed masculine mastery of logical thought.

The dichotomy between intuition and reasoning builds on conventional associations of the female with the body and the male with the mind.

As anthropologist J. McGrigor Allan—one of the most acerbic critics of women's mental capacities—characterized the distinction in 1869, "man's realm is the intellect—woman's the affections" (cci). Fellow anthropologist Luke Owen Pike typified numerous evolutionists by claiming that "it will hardly be denied that in all ages" women "have been more prone to the display of emotion than of pure reason" (85). Indeed, he asserted, "[i]f man's highest prerogative is to think, woman's noblest function is to love" (86). Building on such presumptions at the end of the century, Campbell accounted for the difference between the sexes by characterizing them "somewhat in inverse ratio" with regard to the "emotional and intellectual portions of our being" (84). In an article on the "psychology of feminism" appearing the same year as *The Beth Book*, Hugh E. M. Stutfield commented that even though women's intellect had been stimulated in recent years, they remained "being[s] of transient impulses and more or less hysterical emotions" (106).

The Beth Book views the traits that such theorists associated with the female body as valid rather than vapid, particularly through an iconoclastic valuation of the traditionally gendered forms of written and oral language. Following Darwin, the evolutionary psychologists appropriated science to bolster the presumption that writing represented a male province, pointing to the scientific, philosophical, literary, and other texts that men produced over the centuries to advance human progress.[16] Indeed, biologist and novelist Grant Allen went so far as to pronounce "confidently" that "the males are the race" because "[a]ll that is distinctly human is man" ("Woman's Place" 263). Though adhering to the customary labeling of written texts as a masculine purview and orality as its feminine counterpart, *The Beth Book* inverts the traditional privileging of the former, not only by deeming feminist oratory as the culmination of Beth's genius, but also by tracing the positive influence of women's speech upon her development.

Through numerous examples, *The Beth Book* allies its protagonist with the oral rather than the inscriptive tradition. In early childhood, Beth accedes to the command to learn prayers and hymns by choosing to listen to the supplications of the servant Kitty rather than inculcating them through the written word. "[L]earning by heart from a book did not come naturally to her," the narrator asserts in describing the incident; Beth "learned by ear easily enough, but not by sight" (47). Similarly, in later childhood, Beth avidly absorbs the tales told by the servant Harriet, characterized as "a woman of well-marked individuality and brilliant imagination" who was incessantly "recounting something" (122). Continually demonstrating that "narrative was her speciality," Harriet spins endless stories so compelling that Beth follows the servant from room to room while she works, "listening with absolute faith and the deepest interest to the stream of narrative which flowed on without interruption." The array of novels with which Beth becomes familiar as a child are mediated by the voice of her mother, who reads them aloud since Beth "would not read to herself if she could help it" (119).

Beth's preference for orality over textuality likewise emerges through her disinclination to learn through the printed word. Unlike her older sister Mildred, whose rapid acquisition of reading skills is figured as an intellectual dullness, "books to be deciphered remained a wonder and a mystery to Beth" (46). Ignored by their tutor in favor of the "docile and studious" Mildred, Beth "soon wearied of the dull restraint" and responded with a rebelliousness manifested in such subtly telling acts as a threat to destroy the teacher's ink bottle. By age eight, Beth's facility with written texts had progressed only to the point of being "able to follow the church-service in the prayer-book, and make out the hymns, but that was all." Despite her scholarly obtuseness, however, "Beth's intellect advanced with a bound at this period" as she turned to "interesting observations of men and manners" to follow her own version of the educational process in preference to constrictive schooling (48). In contrast, the hapless Mildred—"an artificial product of conventional ideas"—not only "lived upon books," but "very literally died of them eventually" (123).

Beth's distaste for written texts extends beyond reading to the act of writing itself. Beth composes and shares her remarkable verses "long before she could commit them to paper intelligibly" (169); "hated writing copies, and did them disgracefully" (123); and pens the first note she has ever written voluntarily only by imitating an aunt's delicate handwriting (169). Beth is so unschooled in punctuation that she asks her youthful companion Sammy to teach her, even though he scoffs at the necessity to do so, since "[m]en write books, . . . not women, let alone gels!" (172).

Music, too, serves as a marker of the feminine oral tradition, representing "the very voice and articulation of emotion" (10), according to Devereux's 1896 feminist evolutionary treatise, *Ascent of Woman*. We are reminded, for instance, of Tennyson's "The Princess," in which successive male narrators tell the tale of a doomed women's college, allowing the female listeners merely to sing ballads in the gaps of their stories, "[l]ike linnets in the pauses of the wind" to provide "breathing-spaces." In *The Beth Book*, however, a feminine propensity toward music is reconceptualized as originality rather than repetitive marginal art.

When Beth bursts into a song she has made to mimic nature, for instance, the creative process she describes to her father validates feminine insight over masculine cognition:

> [N]o one taught me, papa.... I used to listen to the sea in that shell in the sitting-room, and I tried and tried to find a name for the sound, and all at once *song* came into my head—*The song of the sea in the shell*.... I used to try and think it, but you can't sing a thing you think. It's when a thing comes, you can sing it. (68)

Beth's creative talents, demonstrated in both her sung and spoken verses, serve to undercut the evolutionist doctrine that females lacked originality. Women's inferiority, as psychologist Romanes explained the concept, "displays itself most conspicuously in the comparative absence of originality"—particularly, he added, "in the higher levels of intellectual work" (655). Campbell similarly remarked that women are "only to a limited extent original" (162). Yet Beth is unquestionably the most gifted character in the novel, rejecting the traditional female role of silent muse to become a poetic voice. In inverting the conventional relationship, Beth appropriates a male—her dull companion Sammy—as her own muse. Serving as the impetus for her "fine flights of imagination," Sammy, "[s]o long as he was silent," provided "a source of inspiration" (174); even that role is minimized, however, since merely "her feeling for him was inspiring." In *The Beth Book*, women's imaginative capacity is refigured as a sign of prowess rather than arrest, belying Spencer's commonly accepted notion that female imagination cannot adequately accommodate complexity and subtlety ("Psychology" 36).

In favoring sensory impression and resisting, at least to a limited extent, an interpellation into language, Beth struggles against a linguistic construction of reality that offers her little opportunity to contest established norms. Mimicry of language, as Luce Irigaray cautions, perpetuates a specular perspective since in repeating its master discourses a woman becomes only, in effect, "a lesser male" (Moi 135). Yet, as Irigaray also asserts in her theorization of language, mimicry can be perceived not only as submission but as assertion (*Irigaray Reader* 124); through mimetic play, a female can bring "new nourishment" to discourse (125) without simply being reabsorbed by it. Though one can never truly step outside of culture and escape the linguistic milieu that reinforces masculine superiority, as the French feminists have so convincingly argued, Beth's early experiences evidence an attempt to do so. By choosing a more expressionistic mimicry derived from an attentiveness to the body, Beth can at least act out alternate roles that provide some measure of freedom from the narrow possibilities offered one of her gender and class.[17] The body thus serves as a liberatory text, providing its own form of syntax through gestural and performative codes. In valuing somatic over written texts, *The Beth Book* again privileges the feminized link to the body, with its complex lexicons transmitted both orally and silently, over masculinized rationality.

Rather than readily absorbing cultural scripts, Beth creates her own texts from the sensory impressions she has stored, shaping her perceptions into performative roles that open up new interpretive possibilities. She learns "to read a countenance long before she learned to read a book" (20) and applies this knowledge to act out a range of subject positions through impersonation and improvisation; most of her time, the narrator informs us, was devoted to "a curiously close, but quite involuntary study of those about her" (48). Attuned to both the ear and the eye, Beth gleans from snatches of overhead conversations the makings of narrative, finding that "a few chance phrases were already enough for her to construct a whole story upon" (63). Transforming these highly imaginative fantasies into enacted roles allows Beth to become "generally somebody else in these days, seldom herself" (131). Even though Beth cannot avoid entering language, then, she can attempt to appropriate it to her own uses.

Many of Beth's early roles reflect the cultural conditioning that Judith Butler attributes to gender performance, in that "the body is always an embodying *of* possibilities both conditioned and circumscribed by historical convention" ("Performative Acts" 272). Thus, Beth dons an array of female subject positions, particularly as a heroine of romance: she becomes a princess confined in a witch's castle, awaiting release from a fairy prince (20); a courageous woman "going to do a great deed" (137); "an ill-used heroine now, in the hands of her knightly deliverer" (150); and "the sad central figure of a great romance" (180). Yet she also pushes these gendered roles to their limits. She becomes "Norna of the Fitful Head"—a mysterious figure in Sir Walter Scott's *The Pirate*, who believes she wields supernatural powers—in preference to two other Scott characters who were "too insipid for her taste" (132). Norna, in contrast, "was different," an unconventional role model who "did things, you know, and made charms, and talked poetry, and people were afraid of her." Indeed, Beth creates an entire "play" of sorts, featuring herself as the leader of a secret society, which is so convincing that her young friend Charlotte Hardy never perceives it as imaginary.

Nevertheless, such performative roles tend to coincide with gender expectations: evolutionist Campbell identified a propensity toward romance as a particularly feminine trait (163), one evinced especially in hysterics (170). Campbell more broadly pointed to mimicry as a gendered quality, citing a characterization of women as "born actors" (54). Moreover, the "markedly imitative" quality of the female presumably served as evidence of her lower evolutionary state, since in this respect she resembled a child (162).

In *The Beth Book*, however, mimicry is validated as a marker of both originality and possibility. The sensory tools of sight and hearing that Beth exercises in preparing for her roles are not indicative of inferiority, as the male psychologists asserted, but "the most refined" of the senses (69) in the contrary view of feminist dissenter Gamble, which reveal instead the female's evolutionary superiority. "[E]ntranced ... by acting" (329), Beth "can act anything" (144); through her performances, she assumes not only female subject positions but also male roles, which enable her to experiment with alternate gender scripts. Beth, for example, imagines herself as an Indian scout (23); dons a mask and her father's sheepskin cloak as she elevates herself to a position of power on an imaginary throne (138); and borrows a soiled sheet and a shawl to become a parson readying his sermon (140). In Butler's terms, such experimentation offers an avenue for challenging the "reified status" of conventional roles (271), suggesting the possibility of interruption or "subversive repetition" of gender's performative acts. Such role-playing, though, is perceived as a dangerous maneuver, as Butler likewise comments, for a "transvestite" act blurs the division between theater and "reality" (278). For Beth, this theory becomes praxis through an adolescent prank in which she cross-dresses to attend a menagerie with two male friends, tucking her hair into a cap and placing her arm around a girl in her mimicry of youthful masculinity. Through that act, her distraught mother informs her, Beth has "done just about as bad a thing as you could do," turning herself into a spectacle who has "made the whole place talk about you" (255). Beth's cross-dressing is so threatening that the two youths are banished from her life in punishment for participating in her scandalous drama.

The transgressive component of performance that Butler identifies can be partly attributed to another factor as well: performance allows the female body to speak, in a sense, in contrast to the written word that instead tends to erase the body. In Julia Kristeva's terms, performance allows access to the semiotic, the utterances of the body silenced by the written word. As Hélène Cixous argues, theatricality represents a contestation of the linguistic order, allowing new meanings to emerge (Shiach 109). Through performance, then, Beth can sporadically transcend the restrictions of masculinist language, exploiting the gaps between rote mimicry and imaginative possibility.

Beth's eventual vocational choice of oratory continues that challenge to the linguistic order in allowing the body to participate in the construction of meaning. Again, the "gestural code of women's bodies," to invoke Irigaray's phrase (136), enables a limited escape from the restrictions of masculine language. Though oratory requires the speaker to follow certain linguistic conventions—to become a mimic, in effect—the circumstances in which Beth's mimicry is enacted represent a shift in its ideological register. As Toril Moi argues, the "context" in which a woman uses "a particular rhetorical strategy" is crucial in judging its "political effects" (141). For Beth, the context of feminist oratory suggests not merely a woman "imitating male discourse," in Moi's formulation (143)—thus simply masquerading as a man—but an alternate positionality that allows linguistic conventions to work against themselves by opening up meanings that masculinist language seeks to foreclose. In Butler's terms, Beth cannot avoid employing "discursive practices"; her choice thus "is not whether to repeat but how to repeat" as a strategy for undermining "the very gender norms that enable the repetition itself" (*Gender Trouble* 148). Through oratory, then, the feminized quality of orality is transformed from verbal ineffectuality into transgressive authority.[18]

Education Versus Biology

As my discussion of *The Beth Book* has argued thus far, Grand recasts the evolutionary psychologists' assertions of female inferiority by reinterpreting women's essentialized traits as strengths rather than weaknesses. Yet the novel also assigns a pivotal role to culture, rather than biology, as the determining factor for the arrest of development that the evolutionists perceived in women. Masculine intellectual superiority, the text asserts, stems from male control over and access to the nuances of language. As Beth increasingly comes to realize, a facility with language represents a male prerogative and ideological tool. As a child, Beth gradually absorbs the rudiments of masculine language: her father, for instance, approvingly notes that she has amassed "quite a vocabulary" (69) by age eight; she becomes intrigued by the workings of metaphor and rhetorically comments, "Isn't it nice when you see that one thing's like another?" (69); and she recognizes the power of the word when overhearing the smallest of a group of carpenters silencing his fellow laborers "instantly" (83). Within a few years, Beth vaguely begins to perceive that men control language, realizing that "all the bad words in the language were made for the men" (190). Women, in contrast, can participate in language only tangentially, conveying their ideas in euphemisms and other approved forms. As Beth learns when chastised by an aunt for referring to tourists as "confounded trippers" (189), a female must couch her meaning in the modes allowed her; Beth thus dutifully responds that "I shall say 'objectionable excursionists' in the future" (190).

Only when on the verge of adolescence does Beth fully realize that linguistic skill—and the power it confers on its practitioners—is acquired, not biologically determined:

> Beth learnt a good deal from her young men that summer.... She found one trait common to all of them when they talked to her, and that was a certain assumption of superiority which impressed her very much at first, so that she was prepared to accept their opinions as confidently as they gave them.... Beth, perceiving that this superiority was not innate, tried to discover how it was acquired that she might cultivate it. Gathering from their attitude towards her ignorance that this superiority rested somehow on a knowledge of the Latin grammar, she hunted up an old one of her brother's and opened it with awe, so much seemed to depend on it. (273–74)

Though initially puzzled by the unfamiliar structure of Latin, Beth discovers through scholastic drudgery that "even in that there was nothing occult" (274). Instead, "[a]ny industrious, persevering person could learn a language." More significant, however, is Beth's realization as she struggles through her Latin studies that men control the valuation of gendered traits through language. To men, Beth muses, "feminine attributes are all inferior to masculine attributes" (274). If a feminine quality could be interpreted as a strength, "they managed to discount" it through their words. Pondering the example of endurance to understand how language guides interpretation, Beth recognizes that women were considered to excel in this respect "not because their fortitude was greater, but because they were less sensitive to suffering." Masculine control over language and interpretation provides the vehicle for maintaining women in an inferior position, Beth realizes, for even intellectual acuity could be translated into biological anomaly: "[a]ny evidence of reasoning capacity in a woman they held to be abnormal, and they denied that women were ever logical."

For the evolutionary psychologists, the innate mediocrity of women's mental faculties stemmed not only from physiological organization but physical necessity, regardless of the workings of linguistic or other cultural forces. In arguing that reproduction was the paramount female function, the evolutionists could demand that intellectual pursuits be sacrificed to ensure a sufficient supply of the body's finite energy for bearing and nurturing children, thereby ensuring the perpetuation of humanity. Spencer, for example, moved from an "*a priori* inference" that "their respective parental functions" explained the sexes' necessary differences in mental ability and pursuits ("Psychology" 35); Allen, noting that "all that is truly woman is merely reproductive," cautioned that women who strive to develop male faculties "unsex themselves" and "fail to perform satisfactorily their maternal functions" ("Woman's Place" 263). Such tenets informed Victorian pedagogical theory as well. Education of the sexes, the evolutionary psychologists asserted, must be designed appropriately and distinctively to compensate for inherent physiological differences and thus avoid damaging a female's reproductive capacities and therefore future generations. Science thus bolstered traditional pedagogical philosophies that considered a masculine educational program far too dangerous for the weaker sex—a point that we will address again when we turn to *The Heavenly Twins*.[19]

Perhaps no proponent of this approach was more adamant than Henry Maudsley, whose 1874 "Sex in Mind and in Education" was based on the premise that feminist attempts to reform female schooling were scientifically unsound. Relating the results of several American studies, Maudsley recapitulated the harmful effects of masculine educational programs on female health by quoting such sources as Dr. Edward Clarke's "Sex in Education," which Maudsley read with "the gravest alarm" (474), and an American physician's findings that the female instinct to nurse diminished with education (476). To Maudsley, the issue was definitive: "it would be an ill thing, if . . . we got the advantages of a quantity of female intellectual work at the price of a puny, enfeebled, and sickly race" (472). Asserting that it "will not be possible to transform a woman into a man" (466), Maudsley warned that the educational period came at a particularly crucial time, when a female's "sexual system" began developing (467). Maudsley's sentiments were echoed more than a decade later by the head of the British Medical Association, William Withers Moore, who saw dire effects on future generations if women performed rigorous intellectual work. Advanced education, he told his fellow physicians, "indisposes [women] to matrimony, and unfits [them] for maternity" (qtd. in "The President's Address" 338). Physician Benjamin Ward Richardson also cautioned in 1886 against the educated woman being a third sex, fearing "a powerful tendency for leaving the responsibilities of maternity to the weakest mothers, about as bad an evil as could befall the human race" (619).

The Beth Book assails such conclusions by demonstrating that the current educational and evolutionary philosophy served primarily as a vehicle for reinscribing male dominance and continuing female subjection. The evolutionists, the novel suggests, have inverted the causal relationship between biology and culture; female schooling does not respond to physiological dictates but creates and continues the very deficiencies that the evolutionists attributed to sexual difference. A girl's education, the narrator remarks, thus "was eminently calculated to cloud her intelligence and strengthen every failing developed in her sex by ages of suppression" (125). The novel's critiques of an educational theory buttressed by evolutionist presumptions are invariably pointed and negative, beginning with Beth's brief attendance at a day school and the home tutelage of her mother, whose own mental faculties "had been successfully compressed into the accustomed groove" (125). Acridly noting that "what her parents would have called [Beth's] education had begun" (16), the narrator identifies a further potential harm that perfunctory schooling poses for female development. When the narrator marshals another doctrine of the evolutionary psychologists—the moral mission of Woman and the transference of sound principles to offspring—it is only to indicate the threat that inadequate education poses to this female function.

Eventually sent to a boarding school when she proves too unruly at home, Beth discovers that the educational approach there is merely a continuation of the lesson conveyed by her mother: females are not to reason but to absorb the scraps of learning they are allowed. Girls' schools simply reinforce the ideological message of the home by preparing females for their approved roles as breeders and nurturers. Such schools continue the chain of ignorance unbroken, for they are operated by women who transmit their own limited learning. The primary goals of a masculine education—linguistic deftness, mathematical aptitude, and historical consciousness—receive only passing attention at Beth's institution. In the text's scathing criticism of pedagogical philosophy, Beth's teachers evidence merely "the trumpery education provided everywhere at that time for girls by the part of humanity which laid undisputed claim to a superior sense of justice" (296). With their own rudimentary educations, Beth's teachers "were not taught one thing thoroughly, not even their own language." Noting Beth's arithmetical deficiencies with sums as she does "every one wrong" (285), they can merely chastise rather than appropriately instruct her. Restricted to a cursory view of history, they had not progressed sufficiently themselves to understand even a reasonably "comprehensive result of the battle of Hastings" (296).

In preparing girls to become docile wives and mothers rather than analytical reasoners, the educational establishment could again point to evolutionary doctrines for justification. As Spencer argued, "the genesis of the family" across the centuries—culminating in the prototypical Victorian model—"fulfils the law of Evolution" (*Principles of Sociology* 745); in the "highest societies," women's responsibilities are confined to "domestic duties and the rearing of children" (756). The self-abnegation and altruism demonstrated by the ideal mother were evolutionarily determined, numerous theorists asserted, even feminist commentators such as Antoinette Brown Blackwell. Yet, as Blackwell added in advocating equal educational opportunities for girls, evolutionists had offered no proof that the same regimen of study would harm one sex more than the other.

Ironically, *The Beth Book* argues, current educational modes are both delimiting and damaging to the girls they seek to protect, stifling and occasionally destroying natural ability through the narrow outlets allowed to female potentiality. Beth's "excellent musical memory" and delicate touch, for example, are lost "entirely" through a system of practicing that "made it impossible for her to feel what she was playing or put any individuality of expression into it" (295). Ensuring that females maintain their traditional dependent postures, "minds were starved on books suited to the capacity of infants and imbeciles" (314). Beth's teachers allow learning to proceed only within prescribed parameters by discouraging intellectual curiosity and original interpretation:

> [Beth] could have told the whole history of William the Conqueror in her own language after once reading it over; but the answers to the questions had to be learnt by heart and repeated in the exact language of the book, and in the struggle to be word-perfect enough to keep up with the class, the significance of what she was saying was lost upon her. It was her mother's system exactly.... These pillules of knowledge only exasperated her; she wanted enough to enable her to grasp the whole situation. (295)

Rather than being encouraged to develop a cognitive context in which she could make her own judgments, Beth is warned that "it was absurd for a girl of her age to call in question the teaching of the best and greatest men that ever lived" (305).

The sole practicable alternative to such an educational model, *The Beth Book* implies, is to amass the few intellectual tools offered and apply them in other directions. Borrowing Butler's terminology, the appropriate strategy is to "perform" learning, as Beth does:

> Beth played very diligently at learning during this experiment, but only played for a time. The mind in process of forming itself involuntarily rejects all that is unnecessary, and that kind of knowledge was not for her.... All she cared to know was what it felt like to have mastered it .... [S]he learnt only enough of anything to express herself; but it was extraordinary how aptly she utilised all that was necessary for her purpose, and how invariably she found what she wanted. (276)

Beth circumvents the limitations of her culture, then, by manipulating the "pillules of knowledge" she is provided to achieve her own objectives. Adopting the few tools that enable her to become an adept reader and writer, Beth resists their implicit perpetuation of a masculinist perspective by employing them to assume a different voice and promote a feminist philosophy.

The fruits of that labor emerge after her marriage to the unsavory Maclure, when Beth isolates herself within the domestic sphere to launch a career as a writer. When a male acquaintance reminds her of the "formidable" power of language to construct reality by "set[ting] the tune to which men insensibly shape their course" (351), Beth borrows those linguistic techniques to open up alternative possibilities for her female readers. She rejects fiction as her model because of its reinscription of female stereotypes and turns to biography for her instruction—preferring life as its authors "had lived it, not as they had observed and imagined it" (370). Determined to present life experience with an attentiveness to content over style, Beth rejects the focus on the latter that was privileged by the aesthetes, noting that "[m]anner has always been less to me than matter" (460).[20] Instead, in "[h]er own language, strong and pure" (423), Beth encourages women to recognize their duty to themselves, not merely to their husbands.

In terms of evolutionary psychology, Beth's achievements as a writer come at a significant point in her lifetime, the end of adolescence. Beth's literary success represents the first step in an illustrious career, foreshadowing her intellectual development over the coming years. By situating this accomplishment at the verge of Beth's adulthood, the novel contests another evolutionary truism. Females, the psychologists claimed, matured more rapidly than males but ended their mental growth by late adolescence. The slower development of males, achieved in their late twenties, ostensibly stemmed from their greater intellectual complexity. Like Darwin, Spencer, for example, based his psychological theories on the principle of an "earlier arrest of individual evolution in women" ("Psychology" 32). Campbell tended to agree that "the mind of woman does not continue to evolve as far on in life as the man's" (172). A contributor to the influential *Popular Science Monthly*, identified as G. Delauney, similarly contended that "[g]irls grow faster than boys till they are seventeen," but men continue their development while "the woman remains at a stand-still" (189). In *The Beth Book,* however, Beth's mental development is intensifying at the very time that psychologists said it should cease. Indeed, the end of adolescence marks the point at which her "genius" gradually garners public recognition.

Genius Regendered

By designating Beth a "woman of genius," the text disputes a related psychological principle prominent in the *fin de siècle*. Genius, the argument went, was virtually non-existent among women; in its isolated instances, female genius was less an attribute to be admired than a sign of physiological deviance.[21] Limited to rare cases, according to Campbell, female genius was convincing proof of the "intellectual disparity of the two sexes" at that level (173). Campbell argued that "[g]enius of the highest order is practically limited to the male sex," a phenomenon that he claimed could not be attributed to women's lesser opportunities. In an 1891 text pointedly titled *The Man of Genius,* Italian criminologist and anthropologist Cesare Lombroso reiterated the view that "[i]n the history of genius women have but a small place," representing only "rare exceptions" (137). Like Darwin in *The Descent of Man,* Lombroso pointed to the dearth of female accomplishments in music and other fields to support his argument. Since there were "no women of genius," according to Lombroso, such a biological anomaly could be considered a kind of intellectual cross-dressing, for "the women of genius are [actually] men" (138).[22] Attesting to the assumed absence of women geniuses, Francis Galton's lengthy 1869 treatment on *Hereditary Genius* noted more than "four hundred illustrious men" throughout history (v), but barely mentioned women. Instead, women's role was generally restricted to exerting positive influences upon their sons, but Galton diminished even that limited accomplishment. Despite the "common opinion that great men have remarkable mothers," he maintained, that view "ascribes an undue and incredible share to them," since male geniuses "naturally" demonstrated "extreme filial regard" and "exaggerated praise" of maternal influence (319). In attributing instances of women's so-called genius to "a disease of the nerves," *Fortnightly Review* commentator Janet E. Hogarth conferred upon female genius decidedly adverse connotations, remarking that "if abnormal nerve excitement can be made to spell genius, what is to hinder every woman from obtaining the coveted distinction?" (587).[23]

Like other *fin de siècle*, writings, *The Beth Book* distinguishes genius from talent, which "may manufacture to order" (233), but there the similarity ends. In *The Beth Book*, genius in women is not only enthusiastically approved, but the concept of genius itself is emphatically gendered as feminine.[24] Beth's intellectual capacities, for example, are developed by her kinship with and early inspiration from a feminized Wordsworthian nature. As the narrator informs us in the novel's opening pages, nature caused "the first stirring in herself of the creative faculty" (16), and throughout her life, Beth was "keenly susceptible to outdoor influences" (22). The moments when Beth "passed from conscious thought into a higher phase of being" coincide with her yearning for and absorption in nature (308). The novel strives to emphasize the specifically feminine quality of Beth's genius, however, by invoking the Burkean distinction between the beautiful and the sublime. Only the feminized beautiful draws forth Beth's highest powers, while the masculinized sublime triggers fear and anxiety:

> For a happy interval the scenes which had oppressed her—the desolation, the sombre colours of the great melancholy mountains, the incessant sound of the turbulent sea, the shock and roar of angry breakers warring with the rocks, which had kept her little being all a-throb, braced to the expectation of calamity—lapsed now into the background of her recollection, and under the benign influence of these lovelier surroundings her mind began to expand in the most extraordinary way, while her further faculty awoke. (101)

An additional feminization of genius comes in the text's definition of the term itself. Resonating with conventional views of women's altruistic and compassionate qualities, genius represents "sympathetic insight made perfect" and "touch[es] on every human experience" (80).

Also telling is the inexplicable, irrational quality of Beth's genius, which similarly evokes traditional designations of female impulsiveness. Identified as her "further faculty," Beth's genius was to her "only another word for soul" (16), which is opposed specifically to reasoning ability: Beth "possessed a power of some kind in her infancy which gradually lapsed as her intellectual faculties developed" (28), a power that could be reinvigorated only through an immersion in the beauty of nature. This contrast between emotionality and rationality emerges more forcefully in Beth's comparison of the two states:

> All through life, when she was in possession of her further faculty, and perceived by that means—which was only at fitful intervals... she was calm, strong, and confident.... But when she had only her intellect to rely upon, all was uncertain, and she became weak, vacillating, and dependent. (28)

The Beth Book takes issue with the evolutionary psychologists not only by feminizing genius, but also by intimating that female genius is no more rare than male genius and indeed represents the future development of the species. Again distinguishing Beth's genius from male rationality, the narrator wonders if there exists "some more perfect power to know than the intellect—a power lying latent in the whole race, which will eventually come into possession of it; but with which, at present, only some few rare beings are perfectly endowed" (27). By implying that this feminized power rests latently in the human race as a whole, the novel positions Beth as an evolutionary pioneer, whose particular quality of genius will eventually emerge in humanity through the workings of natural selection.

The presumption of superior female development emerges in another respect as well in the text's assessment of women's moral qualities, reminding us of Auguste Comte's contention that women are "morally the purest portion of humanity" (166) and "in every respect adapted for rectifying the moral deviations" of society (185).[25] Rather than according to women the relatively passive role of positive familial influence, *The Beth Book* interprets this function as a crucial power directing human evolution. As one of Beth's acquaintances explains, "We women have in our minds now what will culminate in the recognition by future generations of the beauty of goodness. Woman is to be the mother of God in Man" (414). New Women will perform an integral function in that mission, a critical point stressed in the novel through the remarks of another enlightened female character, for they initiate evolutionary progress:

> [T]his woman movement is towards the perfecting of life, not towards the disruption of it. . . . I am sure it is evolutionary. It is an effort of the race to raise itself a step higher in the scale of being. For see what it resolves itself into! Men respond to what women expect of them. . . . Now women want husbands of a nobler nature, strong in all the attributes, moral and physical, of the perfect man, that their children may be noble too, and thus the ascent of man to higher planes of being become assured. (412–13)

In finding her voice as a feminist orator in the novel's final pages, Beth reinforces the message that has permeated the text: female development is not a lesser but an alternative—indeed, the paramount—mode of maturation. The evolutionary psychologists' definition of recapitulation is reversed, for the female, not the male, proceeds through and surpasses the highest point of progress achieved by lesser specimens of the species. By valuing the feminized spoken word over the written, *The Beth Book* implies that the linguistic signifier of male maturation simply represents an intermediate step in Beth's development. In fact, "[i]t was as if she did not come into full possession of her true self until she had experienced numberless other phases of being common to the race" (320). By validating female genius, calling for a resistance to an uncritical linguistic interpellation, and privileging the oral tradition, *The Beth Book* argues for a reevaluation of psychological assumptions and echoes Victorian feminist critiques pointing to the flaws of this self-designated empirical science. Like Gamble, who viewed Darwinian theory as an apologia for cultural norms, *The Beth Book* exposes scientific conclusiveness as ideological reinforcement. In so doing, *The Beth Book* reiterates Gamble's contention that "the time has at length arrived when the current opinions concerning sex capacity and endowment demand a revision, and when nothing short of scientific deductions, untainted by the prejudices and dogmatic assumptions of the past, will be accepted" (viii).

Environment and *The Heavenly Twins*

With *The Heavenly Twins* we shift emphasis to the cultural forces generally ignored by the evolutionary psychologists but identified by Grand as equally significant determinants of behavior as biology. The epigraph launching the novel's first chapter serves as an ironic announcement of this project, with a telling assertion from Darwin that "education and environment produce only a small effect on the mind of anyone," since "most of our qualities are innate" (2). *The Heavenly Twins* represents a vigorous denial of this claim, arguing that, for women, the converse is true: education and environment carry enormous consequences for the development of women's innate mental capabilities, either misdirecting or promoting cognitive growth. In *The Heavenly Twins* the natural order of time is figured not as the signifier of progress that Victorians approvingly identified, but as an anti-evolutionary force threatening the viability of the entire human species through the arrest of female development.[26]

Like *The Beth Book*, *The Heavenly Twins* follows a *Bildungsroman* format but broadens its scope to explore the environmental influences acting on three female characters: the primary protagonist, Evadne, who is compelled by social conventions to conform to the appearances of marriage by living with a spouse whose disreputable past she discovers moments after her wedding; Angelica, whose development is contrasted against that of her twin brother Diavolo; and Edith, the least prominent of the three female characters, whose ignorance of social evils allows her to marry a syphilitic philanderer who subsequently transmits the disease to her with fatal results.[27] In *The Heavenly Twins* childhood is relatively unproblematic, a kind of free space in which girls are generally allowed to follow their intellectual and behavioral inclinations. It is in adolescence that cultural pressures are most definitively brought to bear upon the female characters, compelling them to assume traditional roles in the domestic sphere.

The Heavenly Twins responds to a pronounced *fin de siècle* fascination with adolescence that was especially evident in psychological discourse. From a modern perspective, historian John Neubauer credits a confluence of social discourses—psychological and psychoanalytic, as well as educational and sociological—for the burgeoning interest in and specific references to the adolescent span of human growth. Coming into recognition in the final decades of the nineteenth century as a distinct developmental stage, adolescence offered a rich field of study for the evolutionary psychologists.[28] Indeed, adolescence became "the focal point of all psychology" (119), E. G. Lancaster remarked in an 1897–98 edition of *Pedagogical Seminary*, a journal established by developmental psychologist G. Stanley Hall. As William H. Burnham noted in the same journal in 1891, adolescence was worthy of study because it signaled "a great influx of hereditary strength and character" (180). Perhaps the most influential theorist on the subject, Hall based his 1904 two-volume study of adolescence on a compilation of prevalent notions that had appeared "in less systematic form" throughout the century, characterizing adolescence in specifically Darwinian terms, as John Springhall observes (29). Defining adolescence as ages fourteen to twenty-four (30), Hall gave a biological rather than cultural reading to the emotional traumas and stresses of this period. Yet, as Carol Dyhouse points out in her discussion of late-Victorian girlhood, assumptions about adolescence were based on generalized observations about boys, with the few specific references to girls limited to "value-laden and stereotyped" conclusions (116). *The Heavenly Twins* redresses this common omission by its predominant concern with female adolescence, analyzed within a cultural rather than physiological register to question Darwinian presumptions about female development.

For all three protagonists, the environmental influences exerted during adolescence—not the innate qualities that Darwin considered most significant—determine the course of their bleak and unsatisfying lives. Central to the text's investigation of these social forces is a recurrent image that calls attention to the powerful influence of the natural order of time in validating them: a chime that sounds after the striking of the hours from a cathedral tower in the central locale of Morningquest. Introduced graphically in the proem as a bar of Mendelssohn's "Elijah," the chime punctuates the passage of masculine linear time as a musical and plot refrain with its trenchant message, "He, watching over Israel, slumbers not, nor sleeps" (xxxix). As the text's opening image, the chime is positioned as a monolithic presence that pervades Morningquest "day and night" (xxxix), conveying its power through a "regularity which suggested something permanent in this weary world of change" (xl). Although variously interpreted by the village residents—most compellingly as characterizing "a God essentially masculine" (xli)—the chime is universally deemed significant: "It meant something! It was not a mere jingle of bells, as most chimes are, but a phrase with a distinct idea in it which they understood as we understand a foreign language when we can read it without translating it" (xli).

Reappearing at those moments in the text when cultural forces are particularly critical to the workings of the plot, the chime stresses masculine temporality's control over personal destiny, despite the vagaries of individual circumstances and events: even though "[c]hange followed change," as "time passed," the tolling of the chime remained "immutable" (xlvi). For those individuals who embrace the ideological associations of the natural order of time, the chime is a comforting presence; for others, however, the chime carries troubling undertones, connoting an oppressive temporal order that forces women to follow constrictive social conventions.

Yet the proem also holds promise that the hegemony of the masculine temporal order can be attenuated and even dismantled:

> In these latter days, however, it began to appear as if the supremacy of the great masculine idea was at last being seriously threatened, for even in Morningquest a new voice of extraordinary sweetness had already been heard, not *his*, the voice of man; but *theirs,* the collective voice of humanity, which declared that "He, watching," was the all-pervading good, the great moral law, the spirit of pure love, Elohim, mistranslated in the book of Genesis as "He" only, but signifying the union to which all nature testifies, the male and female principles which together created the universe, the infinite father and mother, without whom, in perfect accord and exact equality, the best government of nations has always been crippled and abortive. (xliii)

For the female protagonists of *The Heavenly Twins*, however, this more optimistic interpretation of the chimes remains only an unfulfilled promise.

Intellectual Development

With its title of "Childhoods and Girlhoods" framing the story within the discourses of evolutionary psychology, the first of the novel's six books centers on Evadne's innate intellectual powers and the influences that shape and retard them in adolescence. Characterized in the opening paragraph as one who "wanted to know," the nineteen-year-old Evadne "looked out of narrow eyes at an untried world inquiringly" (3), one of numerous references to her naturally searching mind. As this initial comment suggests, *The Heavenly Twins*—in contrast to *The Beth Book*, with its privileging of feminine qualities as markers of developmental superiority—begins its assault on the evolutionary psychologists by undermining the premise that women inherently demonstrated limited reasoning abilities and a disinclination for abstract thought. Instead, Evadne found "[t]he acquisition of knowledge" to be "her favourite pastime, her principal pleasure in life" (24).

Absorbing her lessons "with interest and intelligence" (3), Evadne reveals an intellectual precocity through complex analyses of the texts she peruses rather than an indiscriminate acceptance of their messages.[29] She acquires a "proper appreciation of masculine precision of thought" (5) and "experiment[s] with every item of information" her mind amassed "to test its practical value" (4). Though she appears to embrace "every article of faith in God and man which had been offered for her guidance," Evadne instead accepts them "only provisionally" (3) and disputes troubling assumptions in dialogic marginal notes. She demonstrates a linguistic sophistication traditionally linked with the male in displaying a propensity for writing—"her best mode of communication" (14)—as well as a deftness with oral expression and a "special aptitude for languages" (39). She contests presumptions of biological difference in the sexes' mental acuity as she determines that "women had originally no congenital defect of inferiority" (13). Indeed, Evadne's own intellectual ability is characterized as a natural product of evolutionary movement. Her questioning mind is attributed to "[a]ges of education, ages of hereditary preparation" that "rendered its action inevitable" (3)—a statement that belies assumptions that intellectual prowess represented a sex-linked trait. Evadne's mental powers are fostered by a kind of hereditary memory, which reinforces the notion that a capacity for ratiocination is as natural in women as in men, for "[i]t was as if she only required to be reminded of things she had learnt before" (3).

The contrast between the narrator's assessment of innate female ability and the Darwinian position becomes strikingly apparent through the pronouncements of Evadne's father. Warning of the perils of original thought, Mr. Frayling informs his daughter that "[o]nly confusion comes of women thinking for themselves" (5); instead, Evadne "must let me decide all such matters for you" until coming under a husband's "control." Frayling reiterates psychologists' beliefs that female intellectualism is anomalous rather than representative as he asserts that "you can't argue from exceptional women" (11). Instead, a woman more convincingly "resembles a parrot in her mental process," since she amasses bits of information "with a parrot-like sharpness" but lacks the intelligence "to make any practical application of them" (12). In positioning the obtuse Frayling as a mouthpiece for Darwinian psychologists, *The Heavenly Twins* converts their proclamations into parody by exposing the manipulation of scientific discourses to reinscribe tradition. "[R]eady to resent even the upward tendency of evolution" when it means alterations in women's position and influence, Frayling becomes "rabid" upon the "mere mention of the subject" and responds to it with "apoplectic" fervor (6).

The text, however, proceeds to demonstrate that such patronizing preconceptions themselves endanger evolutionary progression, particularly through the pedagogical theories that reflect them. As in *The Beth Book*, Evadne's experiences belie the guiding tenets of such educational philosophies, which strove to protect the female from a dangerous exertion that could threaten reproduction—"the end and aim of all life everywhere," according to Havelock Ellis (*Women and Marriage* 15). As physician Henry Maudsley cautioned in 1874, "When Nature spends in one direction, she must economize in another direction" (467); education must accommodate the "special functions" of womanhood that can develop only in "a special sphere of development and activity determined by the performance of those functions" (466). For Evadne, the reverse holds true. In contrast to conservative assumptions, not the presence but the lack of the rigorous education that Victorian males received, beginning in childhood and extending through adolescence, produces an adverse effect on her development that presumably would bode ill for future generations. Indeed, as she realizes, "[w]ithholding education from women was the original sin of man" (24). Confined to the "accustomed education for a girl in her position" (25), Evadne can broaden her cognitive scope only by solitary reading once her perfunctory schooling has ceased. Without the guidance provided through disciplined schooling, though, Evadne cannot mature appropriately. Her intellectual labors are stunted through marriage to the conservative George Colquhoun and a resulting consignment to the domestic sphere for which her cursory education presumably has prepared her. The domestic activities that Maudsley and later thinkers viewed as the healthy applications for female education instead precipitate an intellectual degeneration and emotional breakdown.

The flawed reasoning and specious conclusions underlying evolutionary psychology emerge most dramatically in the novel's final chapter, which centers on the musings of Dr. George Galbraith, a nerve-disorder specialist who treats and subsequently marries the widowed Evadne. In an introductory note to the chapter, the narrator attests to the limitations of the psychological discipline that Galbraith's study of Evadne will reveal:

> [T]he reader, better informed than himself with regard to the antecedents of his "subject," will find it interesting to note both the accuracy of his insight and the curious mistakes which it is possible even for a trained observer like himself to make by the half light of such imperfect knowledge as he was able to collect under the circumstances. (554)

Galbraith's opening comments reiterate the limitations of psychology and negate its pretensions to be an exact science:

> Evadne puzzled me. As a rule, men of my profession, and more particularly specialists like myself, can class a woman's character ... while he [sic] is diagnosing her disease.... But even after I had seen Evadne many times, and felt broadly that I knew her salient points as well as such tricks of manner or habitual turns of expression . . . I was puzzled. (555)

Nevertheless, Galbraith becomes a sympathetic figure in this text, primarily by identifying cultural influences as the cause of Evadne's mental distress. Diagnosing Evadne as a hysteric, Galbraith attributes this conventionally feminine disorder to a "want of active occupation" (626). Comparing Evadne's condition to "the old story of these cases in women," Galbraith blames cultural conditioning for her fragile mental state, since "[t]he natural bent has been thwarted to begin with" (639). Subtle allusions to the natural order of time reinforce the point that Evadne's hysteria is induced not by an innate physiological propensity but by a suffocating patriarchal culture that provides men with meaningful occupation and middle-class women with only desultory leisure. Evadne finds "many spare hours of every day on her hands" (639)—a condition so disorienting that she loses "all count of time" (581)—in sharp contrast to Galbraith's satisfied recognition that "my time was fully occupied" (624).

Evadne herself alludes to the cause of her mental imbalance in condemning "[t]he wisdom of ages" that "is brought to the training of each little girl" to instill the idea "that a woman's one object in life is to be agreeable" (612). The disastrous effects stemming from such environmental pressures emerge in Evadne's final attempts to preserve her tenuous hold on sanity by rejecting all intellectual pursuits, as she informs Galbraith:

> All my endeavor is not to think. Let me live on the surface of life, as most women do. I will do nothing but attend to my household duties and the social duties of my position. I will read nothing that is not first weeded by you. . . . But do not ask me to think. I can be the most docile, the most obedient, the most loving of women as long as I forget my knowledge of life. (672)

Unable to effect a cure, Galbraith asks in the novel's final sentence only for "the power to make her life endurable" (679).

Evadne's tragic story gains much of its impact not only from her individual plight, but also for its broader evolutionary implications. Evadne, Galbraith laments, "should have been a representative woman such as the world wants at this period of its progress," one who would make "a name for herself and an impression on the age" (556). In his earliest acquaintance with Evadne, shortly after her marriage to Colquhoun, Galbraith recognizes the possibility that Evadne is part of the "seventh waves of humanity" that ensure its forward movement:

> [I]t has always seemed to me that the tide of human progress is raised at intervals to higher levels at a bound. . . . The seventh waves of humanity are men and women who, by the impulse of some one action which comes naturally to them but is new to the race, gather strength to come up to the last halting place of the tide, and to carry it on with them ever so far beyond. (99)

That power, the text subsequently implies, rests in the New Woman. In depicting Evadne as a stunted New Woman figure, *The Heavenly Twins* suggests that the societal refusal to allow such visionary potential to flourish holds perils for humanity.[30] Using male characters to transmit the message of the New Woman's progressiveness—Galbraith and Mr. Price, for example, an elderly American with whom Evadne socializes during her marriage to Colquhoun—the text argues that furthering women's evolution benefits men as well. As Price explains to a dubious acquaintance:

> I believe myself that all this unrest and rebellion against the old established abuses amongst women is simply an effort of nature to improve the race. The men of the present day will have a bad time if they resist the onward impulse; but, in any case, the men of the future will have good reason to arise and call their mothers blessed. . . . Don't interfere with Evadne. (219)

In this contention, Price echoes the dissenting voice of evolutionist David Ritchie, whose 1889 critique of the ideological implications of Darwinism led him to conclude that "[a] people, *all* whose members become superior in mental qualities, will have the advantage over those" whose "development is partial and one-sided" (81).

Yet the evolutionary movement of humanity that Price attributes to women's leadership is impeded by environmental forces—not only the education and marital restraints we have witnessed, but also the teachings of Christianity that are marshaled to maintain women in an inferior position. "With fair play," Price argues, women "should continue on," but through the influence of the clergy, their "development may be entirely arrested" (218). Characterizing religion as an anti-evolutionary ideological apparatus, Price tells a cleric:

> It is curious that priesthoods, while preaching perfection, invariably do their best to stop progress. You will never believe that any change is for the better until it is accomplished, and there is no denying it, and so you hinder forever when you should be the first to help and encourage. (218)

That sentiment is placed firmly within an evolutionary context by Dr. Shadwell Rock, an eminent nerve-disorder specialist whom Galbraith calls in for consultation in his early treatment of Evadne. "My own idea," Rock asserts, "is that a woman is a human being; but the clerical theory is that she is a dangerous beast, to be kept in subjection, and used for domestic purposes only" (639). This stance, Rock warns, imperils human evolution, since "[t]he restrictions imposed upon women of ability warp their minds, and the rising generation suffers."

Invariably reactionary, the clergymen who periodically enter the narrative demonstrate a paternal condescension, proclaiming the natural superiority of the male and the responsibility of women to accept their lowly status. In valorizing the "old exquisite ideal of womanhood," one cleric muses, "What can be more admirable, more elevating to contemplate, more powerful as an example, than her beautiful submission to the hardships of her lot?" (179). Antithetical to that image is the threatening figure of the New Woman with her vision of a "New Order" (489). "[N]o good can come of that kind of thing," asserts an elderly clergyman (489), sharing the view of a younger cleric that "[t]he way in which women are putting themselves forward just now on any subject . . . is quite deplorable" (193). The elderly clergyman assails the hubris that leads women to question ecclesiastical authority because they perceive that the church is "a distinctly masculine organization" and characterizes such heresy as not only "the height of folly" but "absolutely dangerous" (490). Yet New Women who contest the church's authority are otherwise deemed by another character as "[n]ot 'revo'—but evolutionary" (230).

The church's complicity in maintaining women in a posture of submission becomes especially apparent in the text's treatment of Evadne's close acquaintance, Edith. Periodic iterations of the cathedral chime signal the role that the ideological associations of the natural order of time play in Edith's horrific fate. An Old Woman figure who initially embraces conventional religious and social teachings promulgated by her bishop father and conservative mother, Edith grows up "under the protection of the great cathedral . . . and the influence of its wonderful chime" (154). Reflecting the power of Mariolatry to reinforce female subjection, Edith's bedroom, architecturally Gothic like a church, contains a virtual gallery of Madonna paintings and other religious icons that convey a sacrificial message (158). Because she is kept in the state of "complete ignorance" (156) that the church believes appropriate for female innocence, Edith readily agrees to the marriage proposal of Sir Mosley Menteith, accepting her parents' enthusiastic assessment of him as a desirable mate despite Evadne's repeated warnings about his disreputable character. Within a year of marriage, Edith contracts Menteith's syphilis, which carries not only individual consequences but augurs poorly for the viability of future generations, as evidenced by the hideous child she bears shortly thereafter.

A biological anomaly, Edith's infant has an "old, old" face (289); "[r]apidly degenerat[ing]" after birth (277), the child displays such a ghastly demeanor that its own mother wants to kill it (304).[31] Described as "a speckled toad" (301), the infant more convincingly represents an evolutionary throwback than a human child. The conclusion to be drawn, the text therefore suggests, is that humanity cannot evolve unless women are allowed to advance beyond the condition of ignorance in which Victorian culture seeks to maintain them. Had Edith been apprised of the social realities that permit a man to marry regardless of an unsavory past—with no concern for the repercussions his debauched activities could carry for a wife and offspring—she would have attended to Evadne's warnings.[32] The future of humanity, *The Heavenly Twins* cautions, depends upon the ability of women to choose their husbands appropriately, following a kind of Darwinian selection that would enable the morally as well as physically fittest to prevail.[33]

To denounce the flawed perspective that allows marriages like

Edith's to take place, the text brings in the image of the chimes at two critical moments. In a blasphemous identification of God as a "demon," Edith responds to the chiming of the bells that sound soon after her child's birth with the plea that "I wish those bells could be stopped! . . . They deafen me" (285). When she ventures outdoors shortly thereafter as she attempts to recover from the difficult birth, Edith inadvertently discovers Menteith's illegitimate child, a "small and rickety" boy whose "unhealthy appearance" (290) is as repellent as that of her own infant. Relapsing into the nervous and delirious state into which she first succumbed after giving birth, Edith again hears the chime, sinister and oppressive. The chime "rolled through the room, a deafening volume of sound, in long reverberations" (293), as Edith lies dying—"gray and ghastly, and old" (300).

Nature or Nurture

The novel's presumption that female development is both determined and constricted by environment becomes particularly convincing when the narrative focus shifts to the aristocratic Angelica. Her story, beginning with childhood and concluding in late adolescence, demonstrates that her skepticism of "hereditary predisposition" (496) is an appropriate response to evolutionists who deny that culture is a powerful influence on behavior. By presenting Angelica as a different-sex twin, the text can trace the environmental factors that both distinguish her development from that of her brother Diavolo and ignore the individualistic qualities that ill suit her for a woman's conventional role. Twins have traditionally provided women authors with a strategic literary device, allowing these writers to chart the gendering process and the harm to both sexes that such cultural conditioning entails.[34] In the context of evolutionary psychology, however, the choice of twins is a particularly ironic one. In his lengthy 1883 study on such siblings, eugenics pioneer Francis Galton questioned "whether nurture can do anything at all," concluding that nature was the primary factor directing behavior (172). Though Galton's treatise focused on identical twins, not the opposite-sex fraternal twins that Grand portrays, Darwin's claim that nature overshadows nurture loses credence through the novel's extensive examination of acculturation.[35]

As critical commentary on *The Heavenly Twins* has noted, Angelica and Diavolo reverse traditional gender roles.[36] A nascent New Woman, Angelica is the cleverer of the two, the initiator of their activities, and the dominant personality, who in her "rage to know" pulls "Diavolo on with her" (126). In a chapter significantly titled "Development and Arrest of Development," the text traces the unsuitability of gender roles for Angelica, who will be consigned to the domestic sphere despite her undeniable talents, and Diavolo, who will be prepared to assume his place in the patriarchal structure despite an absence of professional aspirations that, as Angelica scoffs, makes marriage "the best profession for you" (319). To the twins' grandfather, the duke of Morningquest, Angelica's precocity merely attests to the truth of evolutionary psychologists' pronouncements on female development. In the duke's estimation, "women mature earlier . . . [b]ut their minds never get far beyond the first point at which they arrive" (259).[37] Yet that contention is immediately reinterpreted as a cultural effect, for Diavolo himself attributes the abrupt cessation of female maturation to the social norms that either "they marry at seventeen, or their education" is discontinued "just when a man is beginning his properly."

The text more directly interrogates the acculturation process during Angelica's later adolescence, when she experiments with cross-dressing to establish a close relationship with a gifted tenor who briefly enters the narrative after Angelica has married. Borrowing Diavolo's clothing to assume her brother's identity and attain greater freedom of movement, Angelica gains the Tenor's respect and friendship during their frequent meetings. Contrasted to the Tenor's close relationship with the Boy, his term for the disguised Angelica, is his idealization of the real Angelica whom he observes regularly in the church where he sings. Viewing Angelica as an unapproachable Beatrice who seemingly embodies all the qualities of womanly perfection as "his ideal of purity, his goddess of truth, his angel of pity" (446), the Tenor shrinks from an actual encounter. His divergent valuations of the same person, solely on the basis of perceived gender difference, attest to culture's role in shaping conceptions of subjectivity, culminating with a boating accident that reveals Angelica to be female. Immediately the Tenor's attitude toward her alters, as he attempts to revive her with a hot drink into which he pours only "half the quantity of brandy he would have used five minutes before for the Boy." With the Tenor's vague dreams of wedding his feminine icon shattered by this revelation, even before he learns of her existing marriage, the narrator muses:

> It was only a change of idea really, the Boy was a girl, that was all; but what a difference it made, and would have made even if there had been no question of love and marriage in the matter! At any

other time the Tenor himself might have marvelled at the place apart we assign in our estimation to one of two people of like powers, passions, impulses, and purposes, simply because one of them is a woman. (446–47)

Angelica similarly attests to the power of gender roles as she ponders the effects of cross-dressing on her own sense of subjectivity. Denying that she merely imitated Diavolo, Angelica instead asserts that she became Diavolo, adopting his point of view so completely that "my difficulty was to remember that I was not him" (452). As she ponders the transformation that her disguise prompted, Angelica informs the Tenor: "having once assumed the character, I began to love it; it came naturally. . . . I tell you I was a genuine boy. I moved like a boy, I felt like a boy; I was my own brother in very truth. Mentally and morally, I was exactly what you thought me" (456). Only through cross-dressing, Angelica stresses, could cultural preconceptions be overcome and the Tenor accept her under the identical terms accorded men:

> I have enjoyed the benefit of free intercourse with your masculine mind undiluted by your masculine prejudices and proclivities with regard to my sex. Had you known that I was a woman—even you—the pleasure of your companionship would have been spoilt for me, so unwholesomely is the imagination of a man affected by ideas of sex. (458)

Blaming social conditioning for this narrow perspective, Angelica castigates the "training" that educates men to view women as "the opposite sex," thereby creating a binary that identifies and diminishes female difference.

Central to the examination of acculturation in these scenes are the frequent iterations of the Morninquest chimes, marking each signal moment inscribing gender positions. Unlike the Tenor, who found solace in the chime's mellifluous refrain at trying times in his life, "the Boy hated the chime," considering it "importunate, like an ill-bred person" (409). Insidious and vengeful, the chime "mingled inopportunely with everything" and demonstrated "a spite against him, and would do him an injury if it could." Rebelling against the dictates of the chime, the Boy imagines destroying it, but resistance is futile—the Boy's desire of "upsetting the chime" is merely "one of his impossible threats" (410). By hailing the reinscription of gender positions, the chime reflects a culture that allows no fluidity in those roles; indeed, the Boy is prevented from revealing his dual identity on one occasion by the sounds of the "beastly chime," which "made it impossible" for the acknowledgment to proceed (436). Silenced by the chime while attempting to admit his gender play, the Boy can only respond ineffectually with rage by repeating: "I hate it. I loathe it. It is cruel as eternal damnation. It is condemnation without appeal."

The veracity of the Boy's observation is proven through Angelica's ineffectual efforts to alter her gender destiny within Victorian culture. Uninterested in marriage, she nevertheless recognizes that it is her only option. Though pushing her power as a woman to its limits by making a marriage proposal herself—demanding of her choice, the amiable Mr. Kilroy, that he *"let me do as I like"* (321)—Angelica nevertheless is trapped by cultural expectations that she become a conventional wife. In a scene with her religious Aunt Fulda shortly after the Tenor's sudden death, the chime marks the moment that Lady Fulda identifies as "a time [that] comes to us all—an hour when we are called upon to choose between good and evil" (537). Although the definition of those relative terms is left ambiguous, the fact that Angelica has "sinned against the whole spirit of uprightness" suggests that a reluctance to assume her appropriate gender role represents the source of her transgressions. The striking of the hours by the cathedral clock mingles with the tolling of the city clocks, as the religious signifier blends with its secular counterpart to convey the monolithicism of the natural order of time. Angelica's acquiescence to her aunt's dictum that she choose goodness comes "almost at the same moment" as the clocks strike and the chime begins to toll, ushering in the dramatic change in her life: "The hour was over which had been her hour; a chapter of her life had closed with it forever; and when she looked up then, she found herself in another world, wherein she would walk henceforth with other eyes to better purpose" (540).

The reference to Angelica's "better purpose" can only be read ironically, for an announced objective to "[l]ive for others" is implicitly translated as an edict to live through others. After Kilroy has received her promise that she will confine her musical talents to the domestic sphere rather than pursue a professional career, Angelica's only conduit to the public world is through her husband, as she anonymously writes the speeches he delivers in Parliament. Self-abnegation becomes a marker of regression, as Angelica reveals through an unsettling propensity to call her husband "Daddy" and indulge in childish behavior that prevents him from working in peace.[38] Oppressive rather than opportune, time becomes merely a "long vista of weary days, through which she must live . . . to no purpose" (486).

Angelica's fate, like that of Evadne and Edith, is directed by the cultural forces that are reified by the natural order of time; in none of these *Bildungsromane* does a biological propensity bring the physical or psychological disaster the characters incur or allow them to develop into adulthood unimpeded. In demonstrating the consequences of stunted development, *The Heavenly Twins*—like *The Beth Book,* in its own way—turns the Darwinians' doctrines against the guiding premise that the mechanism of evolution reflects and requires female inferiority. Instead, Sarah Grand insists, the advancement of the human species depends on the recognition and rejection of the dangerous limitations imposed on the development of half of its numbers. Through her fictional vehicles, Grand adds her voice to the murmurs of dissent that feminist evolutionist Devereux articulated: the common tendency to consider the New Woman an "excrescence on the face of society" denies her an advanced and "inevitable" evolutionary status (18). As Grand stresses, only through a valorization of a new ideal of woman—embodied in the New Woman—can the human species hope to progress and thrive.

Chapter 5

Controlling Women's Time: Regulatory Days and Historical Determinism in *The Daughters of Danaus*

> There is nothing to be really alarmed at in her ideas, regrettable as they are. . . . No use to oppose her now. Nothing but experience will teach her. She must just be humoured for the present. . . . Time will cure that. . . . What can she do against all the world? She can't escape from the conditions of her epoch.
> —Caird, *The Daughters of Danaus*

Mona Caird's 1894 *The Daughters of Danaus* not only addresses the broad theoretical implications of time that we have examined thus far, but also its minutely practical applications. With the writings of Florence Nightingale, Dinah Mulock Craik, and other Victorian essayists providing a didactic framework to which it is apparently responding, this New Woman novel traces the ruinous effects wrought by a patriarchal culture's stringent regulation of a woman's time through numbing domestic routine. Coupled with this everyday control over her time is the historical pattern that validates it—"the conditions of her epoch," in the epigraph's terms. Temporality is thus accorded a double focus in this text through which daily disciplinary constraints on the exercise of time are contextualized within the oppressive burden of history. As the mythic reference in Caird's title suggests, temporal regulation consigns Victorian women to an existence as futile as that of the daughters of Danaus in Greek lore who were eternally condemned to draw water with sieves from bottomless wells.

The Daughters of Danaus traces the fortunes of the outspoken Hadria Fullerton, a New Woman whose ambition to become a renowned musical composer is thwarted by perpetual claims on her time as a daughter, wife, and mother. As the sole daughter remaining in the middle-class home of her conservative parents, Hadria can devote time to her musical studies only in the rare moments that her domestic obligations leave her. Dismayed over her unsatisfying life in the Fullerton household, Hadria eventually agrees to the marriage proposal of Hubert Temperley, but she soon discovers that marital life and motherhood are equally enervating. Hadria instead advocates a woman's right to a genuinely free choice to rear children, which she puts into practice by informally adopting Martha Jervis, the illegitimate child of a local schoolteacher who had died without revealing the father's name. Eventually rebelling against the marital state she compares to a barbaric rite, Hadria travels to France with Martha to pursue her vocational interests. Yet her freedom is short-lived, for her mother's serious illness forces her to return home. Again ensconced within the domestic sphere, Hadria is pursued by Professor Theobold, reluctantly returning his interest until he reveals that he is Martha's father. Theobold, incensed at Hadria's rejection of him once the revelation has been made, extracts his revenge by taking his daughter from Hadria to raise her as a traditional wife and mother, the figure whom Hadria has inadvertently become.

Setting *The Daughters of Danaus* apart from the novels we have investigated is the protagonist's ambivalent response to masculine temporality: she chafes at the endless time-consuming duties that it imposes on a woman of her class yet evidences an irrepressible desire to participate in its civilizing endeavors as a composer. Hadria's first name suggests her problematic link with the masculine time she avidly wishes to share. Derived from the prominent Roman emperor Hadrian, "Hadria" both associates the protagonist with the linear time of history and separates her from it as a feminized variation. In effect, Hadria Fullerton is a frustrated aspirant to the goals of early feminists, seeking to become part of the first wave of the woman's movement that Julia Kristeva characterizes as motivated by an ambition "to gain a place in linear time as the time of project and history" ("Women's Time" 18)—the time, Kristeva remarks, that feminism "both inherits and modifies" (15) through participation within it. Substantive involvement in masculine temporality, Kristeva adds, necessitates a denial of traditional conceptions of femininity and maternity "insofar as they are deemed incompatible with insertion in that history" and the culture's "logical and ontological values of . . . rationality" (19). Hadria's failing comes in taking only tentative steps in that direction.

Despite the novel's intriguing analysis of the cultural forces that reify women's subordinate status and a compelling character who battles against them, *The Daughters of Danaus* has received less attention in modern critical discourse than it deserves. Caird's work is important to consider because she was a prominent feminist author in the *fin de siècle*.[1] Her essays on marriage, human development, and history gained wide audiences in Victorian journals, with one controversial article on marriage garnering twenty-seven thousand replies from readers.[2] Biographical data identify Caird as a significant reformer and celebrated polemicist of the period and *The Daughters of Danaus* as a popular novel, one of several she published around the turn of the century.[3]

When assessed within a literary economy, *The Daughters of Danaus* offers a prime example of the 1890s aesthetic project of New Woman writers—a rare successful blending of "the demands of art and propaganda," as Gail Cunningham characterizes the text (69–70). In a detailed study of feminist novels in the nineteenth-century's final decade, Rita Kranidis points to the sharp division between art and social issues that Walter Pater and other aesthetes valued in their appraisal of high culture and their identification of the best exemplars of the artistic process as those ignoring social concerns (25). Yet Kranidis locates the importance of the feminist novelists precisely in their appropriation of and experimentation with the genre to articulate gender issues, manipulating novelistic conventions to expose widespread cultural myths (72). Through its negotiations between form and content, the late-century feminist novel strove to incorporate polemicism and aesthetics as a "means of intruding on the cultural imagination," as Kranidis describes the phenomenon, and rewrite "the 'story' of women's lives . . . from a radically politicized perspective" (73). Though we have seen this approach at work in Sarah Grand's novels, *The Daughters of Danaus* offers one of the most explicit and pronounced manifestations of the strategy in the entire body of New Woman texts, for the narrative derives both its initial impetus and ongoing momentum from the protagonist's continual and vocal conflicts with the gender ideology of the late-Victorian period.

Perhaps one reason that *The Daughters of Danaus* has appeared infrequently in critical discourse is the novel's narrow focus, for the narrative presents its social commentary through a specifically temporal lens to become an obsessive analysis of the workings of time.[4] Yet that very singularity makes *The Daughters of Danaus* an ideal choice for an examination of temporality and gender and the impact their interrelationship had on the *fin de siècle* woman and her descendants. One daughter of the period, Virginia Woolf, would later articulate in her feminist treatise *A Room of One's Own* the two pressing concerns that Caird identifies: a woman's day does not provide "long hours of steady and uninterrupted work," since "interruptions there will always be" (78); and a woman "is all but absent from history" (43), seen only "in the lives of the great, whisk[ed] away into the background" (45).

The Cultural Context

The Daughters of Danaus responds to the same concerns articulated by Victorian women writers who decried the incessant claims of domestic and social routine upon their time, thereby limiting or precluding the pursuit of other interests. Socialist Beatrice Webb, for example, laments in her 1926 autobiography "the rival pulls on time and energy" in which a domineering "Victorian code of feminine domesticity" perennially clashes with an intellectual "curiosity into the nature of things" (100). Noting that "the current code" requires that "the entire time and energy" of a daughter be directed to serving her familial and social circle, Webb contends that "the right to end this apprenticeship" could be attained only through marriage (101)—which merely repeats rather than resolves the problem by substituting a comparable set of demands on a woman's time. Webb's diary entries attest to the social monopolization of a woman's day through a detailed record of the calls and events that occupied her during the London season, splitting her life "sharply into the thoughtful part and the active part, . . . completely unconnected one with the other" (105). With such time-consuming schedules, Florence Nightingale similarly argues in the 1852 *Cassandra,* "[w]omen never have half an hour in all their lives . . . that they can call their own" (34) and are given "no means" with which to "resist the 'claims of social life'" (35).

Because "no time is appointed for thought" (31), Nightingale further stresses in her 1860 *Suggestions for Thought,* women are left with only "odd moments" for non-domestic pursuits (71) and limited energy to devote to them. Webb concurs, complaining that social preoccupations left her "absolutely useless in the way of brain-work" for "the little time and energy left" (106) after performing her duties. Harriet Martineau makes precisely the same point in her 1879 autobiography, observing that when social events left only evening hours for work, she could rarely write "any thing more serious than letters" (145). Nightingale contests a related and popular preconception in arguing that "[t]he maxim of doing things at 'odd moments' is a most dangerous one" (71), since one cannot muster the intellectual stamina necessary for anything "requiring original thought" (72) or "a form, a completeness." Genius, Nightingale cautions, cannot be exercised in spare moments; as a result, women traditionally have been "dilettanti," with few producing substantive achievements. Domestic and social routine, these writers say, prevents women from achieving their potential and attaining creative or professional goals.

The essayists further indicate that the problem is exacerbated by a gender-specific difference in the very perception of time. Women's rights advocate Dinah Mulock Craik illustrates the distinction by noting in 1858 that "[m]en are taught as a matter of business to recognise the value of time," but "women rarely or never" are given that lesson (18). Nightingale agrees that "[w]omen's life is spent in pastime, men's in business"; women's chief occupation is simply "to find something to '*pass*' the '*time*'" (*Suggestions* 131). Poet Augusta Webster also comments on the assumption that women's time is unimportant, remarking that it is "reckoned needless to the owner and free to whoever takes it, like blackberries in a hedge" (160). The failure to recognize the importance of time begins well before marriage, Craik warns, for daughters' "whole energies are devoted to the massacre of old Time," whom they "prick . . . to death with crochet and embroidery needles," and "strum him deaf with piano and harp playing—*not* music" (17). Significantly selecting the masculine pronoun in discussing time, Craik adopts particularly violent imagery to convey the gravity of the issue:

> [Women] cut him up with morning-visitors, or leave his carcass in ten-minute parcels at every "friend's" house they can think of. Finally, they dance him defunct at all sort of unnatural hours; and then, rejoicing in the excellent excuse, smother him in sleep for a third of the following day. Thus he dies, a slow, inoffensive, perfectly natural death; and they will never recognise his murder till, on the confines of this world, or from the unknown shores of the next, the question meets them: "What have you done with Time?" (17)

A cursory reading of Craik's observations suggests that women exercise agency in their relationship with time, for the sequence of active verbs repeatedly places women in the subject position as they cut, leave, and smother time. Yet the forceful predicates instead signal the opposite interpretation by reflecting back upon their subjects. Since a woman's life is itself grounded in time, "his murder" represents a form of self-destruction. The "slow, inoffensive, perfectly natural death" experienced by time mirrors that of the women who squander it as they languidly proceed toward death through years of innocuous and expected feminine activities. Underlying Craik's assertions, however, is the inference that women, on some level, recognize their inadvisable response to time, since their "rejoicing" in an "excellent excuse" for continuing its waste translates into unwitting rationalization. Only when it is too late, if at all, does even a glimmer of understanding emerge that the potential of their lives has been lost.

Besides such prominent figures as Webb, Nightingale, Martineau, and Webster, long-forgotten contributors to Victorian periodicals condemned the temporal demands on women. Catherine Milnes Gaskell asserts in an 1889 number of the *Nineteenth Century* that "[n]obody looks on a woman's time as sacred" (779), noting that "perhaps the hardest burden of all is the vast number and constant change of subjects and occupations that a woman has to get through in a day" (778). An 1887 essay in the *Westminster Review* lambasts the "unremitting claims upon the time and thought, ceaseless small duties, unrelieved by any space of time when the work is done and the mind is free to throw aside its worries, and recruit itself with study or recreation" ("What Woman" 212). In 1894, Alys W. Pearsall Smith writes that "[t]he time of unmarried daughters at home is often entirely spent in domestic and social duties or pleasures" (443); because "the girl can never sit down to read or write without fear of being disturbed," she "can never undertake any definite work or pursuit, lest it might interfere with some of these unceasing claims" (444–45). As a result, "[s]he never, in fact, has an hour that she can call absolutely her own free from the danger of interruption."[5]

My discussion thus far alludes to a troubling predicament for a Victorian woman: since she spent her days attending to social obligations or household duties, her time was never truly her own but instead directed by cultural expectations. The ideological implications of this monopolization of women's time are staggering, for temporal control became a vehicle for social control in reinforcing the separate spheres. With hours of the day apportioned to domestic tasks, women had little opportunity to develop cognitive and vocational talents that would allow them to move beyond traditional roles. To borrow Michel Foucault's terminology, temporal regulation kept women in a state of subjection in much the same way it did the prisoners, workers, and soldiers addressed in *Discipline and Punish*. Time in all of these cases served as a disciplinary mechanism whereby the dominant culture could exercise its authority; power, as Foucault argues, could be "articulated directly onto time" through "a detailed control and a regular intervention . . . in each moment" (160).

The domestic routines foisted on Victorian women, like the elaborate schedules that Foucault describes for French prisoners in 1838 or industrial workers in the early years of the century, provided a "continuity and constraint" (161) that unobtrusively promoted cultural stability. Indeed, the position of women recalls Karl Marx's discussion of temporal oppression among the working class in his 1867 *Capital*, in which Marx decries the "small thefts" of time in a worker's day (145). Like the factory laborers Marx defended, Victorian women needed a limited working day that would clarify "when the time which the worker sells is ended, and when his own begins" (175). As Havelock Ellis remarked some twenty years later, "A healthy life is more difficult to attain for the woman of the ordinary household than for the worker in a mine, for he at least, when the work of his set is over, has two-thirds of the twenty-four hours to himself" (*Women and Marriage* 10). In an analogy that Caird also employs in her novel, Ellis adds that the Victorian female "is bound by a thousand Lilliputian threads from which there seems no escape."

Evidence of the careful regulation of the middle-class woman's time comes from popular manuals on household management, descendants of the conduct books of the two preceding centuries. Late-Victorian mothers presumably would have read the nineteenth-century versions in their youth, sharing with their daughters the texts' dubious wisdom about breaking the day into designated segments. More recent manuals brought a "scientific approach" to domestic routine, according to Patricia Branca, covering virtually "every aspect of domestic life" (13), as did their predecessors. Although the manuals throughout the century differed markedly depending on the economic situation of their intended audiences, they shared an interest in systematically governing a woman's day and inculcating conceptions of her appropriate role. Household manuals offered "explicit information on the expenditure of time" (21–22), says Barbara Stein Frankle, and their "heavy schedules" provided a convenient tool for "adamant supporters of the domestic ideal" (178). Often written by women, the manuals reflect the force of domestic ideology, absorbed and promulgated by representatives of the very sex it seeks to control.[6]

Mrs. Warren's 1864 manual, in particular, stresses the value placed on the appropriate management of a woman's time.[7] Indeed, she indirectly credits a newfound appreciation of punctuality in household routine with saving her marriage (31), turning to no less a figure than Lord Nelson to emphasize the importance of an acute awareness of time:

> I endeavoured to become punctual, and this was my hardest task. Again and again I tried, and failed—I could not be exact. One day I was reading the Life of Nelson, and it was said that he owed all his success to being always a quarter of an hour beforehand for any appointment or object that he had in view; not that he actually kept the appointment at a quarter before time, but was always *ready* for it. The words seemed to stand luminously out from the page, and forced themselves upon my sense, so that they recurred continually to my memory, and could not be forgotten. (32)

Mrs. Warren concludes her treatise on household management with an itemized schedule of a week's work, advising her readers that "[a] woman who means to play her part well ... must be a good manager, so that every duty shall have its allotted time" (92).

For such discerning social observers as Webb, Martineau, and Nightingale, temporal restraints could be loosened by manipulating or rejecting quotidian routines they found impossibly confining. Webb, for instance, rose at dawn to perform her "intellectual work" before turning to a full day of "domestic cares and social duties" (101). Martineau considered her "morning hours ... sacred," refusing to make social calls and receiving visitors only for two hours in the afternoon (145). Nightingale found that invalidism offered an escape from routine, enabling her to write extensively while bedridden.[8] For most Victorian women, however, such strategies seemed neither imaginable nor practicable. Their more typical experience provides the foundation for *The Daughters of Danaus*, although conveyed through the life of an atypical female genius whose potential is thwarted by her inability to wrest control over her time. In selecting an extraordinarily talented woman as the protagonist of this failed *Künstlerroman,* Caird could foreground and decry, through a technique of defamiliarization, the insidious temporal demands that the Victorian Everywoman daily faced.[9]

Limited Time in the Parental Household

The opening chapter of Part One sets the tone for the novel's scrutiny of temporal impediments as Hadria and her siblings debate Ralph Waldo Emerson's dictum that an individual can always conquer circumstances and achieve desired goals. Hadria argues, however, that "Emerson never was a girl" (14) facing the "prejudice and custom" inflicted specifically on women (15). Contrary to a brother's assertions that merely "a little force of will" would allow her "to occupy your life in the manner you think best," Hadria responds that a true choice "is often impossible for a girl." Once her only sister becomes a rare exception to that rule by leaving home to aid the urban poor, Hadria is beset by the domestic occupations that her mother considers necessary for a British middle-class daughter. Emerson's pronouncements on circumstance are translated into temporal terms as Hadria finds her household duties consuming virtually all of her time. Her experience provides a personal gloss on the lines of Emerson's poem, "Days," that her brother quotes to her, with its references to "hypocritic days" that are "[m]uffled and dumb" and proceed in "an endless file" (43).

Indeed, that "endless file" presents Hadria with an "underrated" rather than "exaggerated" problem as she attempts "to force circumstance to yield a harvest to her will" (44) and counter the continual demands on her time imposed by her mother. As Mrs. Loftie warns in her *Social Twitters* household manual, a mother carries on the "traditions of rigorous dependence" (116) with her daughters by "assum[ing] complete control over their time" (117), a pattern that Hadria readily discovers in striving to balance musical study with domestic duty:

> Her mother would keep her for hours, discussing a trivial point of domestic business, giving elaborate directions about it. . . . She spent her whole life in trifles of this kind, or over social matters. . . . Hadria, fighting against a multitude of harassing little difficulties, struggled to turn the long winter months to some use. But Mrs. Fullerton broke the good serviceable time into jagged fragments. (44)

Seeking to manage her time—"to set apart certain hours for household duties, and to have other portions of the day to herself" (44)—Hadria gains her mother's reluctant agreement, yet the domestic tasks never substantively ease. Instead, "the weeks went by, in dreary, troublous fashion, cut into a hundred little barren segments" (45); without free time, "[t]he mind had no space, or stretch, or solitude," and "its impetus was perpetually checked." Consequently, Hadria's "greatest effort" in developing her art is devoted "not to the work itself, but to win opportunity to pursue it" (109). Because she is "unable to command any certain part of the day" (109), Hadria necessarily postpones her musical endeavors until late in the night, the only "fruitful hours of the twenty-four" (46).

As the Victorian women prose writers observed, however, snatching such "odd moments" for intellectual work does not come without a price. For them, the cost was a depleted store of energy remaining after performing diurnal responsibilities. Hadria likewise brings diminished energy to her musical studies. She initiates a cycle in which the strain of daytime and nighttime activities—coupled with Mrs. Fullerton's resistance to what she terms Hadria's desire "to be selfishly pre-occupied" and a reluctance to do a woman's duty (109)—leaves Hadria exhausted:

> If Hadria yielded the point on any particular occasion, her mood and her work were destroyed: if she resisted, they were equally destroyed, through the nervous disturbance and the intense depression which followed the winning of a liberty too dearly bought. The incessant rising and quelling of her impulse and her courage... represented a vast amount of force not merely wasted, but expended in producing a dangerous wear and tear upon the system. The process told upon her health, and was the beginning of the weakening and unbalancing of the splendid constitution which Hadria... enjoyed as a birthright. The injury was insidious but serious. (109)

Appropriately, Hadria adopts the title "Futility" for the composition on which she labors in those dearly purchased hours.

Hadria's unending struggle to gain time for her musical work carries broader repercussions than the physical and emotional toll exacted upon her, however. Prevented from exercising her musical talents during lengthy periods, she cannot become more than one of the "dilettanti" whom Nightingale identifies in a pertinent analogy:

> When Beethoven wrote a bar, he must have had the phrase, the movement, the quick time which was to succeed, the slow movement which came before—the whole piece, in short, in his thought. And could he write a bar now, a bar then, at an "odd moment"? This is what we call being a "dilettante," when a man does work in that way.... Women are almost always dilettanti, and have women

ever produced any original work, any, with a *very* few exceptions, which the world would not be as well without? (*Suggestions* 72)

Nightingale was not alone in this view. In the 1869 *Subjection of Women,* John Stuart Mill also attributed the dearth of noteworthy female composers to their lack of time. "[W]omen remain behind men, even in the pursuits which are open to both," Mill asserts, because "very few women have time for them" (79). Itemizing the numerous activities that occupy the "time and thoughts of every woman," Mill establishes that the notion of free time is more of an oxymoron than a truism:

> The superintendence of a household, even when not in other respects laborious, is extremely onerous to the thoughts; it requires incessant vigilance, an eye which no detail escapes, and presents questions for consideration and solution, foreseen and unforeseen, at every hour of the day. (79)

As Hadria sarcastically comments in making the same point, "People are surprised that women have never done anything noteworthy in music. People are so intelligent!" (110).

With such limitations on their time, Mill implies, women will always remain "amateurs" in the arts (77). Yet Mill hints at the high social cost exacted by furthering amateurism at the expense of professionalism in his extended discussion of the broader "injustice of excluding half the human race" from meaningful occupations (53), which denies others the stimulating effects of competition (55). In Hadria's case, the temporal restraints that curb artistic prowess are similarly figured as social harm, implicitly through such a competitive impetus lost and explicitly through "real musical genius of the first order, going to waste" (267), as one acquaintance characterizes the situation. Hadria's "unique power," a renowned musician more forcefully claims, "is a gift supreme to the world, which the world must not lose" (335).

Marriage, Motherhood, and Music

For Hadria, marriage seems to offer hope of escaping the burdensome domestic schedule of the parental household. She initially refuses the proposal of Hubert Temperley, a lawyer and amateur musician with whom she occasionally practices, but accedes to his persuasive second request in the belief that "he too regarded the ordinary domestic existence with distaste" (122). Hubert, who managed "to be very convincing," offers the tacit promise that Hadria's time would become her own, explaining that "life in her father's house is far less free than in her own home," where "existence could be moulded to any shape she pleased" (140). To her endless regret, Hadria misreads Hubert's estimation of her as an exception to his general perceptions of women, interpreting his regard for her "as a great compliment" (122) rather than a sign of his stultifying conservatism. Lurking beneath Hubert's "subtly critical" views of "feminine qualities" is a contempt for women who reject traditional responsibilities in favor of Hadria's conception of more fulfilling work. "We hear a great deal about rights," Hubert says, "but we hear nothing about duties" (77). Hubert has "scant patience with these interfering women" and rails at their desire "to turn everything upside down, instead of quietly minding their duties at home." As Hubert's surname Temperley hints, Hadria will soon discover that marriage brings not an escape from but a continuation of the temporally based restrictions experienced in her parents' home.

Images of death initiate the narrative shift to Hadria's marital life in Part Two, opening five years after her wedding—a temporal gap hinting that since all of Hadria's days are alike, the story can recommence at any arbitrary point. In the initial scene, Hadria wanders to a cemetery in the tiny English hamlet where she resides with Hubert and her two children, a stagnant and virtually timeless environment that "had forgotten to change . . . for at least a hundred years" (145). As Hadria listens to a gravedigger laboring in the churchyard, each stroke of the pickaxe alternates with the sound of a clock striking from a nearby tower:

> The sound of his steady strokes fell on the stillness. Presently, the clock from the grey tower gave forth its announcement—eleven. One by one, the slow hammer sent the waves of air rolling away, almost visibly, through the sunshine, their sound alternating with the thud of the pickaxe, so as to produce an effect of intentional rhythm. One might have fancied that clock and pickaxe iterated in turn, "Time, Death! Time, Death! Time, Death!" till the clock had come to the end of its tale, and then the pickaxe went on alone in the stillness—"Death! Death! Death! Death!" (149)

The sibilance of the first sentence establishes the cadence of the pickaxe's strokes, which the tolling clock immediately mimics to create a syncopation suggestive of a symbiotic relationship between them. The scene recalls the sinister chime of the Morningquest clock tower in *The*

Heavenly Twins and evokes the gender ramifications that Sarah Grand's text conveys: women are both controlled by and separated from the masculine temporality that the chimes mark. As the clock and pickaxe in Caird's novel alternate their sounds, "time" and "death" become virtually conflated in the harmonious refrain produced. That Hadria makes the connection between masculine temporality and death is intimated through the ironic smile, "not easy to be accounted for," with which she reacts to the sounds.

The negative connotations of masculine time established in the passage shape the critique of marriage and motherhood that unfolds in subsequent chapters. Since Hadria's time is governed by these twin responsibilities, Caird's estimation of domestic life, established in her nonfiction prose, offers an appropriate context from which to read Hadria's experience. Like Mill, Caird identifies marriage as a form of enslavement and a barbaric sacrificial rite.[10] In "Emancipation of the Family," for example—an 1890 journal contribution later included in Caird's 1897 collection, *The Morality of Marriage and Other Essays*—Caird argues that marriage is merely "a lineal descendant of crystallized barbarian usages" (2:33). "[C]ruel and absurd" (33), marriage depends upon a "subjection of women" (34), Caird contends in invoking the title of Mill's controversial text.[11] In another allusion to Mill, Caird asserts in the 1888 "Marriage" that women have long been "enslaved" (189), a point reiterated in the novel through Hadria's scathing reference to the Aristotelian notion that she quotes: "a wife ought to shew herself even more obedient to the rein than if she entered the house as a purchased slave" (170–71). Victorian culture has adopted such a view virtually unaltered, Hadria claims, for "Aristotle doubtless professed a high respect for women who followed his precepts—as men do now when we are obedient" (171). Denying that an essentialized female nature necessitates that women be held "in thrall," Hadria attributes their situation to the "mere brutal necessity" of accommodating themselves to an "inexorable logic of conditions" (169).

Motherhood, the novel additionally argues, perpetuates women's enslavement by providing "the sign and seal as well as the means and method of a woman's bondage" (341). Women accept thralldom by trading their bodies for food, shelter, and social approval, accepting their responsibilities even when the prospect of motherhood directly counters their own desires (343). "Throughout history," Hadria says, "children had been the unfailing means of bringing women into line with tradition," becoming "little ambassadors of the established and expected" (187). In

"Emancipation," Caird suggests that the solution rests in motherhood becoming an informed choice rather than an ordained responsibility (2:35), a theme that the novel similarly expresses. Hadria considers the two boys she has borne to Hubert as "the tribute exacted of my womanhood," through whom "I am to be subdued and humbled" (190), in contrast to the illegitimate Martha Jervis whom she freely adopts in "opposing the world and the system of things that I hate" (188).

Insidious and inescapable, the "tethers" of marriage and motherhood fasten upon women surreptitiously, leaving "no interval for breathing, and scarcely time or space to cope with the legions of the moment" (169–70). The general condition of Victorian women that Hadria identifies here takes on individualized dimensions as the minutiae of domestic life threaten to overwhelm Hadria herself. As in her parents' household, a full domestic routine leaves little time for musical pursuits, but Hadria clings to the slender hope that she can eventually balance familial responsibilities and artistic aspirations. Yet Hadria's "pathetic" wish (190) clashes repeatedly with the realities of daily activity that prevent her from setting aside domestic duties, however briefly:

> The details of practical life and petty duties sprouted up at every step. If they were put aside, even for a moment, the wheels of daily existence became clogged and then all opportunity was over. . . . And yet it was so foolish. Each obstacle in itself was paltry. It was their number that overcame one, as the tiny arrows of the Lilliputs overcame Gulliver. (191)

Victorian culture overlooks the temporal demands placed upon a wife and mother, the text stresses, to apply instead a faulty logic that attributes a lack of professional accomplishments to a "passive and reflective nature" (371). In one telling scene that illustrates this widespread misconception, Hadria listens to "a callow youth" decry New Women's ambitions to move "out of their sphere, and put themselves forward . . . and all that sort of nonsense" (371). Noting the "absurd" assumption "that women could do work that was peculiar to men," the youth purportedly proves his contention by citing a "failure in original work in every direction" (372). He argues that "[w]omen's strength lay in a different domain—in the home" and confidently asserts that "[i]t was of no use to try to fight against Nature." Unaware of Hadria's avocation, the youth coincidently selects the example of music to make his point and proclaims that "one required no particular liberty to pursue *that* art, yet where were the women-composers?" As final proof that women's nature was responsible for their artistic omissions, he rhetorically demands: "If there was so much buried talent among women, why didn't they arise and bring out operas and oratorios?" Hadria, however, immediately situates his remarks within the appropriate temporal context in pretending agreement, acridly replying that "the domestic life was arranged, one might almost say, with a special view to promoting musical talent in the mistress of the household."

The impossibility of balancing domestic duties with artistic work—which Hadria increasingly comes to realize and Hubert confirms by complaining that "I judge the presence of oratorio by the absence of food" (161)—is corroborated by the experiences of an acquaintance, Lady Engleton. A talented painter, Lady Engleton similarly struggles to find sufficient time for her creative work, since social responsibilities consume an inordinate share of each day. More an Old than a New Woman, whose occasional modern pronouncements are neutralized by her general approval of traditional gender roles, Lady Engleton bemoans the repeated interruptions that prevent her from completing her latest picture, unironically identifying "the worst [aspect] of visitors" as the result that "[o]ne's little immortal works do get put aside, poor things" (176). Although she admits that her friends do not begrudge the time she spends in her studio "so long as I give them as much time as they want," Lady Engleton unwittingly articulates her dilemma by adding that very qualification. Reminding us of Webb's complaints about burdensome social schedules, Lady Engleton regrets that "I have to apologise and compromise, don't you know," since "society does ask a good deal of attention, doesn't it?" Even though she claims that "with a little management, one can get on," Lady Engleton's own situation belies the truth of that remark. Immediately thereafter, she decides to ask a friend for permission to "pursue my art in peace and quietness" at his secluded home, "beyond the region of visitors" (179). Similarly underlining the incompatibility of duty and art, Lady Engleton's own visitors begin to depart so that she can "have some time to herself" and begin a new picture (401).

As Lady Engleton and Hadria's experiences confirm, only by divorcing oneself from the domestic sphere—establishing a geographic as well as psychic distance, as a Victorian man is allowed to do—can a woman pursue other interests successfully. In contrast to the two women, Hubert "went every day to town to attend to his legal business," returning "by the evening train to the bosom of his family" (146). Women, the novel implies, need the same separation from the home to focus rather than divide their attention and prevent the concerns of domestic life from intervening in their work. The train that Hubert daily takes—a signifier of male temporality, with its linear movement and strict schedules—itself serves to foreground the sharp contrast between the figuratively and literally separated spheres. In "widening the physical gap between home and workplace," Carol Dyhouse has observed in her study of Victorian girlhood, the railway punctuated "the sexual division of labour" (4) typifying the era. To Dyhouse, the train emblematizes "[t]he distinction between mother's world" and "father's world—distant, invisible—a public world of regular time-keeping" (4–5). The division between the two worlds is further illustrated by one late-century resident of Alderley Edge, near Manchester, who remarks that once "the 9.18 [morning] train had pulled out of the station the Edge became exclusively female" (qtd. in Dyhouse 4).

A corollary notion—that a comparable division between a woman's domestic life and intellectual life holds the key to emotional well-being—emerges indirectly in *The Daughters of Danaus* through the unusual life path chosen by Hadria's sister, Algitha. Characterizing "[t]he change in Algitha" as "striking" once she has left the Fullerton household to aid the poor, the narrator notes that Algitha was "gentler" and "more affectionate," while her "tendency to grow hard and fretful had entirely disappeared" (132). An earlier reference hints that Algitha's improved condition has come through a judicious division of her time, as she explains to Hadria:

> With all its drawbacks, this existence of hard work (yet not too hard) suits me exactly. It uses up my energies; yet, in spite of the really busy life I lead, I literally have more leisure than I used to have at home, where all through the day, there was some little detail to be attended to, some call to make, some convention to offer incense to, some prejudice to respect. Here, once my day's work is over, it *is* over, and I have good solid hours of leisure. I feel that I have earned those hours when they come. (48)

The typicality of Hadria's situation for Victorian women, immersed in the continual drudgery of domestic routine rather than Algitha's fulfilling and temporally demarcated labor, is underscored in one of the novel's most compelling scenes, centered on the overdetermined symbol of a man's watch. Aside from its primary function of designating the passage of linear time, the watch is owned by Professor Theobold, "a great archaeologist" (178) "profoundly" interested in history (216) whose work immerses him in the study of temporal events. With Theobold's strong links to the masculine time from which she feels excluded, Hadria's marked dislike and distrust of the professor during their early acquaintance—she reacts with "intense enmity" when he approaches her on one occasion, as "[e]very instinct rose up as if in warning" (215)—appears neither coincidental nor insignificant. During a subsequent encounter, Hadria's adopted daughter Martha grabs Theobold's watch, refusing to release the tight grasp through which she holds the professor "helplessly tethered by his own chain" (241). Multiple references build on the yoking of time and entrapment that this phrasing establishes. Theobold is Martha's "captive" (241), "prisoner," and "victim" as he "struggle[s] in the toils" but remains confined by "these tender moorings" (242). As Hadria observes Theobold's powerless state, she acidly remarks, "I hope you are not pressed for time," before proceeding to her interpretation of the incident.

Instructing the professor that he "now stand[s] for an excellent type of woman... strong but chained," Hadria designates the child as "Society with all its sentiments and laws, written and unwritten" (243), accentuating Society's omnipotence through verbal capitalization. The watch, Hadria continues, represents "[w]oman's life and freedom," while the chain connotes "[h]er affections, her pity, her compunction, which forbid her to wrench away her rightful property" held by "ignorant and tender hands." The comparison is important, for by describing the watch in these terms, Hadria suggests that participation in the projects of masculine time is both a woman's prerogative and the key to her survival, inappropriately denied by a myopic Victorian culture. In restricting rather than nurturing women, masculine temporality signifies a form of death—a point to which Theobold unwittingly attests in demanding, "Come, come, life is passing; I have but one; relax these fetters, or I die." For a Victorian woman, Theobold's comment implies, "life" within masculine time simply produces an unbearable and insolvable tension that can lead only to destruction.

The scene additionally demonstrates that masculine temporality's control over women is perceived as natural by the victims themselves, who absorb the unstated cultural edict that any attempts to alter their position are deviant and punishable. In one telling comment after Theobold has finally freed himself from the chain, Hadria continues her "lovely allegory" (244) to make that message abundantly clear:

> [Y]ou can say you are sorry you made so free with your own possessions, and you wish you had done your duty better, and are

eager to return and let Her Majesty hold you captive. Your prototype always does, you know, and she is nearly always pardoned, on condition that she never does anything of that kind again.

... In one respect you have not yet achieved a thorough fidelity to your model; you don't seem to enjoy sacrifice for its own sake. That will come with practice. (244-45)

The ironic gender reversal in the watch scene serves, then, both to defamiliarize the temporal constraints exerted upon women and to highlight the damage those restrictions cause. In effect, the scene glosses and elaborates upon the graveyard incident that opens the discussion of Hadria's marital life. As in the earlier episode, time is equated with discipline and death; Theobold's plea that his fetters be loosened "or I die," implicitly provides the connection here. In casting Theobold's plight as female allegory, however, the text solidly forges the gender connection only intimated in the earlier scene.

Rejecting Temporal Constraints

For Hadria, the opposing pulls on her time and the tensions that result from her futile endeavors to balance domestic duties and musical aspirations can be resolved only by the outright rejection of one set of these demands. Hadria chooses to spurn her household responsibilities and decides to leave England to devote full time to composition in France. In a move that anticipates modernist manipulations of time through space, Hadria begins her journey through a dreamlike train ride that inaugurates Part Three of the novel, ushering in a narrative turn that signifies Hadria's attempts to break down time as a construct. Blending past, present, and future, the train ride unsettles conventional notions of time as an ordering principle to open up an alternative imaginative space:

> The speed was glorious.... Back flew iterative telegraph posts with Herculean swing, into the Past, looped together in rhythmic movement, marking the pulses of old Time. On, with rack and roar, into the mysterious Future. One could sit at the window and watch the machinery of Time's foundry at work; the hammers of his forge beating, beating, the wild sparks flying, the din and chaos whirling round one's bewildered brain;—Past becoming Present, Present melting into Future, before one's eyes.
>
> ... Disjointed, delicious impressions followed one another in

swift succession, often superficially incoherent. . . .
Images of the Past joined hands with visions of the Future. (294–95)

In its blending of temporal states, the passage confuses and breaks apart the discrete units of linear time, mirroring the similar vignette in *Tess of the d'Urbervilles* in which the protagonist strove to transcend time itself as she drove the family wagon to the marketplace moments before the fateful collision with the mailcart. In Caird's scene, orderly linear images are immediately undercut by circular and anarchic forces. The "iterative telegraph posts," for instance, lose their precise linear positioning as they are "looped" through "rhythmic movement." The repeated strokes of time's hammers, "beating, beating" in their systematic rhythm, dissolve into a "whirling" pattern that mimics the internal "chaos" and bewilderment created by the breakdown of linear consistency. The only vestige of the methodical movement of linear time—the "swift succession" of impressions—is undercut by the "disjointed" and "superficially incoherent" quality of the impressions themselves.

The irony of the passage comes, of course, in the choice of a train—a polysemic symbol of masculine temporality—to disrupt rigid conceptions of time. Yet in this and subsequent passages, the train is reconceptualized and manipulated to transform it from a sign of confining order to a vehicle of liberatory disorder. In effect, masculine time participates in its own attenuation, suggesting that its seeming monolithicism instead points to intrinsic weaknesses that can be exploited to allow a measure of escape from its control. Linear hegemony continues to deteriorate as the train proceeds through the countryside:

> The patient monster began to move again, with a gay whistle, as if he enjoyed this chase across country, on the track of Time. He was soon at full speed again, on his futile race: a hapless idealist in pursuit of lost dreams.
> . . . What a speed the train was going at! One could scarcely stand in the jolting carriage. Old Time must not make too sure of his victory. (296)

The movement of linear time is transformed from an unstoppable momentum to a doomed competition, no longer exercising firm authority but demonstrating the ineffectuality of a dreamer. The "jolting" movement of the train accentuates the breakdown of linear control, as passengers are physically and psychically severed from its signifier, barely able to stand in the swaying carriage. The conventional construction of temporality—"Old Time"—increasingly loses its hold on Hadria's life as the train continues its journey, less and less assured of "his victory." Her domestic past takes on the insubstantiality of a "dream" that "seemed to be drifting away already," becoming a veiled memory unable to withstand "the emphatic present" (297). Experiencing a "joy of freedom and its intoxication," Hadria contextualizes the emancipatory feeling explicitly in temporal terms: the "sheer relief" that stems from the luxury of "stretch[ing] oneself in mental liberty" comes from the ability "to possess one's days, one's existence for the first time, in all these long years!" Such a command over time is figured as a natural state that Hadria regains, one that men assume as a birthright.

Hadria's flight to France can be read, then, as an entry into a kind of green world—a space that Annis Pratt theorizes as a "landscape of the psyche," an "essentially apatriarchal" milieu offering "possibilities of personal development" (127)—in which Hadria wrests control over her own time. Hadria initially rejects any form of schedule once she arrives on French soil and "bask[s] and bathe[s] in the sunny present" (304), rarely making "definite plans the day before, unless it were for the pleasure of changing them" (305). The schedule that she eventually adopts is one of her own making, devoted to the exigencies of musical study under the tutelage of the genius Jouffroy. Significantly, Hadria brings only Martha of her three children to France, transforming motherhood from an unavoidable duty to a volitional act that can be balanced with other interests. Once Hadria has accommodated herself to a self-designated timetable, "[c]omposition went on rapidly" (320).

Hadria's selection of music as a vocation itself carries intriguing implications that help inform her relationship to masculine temporality, in France as well as her earlier life. In an analysis of music as a "scaffolding of time" that offers pertinent applications for *The Daughters of Danaus,* Walther Dürr argues that "music is a temporal art"; because it "begins, progresses, and ends," music always "moves in time" (181). Invoking German critic Gotthold Lessing's influential eighteenth-century postulation in *Laokoon* that art's relationship with time and space is "its foremost characteristic," Dürr distinguishes the temporal valences of music from the spatially informed pictorial and plastic arts, albeit noting that music does evidence "certain spatial concomitants" through such characteristics as the expansion of sound waves in space. Dürr places dance amid the temporal and spatial arts, whereby "artistic realization in space is combined with music."

Using Dürr's thesis as a model, coupled with Kristeva's theorization of the symbolic order, allows us to examine the polyvalent associations that music—and, to a lesser extent, the related art of dance—brings to a reading of time in the novel. My approach thus is twofold here, providing a temporal reading that is in turn mapped onto a linguistic matrix to assess music as a form of language, both participating in and defying the law of the Father. The point of intersection is Kristeva's designation of the symbolic order as doubly paternal and temporal, "provid[ing] the reference point, and, consequently, all possibilities of measurement," by establishing the distinction "between a before, a now and an after" ("About Chinese Women" 152–53). As a temporal art, Hadria's music functions in one sense as a signifier of the symbolic order, but in another regard as an insurgent force acting against that order. These vying interpretations are replicated by the nature of music itself, which evinces both temporal and historical tensions. Subject to the discipline and regularity of time, music nevertheless carries an ethereal and dreamy component; generally the vocational province of the male in Western culture, musical composition, as we have seen, rarely was embraced successfully by women as a profession.

In effect, Hadria's music represents an invasion of the masculine symbolic order by Kristeva's corresponding notion of the semiotic—the rhythms, inconsistencies, and disturbances that reflect the forces marginalized by the symbolic. Throughout the text, Hadria's compositions are characterized as iconoclastic: invariably "bizarre" (166), they "shocked" Hubert "painfully," for example, and to concertgoers in France they represent "rebel music, offensive to the orthodox" (321). Most compellingly, however, the compositions "invaded fresh territory," creating "a new language" in the narrator's terms. Though Caird does not specifically confer a gender designation on the "new language," I suggest that it is a kind of female language, which allows suppressed elements to surface and be recognized.

Hadria's choice of music as a profession, then, can be assessed as a desire both to participate in and undermine the Father's law that undergirds language as well as the cultural construction of temporality. Those paradoxical twin goals are manifested in Hadria's resistance to the natural order of time through her rebellion against its gender-specific constraints in England and in her desire to insert herself within that order through the schedule she fashions in France. Hadria acts to establish a kind of dialectic that enables her to reshape the masculine temporal order and the "syntax" that underlays it, infusing it with a "new language" whose own codes challenge masculinist rules. Through that dialectic, the temporal construct can be reconfigured to allow women to structure their time under their own terms and accommodate their own desires.

The spatiotemporal art of dance suggests a preliminary stage toward that goal in the novel, for an early fascination with dance represents Hadria's initial attempt to manipulate time for her own uses. If we again shift to a linguistic register, dance, like music, articulates its own form of language—though, as Arthur Symons implies in his 1898 essay, "The World as Ballet," in dance "[n]othing is stated, there is no intrusion of words" (261). In an extensive discussion of *fin de siècle* language, Linda Dowling characterizes Symons's assessment of dance as one that "specifically challenges verbal language" (*Language* 239) and provides, along with music, "alternative human languages" (240). The pertinence of those assumptions in temporal terms begins to emerge in the first paragraph of the novel through an attentiveness to Hadria's compulsion to dance. Inspired by "intoxicating primitive music," Hadria glides with her siblings "excellently well, as to the manner born," occasionally emitting "that wild Celtic shout or cry that sets the nerves athrill" (5). Hadria, however, moves with a "peculiar spirit and brilliancy" that one observer considers "no 'right canny'" (6). Within the spatiotemporal continuum that Dürr identifies, dance both participates in and is distanced from the temporal art of music, a positioning that replicates Hadria's relationship with the natural order of time. Hadria's interest in dance soon metamorphoses into an obsession with music, suggesting a continuum in which an initial experimentation with a new "language" of rebellion will reach maturation through her music. The movement from dance to music, followed by the gradual honing of compositional skills that continues Hadria's development, similarly can be read as an emblem of her increasing sophistication about time, paralleling a growing understanding of the constraints that masculine temporality imposes upon her and the possibilities of circumventing them.

Yet the green world that France represents as the culmination of Hadria's temporal freedom is not wholly idyllic. Gradually, the social responsibilities that exhausted Hadria in England take on similar form in France, as "the demands of an enlarging circle swallowed an astonishing number of hours" (322). Through these intrusions, "the life that had been so full of serenity, as well as of regular and strenuous work," instead presents "anxiety and hurry." The text again accentuates the incompatibility of social duties with professional life, for Hadria muses that "there were only a certain number of hours in the day, and only a certain number of years in one's life, and art was long." As in England, the problem is contextualized in gender terms:

> Insidiously, treacherously, difficulties crept up. Even here, where she seemed so free, the peculiar claims that are made, by common consent, on a woman's time and strength began to weave their tiny cords around her. She took warning, and put an end to any voluntary increase of her circle, but the step had been taken a little too late. The mischief was done. To give pain or offence for the sake of an hour or two, more or less, seemed cruel and selfish, yet Hadria often longed for the privilege that every man enjoys, of quietly pursuing his work without giving either. (322)

The "difficulties" that Hadria experiences in attempting to balance her time in France directly stem, the novel argues, from the cultural conditioning that the natural order of time exercised upon her as a woman of patriarchal England. Through repeated references to the hold of past influences, the text conveys the enormous power of the masculine temporal order and the irrecuperable damage that it can exact on a woman's sense of subjectivity. Hadria, for example, "struggle[s] to get round and beyond that past-fashioned self" (307); recognizes that "even now there are strange thick wrappings from the past that cling tight round," despite attempts "to strip off that past-made personality" (306); and regrets that "[t]he Past is never past" but "lives enthroned in the Present, and sets its limits and lays its commands" (308). Though realizing that "Time must be gained, at all hazards" (326), Hadria lacks the culturally inculcated strategies that would allow her to convert that theory into practice and thus participate in masculine temporality.

Before Hadria can attempt to resolve her dilemma, however, her mother's serious illness compels her to return to England. Admonished by her mentor Jouffroy that remaining in France would offer "a stupendous future," whereas retreating to "your fogs and your tea-parties" would cause her genius to wither (336), Hadria gradually comes to realize the veracity of his statement. Once in England, a ticking clock presages Hadria's fate as her delirious mother announces that Hadria's "duty" rests in her reinsertion within the domestic sphere. Accepting that edict for fear that her mother's health will worsen if she refuses, Hadria faces redoubled responsibilities as she attempts to manage both her parents' household and her own. With her time "filled more and more with detail" (370),

Hadria has even less opportunity than in her earlier married life to work on her compositions. Though not completely abandoned, her music nevertheless "had, perforce, to fall into abeyance," making progress "scarcely possible" (371). As her mother gradually recuperates, time represents an increasingly unbearable monotony, for repetitive daily duties precede equally exhausting nocturnal cardplay in which "[h]ours and hours were spent" (369). A mantelpiece clock ticks in the background as Hadria immerses herself in ceaseless routines that "already seemed a hundred years old," causing not only a "disastrous effect on her nerves" but auguring "wild and desperate impulses" (369).

These impulses, manifested in a manipulative flirtatiousness, point to yet another aspect of the injurious effects of the natural order of time. Deprived of the opportunity to nurture her musical potential, Hadria assumes the traditional female role of temptress along with self-sacrificial wife, daughter, and mother. Wielding the sexual power of "ornamental womanhood" (382), Hadria responds to an acquaintance's criticism of her behavior with the exasperated comment, "If a woman might not do this, what, in heaven's name, *might* she do?" (394). Since women are perennially associated with their "influence" and "kingdom," Hadria justifies her actions in remarking, "Surely a day's somewhat murderous sport was allowable in *that* realm!" In effect, Hadria performs the kind of "masquerade of femininity" that Luce Irigaray theorizes as a way to recuperate lost desire (*This Sex* 134), but it is a strategy that exacts a high cost; women "participat[e] in man's desire," Irigaray cautions, "at the price of renouncing their own" (133). Once her personal moorings of musical study have been broken, Hadria enters "into a system of values that is not hers," in Irigaray's terms, and can "'appear' and circulate only when enveloped in the needs/desires/fantasies of others, namely men" (134).

In casting Hadria as a femme fatale, the novel intimates that the ostensible objective of controlling women's time to promote familial stability instead has the opposite effect. By depriving women of the time to exercise their talents and find stimulating outlets for their energies, Victorian culture undermines the integrity of the very domestic structure it labors to protect. As proof, the text attributes Hadria's untoward conduct to a desire to discover "some emotion to take the place of my lost art" (396), an amusement to "fill the empty throne" (398) remaining once "the pre-occupying ideas of her life had been chased from their places" (397–98). The intellectual void is directly blamed for Hadria's ultimate defiance of "the world's laws" (397), for she enters into an improper relationship—mentally, if not physically, consummated in the gaps of the text—with the once-detested Theobold. Able to ward off the "strange, unpleasant fascination" (387) Theobold held in their first encounters, which came as she was preparing for her flight to France, Hadria discovers that "now everything had changed" (388). With the "present moment" no longer "exciting," lacking "plans and projects," Hadria turns to Theobold as a means of easing the "burden of life [that] weighed upon her" and thereby "drag through the day."

The psychic toll caused by such unproductive use of time is figured as a corresponding physical degeneration, which magnifies as the repetitive days proceed uneventfully. Indeed, Mrs. Fullerton's ironic exclamation of "[h]ow the time flies" when she recognizes that a year has passed since Hadria returned to England becomes disturbing when juxtaposed with the narrator's remark that Hadria "looked worn and white, and dreadfully thin" (378). Physical diminution and a sepulchral pallor reflect a deteriorating sense of subjectivity that culminate in Hadria's own recognition of the effects that time has wrought:

> Nothing remained but the endurance of a conscious slow decay; nothing but increasing loss and feebleness, as the surly years went by. They were going, going, these years of life, slipping away with their spoils. Youth was departing, everything was vanishing; her very self, bit by bit, slowly but surely, till the House of Life would grow narrow and shrunken to the sight, the roof descend. (478–79)

A chance discovery of her early composition "Futility" confirms the change in Hadria's sense of self, for an attempt to play the piece "was like trying over the work of some other person" (466).

Returning to the piano in this rare practice session, Hadria realizes that her musical gift has undoubtedly diminished from disuse, as Jouffroy warned it would, while a telltale clock sounds in the background with an ominous and "steady tick-tack" (476). As she appraises the decline of her talent, Hadria censures the natural order of time for her plight, converting the linearity of time into space while recalling past influences:

> She looked back along the line of the past and saw, with too clear eyes, the whole insidious process, so stealthy that she had hardly detected it, at the time. . . . [L]ike a creature accustomed to the yoke, she had found it increasingly difficult to use the moments of opportunity when they came. The force of daily usage, the necessary bending of thoughts in certain habitual directions, had assisted the crippling process. (478)

In effect, the passage reverses the dissolution of linear hegemony that we saw during the train ride with which Hadria began her journey to France. Signifiers of linearity are again dominant, as space reinforces rather than diminishes time's hold. A sense of time's relentless momentum is reasserted through Hadria's spatial perception of "the whole insidious process," as it proceeds gradually but inexorably toward a predetermined fate.

A subsequent passage continues to reinscribe the hold of linear temporality that the train ride unsettled, referring again to "old Time" but in this instance associating it with implacable forward movement. As she visualizes "a panorama of her own life and the general life pass before her" (479) in another spatial allusion, Hadria justifies her defeat by ceding all agency onto time:

> We are possessed by a sentiment, an ideal, a religion; old Time makes no comment, but moves quietly on; we fling the thing aside ... the ideal is tarnished, experience of the world converts us—and still unmoved, he paces on. We are off on another chase; another conception of things possesses us; and still the beat of his footstep sounds in our ears.... [A]nd this and that, and that and this,—like the pendulum of the old time-piece, with its solemn tick—dock the moments of one's life, with each its dull little claim and its tough little tether, and lead one decorously to the gateway of Eternity. (480)

Though the novel attributes Hadria's defeat to the powerful constraints operating specifically on women—Hadria complains, for example, that "I am born a woman, and to be born a woman" means living under "insult ... always, always" (481)—the text does tender the slight hope that succeeding generations in totality can triumph over temporal constraints as Algitha had individually. Occasional references have hinted at a measure of optimism, as Hadria mused, for example, that "[o]ne sees, now and then, in a flash, what the world may some day be" (272) and asserted that "[t]he hope of the future lies in the rising generation" (474). In the novel's final scene, Hadria maintains a vigil at the deathbed of an old friend as a robin comes to the window to warble a gentle requiem. With resonances to the conclusion of *The Story of an African Farm*, and its own arguably hopeful ending as Waldo lay among nestling chickens, *The Daughters of Danaus* is similarly distinguished by a virtual non-closure and unspecified promise for the future. That ambiguity invites us to create a more encouraging scenario than the traditional nineteenth-century realist text accords to its female characters who defy cultural dictates. In departing from the decisive conclusion that characterizes the paradigmatic Victorian novel, *The Daughters of Danaus* advances the possibility that our final glimpse of Hadria signifies not wholly a pessimistic commentary on women's wasted potentiality but the passing on of experience to guide subsequent generations to eventual success.

History as Repetition

Such a positive outcome, however, can result only through a defiance and defeat of a historical determinism that naturalizes women's inferior status. Countering the common Victorian view that history represents a sequence of change and progress, *The Daughters of Danaus* instead argues that history is a cultural construct that reinscribes tradition. Consequently, women are trapped within a historical moment that disguises synchronicity as diachronicity, condemned to repeat the past rather than shape the future. The view of history in which Hadria's struggles are contextualized thus brings us far from the positive valuation accorded to the past we saw in *She*. *The Daughters of Danaus* instead anticipates the Nietzschean discontent with history that would figure so prominently in modernist texts, but the novel conveys history's dictatorial tenor in unequivocally gendered terms. History carries negative associations in *The Daughters of Danaus* solely because it confines women within a totalizing tradition, a point that expands on the concerns we saw raised in preliminary form in *Tess of the d'Urbervilles*. In Caird's novel, history becomes debilitating destiny rather than vibrant change, exercising a firm hold over the present and foreclosing opportunities for reconfiguring the female role. With few examples from previous generations to intimate that departures from an established standard can be achieved and sustained, history presents Hadria with the dilemma articulated by Hélène Cixous: "[W]here am I to stand? What is my place if I am a woman? I look for myself throughout the centuries and don't see myself anywhere" ("Sorties" 75). History is unmasked as a pretender to progress in *The Daughters of Danaus,* creating only the illusion of change while perpetuating static conceptions of womanhood across time.

Caird's essays on history, published the same year as *The Daughters of Danaus,* undermine the notion that women's intrinsic nature foredooms them to repeat the past. Instead, Caird carefully distinguishes between essence and circumstance in the two-part "Phases of Human Development," identifying the spurious logic that blurs the distinction between them. Caird dismisses as "false and superficial" the widespread belief that an "essential and eternal nature of mankind" exists (1:37), arguing that history instead discloses that an individual is a "product" of surroundings, "moulded and modified by them."[12] The essay resonates with Hadria's contention that circumstances, not ability, determine the course of one's life in reiterating that "[i]t is all a matter of conditions" (39). Caird asserts that "[w]e must on no account admit that local 'human nature'" is "a constant factor" and instead stresses that "the character of a man is the product of all the events of his past," both through heredity and the "creeds through which his right and wrong, his ideas and ambitions, became established." For women specifically, the false perception of an essential nature has obscured the fact that history has meant "centuries of man's absolute power over woman, and of his abuse of that power to his own and her age-long injury" (2:170). The popular presumption that "'Nature intended' the whole race of women to occupy precisely the position which they now occupy" (1:45) has served to block tentative moves toward change. "'Practical' philosophy" has assumed "the inevitable necessity of these depradations" and perpetuated the "firmly fixed" belief that "the nature of man demands the martyrdom of woman" (2:170–71), continuing the historical pattern virtually unbroken.

The Daughters of Danaus similarly identifies women's history as a repetition of the same through an untoward reliance on tradition. As one of Hadria's acquaintances bleakly observes, "The centuries are behind one, with all their weight of heredity and habit" (71), a notion that Hadria confirms as she castigates the "dictatorship of tradition" (450). Hadria attests to the power and danger of tradition in equating it with a "thralldom" to which "everybody was more or less subject," instigating a "narrowing process" that she identifies as both "exhausting" and "vampir[ic]." One can never be entirely independent of tradition, Hadria observes, for it either makes individuals "blindly submissive" or "tempt[s] them to act out of an equally blind opposition to its canons" (400).

Invoking Darwinian terminology to decry the barriers to women's development that an enslavement within tradition creates, the novel contends that refusing to allow evolutionary variations to emerge, flourish, and alter the qualities society deems appropriate for women signals a degeneration of the human species as a whole. Like Sarah Grand in *The Heavenly Twins,* Caird decries the consequences of such a narrow cultural view. As Caird notes in her essay on human development, the prospect of productive variations is "obviously unlikely to occur often in a race, when half its numbers are placed in similar conditions, trained in the same fashion" so that "precisely the same set of qualities and instincts—to the discouragement of others—are [sic] called forth age after age" (1:42). Indeed, "the subjection of women" resembles "a vast machine carefully constructed to stamp out and mangle smooth all varieties and all superiorities of the human race." Hadria characterizes the process in similar terms, claiming that "the smallest, meanest, poorest, thinnest, vulgarest qualities" are "selected for survival" (292).[13] Specifically addressing the condition of women, Hadria argues:

> It is cunning, shallow, heartless women, who really fare best in our society; its conditions suit them. *They* have no pity, no sympathy ... *they* don't mind playing upon the weaker, baser sides of men's natures ... *they* don't mind swallowing indignity and smiling abjectly, like any woman of the harem at her lord, so that they gain their object. *That* is the sort of "woman's nature" that our conditions are busy selecting. (347)

Male self-interest, the text claims, has reinscribed this faulty selection process in encouraging women's abasement. Hadria's mother, for example, though "obviously above the average of humanity," evidenced "signs of incomplete development" (32), directly attributed to her husband's intervention: he "had influenced her development profoundly, to the apparent stifling of every native tendency," and condemned her to "a benumbed sort of life" (33). More troubling, the novel suggests, is the continuation of that process across future generations, as demonstrated through the fate of Hadria's adopted daughter. Eventually revealed to be Theobold's child, born of his illicit union with a schoolteacher, Martha becomes a pawn by which the professor can avenge himself on Hadria for deciding to discontinue their clandestine meetings. Theobold informs Hadria that he will publicly acknowledge his fatherhood and take Martha to live with him, outlining his plans for his daughter's training while complaining that Hadria holds "some special views on the education of the little one which I cannot entirely approve":

> After all, a woman has probably to be a wife and mother, on the good old terms that have served the world for a fair number of centuries, when one comes to consider it: it is a pity to allow her to grow up without those dogmas and sentiments that may help to make the position tolerable, if not always satisfactory, to her ....

> [T]he education of a girl should be on the old lines, believe me. . . . My duty is obvious! (439)

That such a destiny is decreed by the natural order of time is stressed through the sounds of a clock shortly before Martha's departure with her father. Martha's fate, the ticking of the timepiece insinuates, conforms to a preordained, naturalized pattern, as Hadria herself recognizes while observing her child:

> The busy, loud-ticking clock was working on with cheerful unconcern, as if this were just like every other day whose passing moments it had registered. The hands were pointing towards seven, and the dinner hour was half-past seven. Hadria stood looking down at the sleeping child. . . . There was a desolate look in her eyes, and something more terrible still, almost beyond definition. It was like the last white glow of some vast fire that has been extinguished.
>
> Suddenly—as something that gives way by the run, after a long resistance—she dropped upon her knees beside the cot with a slight cry, and broke into a silent storm of sobs, deep and suppressed. The stillness of the room was unbroken, and one could hear the loud tick-tack of the little clock telling off the seconds with business-like exactness. (445–46)

The novel's assault on tradition and the reinscription of female history resonates with Nietzsche's cautions on the influence of the past articulated in an influential 1874 essay. In his analysis of the uses and abuses of history, Nietzsche urges the present generation to "serve history only to the extent that history serves life," warning that the valuation and study of the past can proceed "to such a degree that life becomes stunted and degenerate" (59). Claiming that "we are all suffering from a consuming fever of history" (60), a "phenomenon we are now forced to acknowledge . . . in the face of certain striking symptoms of our age" (59), Nietzsche argues that the pressures of the past can become paralytic by impeding "any firm resolve to attempt something new" (75). A skewed sense of the past's importance, Nietzsche adds, precipitates "a kind of inborn grey-hairedness" (101) that undermines "life's plastic powers" (120). Nietzsche employs the metaphor of disease in admonishing that the "malady of history" characteristic of the present "sick" age "needs to be cured" (120); the appropriate response to ensure "the health of an individual, of a people, and of a culture" is to attain a proper balance of the historical and the unhistorical (63).

Caird promotes the same argument in her 1890 essays on "The Emancipation of the Family" in asserting that "our own ideas are merely an inheritance from the past" and criticizing the "changeless order of ideas" that make "a spellbound people, inaccessible to new views of life that would lead to altered action" (1:693). She calls for an analogous equipoise between the historical and unhistorical: "Without irreverence for the past, we must see that the time has fully come for us to throw off the tyranny of surviving superstitions which are holding us back and causing a dislocated social condition" (2:36). Only through "a shaken confidence in the fundamental nature of our institutions," Caird stresses, can they be assessed appropriately and the "true direction of social progress" be recognized (1:693). Caird undercuts the positive Victorian equation of history with progress in arguing that "[p]rogress, indeed, is not inevitable" in contrast to the "disposition to look upon it in that light" and ignore the "danger of crystallizing . . . under the influence of certain fixed ideas" that "exhaust our vitality" (693–94). Indeed, as Caird maintains in another essay, "The Future of the Home," a confidence in the "power of man to choose his direction of change" represents the "mark of the essentially modern thinker" (3) rather than one enmeshed by the chains of the past.

In *The Daughters of Danaus,* Hadria's choice of music as her focal interest tacitly validates the historical skepticism that both Nietzsche and Caird encourage. Hadria's compositions, as periodic references have stressed, depart from the music of the past in their violation of traditional rules. To Hubert, as we have seen, whose "nature is conventional through and through" (267), Hadria's works are jarring and distressing; they "set his teeth on edge" (267) precisely because of their nonconformity to musical tradition. In defying artistic convention, Hadria's music anticipates the avant-garde of early modernism and the rejection of history that such experimentalism connoted. As Art Berman suggests in his discussion of these post-Victorian cultural forces, "artistic creativity can be exercised free from the constraints of the historical past" (160). Works that have "broken free from the causal chain of history" generate the kind of "disorientation, shock, or dismay" that Hubert expresses. In Nietzschean terms, history becomes a point of departure rather than reinscription. Berman's elaboration on the avant-garde and modernism provides an interpretive context in which Hadria's rebellious compositions can be assessed as a denial of historical determinism:

The past may arguably be a resource, but it is certainly not an obligation. The imposition of the past is rejected. The past cannot be totally incapacitated as influence, because the modernist achievement requires the past for comparison.... But the causal efficacy of the past, the burdensome immediacy of its coercion, is relinquished. (160)

In its admonishments to reject an unhealthy reliance upon the past, *The Daughters of Danaus* makes the same argument as Caird's 1889 *The Wing of Azrael*, which systematically identifies the negative ramifications of a pronounced historical dependence. Indeed, the earlier novel reads like a fictionalized version of Nietzsche's treatise, furnishing further evidence that Caird assessed tradition as tyrannical and fatiguing. *The Wing of Azrael* incorporates *fin de siècle* views on the workings of time, history, and organic memory framed within a feminist perspective to reveal the calamitous consequences of tradition through the experiences of its doomed protagonist.

Tradition in *The Wing of Azrael*

The Wing of Azrael chronicles the life of Viola Sedley from childhood through an unhappy marriage to the detestable Philip Dendraith, the son of a parvenu baronet, whom Viola meets in girlhood. Encouraged by her spendthrift father to accept Philip as a suitor in hopes of improving her family's fortunes, Viola accedes to the pressure to perform her filial responsibility, despite her distaste for her future husband. Though Harry Lancaster, a longtime acquaintance and a rival but impoverished suitor, urges her to break off her engagement, Viola must proceed with the marriage when Philip refuses to release her from her promise. With her marital life resembling a Gothic novel[14]—Philip scrutinizes and controls her every move, enlists the housekeeper to watch Viola in his absence, and threatens to imprison his wife if she defies his dictates—Viola eventually agrees to Harry's request that she flee with him to the continent. As she prepares for her departure, however, Viola is surprised by Philip. She fatally stabs him with an ornamental letter opener, Harry's wedding gift to her, in a scene that anticipates Tess's murder of the equally loathesome Alec. Fearful that Harry would suffer harsh consequences, Viola refuses his entreaties to leave England together and disappears into the darkness among the jagged seaside cliffs surrounding her home, presumably throwing herself to her own death.

The force of time in fashioning Viola's life is signalled both by the novel's title and its opening epigraph. As Caird explains in her introduction to the novel, Azrael was an angel of death or destruction who dwelt within "immeasurable, all devouring Time" (xiii). The novel's epigraph, taken from a historically rich text—the twelfth-century *Rubaiyat,* popularized through Edward FitzGerald's Victorian translation—stresses through italicization the temporal connections: "*Yesterday, this* Day's madness did prepare / *To-morrow's* Silence, Triumph or Despair." With the conflation of present, past, and future, the epigraph instructs us to read the novel from a temporal perspective, a dictate reinforced by the text's initial image of a "great stable-yard clock" that presides over the Sedley domicile (1). Though the young Viola ponders the notion of "self," assuming she is "a separate being" having "thoughts of her own, entirely her own" (3), an initial Cartesian sense of subjectivity is subsequently undercut and reconfigured as culturally informed when the narrative shifts to the training Viola undergoes under her mother's influence. Herself a product of tradition, Mrs. Sedley instills in her daughter the identical notions of self-sacrifice and submission that she had practiced with "meek and saint-like endurance" (8), lessons that Viola absorbs unquestioningly to continue the pattern into the next generation. "Endure bravely, and in silence," Mrs. Sedley advises Viola, for "that is the woman's part" (134). Time seemingly stands still as quotidian life repeats women's history: "And the routine of the days! without change, without movement; they were like a stagnant, overshadowed pool, where there was never a glimpse of the blue heaven, never a ripple or a sparkle from dawn to dark" (217).

Viola's marriage represents a continuation of that enervating history. Acceding to Mrs. Sedley's desire that Viola wed Philip despite her own misgivings, Viola reenacts women's traditional acceptance of their duty, "too accustomed to follow her mother's ideal of womanly submission to offer any resistance" to Philip's decision to proceed with the marital plans (2:63). The marriage is contextualized within a historical sequence to highlight Viola's reinscription of an exhausted past. Harry, for example, laments Viola's immersion "in the meshes of a worn-out, lifeless old error" (2:71) that signifies a form of living death as Viola approaches the church where the ceremony is to be performed. The chants of well-wishers expressing "[l]ong life and happiness to you!" assume an ironic tone as Viola walks among tombstones, and wedding bells interrupt the communal blessings as if "ushering in the sorrows of the ceaseless generations" (2:82).

The intimations of historical tyranny and fatigue that suffuse these descriptions of Viola's early experiences, and which gain force in the chronicle of her married life, recall Nietzsche's concerns and Caird's own essays in "Emancipation of the Family."[15] In tracing the course of familial history from ancient times to the present in "Emancipation," Caird confers a masculine cast upon history, arguing that "[i]n more or less modified forms," the "patriarchal idea" has prevailed "with remarkably little change" (2:27). Nietzsche similarly masculinizes history in regarding it as "the eternally manly" (87) and offers an especially pertinent point for a reading of the past in *The Wing of Azrael* as a continuation of male domination over women. History, Nietzsche emphasizes, "can be borne only by strong personalities," for "weak ones are utterly extinguished by it" (86):

> The reason is that history confuses the feelings and sensibility when these are not strong enough to assess the past by themselves. He who no longer dares to trust himself but involuntarily asks of history "How ought I to feel about this?" finds that his timidity gradually turns him into an actor and that he is playing a role, usually indeed many roles and therefore playing them badly and superficially. (86)

Absorbed within women's history, Viola initially feels the pressures of duty to enact her appropriate part without questioning the validity of the institutions that oppress her. As one acquaintance, the socially rebellious Sibella Lincoln—one of Nietzsche's "strong personalities"—remarks, Viola is "the child of her fathers" who exists under "a spell" that causes her to accept her role as "sacred" (2:208). Historical influence thus outweighs present discontent as Viola struggles to perform the primary role of submissive wife in accordance with her mother's traditional training. Despite "all the suffering she had endured," the hold of "[t]he past seemed to be too strong for her, the attitude of feeling to be changelessly fixed" (3:66). As Viola herself recognizes, "I am as I was made and as I was taught!" (39). Unable to "adapt" or "alter," Viola despairs that "I am helpless. Things are too much for me; I cannot bear it!" Though advised by Sibella not to "be frightened to open your eyes and to use your reason," since "the creeds of our youth" should be able to "bear the light" if valid, Viola can respond to Sibella's assertion that "we have really been taught to worship the devil" only with an instinctive dismissal that "Oh! I can never believe so" (8).

The force of women's history in shaping the present is compulsively reasserted in this text to characterize Viola's fate as a predestined repetition of the past. Indeed, as the narrator rhetorically comments, "What could she do to unravel the Gordian-knot, tied and drawn tight by the force of generations and the weight of centuries?" (2:210). As Sibella similarly muses, "The whole machinery of doom is in motion" (208) to condemn Viola, like the women before her, and make "all these time-honoured iniquities possible and successful" (3:11); "these profitable old crimes" will recur "apparently for all eternity." In one significant exchange between Sibella and Harry's sister, the conventional Adrienne, Victorian women are figured as modern versions of druidical sacrifices that extend the historical chain of oppression. Noting that Viola's mother sacrificed her child "open-eyed, in the name of all that is sacred" as did druid priests, Sibella proclaims that "[h]istory repeats itself" (31). Criticized by Adrienne for "fling[ing] over with a light heart, the creeds and the traditions of centuries" (31–32) as Adrienne "entirely dispute[s] the analogy between Viola's case and these Druidical sacrifices" (34), Sibella rejoins: "Therein also history repeats itself."

The assessment of history that unfolds in *The Wing of Azrael* imports *fin de siècle* notions of organic memory to demonstrate the power of the past to determine the future. Developed during the 1870s by scientist Ewald Hering, the theory gained adherents and respectability into the next decade, when Caird was writing her novel.[16] Built on an evolutionary foundation, Hering's theory assumed that memories were carried within the molecules of each individual, to be transmitted from one generation to the next (Otis 4). As enthusiast Samuel Butler explained the workings of organic memory, an individual represents "but a part of the life of his progenitor, imbued with all his memories, profiting by all his experiences—which are, in fact, his own," continuing "already infinite repetitions" (qtd. in Otis 6). *The Wing of Azrael* proffers a similar argument through its iterative emphasis on the hold of the past in shaping Viola's present; the message of submission seemingly is transferred by the body itself, compelling subsequent generations to repeat the experiences of the preceding ones. Indeed, as Viola surmises, "[e]very movement, every act, every thought, was preordained to lead up to misfortune" (3:110).

In that respect, Viola exists within a kind of "specious present," to adopt William James's phrase, in which the influences of the past cannot be severed from the sense of the present or the workings of the future. *The Wing of Azrael* expresses the similar formulation of Henri Bergson to map onto women's experience as a whole the notion of "duration" that he specifically attributed to an individual's internal assessment of time.

Defining duration as a subjective temporal measurement in contrast to the scientific method that ostensibly distorts time by breaking it into discrete units, Bergson theorizes time as a continuous flow that unites past, present, and future. As Bergson explains in the 1888 *Time and Free Will:*

> Pure duration is the form which the succession of our conscious states assumes when our ego lets itself *live,* when it refrains from separating its present state from its former states.... [I]n recalling these states, it does not set them alongside its actual state as one point alongside another, but forms both the past and the present states into an organic whole, as happens when we recall the notes of a tune, melting, so to speak, into one another. (100)

In *The Wing of Azrael,* history is analogously figured as an organic whole in which Viola's life simply participates in an ongoing process. That interpretation gains support through the text's recurring image of the sea, which itself connotes the sense of flow that Bergson links to duration. Indeed, Viola is variously characterized by Harry as a "sea spirit" (2:36), "sea-queen" (37), and "almost a daughter of the sea" (22), designations with which she agrees in recalling that, from childhood, the sea "has sung to me its slumber-song and drawn me towards it." Like history and the movement of "human destiny" (184), the waves represent "big powers at work,... rolling in, centuries old—high, resistless, unbroken" (3:87). The forces of history cannot be conquered, the sea imagery suggests, for each generation is subsumed within the past like an individual wave within the surrounding waters:

> The waves were tossing restlessly, forming for ever in new vigour, like endless generations, to culminate and then roll over and lose their individuality in the waste of waters. How fresh and eager they looked as they climbed up to the breaking-point, wearing their crown of surf for a moment, and then with what a peaceful sweep they sank to the level of the dead waves, broken and gone, losing the fever of their short lives in a gentle annihilation! (2:106–7)

The sea speaks "in parables" to Viola (3:145) by revealing that "[s]uch were the movements of human destiny, the restless everlasting labour without aim or hope" (2:184). Viola's "instinctive fatalism" is merely the "lesson of unresting tides, of the waves, for ever advancing and retreating, blindly obedient" (3:156).

Viola's gradual disillusionment with the historical imperatives that fashion her life—the dissatisfaction that eventually leads to her decision to flee Philip and then impulsively murder him—is also imaged in oceanic terms. Resonances to the persona of Matthew Arnold's "Dover Beach" suggest Viola's comparable dissatisfaction with the beliefs that once guided her. The erosion of those creeds echoes the retreat of the "sea of Faith" and sense of confidence that Arnold's speaker bemoans in charting "the turbid ebb and flow / Of human misery," as the following passage from the novel demonstrates:

> Thus for centuries, the sea had beaten, just as to-day, on the crumbling coast, and probably for centuries after would beat so; while the joy and the anguish of human souls came and passed away as the shadow of a cloud over the sea, or as a tremor in some salt pool left by the resilient waves.
> When the human being fully realises how utterly he is swallowed up and lost in the world of infinities, the moment is always vital and terrible.... [T]he sufferer finds himself shouting to a deaf universe, and hears his own voice dismally echoing through its unending spaces. (3:3–4)

Like the persona of Arnold's poem, Viola, previously "shielded by religious teachings from this conception," finds that the old beliefs no longer offer consolation: though "[r]eligion spoke warningly," the "familiar voice was not heeded" (4). Sharing with Arnold's speaker a sense of being poised between the ages—lacking the comforting creeds of the past but finding no alternative beliefs to replace them—Viola feels cut adrift. With the "old faiths . . . shaken" (50) and the "new" ideas "appalling" (71), Viola can only experience "horrible conflict" as she finds "nothing now to cling to" (82). Unlike the Arnoldian malaise, however, Viola's discontent is attributed directly to the influence of history. Despite her "weakened and uprooted faith," Viola is enmeshed within "feelings and instincts still belonging to the past, still responding to the old dead and gone dogmas."

As one of the unfortunates whom Nietzsche identifies, Viola succumbs to the pressures of the past that the German philosopher characterizes as "a dark, invisible burden" (61). Unable to "employ the past as a nourishing food" (120), as Nietzsche recommends, Viola instead is vanquished by history. Her murder of Philip signifies not a rejection of the past that could usher in a new beginning, but a sign of defeat. It is thus appropriate that the novel's final sentence hints that Viola has plummeted into the sea, drowned within the enveloping history that it represents—"pitch-black, rayless, impenetrable darkness" (3:224).[17]

The pessimistic closure of *The Wing of Azrael* derives, then, from Viola's inability to escape from the determinism of history—the sense that, as Cixous observes, one is "rigidly set within historicultural limits so mixed up with the scene of History that . . . to think or even imagine an 'elsewhere'" becomes a virtual impossibility ("Sorties" 83). *The Daughters of Danaus* is a revision of its predecessor, for the later text does imagine an "elsewhere." The more hopeful conclusion of *The Daughters of Danaus* issues not only from its plea to reject the tyrannical women's history that paralyzes Viola, but its replacement with a vision of the future that does not simply confirm the past. Though the final pages of *The Daughters of Danaus* signal Hadria's personal defeat, the novel hints that history need not be proscriptive; indeed, Hadria eludes the traditional fate of death or a humble admission of error bestowed upon a Victorian female protagonist who challenges social mores. *The Daughters of Danaus* instead suggests that history can tender both a lesson and a warning to the next generation. To invoke Cixous's terminology, the novel leaves its New Woman readers with the tantalizing message that history does not necessarily predetermine one's "destiny."

Chapter 6

Dissolving the Boundaries: Temporal Subversion in *The Story of an African Farm*

> When I am with you I never know that I am a woman and you are a man; I only know that we are both things that think.
> —Schreiner, *The Story of an African Farm*

With Olive Schreiner's treatment of temporality in *The Story of an African Farm* we have traveled to the ideological opposite of the text with which we began, H. Rider Haggard's *She*. Indeed, one irony of literary history is that Haggard included *African Farm* in his pairing of the most significant novels of the *fin de siècle*—a startling assessment, considering that Schreiner's text challenges rather than reinforces the temporal perspective that characterizes *She*.[1] Instead of deploying temporal discourses to solidify gender roles, as *She* attempts, *African Farm* employs gendered notions of time only to deconstruct them, demonstrating their complicity in reifying the natural order of time and illustrating the harm this order posed to men as well as women. Through its temporal maneuvers, coupled with its anomalous response to narrative conventions, the novel problematizes gender construction on both an intimately textual and broadly structural level. Appropriating the prevailing essentialist distinctions between temporal forms, the novel situates masculine linear temporality as a controlling force and simultaneously disrupts its hegemony through the inexorable intervention of feminine time. In the narrative chaos that ensues, *African Farm* creates a liberatory space within which alternate constructions of gender can be imagined and enacted.[2]

The underlying assumption fueling these textual moves is that the New Woman can neither flourish nor survive within the constrictive gender roles of Victorian culture. Instead, as the epigraph to this chapter suggests, *African Farm* argues that the conventional gender economy must be discredited and discarded to allow for a fluidity between masculine and feminine positions. *African Farm* pursues its ideological agenda by manipulating the conventions of the narrative structure that most works against it—the linear novel, particularly the realist novel.[3] Through a teleological format, as narrative theorists like Rachel Blau DuPlessis have reminded us, such texts indirectly reinforce the separate spheres; by offering only limited scenarios for a female character, these narratives implicitly validate them. With its odd syntax, desultory structure, and peculiar characterizations, the 1883 *African Farm* is an iconoclast among the tightly constructed linear narratives that tended to dominate nineteenth-century fiction. In problematizing both the structure and language characteristic of this prevalent fictional form, *African Farm* expands the hermeneutic possibilities that the realist novel seeks to foreclose, revealing gender as a cultural construction rather than a natural law. By establishing an "eternal present" in place of the sequential progression indicative of a realist text, *African Farm* undermines the natural order of time dependent on linear principles and their attendant associations.

Although not seamlessly applicable to Victorian notions of time, as I noted in my introductory chapter, Kristeva's model of gendered time is a particularly useful tool for evaluating the interplay of temporal discourses in *African Farm*. In scene after scene, the novel establishes a stark contrast between the masculine associations of linear time and the feminine connotations of monumental and cyclical time that Kristeva theorizes. While seeming initially to privilege masculine time in the text's vignettes and structure, *African Farm* instead subtly dissolves linear temporality's hegemony through the relentless interventions of feminine time.

Gendered Images of the Watch and Moon

Schreiner firmly establishes the dichotomy between masculine and feminine temporality with the powerful gender-charged images of the watch and moon that dominate the novel's first pages.[4] The moon, through its evocation of monthly cycles and rhythms that resonate with fertility and fluidity, is a conventional emblem of the female that in this text suggests the amorphous qualities of "women's time." The initial paragraphs establish the moon as a signifier of feminine temporality through images that convey boundlessness and procreation; further, these early paragraphs situate "women's time" as a potent force in the narrative:

> The full African moon poured down its light from the blue sky into the wide, lonely plain. The dry, sandy earth, with its coating of stunted "karoo" bushes a few inches high, the low hills that skirted the plain, the milk-bushes with their long, finger-like leaves, all were touched by a weird and an almost oppressive beauty as they lay in the white light.
> In one spot only was the solemn monotony of the plain broken. Near the centre a small, solitary "kopje" rose. Alone it lay there, a heap of round iron-stones piled one upon another, as over some giant's grave. Here and there a few tufts of grass or small succulent plants had sprung up among its stones, and on the very summit a clump of prickly-pears lifted their thorny arms, and reflected, as from mirrors, the moonlight on their broad, fleshy leaves. (35)

In the opening sentence, the first adjective and verb carry inferences of fecundity through the fullness of the moon and its pouring of light, especially in contrast to the barren setting upon which the rays fall. Adhering to the traditional gendering of the sun as male, the text specifically attributes the sterility of the landscape to masculine intervention through the solar leaching of vital fluids. Indeed, a subsequent passage allies the sun with infertility as "[w]eek after week, month after month, the sun looked down from the cloudless sky, till the karroo-bushes were leafless sticks ... and the earth itself was naked and bare" (44). The moon functions as a life-giving force through the markedly different effect its light has on the sparse vegetation of the plain, upon which the beams bestow an unusual beauty rather than a debilitating aridity.

Further implicating the moon in feminine temporality and suggesting lunar potency is the orb's sororal and beneficent bond with the landscape, which is inherently encoded as feminine and subsumed within cyclical time through nature's archetypal designation as procreative mother. Topographical description reinforces the landscape's gender affiliation by subtly depicting the female form, imparted by a combination and sequence of images replicating the downward movement of an eye in scanning the terrain of the body. The African plain is distinguished by "low hills" and the maternally suggestive "milk-bushes with their long, finger-like leaves," as well as by the "few tufts of grass or small succulent plants" that retain life-giving fluids and lie upon the nearby hillock. Moreover, the moonlight seemingly feminizes the phallically redolent vegetation on the landscape, the clump of prickly-pears that assumes a dominant position through its presence upon the "very summit" of the kopje. Although these plants are physiologically distinguished by their barbed spines, the moonlight shifts the emphasis from this masculine register to a feminine one. Thus, even though the prickly-pears initially "lifted their thorny arms," they are immediately feminized through the mirror-like reflection of the moonlight upon "their broad, fleshy leaves." Rather than convey a passive female specularization through this reflective quality, however, the plant seemingly metamorphoses from a phallic column to an active and powerful female force.

Syntax, too, accentuates the relationship between moonlight and "women's time" through the dreamy structure of the sentences in the inaugural paragraphs. Linear time, as Kristeva argues, governs language through the sequential articulation of the typical sentence: the movement from subject to verb corresponds to the pattern of a beginning and ending through which the sentence encounters "its own stumbling block," death, in the very act of enunciation (17). Schreiner, however, bypasses such a linear framework through a sophisticated play with language. In the first two paragraphs of the novel there are no simple linear sentences as such, since all conceal the usual recognizable sequence of noun and predicate among complex descriptions. Verbs follow objects; extensive prepositional phrases and dense strata of clauses appear in unexpected positions; and digressive appositional remarks complicate interpretation. As DuPlessis comments, "[b]reaking the sentence" not only represents "a way of rupturing language and tradition sufficiently to invite a female slant, emphasis, or approach" (32), but also of "delegitimating the specific narrative and cultural orders of nineteenth-century fiction" (34).

In this respect, Schreiner's technique resembles Kristeva's linguistic model of the semiotic—the disruptive force that constantly challenges the symbolic order, the dominant language of patriarchal society built on the underlying opposition of privileged male and peripheral female. Polysemic and mutable, the semiotic serves to keep meaning uncertain rather than tightly defining it. In *African Farm,* semiotic interventions undermine linear form within sentences to suggest a larger problematization of meaning in the demarcation of gender roles. Blending masculinized linearity and feminized chaos, sentences linguistically blur the distinctions between genders that the novel similarly strives to achieve on a structural and thematic level.

The second sentence of the novel exemplifies Schreiner's unusual syntactic approach through its tortuous yet poetic path toward subject and verb, thereby implying the fluidity of monumental time rather than the directness of linear language. First, the placement of the three initial phrases, strewn with commas, creates a languid effect since the phrases delay the sentence's action: "The dry, sandy earth, with its coating of stunted 'karoo' bushes a few inches high, the low hills that skirted the plain, the milk-bushes with their long, finger-like leaves, all were touched by a weird and an almost oppressive beauty as they lay in the white light." Second, the three phrases become disconcerting in their conjunction, for they depict elements whose interrelationship seems neither significant nor logical; no apparent rationale exists for linking the earth with karoo bushes, then demarcating a subset of that earth by remarking upon low hills, and finally proceeding to milk-bushes whose location is left undefined. Next, the first and third phrases are virtually amorphous in their extended descriptions, loosely binding between them the more linear phrase with its relatively straightforward description and its possession of the sole verb form among the sentence segments, albeit part of a subordinate clause. The sentence's departure from parallel and logical structure, combined with an adjectival rather than predicative emphasis ("the dry, sandy earth" and the "long, finger-like leaves"), sanctions ambience in preference to movement. Relegating the verb to the final clause of the sentence reinforces that attentiveness to atmosphere, as does the selection of passive voice and a weak verb ("they lay"). The latter verb choice deprives the earth, hills, and milk-bushes of agency, since they merely "lay" in the moonlight. Preceding the verb clause with the three pictorial layers confers a suffocating and dense effect, amplifying the sense of a "weird and an almost oppressive beauty" that the moon imposes upon the landscape. The diffuseness of the illumination upon the elements of the landscape ("all were touched" by the moonbeams) emphasizes imagistically the departure from linearity that the sentence conveys structurally.

Other syntactic anomalies in the opening paragraphs complicate the linear reading process, for sentences seem to have been written backwards or periphrastically through their massed layers of phrases. Sentences characteristically unfold with a bewildering array of prepositional phrases or embedded clauses that situate predicates in unexpected places or dispense with them altogether. In a continuation of the cited passage, the second paragraph of the novel offers a telling example of this technique:

> At the foot of the "kopje" lay the homestead. First, the stone-walled "sheep-kraals" and Kaffir huts; beyond them the dwelling-house—a square red-brick building with thatched roof. Even on its bare walls, and the wooden ladder that led up to the loft, the moonlight cast a kind of dreamy beauty, and quite etherealized the low brick wall that ran before the house, and which enclosed a bare patch of sand and two straggling sunflowers. On the zinc roof of the great open wagon-house, on the roofs of the outbuildings that jutted from its side, the moonlight glinted with a quite peculiar brightness, till it seemed that every rib in the metal was of burnished silver. (35)

Appearing midway through the passage, for instance, is a perplexing sentence that lacks both verb and sequential movement, even though it presumably establishes a causal chain in its introductory phrase: "First, the stone-walled 'sheep-kraals' and Kaffir huts." The sentence dissolves, however, into a fragment that leaves the reader to grapple with the appropriate perspectival position to adopt in observing the features of the dwelling house, for the sentence contains an implicit command to study the scene despite the predicative void. By contrast, the penultimate sentence complicates reading through extension beyond its expected endpoint. Beginning with a claustrophobic amassing of clauses that draw the reader into progressively smaller spaces ("[e]ven on its bare red walls, and the wooden ladder that led up to the loft"), the sentence ostensibly characterizes the movement of the moonlight in straightforward fashion with active verbs and their respective direct objects. Yet tacked onto the final object is a clause that stimulates a disconcerting afterthought, as if the narrator inadvertently perceived a mundane patch of landscape and digressively commented upon it to shift emphasis from action to atmosphere. The sentence defies a teleological reading, since the ending offers no interpretive cues for deciphering its beginning.

Solidifying the link between the moon and "women's time" in this passage is the mystical cast that lunar luminescence confers upon the stark landscape through the moon's enveloping and transformative qualities. The moonlight falls upon the "bare" surface of the karoo building and bestows upon it a "dreamy beauty" to "etherealize" its brick enclosure, which suggests the intervention of monumental time through the representation of such an unworldly dimension. Moreover, the play of the moonlight, by which the dull spines of a zinc roof metamorphose into "burnished silver," suggests an aesthetic conversion of the mundane into the unusual, connoting monumental temporality by hinting at the infinite duration of artistic creation.

The maternal quality of the moonlight amplifies the association of the moon with "women's time" as it gently sweeps across a bedroom inhabited by two sleeping girls. Within the chamber are the young Lyndall, the novel's central female character who evinces from an early age a contempt for valorized feminine behavior, and her cousin Em, the text's most conventional female figure. The moonlight streams upon them through an opened shutter and is again emblematic of plenitude as it issues forth "in a flood" to make the room as "light as day" (36). The ensuing descriptions of its movement across the children's forms represent a shift in focus, for the language becomes permeated with maternal images to allude to the moon's protective and nurturant elements. Traversing the uncomely face of Em, for example, "the loving moonlight hid defects here as elsewhere, and showed only the innocent face of a child in its first sweet sleep" (36). More definitively, the moonlight assumes a relational bond with the figure in the next bed, for Lyndall "belonged of right to the moonlight" with her "quite elfin-like beauty." Like a mother guarding her innocent young, "the moonlight looked in at the naked little limbs" as Lyndall awakened to "the moonlight that was bathing her." The moonlight's link to the feminine in this passage is reflexively emphasized by its separation from the masculine in a subsequent paragraph: "not a ray of light entered anywhere" in the hut where the overseer of the farm, Otto, rests along with his son Waldo, the main male character whose problematic relationship to masculinity will soon unfold.

As these early descriptive passages reveal, the moon carries a connotation of agency since it is the only active force presented. The verbs ascribed to the moonlight all attest to its force—it pours, touches, casts, etherealizes, glints, looks, and bathes. The structure of the novel's opening paragraph establishes and reiterates that potency, since the first noun is the "moon" and the last noun is the "light" emanating from it. As the initial noun of the novel, the moon is the privileged image that becomes an engulfing force, implying that a powerful presence associated with the female will overlay the text. That implication is borne out in the next segment of the opening chapter, in which linear time becomes absorbed within "women's time." In contrast to the benevolence and dreaminess of the feminine temporality allied with the moon, linear time is depicted as tyrannical and threatening through the image of an interminably ticking watch. Linear time is gendered male and associated with patriarchal heritage by its link to Waldo's father, since "[a]t the head of his father's bed hung a great silver hunting watch" (36). The sound of the watch is relentless and menacing, as linear time conjures death:

> It ticked loudly. The boy listened to it, and began mechanically to count. Tick-tick-tick! . . . He lost count presently, and only listened. Tick-tick-tick-tick!
> It never waited; it went on inexorably; and every time it ticked *a man died*!
> . . . "Dying, dying, dying!" said the watch; "dying, dying, dying!" (36–37)

The passage is replete with sinister images: the adverb "loudly" is harsh and jarring, as it replicates the sound of a ticking clock with the equal stress on the syllables; each string of "ticks" seems monolithic through the conjunction of four monosyllabic words in a single hyphenated sequence emphasized by exclamatory punctuation; and Waldo relinquishes any vestige of control over the "mechanically" ticking watch once he has "lost count" and "only listened" to it. Sentence structure mimics the implacable movement of linear time through the series of clauses separated by semicolons, creating a crescendo effect with the succession of incessant activities ("it never waited"), forward pressure ("it went on inexorably"), and triumphant conquest ("every time it ticked *a man died*!"). The final sentence of the passage affirms the power of linear time through the multiple iterations of the ominous "dying."

Linear time's relationship to masculinity is inscribed by an odd dialogic passage in which the ticking sounds of the watch respond to the words of an overwhelming patriarchal figure—one that is doubly drawn, since the biological father is repeating the words of the spiritual Father in reciting biblical selections:

> [Waldo] thought of the words his father had read that evening—
> *"For wide is the gate, and broad is the way, that leadeth to destruction, and many there be which go in thereat."*
> "Many, many, many!" said the watch.
> *"Because strait is the gate, and narrow is the way, that leadeth*

unto life and few there be that find it."
"Few, few, few!" said the watch. (37)

Mentally hearing the dialogue between patriarch and watch, Waldo equates the two, concluding that the ticking is inalterable, "just like God's will." The dialogue implicitly valorizes linear directness over expansive choice: the "wide" gate and "broad way" bring destruction, while the "strait" gate and "narrow" way ensure life.

Yet even as linear time is being constructed as a controlling force in this passage through the watch, it is being deconstructed by the repeated intervention of "women's time," as intimated in the following passage:

> The boy lay with his eyes wide open. He saw before him a long stream of people, a great dark multitude, that moved in one direction; then they came to the dark edge of the world, and went over. He saw them passing on before him, and there was nothing that could stop them. He thought of how that stream had rolled on through all the long ages of the past—how the old Greeks and Romans had gone over; the countless millions of China and India, they were going over now. Since he had gone to bed, how many had gone?
> And the watch said, "Eternity, eternity, eternity!" (37)

Linear time initially holds the position of authority in the passage: it augurs death with every tick; it evokes a grave through the "dark multitude" stumbling over the world's "dark edge"; and it propels its victims linearly and unstoppably in a single direction. Yet the procession is also illustrative of monumental time through the juxtaposition of past and present, since a timeless "stream" blends ancient Western victims with numberless contemporary counterparts ("countless millions") in the East. Additionally, the change in the watch's mantra signals the immersion of linear time within monumental time as the words "dying, dying, dying" are replaced by "eternity, eternity, eternity."

For Schreiner, a ticking watch or clock serves as a crucial emblem of the destruction and coercion associated with linear time. Indeed, Waldo's frightened response to the sounds of the timepiece is a reworking of a markedly similar scene in *Undine*, Schreiner's earlier novel tracing the unhappy fate of its eponymous character, a nascent New Woman figure who eventually succumbs to the gender role marked out for a female in colonial culture. As a young girl living in South Africa, Undine listens to the unnerving cadence of a great clock that dominates the household:

> "Another week gone, another day gone. What have you done? We never come back, we moments; we fly, but we never return, never, never, tick, tick. What have you done with us? If you do the best you can with all the rest of us, you can never bring one of us back, never, never, tick, tick.
> ... "Tick, tick," cried the inexorable old clock, "what good have you ever done? How are you better able to die now than you were last week? You are nearer death, but are you ready, ready, ready, tick, tick, tick?" (4–5)

Reiterating the clock's incessant marking of the seconds is the succession of the short vowel sounds of "never" and "ready," which mimic the tone of the equally grating "ticks" to which they are yoked in double repetitions. Passage of time becomes almost Gothic in its horror through the inability to recuperate lost moments, for the rhythm of such phrases as "another week gone, another day gone" becomes both a hypnotic and an unsettling mimicry of the clock's litany. With its specific reminder of an individual's brief tenure within linear time ("[y]ou are nearer death") joined with a disconcerting implication that existence is meaningless ("what good have you ever done?"), the clock associates despair, anxiety, and helplessness with this temporal form. Described as a "great red clock overhead" (4), the timepiece suggests a disturbing omniscience ("overhead"), omnipotence ("great"), and violence (the bloodlike "red") that it exercises upon its powerless victims.

As in the *African Farm* scene, the clock is linked with the ultimate Father, interrupting prayers and drowning out the devotions of Undine's family as the words of the clock blend with supplications:

> Undine tried to listen to the prayer again, and she caught these words: "Thousands, O Lord, are going to destruction every moment."
> "Yes, yes, yes," said the clock, "tick, tick, hell, hell, going, going, going, thousands, thousands, thousands, tick, tick, tick, tick." (5)

The tyranny of the clock intimated in the first *Undine* passage is transposed onto Christianity in its successor, as the signifiers of the unstoppable progression of time ("tick, tick"; "going, going, going") are interspersed with reminders of "hell, hell." Unlike the *African Farm* passage, however, the *Undine* version promises no respite or salvation from the intercession of monumental time and its implicit suggestion of eternal life:

> She could kneel there while the old clock told only of her own sins
> and fate, but now—when every tick talked of half the world, for
> whom there was no help, no hope, who were going, going, going—
> she felt as though she were being suffocated and the walls and roof
> were throbbing and coming down on her. (5)

Chastised for her inattention to prayers, Undine is banished to a lightless room where the clock's sounds reverberate in her memory and accentuate the enveloping atmosphere of despair: "[S]he could not forget the old clock; and how dark the room was! Perfect, boundless, endless darkness it might be, for anything she could see; like that silent darkness which surrounds poor lost souls and is all the answer they get when they cry aloud to God" (6–7). No comforting moonlight enters Undine's chamber to relieve the claustrophobic darkness, and no prospect of consolation is offered in her prayers to God.

The clock vignette foreshadows the agonizing fate of *Undine*'s female protagonist, whose "unwomanly" opinions and behavior (137) allow no favorable textual resolution. Caught in a double bind, Undine faces social annihilation if she holds to her masculine opinions and intellectual suffocation if she renounces them to accommodate the wishes of her lover Albert Blair. Choosing the latter course, Undine experiences a psychic death. As she prepares to become the "little wife" (146) who will serve Albert unstintingly, Undine quells her own desires and loses her sense of subjectivity. Rejected by her lover despite her disavowal of the beliefs that had once guided her, Undine marries his unsavory father to ensure that Albert will receive the funds he so desperately needs to cover disastrous speculative ventures, later dividing her inheritance between Albert and his brother after the father's early death. Destitute and disconsolate after Albert marries an heiress, Undine embarks for the diamond fields of South Africa and a difficult life of menial work that ends in a premature and solitary death.

The harsh ticking of the massive clock in the novel's opening pages portends, then, that Undine will be unable to escape a constrictive culture associated with the civilizing and ideological projects of linear time. Through a gender switch in the similar scene in *African Farm*, however, Schreiner creates a textual window through which such constraints can be queried and rejected. In problematizing Waldo's relationship with linear time, *African Farm* demonstrates that the gender restrictions reinforced by linear time are equally destructive to the male. A woman, *Undine* implies, is powerless to alter her prospects alone; the possibility of change, *African Farm* suggests, rests only in a cross-gender effort to reimagine and rearticulate male and female roles.

In *African Farm*, the confusion of linear and "women's time" intimated by the pre-eminence of the moon over the ostensibly masculine image of the ticking watch prefaces the overlapping of gender-linked traits that marks the remainder of the text. Neither of the main characters is inextricably bound to the essentialism implied by either temporal mode. Instead, the characters drift from one form of time to another, and indeed Waldo periodically occupies both linear and feminine time simultaneously.[5] Although such temporal fluidity is manifested almost universally in the text, the unworldly Waldo is the pivotal figure implicated in the transgression of gender barriers. His ambivalent relationship to patrilineal heritage is the crucial exegetical element in this behavior, since it presages his movement into "women's time."

Masculine Roles Problematized

As the presence of moonlight in the girls' chamber and its absence in the male household reveals, the text establishes a distinctive gender boundary in the initial scenes. Though unambiguous in the novel's opening pages, this division is challenged by the end of the first chapter, when Waldo fails to assume his hereditary place in the patriarchal structure. The son's unsuitability for that traditional role emerges in the following passage as he prepares for his ultimately abortive attempt to tender a sacrificial offering to the Father:

> Waldo ... herded the ewes and lambs—a small and dusty herd—powdered all over from head to foot with red sand, wearing a ragged coat, and shoes of undressed leather, through whose holes the toes looked out. His hat was too large, and had sunk down to his eyes, concealing completely the silky black curls. It was a curious, small figure. His flock gave him little trouble. It was too hot for them to move far.... He himself crept under a shelving rock. (39)

Appropriately, the scene begins in sunlight, conveying the masculine tenor of sacrificial ritual, and this gender designation is reinforced by resonances to the Bible and patriarchal Christian tradition as a whole. Yet subtle clues anticipate Waldo's reluctance to enter the patrilineal structure of his culture. He immediately escapes the blazing sunlight by retreating under a rocky ledge while carefully tending his flock, and he evinces qualities conventionally ascribed to the female. Although the role of nurturing shepherd could imply a link to a masculine Christ rather than a feminine nature, and thus a fitting one for Waldo to enact, the novel instead builds upon the latent feminine qualities underlying medieval and other representations of the son of God to problematize gender positions; Waldo's "silky black curls" resonate with iconography that emphasizes Christ's flowing locks. Indeed, an intertextual reference additionally links Waldo to femininity, for Undine enacted a similar unsuccessful ritual in the earlier text. Yet *African Farm* goes further than such representations in depicting Waldo not only as a feminized Christ figure but as shabbily inadequate to perform his Christ-like ritualistic duties. Waldo is dramatically distanced, then, from the Old Testament's version of the masculinized divine Father as well as His feminized son to complicate and undermine Waldo's patrilineal status. Instead of conveying a competent patriarchal presence, Waldo repeatedly reveals his inability to take on that role. He makes "a curious, small figure" rather than appear as a robust man; his coat is tattered and his shoes in disrepair; and his hat falls over his face, as if he were a child ludicrously dressed up in his father's garb.

The paragraph following Waldo's retreat from the sunlight continues to demonstrate his distance from patriarchal practices:

> Soon, from the blue bag where he kept his dinner, he produced a fragment of slate, an arithmetic, and a pencil. Proceeding to put down a sum with solemn and earnest demeanour, he began to add it up aloud: "Six and two is eight—and four is twelve—and two is fourteen—and four is eighteen." Here he paused. "And four is eighteen—and—four—is eighteen." The last was very much drawled. Slowly the pencil slipped from his fingers and the slate followed it into the sand. (39)

Waldo is inept in plying the tools that further the civilizing projects of his forefathers, as indicated by his inability to solve arithmetical sums while his sheep are grazing. He works only with a "fragment of a slate," implying a marginalized relationship to the masculine arts. As he proceeds solemnly through the series of sums, Waldo soon loses interest, drawling his answer and allowing his writing materials to disappear into the sand in a gesture that signals his more tenacious bond to nature than to linear pursuits. He immediately mutters to himself with his head upon his folded "little arms" and is again aligned with nature when a "curious old ewe came to sniff at him."

The sacrificial offering that Waldo futilely attempts with a mutton chop upon the sunny plain is affiliated with masculine temporality not only because of religious tradition, but also because Christian time is itself linear. The primary Christian narrative, the Bible, represents both a patriarchal and a linear story. In its Western typological reading, the Bible creates a pattern of repetition leading to a conclusion, since its significant male figures were commonly considered as precursors of Christ.[6] Waldo participates in linear Christian temporality in his capacity as a "priest" performing a sacred ritual, but it is a role that he can only partially fulfill: "never since the beginning of the world was there so ragged and so small a priest" (40). Thus, despite his imitation of the transubstantiation ritual that a priest performs by thrice genuflecting before an altar, Waldo's sacrificial effort is decidedly unsuccessful. His failure precipitates a movement from "[t]he fierce sun [that] poured down its heat upon his head and upon his altar" to seek refuge in the more companionable shade.

Also problematizing Waldo's link to linear time through Christianity is the gender ambiguity inherent in ritual, for his religious sacrifice melds linear and monumental time. In one sense, ritual implies a validation of the patriarchal structure upon which religion is grounded, since ritual accepts and reifies the order of a masculine divinity (Gorman 230–32). In so doing, ritual evidences a desire to control and dominate, to establish a sense of power over the exigencies of human existence through a repetitive and orderly structure. Moreover, ritual is sequential, for an unvarying performative pattern must be enacted for the ceremony to be concluded properly (27). In a second sense, however, ritual carries mystical and mythological connotations related to feminine time,[7] which in *African Farm* emanate from Waldo's anticipatory ecstasy at consummating a sacrifice: "[s]lowly the dullness and heaviness melted from his face [and] it became radiant" (39).

Waldo's unstable connection to religious tradition contrasts with the priestly role enacted by the paternally parodic figure of Bonaparte Blenkins in a later chapter, "Sunday Services." Though Blenkins is characterized by his self-serving response to religion, he nevertheless performs his clerical functions with appreciably more competence than the inept Waldo. In the first section of the chapter, "Service No. 1," Waldo's religious sensibility is again evocative of a mystical ebullience. Lapsing into quiet after singing hymns, Waldo sees a vision that produces a reaction approaching sexual climax in its eroticized language and pronounced intensity:

> "Oh, God!" he cried, "I cannot wait! I cannot wait! I want to die; I want to see Him; I want to touch Him. Let me die!" He folded his hands, trembling. . . . "I will die any death. Oh, let me come!" Weeping he bowed himself, and quivered from head to foot.
> . . . "I want you; oh, I want you,—soon, soon!" (68–69)

Rather than a masculinized priest, however, Waldo is a feminized supplicant in this passage through his self-abnegation before his God: Waldo "folded his hands" and "bowed"; he weeps, trembles, and quivers; and his ardent pleas situate God in the dominant position.

In contrast, the hypocritical Bonaparte, whose telling first name binds him to linear time, performs "Service No. 2" in more conventional fashion.[8] Bonaparte presumably is an appropriate priest, since previous references have established him as a patriarchal figure: he acts as schoolmaster, becomes overseer of the farm, and tells linear tales associated with history. Yet the text again questions the efficacy of patrilineal heritage, for Bonaparte fulfills his patriarchal responsibilities inadequately. He is an unlearned teacher, a limited master who governs under female authority, and a narrator of highly imaginative lies.

Waldo is distanced from patriarchal tradition not only through his shortcomings as a priest of the divine Father, but also through the impoverished model of conventional masculinity inhering in the earthly father. Like Waldo, the gentle Otto seems an especially elastic figure who continuously traverses gender boundaries by assuming qualities associated with both masculine and feminine temporality. Although Otto precedes Bonaparte as overseer of the farm, his occupation is an ironic one since he never demonstrates dominance but instead perpetually displays "childish" behavior (38). Otto's distance from linear time is evidenced by his lack of participation in the affairs of men and the progress of civilization: he reads a newspaper that is three weeks old (55) and responds to the comment that he is "a student of history" with the equivocal remark, "Well—a little—perhaps—it may be" (58).

Otto's affiliation with "women's time" is far more pronounced, both through his relationship with cyclical time as a surrogate mother and with monumental time through his fascination with the cosmos:

> [Otto's] place was the one home the girls had known for many a year. The house where Tant' Sannie lived and ruled was a place to sleep in, to eat in, not to be happy in.
> . . . [B]est of all, were there not warm, dark, starlight nights, when they sat together on the doorstep. . . . Would they not sit

looking up at the stars and talking of them... and fall to speculating over them? How old are they? Who dwelt in them? And the old German would say that perhaps the souls we loved lived in them; *there,* in that little twinkling point was perhaps the little girl whose stockings he had carried home; and the children would look up at it lovingly, and call it "Uncle Otto's star." Then they would fall to deeper speculations—of the times and seasons wherein the heavens shall be rolled together as a scroll, and the stars shall fall as a fig-tree casteth her untimely figs, and there shall be time no longer. (54–55)

The first part of the passage, establishing Otto's residence as a nurturing environment, not only positions Otto within "women's time" as a maternal presence—his abode is a "home," while that of the detestable maternal surrogate, Tant' Sannie, is a "house"—but it further undermines acculturated gender roles by emphasizing Tant' Sannie's separation from this function. As one who "ruled" her home, the invariably unsympathetic and frequently malignant Tant' Sannie resembles a masculinized authority figure far more than does the feminized Otto. His presence suggests cyclical time through his contiguity to the womblike space elicited by the "warm, dark" tenor of the evenings, and it evokes the cosmos through the reference to "starlight nights." The second section of the passage multiply marks Otto's affinity with "women's time": he is again affiliated with the cosmos through the fantasies he weaves in contemplating the heavens, and he distances himself from linearity by merging temporalities in his stories. In that temporal blending, past lives ("the souls we loved") are recuperated through the imagination and eternalized through celestial reincarnation. Indeed, Otto's fanciful stories about the heavens anticipate his creative rewriting of the Bible the same evening, an act that reinforces his connection to feminine time through its departure from linear narrative; deviating from the words of the Father, Otto alters the text of his "well-worn Bible" by mentally writing Bonaparte Blenkins as Christ. Through his musings upon the stars, Otto similarly causes the children to blur the distinction between reality and imagination by mentally rolling the heavens into a scroll. Such an occurrence necessitates the privileging of monumental time over linear time to effect a condition in which time no longer exists.

Otto not only speculates upon that atemporal condition but seemingly enacts it through his death in a subsequent passage. Otto's demise suggests not so much the abrupt endpoint of linear time as the boundlessness of "women's time" that Kristeva identifies as a "massive presence" lacking "cleavage or escape," a temporality that is "[a]ll-encompassing and infinite like imaginary space" (16). The numerous references earlier in the text to Otto's childlike manner coalesce powerfully at his death in a physical infantilization, intermingling youth and age and thereby unsettling linear temporality:

> The old face was lying there alone in the dark, smiling like a little child's—oh, so peacefully. . . . And it seemed almost as though Death had known and loved the old man, so gently it touched him. And how could it deal hardly with him—the loving, simple, childlike old man?
> So it smoothed out the wrinkles that were in the old forehead, and fixed the passing smile, and sealed the eyes that they might not weep again; and then the short sleep of time was melted into the long, long sleep of eternity.
> "How has he grown so young in this one night?" they said when they found him in the morning. (96)

The sense of fused temporality within this passage proceeds, in part, from the juxtaposition of youth and age in several sentences: an "old face" smiles like a "little child's"; Otto is a "childlike old man"; and wrinkles disappear in favor of youthful skin on the "old forehead." Feminine time dominates the passage through its virtual absorption of linear time. The subsumption of one time by another emerges both through the literal reading of the phrase, "then the short sleep of time was melted into the long, long sleep of eternity," and its alliterative and onomatopoeic effects. The abrupt monosyllables of "short sleep" endure only briefly, whereas the mellifluous "melted," along with the repetition within the "long, long sleep of eternity," suggests the open-ended element of "women's time." In the concluding sentence of the passage, masculine temporality has not only been swallowed by feminine temporality but reversed. Otto does not merely reach a conclusion to his life through death but has "grown young."

Disruption of Linearity

Even though Otto's link to masculine time is tenuous, a bond nevertheless exists, simply by virtue of Otto's identity as a father. His death—along with the subsequent expulsion of Bonaparte Blenkins from the narrative at the end of Part One—removes any patriarchal model for Waldo to emulate. A hint early in Part Two discloses that "women's time" will dominate this segment of *African Farm,* for Waldo periodically leaves his father's house to wander "outside in the moonlight" (144). That movement prefaces his entrance into feminine temporality and rejection of his patriarchal heritage:

> Now we have no God. We have had two: the old God that our fathers handed down to us, that we hated, and never liked; the new one that we made for ourselves, that we loved; but now he has flitted away from us, and we see what he was made of—the shadow of our highest ideal, crowned and throned. Now we have no God. (149)

Waldo's disavowal of his God is, in effect, a denial of the transcendental signified, to borrow Jacques Derrida's term, that governs and reifies the patriarchal system. Waldo breaks his ties to this structure in two ways, as the passage loosely summarizes. First, he distances himself from "the old God," the one "our fathers handed down to us," through his unsuccessful sacrificial offering at the beginning of the novel. Second, he becomes disillusioned by the personal image he has crafted of Christ, the emotionally and erotically charged figure he had visualized during his mystical experience soon after his ineffectual rite. In the later passage Waldo realizes that his subjective vision of Christ—"the new one that we made for ourselves"—is simply a construct. "There is no order," he soon comprehends, since "all things are driven about by a blind chance" (150).[9] Waldo's nihilistic recognition that a logocentric universe is merely a convenient myth is an implicit rejection of telos and its delimiting of interpretation.

By such diminishment of linear time, *African Farm* opens up a textual vacuum through which gender roles can become liquid rather than rigid. This mutability is ensured through the ascendancy of feminine temporality in Part Two, which is achieved through several interdependent routes: gender constraints associated with linear narrative are removed; traditional gender positions are further obscured by Waldo's relationship to artistic works; and gender is exposed as a cultural construction.

The first point, regarding linear narrative, assumes that the dominance of "women's time" in Part Two allows characters to escape scripted gender roles and enter a more imaginative register. That assumption proceeds from the confluence of the Kristevan perspectives on temporality and narrative theory, situating the specific locus in analyses of linear narrative. Most significant for my discussion is the reinscription of conventional gender roles associated with a linear narrative through its inherent privileging of a male reading of a text. This narrative model, as Peter Brooks intimates in *Reading for the Plot* and Jay Clayton observes in an analysis of Brooks's text, "is based almost entirely on a male sexual paradigm" (Clayton 40). Brooks asserts that the beginning of a narrative is an arousal of intention in reading; a middle is kept in a state of tension through postponement or detour; and an ending is a satisfying discharge of textual energy (101–03). As Clayton comments in noting examples of erotic phrasing, Brooks's diction bolsters the contention that linear narrative parallels male desire. Brooks speaks, for instance, of the "forepleasure" of reading, the "pleasuring in and from delay" (103), the threat of "premature discharge" (109), and the ultimate "gratification of discharge" (102).

In a linear narrative, then, the male takes on a subject position and the female, by default, assumes the object position. She is governed by the agency of the male, which has the effect of permitting him to "write" her story and chart her appropriate conduct, especially in the context of the prototypical Victorian marriage plot. As DuPlessis argues, "All forms of dominant narrative ... are tropes for the sex-gender system as a whole" (43). *African Farm* departs from that narrative model through its preoccupation with "women's time," which suggests female sexuality through its evocation of the "unnameable *jouisssance*" that Kristeva attributes to cyclical and monumental temporality (16). As Susan Winnett argues, alternate models of female desire can be posited in opposition to the pattern of male desire to present a "different narrative logic" (509). Exchanging "the male experience [for] an analogously representable female one" (580) allows for a reevaluation of narrative "incipience, repetition, and closure" that is indicative of "*an* experience (not *the* experience) of the female body" (509).[10] Indeed, as Hélène Cixous remarks, one cannot "talk about *a* female sexuality, uniform, homogeneous, classifiable into codes" ("Laugh of the Medusa" 876). Applied to narrative, the multifariousness of female desire implies a broad textual space that allows for a multiplicity of interpretation.

One technique that enables *African Farm* to expand hermeneutic alternatives is allegory, a narrative approach that leads to the second route by which feminine time dominates Part Two. Allegory resonates with female temporality through the sense of infinity that this emblematic narrative form imparts, since an allegory both enlarges one text to create others and, as Scott McCracken argues, represents a kind of *écriture feminine*.[11] In its allegorical moments, *African Farm* departs from the pragmatic concerns and realistic constraints of linear narrative to privilege heterogeneity over homogeneity and generate an endless signifying chain that undermines the teleological reading experience. In Roland Barthes's terms, the text becomes "a galaxy of signifiers" instead of "a structure of signifieds"; the reader encounters the text through "several entrances, none of which can be authoritatively declared to be the main one" (5). Rather than a univocal text that constricts meaning, *African Farm* problematizes and extends meaning.

Allegory thus encourages a transgressive form of reading—a feminine form of reading, if juxtaposed against the appropriate response to the ultimate patriarchal narrative, the Bible. In nineteenth-century culture, the Bible generally was to be read as a historical account, devoid of readerly interpretation; Victorians tended to view allegory negatively because of its implication that the literal meaning of the text was not necessarily verifiable.[12] In *African Farm,* both Waldo and his father are transgressive Bible readers, for both apply subjective interpretations: Otto, through his writing of Bonaparte Blenkins into the text; and Waldo, by extending beyond the Bible to create his own vision of Christ. In effect, then, allegory provides a means of rewriting the quintessential patriarchal story and opening up interpretive possibilities. By allying allegory most definitively with Waldo, the text distances him even further from masculine time and the prescriptive gender roles that linear narrative enforces.

The most striking example of allegory in the novel proceeds from one of Waldo's artistic works, a carved cenotaph. Temporal associations immediately undercut the phallic inference of a columnar grave post, for the cenotaph not only suggests monumental time through the permanence of art, but also signifies cyclical time through the similarity of the creative to the procreative process. Like Waldo's first work in Part One, a model of a sheep-shearing machine, the cenotaph is depicted in maternal terms; as critical commentary has noted, both works required nine months to complete. For his first procreative effort, Waldo "made a machine" (77), paralleling the notion of "making a baby," and he treats it as would a tender mother. The tiny model is kept in his breast; the machine is "his first-born"; and like any mother, he heard no "deception in the voice that praised his child" (106). Unlike the cenotaph, however, the sheep-shearing machine is associated with linear temporality through its utility, thereby serving the civilizing projects of linear time. As such, the sheep-shearing machine is not allowed to survive into Part Two, since the textual environment is purged of conventional masculine characters and influence. The machine's destruction ironically comes through the foot of Bonaparte Blenkins, the character most closely bound to masculine time, in the closing pages of Part One.

Conversely, the cenotaph is separated from the realm of linear time, both through its status as a marker of the dead father and through its primarily aesthetic rather than utilitarian purpose. Moreover, the cenotaph serves as a polysemic symbol of feminine temporality: the post is doubly associated with cyclical time through its "*laboured* resemblance to *nature*" (157, emphasis added); and the work is bound to monumental time through the eternalizing role of art, since art provides a vehicle for recuperating all manifestations of time. As Gilles Deleuze stresses in another context, "the signs of art define time regained: an absolute primordial time, a veritable eternity" (86).

The cenotaph's connection to allegory devolves from the musings of "Waldo's stranger," who briefly wanders onto the karoo and considers the hermeneutic possibilities of the carving:

> "Certainly," said the stranger, "the whole of the story is not written here, but it is suggested. And the attribute of all true art, the highest and the lowest, is this—that it says more than it says, and takes you away from itself. It is a little door that opens into an infinite hall where you may find what you please. Men thinking to detract say, 'People read more in this or that work of genius than was ever written in it,' not perceiving that they pay the highest compliment.... There is nothing so universally intelligible as truth. It has a thousand meanings, and suggests a thousand more.... Your little carving represents some mental facts as they really are, therefore fifty different true stories might be read from it." (169)

Truth, the stranger implies, is subjective rather than Cartesian, recalling Waldo's denial of the existence of a transcendental signified. Meaning thus is not imposed by the creator of art but is produced by its observers, each of whom may read a different story from it. The stranger's conception of art favors a reading that resembles Barthes's notion of the writerly text, one through which "everything signifies ceaselessly and several times, but without being delegated to a great final ensemble, to an ultimate structure" (12). The stranger, in effect, is advocating that all art be read as allegory. In that way, narrative escapes the constraints of a Barthesian readerly text and its limitation of signifying activity through an implicit claim that it always already reproduces "reality."

The verbal art of allegory is particularly suggestive of monumental time in its departure from the realistic settings that tend to characterize nineteenth-century linear novels. As Cherry Clayton observes, "Schreiner saw allegory as an impassioned rhythmical utterance which blended thought and feeling," inserting allegorical sections into her body of texts (*Woman's Rose* 7). Indeed, Schreiner's allegories were themselves likened to paintings. An anonymous review in the *Athenaeum* attributed to Arthur Symons compared Schreiner's written allegories to George Watts's painted allegories, praising Schreiner's vision in her "poems in prose" (46). Allegory, according to the review, "may be considered the essence of all art, all art being symbol, and allegories themselves pure symbols." Schreiner "seems to have put the soul of her soul" into her allegories: "they express, in the only form possible, that passion for abstract ideas which in her lies deeper than any other."

In *African Farm,* the connection between verbal and pictorial art arises not only through the allegory of Waldo's stranger, but also through Schreiner's novelistic technique. Through the erratic use of dreams, digressions, and episodic dead-ends, the text as a whole seems allegorical[13] and subsumed within monumental time rather than the linear time that tends to dominate narratives. Verbal pictures defamiliarize quotidian events and, in effect, transform them into art. Monumental time is transposed onto linear time as the ordinary is converted into the extraordinary.

Yet the problematization of linear narrative time serves also to interrogate the prevalent notion of progress. With its sequential movement from quiescence to a series of interrelated activities that propel it to a resolute conclusion, a linear narrative mimics the conception of progress embraced by Victorians, which similarly presupposed a chain of events moving to a desired end. Each link in that chain represented a segment of a teleological pattern in which civilization advanced to a more complex and elevated position. Schreiner parts company with this view, however, in questioning its Darwinian premise that the "fittest" members of a species form the vanguard of progress.[14] Translated into gender as well as class and racial terms, the "fittest" represent the harbingers of each advanced era: the men of the dominant culture who guide the destiny of British evolution. For Schreiner, this elitist view stems from erroneous assumptions that the advancements of the few overshadow the static plight of the many. Progress, in her estimation, requires the betterment of all: "permanent human advance," Schreiner proclaims in *From Man to Man*, "must be united advance" (166).

Dissolving the Boundaries 211

Schreiner's perception of progress is articulated at length by the South African protagonist of *From Man to Man,* an unfinished text penned in the *fin de siècle* and early years of the next century.[15] Despite an intellectual precocity demonstrated through an early fascination with reading and biology, Rebekah enacts the traditional fate of a Victorian heroine: marriage, motherhood, and self-sacrifice. Wed to a philandering cousin whose frequent absences and domestic indifference leave her to shoulder familial responsibilities alone, Rebekah can indulge her voracious interest in books, science, and writing only in the occasional moments her duties leave free. During one rare interlude, Rebekah ponders the extinction of past civilizations and its implications for progress:

> It was the old, old problem that had always fascinated her: why, when a nation or a race or a dominant class has reached a certain point of culture and material advance, has it always seemed to fall back from it, and the nation or race or class to be swept away? Always the march of human progress has died out there, to be taken up again by some other race or class . . . to die out there also after a time, never proceeding persistently in a straight line. . . . Was it futile for us to hope that human advance might ever proceed persistently and unbroken in one direction? (162)

Discarding her previous belief that this pattern was "organic and therefore inevitable" (163), Rebekah surmises that progress exists only when each societal segment is included. We are reminded here of Auguste Comte's view of progress, in which women would significantly participate in the upward movement of humanity.[16]

> That such a minute section of humanity has never been able to maintain its advance proves nothing except that humanity, being intimately in its nature a solidarity and a whole with all its parts reacting on one another, one minute fragment can never move very far ahead of the mass without ultimately being drawn back, either by internal disintegration, brought about through that body in the society itself which has not been included in the advance, or through external and violent contact with other parts of the race which have not shared its advance. (*From Man to Man* 163)

From Man to Man, however, offers no hope that Rebekah's notion of progress can be achieved, specifically in relation to a woman's prospects. In following the customary form of the linear narrative, *From Man to Man* reinscribes the textual destiny characteristic of other Victorian heroines whose "unwomanly" interests must be channeled into the proper gender role. *African Farm,* however, does hold promise that other possibilities can be realized in future generations. By breaking apart the sequential movement of narrative through its interjections of allegory, stray characters, dreams, polemical pronouncements, and desultory asides, *African Farm* converts textual time into an eternal present. There is no sense of advancement in this novel, for each incident or tangent connects only loosely to other narrative components, creating an amorphous whole rather than a series of progressive steps. The novel's formless structure more closely resembles Schreiner's conception of the true definition of progress: a rejection of dominant evolutionary presumptions in favor of an organic human community that endures across time. Science, Schreiner hints in *From Man to Man,* can offer a vehicle for reimagining progress if its tenets are applied iconoclastically. Rather than reifying a teleological philosophy, science can position the past as a vibrant and inseparable part of the present:

> Slowly advancing knowledge has forced on us an entirely new view of the Universe.
> ... For us once again the Universe has become one, a whole, and it lives in all its parts. Step by step advancing knowledge has shown us the internetting lines of action and reaction which bind together all that we see and are conscious of.
> ... [T]he fossil I dug out on the mountain side this morning, rightly studied, may throw light on the structure and meaning of the hand that unearths it. ... I can see long unbroken lines of connection.... [B]etween the life that has been and the life that is, I am able to see nowhere a sharp line of severance, but a great, pulsating, always interacting whole. (154–55)

Through its negative response to the progressive and realist conventions found in *From Man to Man, African Farm* has drawn divergent critical commentary. Some critics firmly place *African Farm* within a realist tradition,[17] often citing the text's sexual component as a harbinger of the "new realism" that preoccupied such figures as Thomas Hardy, Eliza Lynn Linton, and George Moore.[18] My reading of *African Farm* emphasizes its departure from formal realism. Although the categorization of texts as "realist" is itself problematic, since plot trajectories and closures differ widely, the texts nevertheless tend to reach a decisive conclusion, whether satisfactory or not. *African Farm*'s preface ambiguously situates the text on the boundary of realism, both conveying and denying that the novel fits the generic pattern to allow for a play with its conventions. In one respect, the preface characterizes its subject matter as "far removed from the round of English daily life" and "the ideal representation of familiar things" (27). In critiquing the "stage method" of narrative in which "we know with an immutable certainty that at the right crises" every character will "act his part" to impose a "sense of satisfaction" and "completeness," Schreiner opts for "the method of the life we all lead" in which "nothing can be prophesied" so that "[w]hen the curtain falls no one is ready." That critique, however, both rejects the teleological plot—the "stage method"—and embraces realism's desire to capture vignettes of "the life we all lead." Similarly, Schreiner elusively situates her text by commenting that the realist novelist "paint[s] the scenes among which he has grown," confined to "the facts [that] creep in upon him" (28). Restricted to the real—"the grey pigments" of the narrative palette—such a novelist cannot explore other possibilities, for "[t]hose brilliant phases and shapes which the imagination sees in far-off lands are not for him to portray." For Schreiner, however, the latter scenes are the very ones that a novelist should depict; her textual project is to promote a Barthesian signifying play that allows imaginative hermeneutic alternatives to emerge.

The Role of Acculturation

The interpretive space that unfolds in *African Farm* through the breakdown of linear narrative is presaged by the discussion of temporality that launches Part Two. Like the introductory paragraphs of Part One, the "Times and Seasons" chapter initiating Part Two both establishes and undercuts the prominence of linear time. That attenuation assumes added significance in Part Two, however, through the implications for the cultural production of gender, which represents the third route by which "women's time" undermines its linear counterpart.

The chapter begins with a reference to linear time—"three years had passed" since Waldo had "howled to his God"—and immediately questions its control over human existence: "They say that in the world to come time is not measured out by months and years. Neither is it here. The soul's life has seasons of its own; periods not found in any calendar, times that years and months will not scan" (137). The preeminence of linear time over individual lives is undercut by the insertion of monumental temporality, since the time in which the "soul's life" is measured predominates over the methods used to gauge mortal life. The passage posits an opposition through these dissimilar forms of measurement. Linear time is calculated methodically in specific units through "months and years," while the "soul's life" cannot be divided into neat calendrical categories. Instead, it is governed by the more primal rhythms of the seasons and the cyclical time of nature. The dichotomy between the two temporal forms is immediately resolved in favor of the monumental time of the soul, for linear time lacks the power even to "scan" or comprehend it. Such a resolution is crucial to a reading of the remainder of the chapter in its assessment of the development of subjectivity, for that discussion calls into question the formation of gendered roles.

The first stage of the developmental pattern unveiled in the chapter associates Waldo's early years with sensory experiences.[19] The first year of life issues from a "shadowy background" into "pictures of startling clearness" that are "indelibly printed in the mind" through sensory activity: "the taste of the bread and milk in our mouth," "the red sunset . . . reflected in our basin" (137), and "the feel and smell of the first orange we ever see" (138). The significance of these sensory memories comes from their association with lack, in the Lacanian sense, in this early stage. "[A] feeling of longing comes over us," the text asserts, "unutterable longing, we cannot tell for what . . . and oh, we want it, we want—we do not know what." The implication here, reinforced elsewhere in the text, is that desire is not innate but culturally shaped by the Other.

In the next developmental section, culture's decisive role in determining subjectivity emerges more overtly. Kristevan linear time intersects with both psycholinguistic and psychoanalytic valences by situating a simulacrum of the mirror stage within language, thereby foregrounding the influence of the symbolic order in recognition of the self:

> In the day we learn our letters, and are troubled because we cannot see why k-n-o-w should be know, and p-s-a-l-m psalm. They tell us because it *is* so.
> . . . [S]uddenly it strikes us, Who are we? This I, what is it? We try to look in upon ourself, and ourself beats back upon ourself. Then we get up in great fear and run home as hard as we can. We can't tell anyone what frightened us. We never quite lose that feeling of *self* again. (138–39)

Subjectivity is determined within the language of the Father: one comes to "know" through the "psalm," a signifier of patriarchal culture through its connection to Christianity. This culture is represented as natural and impervious to challenge, since a child's questioning of its logic can be indisputably countered, "because it *is* so." With the mirror stage positioned in the symbolic order in this passage, the self is indistinguishable from the Other; the question of "who are we?" can be answered only through the image of the culturally reflected Other as "ourself beats back upon ourself." The unlikelihood of escaping from that reflection is perhaps the source of the "great fear" that the child experiences through the suspicion that one never loses the culturally determined "self" again.[20]

That conjecture is borne out elsewhere in the text, in a much later passage focusing specifically on Lyndall. As she ponders her reflection in a mirror, the mature Lyndall gazes at "[t]he large dark eyes from the glass [that] looked back at her" as "[s]he looked deep into them" (242):

> There was a world of assurance in their still depths. So they had looked at her ever since she could remember, when it was but a small child's face above a blue pinafore. "We shall never be quite alone, you and I," she said; "we shall always be together, as we were when we were little."
> ... "Dear eyes! We will never be quite alone till they part us; —till then!" (242–43)

As in the "Times and Seasons" passage, the self and its mirrored Other are inextricably linked, from earliest memories to eventual death.

Yet, as in earlier references to its tyranny, linear time is conquered by monumental time. The "Times and Seasons" chapter heightens that effect through the insertion of monumental time within the final stage of development, suggesting that the cultural influences bound to linear time are attenuable. In the "new life" that proceeds from the "new time" (149), the characteristics traditionally linked to female subjectivity enervate the abilities conventionally connected with linear time:

> Has a new soul crept into this old body, that even our intellectual faculties are changed? We marvel; not perceiving that what a man expends in prayer and ecstasy he cannot have over for acquiring knowledge. You never shed a tear or create a beautiful image, or quiver with emotion, but you pay for it at the practical, calculating end of your nature. You have just so much force: when the one channel runs over the other runs dry. (151)

Feminine time seems pervasive and insinuative, quietly contesting the omnipotence of linear time as the former "crept" into the body. Through its influence, "women's time" alters the temper of mental capacities by reallocating intellectual energy from linear pursuits ("acquiring knowledge" to serve one's "practical, calculating end") to the emotional register conventionally indicative of female subjectivity. "Ecstasy" is linked with mysticism; the shedded "tear" and "quiver" call attention to female physicality as opposed to male rationality; and the "beautiful image" is provided through art. Monumental time is immediately favored as the channel "that runs over," since the next paragraph begins: "And now we turn to Nature. All these years we have lived beside her, and we have never seen her; now we open our eyes and look at her" (151).

The chapter reiterates the relative power of monumental time as death within nature signifies not an endpoint but part of an infinite whole:

> This thing we call existence; is it not a something which has its roots far down below in the dark, and its branches stretching out into the immensity above, which we among the branches cannot see? Not a chance jumble; a living thing, a *One*. The thought gives us intense satisfaction, we cannot tell why. (153)

In the chapter's final sentence, the dominance of linear time is vanquished, for "we begin to live again" (154).

The effect of culture in shaping gender positions, suggested briefly in "Times and Seasons," emerges elsewhere in the novel through Lyndall's musings as she discusses the subject with Waldo:

> We all enter the world little plastic beings, with so much natural force, perhaps, but for the rest—blank; and the world tells us what we are to be, and shapes us by the ends it sets before us. To you it says—*Work*! and to us it says—*Seem*! . . . And so the world makes men and women.
> . . . They begin to shape us to our cursed end . . . when we are tiny things in shoes and socks. . . . We fit our sphere as a Chinese woman's foot fits her shoe, exactly, as though God had made both—and yet He knows nothing of either. (188–89)

Recognizing that childhood is the formative period in which culture inculcates gender roles, Lyndall later comments, "The first six years of our life make us; all that is added later is veneer" (193). In expressing such sentiments, this New Woman figure anticipates the views Schreiner would elucidate in her 1911 *Woman and Labor*. Asserting in the nonfictional text that there is "no difference" between the sexes at birth (187),

Schreiner instead attributes gender roles solely to cultural influence:

> If we examine the physical phenomenon of sex as it manifests itself in the human creature, we find, in the first stages of the individual's existence, no difference discernible... between those germs which are ultimately to become male or female.
> ... The intelligence, emotions, and desires of the human infant at birth differ not at all perceptibly, as its sex may be male or female; and such psychic differences as appear to exist in later childhood are undoubtedly very largely the result of artificial training. (187–89)

If Waldo's experiences in "Times and Seasons" and elsewhere in the novel impart a sense of redemption issuing from the breakdown of culturally imposed gender roles, then Lyndall's experiences attest to their oppressiveness. Like the mild Waldo, the restless Lyndall is unsuited for the gender role imposed upon her. While the maternal and unambitious Waldo manifests qualities linked with female subjectivity, the forceful and ambitious Lyndall reveals a predilection to the traits associated with male subjectivity. The distance between the two characters is marked early in the text through their divergent relationships to art when, surrounded by ancient Bushman paintings, Waldo expounds upon his relationship to the aesthetic renderings:

> "Sometimes I lie under that little hill with my sheep, and it seems that the stones are really speaking—speaking of the old things, of the time when the strange fishes and animals lived that are turned into stone now.
> ... "But we will be gone soon, and only the stones will lie on here, looking at everything like they look now. I know it is I who am thinking," the fellow added slowly, "but it seems as though it were they who were talking. Has it never seemed so to you, Lyndall?"
> "No, it never seems so to me," she answered. (49–50)

Waldo recognizes not only the eternal element of art in that the stones will outlive human existence, but also displays imaginative capacity in listening to them "really speaking." Further binding Waldo to "women's time" is his customary immersion in nature when contemplating the Bushman drawings, since he habitually does so while lying beneath a hill as he tends his sheep. Lyndall, however, lacks the imaginative component to fathom artistry and infinitude, considering the drawings literally and remaining oblivious to their creators' voices. Significantly, Lyndall sits with her back to the paintings (44) as she and Waldo discuss their implications.

As critics have noted, Lyndall is Waldo's converse, since she far more convincingly embodies the masculine traits encountered in Victorian texts. The contrast between Lyndall's pragmatism and Waldo's imaginativeness is particularly perceptible in the juxtaposition of the narratives related by the two characters in the Bushman chapter. Preceding Waldo's discourse on art is Lyndall's encomium on Napoleon, "the greatest man who ever lived" (47), which mirrors her pragmatism and literality in its formal similarity to a sequential historical account. Lyndall claims to "*know* what [Napoleon] thought" (48), underscoring her affinity to the male ambition that Napoleon so definitively represents. To Lyndall, only a narrative's single "truth," rather than its interpretive valences, carries meaning.

Lyndall's preference for the drive and directness underlying the projects of linear time becomes apparent when she chastises the desultory Waldo:

> If you go into the world aimless, without a definite object, dreaming—dreaming, you will be definitely defeated, bamboozled, knocked this way and that. . . . It does not matter what you choose—be a farmer, business-man, artist, what you will—but know your aim, and live for that one thing. . . . Anything is possible to a man who knows his end and moves straight for it, and for it alone. (215)

Lyndall crafts her admonition in words and images signifying linearity, which she favors over the denigrated opposites of reverie and uncertainty: "definitely," "aim," "one thing," "end," "straight," "alone," and even the verb "will" entail forceful movement in a single direction. Yet Lyndall's acculturation as a "non-linear" female pervades her syntax in this passage, intimating that she is herself blocked from such linear pursuits. In the first sentence of the passage, for example, Lyndall attains her point indirectly, reiterating the notion of dreaminess by piling on synonymous terms ("aimless," "without a definite object") and even repeating the word "dreaming," before proceeding to another string of substitutions for failure ("bamboozled, knocked this way and that"). The next sentence follows a similarly circuitous pattern. Though Lyndall affirms that "[i]t does not matter what you choose," she nevertheless elucidates a brief vocational catalog from which Waldo could select and concludes the sentence by repeating the mandates of knowing one's aim and living for it.

Dissolving the Boundaries 219

Despite her fascination with the trappings of masculinity, Lyndall reveals her interpellation within conventional gender roles, for she desires material success to fulfill the culturally created picture of an ideal woman:

> "When I am grown up," she added, the flush on her delicate features deepening at every word, "there will be nothing that I do not know. I shall be rich, very rich; and I shall wear not only for best, but every day, a pure white silk, and little rosebuds, like the lady in Tant' Sannie's bedroom, and my petticoats will be embroidered, not only at the bottom, but all through."
>
> The lady in Tant' Sannie's bedroom was a gorgeous creature from a fashion sheet, which the Boer-woman, somewhere obtaining, had pasted up at the foot of her bed, to be profoundly admired by the children. (46)

Lyndall's desire for the knowledge and power of the male immediately collapses into a yearning for the signifiers of femininity, the magnificent clothing that she covets. Her description of the gown is itself telling, for it further binds her to the cultural vision of feminine apotheosis through its Marian resonances: the "pure white" of the silk conjures the virginal purity of the Madonna, while the "little rosebuds" recall traditional allusions to that female icon. The cultural influences defining Lyndall's image of feminine perfection are foregrounded by the reference to Tant' Sannie's "fashion-sheet," since notions of appropriate garb are wholly shaped by social opinion. Indeed, the picture emblematizes the transmission of cultural values across generations. It holds almost iconic status in the household, placed upon an altar-like bed where it can be worshipped.

The oppressiveness of gender roles is further apparent through the mode of Lyndall's death, which seemingly ensues from her entrapment within essentialist conceptions of the female. Lyndall's fatal assumption of the maternal role proves deadly to her child as well. The baby survives merely two hours after birth "and the mother herself almost went with it" (269), for Lyndall cannot fulfill the part of the nurturing mother and participate in the eternalizing project of procreation. Maternity indirectly causes her death, as she visits the baby's grave on a "drizzly day," where she sits on the "wet ground" with "the rain dripping from her hat and shawl" (269). The dominant water imagery ironically suggests the female's life-giving amniotic fluid that permits gestation and birth. Enveloped by water, Lyndall herself becomes a kind of fetal entity, implying that the traditional perceptions of motherhood bring forth a psychic regression in terms of female subjectivity. Indeed, the dampness initiates the debilitating illness that eventually takes Lyndall's life.

The deleterious effects of motherhood on female subjectivity traced here resonate with similar scenes in *Undine*. While meandering through the countryside, Undine chances upon a socially outcast woman carrying a newborn infant, the illegitimate son of Undine's former lover. The imminent death of the sickly infant presages Undine's own experience with motherhood, for both she and the child she bears for her husband hover near death after the birth. Though both survive the natal crisis, Undine's baby, "a puny shrivelled thing" (203), never thrives. The connection between motherhood and death becomes stronger when the baby lies dying, its short breaths muted by the sounds of another manifestation of Schreiner's ominously ticking timepieces:

> On the mantelpiece the bronze clock ticked regularly, but the breathing of the child was so low it could not be heard.
> ... She did not hear the clock strike or know how the moments passed, till the white lids dropped slowly. There was no sigh, there was no change, but when she laid her hand upon its breast she knew that the baby was dead. (210)

The indictment of gender roles underlying this scene, as well as in the exposition of Rebekah's suffocating existence in *From Man to Man*, takes on harsher, even violent overtones in Schreiner's late-century allegorical short stories. Responding specifically to motherhood, "Three Dreams in a Desert" presents a nursing mother who is bitten so savagely by the son at her breast "that the blood ran down on to the ground" (66). In the more generalized treatment of gender characterizing "I Thought I Stood"—a brief vignette consisting of only four paragraphs—an unidentified speaker stands before God's heavenly throne to arraign Man for his crimes against Woman: "He has taken my sister . . . and has stricken her, and wounded her, and thrust her out into the streets; there she lies prostrate. His hands are red with blood" (109). Yet the short narratives do promise redemption if gender roles are contested, as in the optimistic "Life's Gifts." In this one-page story, the personification of Life offers a dreaming woman her choice between love and freedom. When she selects the latter, Life advises that she has chosen wisely, for "the day will come" when Life will "bear both gifts in one hand" (99). The reader is to infer, of course, that love and freedom need not be mutually exclusive; instead, a reconception of gender can lead to a beneficial rather than harmful union of the sexes. "In A Far-Off World" makes a similar point, since the narrator envisions an idyllic world in which "a man and woman . . . had one work, and they walked together side by side" (45).

In *African Farm*, Schreiner's response to the female condition is to undo restrictive gender constructions by contesting the cultural identification of traits as specifically masculine or feminine. In effect, the text advocates the recuperation of the "classical conception of bisexuality" that Cixous posits (883)—one premised not upon the notion of fullness and lack but upon the internal coexistence of both sexes, "variously manifest and insistent according to each person, male or female" (884). Such a notion of bisexuality assumes the "nonexclusion either of the difference or of one sex," presupposing a continual movement between gender positions. Schreiner's *fin de siècle* short stories demonstrate that she considered the psychic bisexuality posited in *African Farm* as the apex of human development. In "The Sunlight Lay Across My Bed," for instance, a dreaming protagonist visits heaven and converses with God, who advises that "[i]n the least Heaven sex reigns supreme; in the higher it is not noticed; but in the highest it does not exist" (156–57).[21] Similarly, "Three Dreams in a Desert" hints that women's struggle to break down gender roles—though a hard-fought battle by which a "bridge ... shall be built with our bodies"—will eventually benefit "*[t]he entire human race*" (68). The result will be a form of "heaven ... [o]n earth" where "brave women and brave men" will stride "hand in hand" (69).

Schreiner explored a similar gender fluidity in *From Man to Man*, again employing a dream motif to allow Rebekah to shift between male and female personas:

> Her thoughts ran around in a dreamy way now. How nice it would be to be a man. She fancied she was one till she felt her very body grow strong and hard and shaped like a man's. She felt the great freedom opened to her, no place shut off from her, the long chain broken, all work possible for her, no law to say this and this is for women, you are woman. ... Oh, how beautiful to be a man and be able to take care of and defend all the creatures weaker and smaller than you are. (202)

As we have seen, however, *From Man to Man* offers no practical transcendence of gender roles. Yet in *African Farm* such a possibility is not only envisioned but realized by altering the sex of the desiring subject. In ascribing to a male character the wish to cross gender boundaries, *African Farm* suggests in this regard—as in the earlier contrasting scenes featuring unnervingly ticking timepieces, both in *African Farm* and *Undine*—that only males can successfully contest cultural mores and, through their pioneering efforts, enable women to follow in their paths. This supposition intersects with Schreiner's view of progress, predicated on the notion that only through a commonality of interests can both male and female advance. As articulated in *Woman and Labor*, the sexes are like oxen yoked together; "they must ultimately remain stationary or move forward together" (264). To achieve progress, then, the New Woman must join with the revolutionary figure that Schreiner identifies in *Woman and Labor* as a "New Man" (272), a "perfect ideal" (271) who can work "side by side" with the New Woman (267).

In *African Farm*, the itinerant farm-worker Gregory Rose provides an inchoate model of the New Man. An especially mutable character in terms of gender roles, Gregory is variously described as a "new man" (174, for example), "a true woman" (197), and "a man-woman." Rejecting his patriarchal legacy and an attendant sense of history, Gregory chooses feminized pink stationery "as more suitable to the state of his feelings" than the sheets displaying his family crest (175). His sampling of different initials before his name (205) attests to his protean identity, but more indicative of his sexual ambiguity is his proclivity for cross-dressing, which represents the most overt and literal experimentation with gender in the novel. Gregory adopts the guise of the traditional female profession of nurse and establishes an oddly bisexual relationship with the dying Lyndall whom he attends. Assuming that Gregory is female, Lyndall asks him to caress her foot, remarking that "[i]t makes it better when you kiss it" (280).

That incident opens the way for the text to explore a new approach to considering gender. We can read Lyndall's illness as providing the vehicle for recuperating this "original bisexuality"; by reversing linear time, Lyndall can retrace and undo the Lacanian mode of maturation and cultural development elucidated in "Times and Seasons." Through the pre-Oedipal regression impelled by her illness, Lyndall can return to the inherently bisexual state that Cixous contends all human beings occupy, one marked by multiplicity and changeability. Such a conception of bisexuality breaks apart phallocentric binary oppositions by allowing a Derridean play of difference through which "meaning" is never rigidly imposed upon gender but instead is made only tentative.

The lengthy passage in which Lyndall reverses linear time takes place soon after she falls fatally ill from maintaining her rainy vigil at her child's graveside. Interspersed through the passage are multiple references to the gradual infantilization process that parallels her illness: thus, for example, "day by day the body grew lighter" (273). Lyndall progressively becomes more childlike, distinguished by her "little hands" (274) and "tiny foot" (280), and at one point she assumes a fetal position with "her body curled up, and drawn close to the wall" (275). The body continues to shrink, decreasing to the size "of a small child over its first shoes" before becoming "so small and slight" that Lyndall resembles "a small doll" (281). At that point Lyndall figuratively returns to the mirror stage as she literally gazes into a mirror at her reflected Other:

> She looked into the glass on the opposite wall. Such a queenly little figure in its pink and white. Such a transparent little face, refined by suffering into an almost angel-like beauty. The face looked at her; she looked back, laughing softly.
> . . . "I am nearly there," she said.
> Then she groped blindly.
> "Oh, I cannot see! I cannot see! Where am I?" she cried. (281–82)

The splitting of the infant between self and Other is uncannily reproduced as the passage unfolds and Lyndall regards the face peering back at her. The scene resonates with the description of this developmental stage in "Times and Seasons" but signals an important change in suggesting a feminist reworking of the Lacanian model of maturation. In the latter passage, Lyndall returns to the state preceding entry into the symbolic order and the cultural construct it reinforces. At this point, the regressive process is almost complete ("I am nearly there"). As death comes upon her, Lyndall concludes her backward journey through the symbolic order, losing the power of speech:

> The dying eyes on the pillow looked into the dying eyes in the glass; they knew that their hour had come. She raised one hand and pressed the stiff fingers against the glass. They were growing very stiff. She tried to speak to it, but she would never speak again.
> . . . The dead face that the glass reflected was a thing of marvellous beauty and tranquillity. (284)

The implications for female identity presented in Lyndall's final scene gain clarity when mapped onto Garrett Stewart's model of Victorian death theorized through the mechanisms of epitome and displacement. Death by epitome, Stewart argues, "condense[s] . . . a character's psychology" (11) in that "essence [is] tested and found true (to itself), life raised to the power of its own (however negative) potential" (14). Death by displacement represents "a death undergone by proxy," which is "overseen by a surviving protagonist" (17). In the first case, Lyndall's "deathbed consciousness," to borrow Stewart's terms, becomes a "revelation (just) in time of the self in time," and thus "identity's fullest because final (and so complete) unfolding to itself" (16). Only in death can Lyndall attain a full comprehension of herself as ungendered subject, attaining the sole moments of peace she achieves in the novel. In the second case, Lyndall's mirrored Other becomes a kind of self-proxy, an alter ego who observes her as she observes it in her dying moments. The mirror serves, in effect, to distance Lyndall from herself as a separated entity through which the psychic trauma of death shifts from a paralytically frightening immediacy, signaled by her anxious cry as she "groped blindly," to a more ontological register in which the whole notion of identity becomes the primary issue. In that way, the novel turns the reader, too, into a proxy for Lyndall, enabling us to move beyond a localized death to a more complex questioning of acculturation and identity.

Because Lyndall's reverse progression through the developmental process ends in death, however, *African Farm* stresses the difficulty of challenging conventional gender roles. Like other Victorian heroines who defy patriarchal dictates—George Eliot's Maggie Tulliver, Emily Brontë's Catherine Earnshaw, or Bram Stoker's Lucy Westenra—Lyndall must be condemned to death. As a successful rebel against gender norms, there is no space she can ultimately occupy in nineteenth-century culture. In DuPlessis's terms, "Death comes for a female character when she has a jumbled, distorted, inappropriate reaction to the 'social script' or plot designed to contain her" (15). Lyndall's regression to a preverbal state of silence suggests that women who contest Victorian standards neither have a voice within the culture nor are able to effect substantive changes in the perception of gender roles.

The text's condemnation of gender positions in Lyndall's death scene and in other explicated passages is ultimately underscored by the novel's approach to closure. The text ends through a virtual non-closure, suggesting the open-ended textuality that Cixous and other feminist theorists advocate to oppose linear narrative. The novel's final paragraphs ambiguously situate Waldo in an unconscious state that could signify either sleep or death. Marked by equivocation rather than certainty through this irresolution of the plot, the novel's ending refuses to allow meaning to be teleologically imposed on the narrative as in a Barthesian readerly text; there is no climatic resolution as in the paradigmatic linear narrative that retrospectively validates a narrow gender script.

Rather, the text implies through Waldo's uncertain fate that the story does not end within linear narrative time but instead extends beyond the conclusion within the realm of "women's time." There is a sense that the story of Lyndall and Waldo needs to develop beyond the arbitrary endpoint the novelistic form imposes. Indeed, a plot thread earlier suggested the pair's eventual union before being abruptly severed: Waldo unknowingly directed an epistolary outpouring of devotion and support to an already lifeless Lyndall. In Lyndall's death scene, however, the narrator had asked the provocative questions: "Had she ceased from being? Who shall tell us?" (284).[22] Similarly, Waldo's musings on death in the novel's final pages indirectly raise the possibility of narrative continuation in noting, "[T]here is that which never dies—which abides" (290). Thus, the novel is seemingly a segment of an extended story that can be continued within the reader's imagination.[23] In its ending as in its beginning, then, *The Story of an African Farm* valorizes the fluidity of "women's time" over the rigidity of linear time. In so doing, the novel strives to defy the claustrophobic role thrust upon the Victorian woman and her male counterpart, offering a glimpse of hope that someday the New Woman will join with the New Man to chart a more liberatory future.

Afterword:
Pointing the Way to Modernist Time

> Time, unfortunately, though it makes animals and vegetables bloom and fade with amazing punctuality has no such simple effect upon the mind of man. The mind of man, moreover, works with equal strangeness upon the body of time.
>
> —Woolf, *Orlando*

As suggested in my opening chapter, our contemporary critics have frequently labeled the Victorian *fin de siècle* as a prescient manifestation of the disillusionment and literary experimentation that would characterize modernism. Some scholars have even placed the origin of modernism in the 1890s or as early as the 1880s, locating in the final years of Victoria's reign the germ of a preoccupation with a dehumanizing and bewildering society. Only in recent years have fiction writers responding to the New Woman been viewed as nascent modernist authors whose contributions to the genre of the novel have remained unrecognized.

Ann Ardis, for example, credits late-Victorian women writers for innovations in narrative form associated with modernism. Gerd Bjorhovde calls the century's final decades "a pioneering period in the rise of Modernism" (16). Lyn Pykett remarks on the intriguing "points of connection" between New Women texts and modernism (*Engendering Fictions* 57).[1] As important as these attempts to recuperate the contributions of New Woman novelists, however, is the texts' focus on time as an ordering principle exercising an enormous effect on the course of an individual's life, which the modernists were to examine exhaustively in the coming decades.

It is tempting to use a conclusion for a project such as mine to chart the thematic and formal directions that the next generation of novelists would take as they built upon or demystified the achievements of the previous one. The problem, of course, is that such conclusions cannot avoid oversimplifying and homogenizing the complex individualized approaches that emerge in a particular literary period. Nevertheless, with that caveat in mind, it is possible to identify prominent concerns that appear throughout a body of fiction, and the autocracy of time was, for modernists, one of those preoccupations. To do justice to modernist perceptions of time would itself require a study at least as lengthy as this one on the New Woman, but we can, in broad strokes, set out some of the issues that engrossed early twentieth-century novelists.

Modernists, for example, feared that time was ominously becoming a way to commodify existence, with an individual's value being assessed in terms of production and consumption in an increasingly mechanized society. Early twentieth-century writers thus turned to a privileging of the subjective assessment, rather than the public measurement, of time as a strategy for reasserting individuality. In a related vein, modernist texts reveal a fascination with the play of memory within this individualized experience of time. Novels of the period similarly display an anxiety over the despotic effects of a strong historical consciousness, deeming it a stultifying force on the human spirit. Most interesting, perhaps, was the modernists' problematization of the linear form to undermine the tyranny of public time.

The modernist view of time, as Ricardo J. Quinones explains, represented a dramatic departure from the Renaissance sense that time was a series of discrete and precise units—the theorization that enabled subsequent industrial and technological societies to measure productivity in temporal terms. In both eras, Quinones argues, time represented the "forward point of the changing consciousness" (4) that would distinguish the periods. For modernists, however, time came to seem more and more threatening as a vehicle for regimenting existence. As Hans Meyerhoff observes in *Time and Literature*, since time was "looked upon as a commodity like the goods produced in time," it "ultimately converts man himself into a commodity" (115). In contrast to the prevailing view of the nineteenth century, time in the modernist period seemed a force of inevitable dehumanization rather than potential invigoration.

Unlike the Victorians, who turned to "the values of history and continuity" for comfort—locating themselves within a historical span that allowed them to participate in a collective whole of humanity (Quinones 31)—modernists also considered time not as a solacing continuity but a numbing sameness. Spurred by Nietzsche's writings on the abuses of history, modernists saw a veneration for the past as a debilitating drain on contemporary society that foreclosed opportunities for needed change. Quinones assesses the former "triumph of time in history" as instigating "the death of history," for time no longer connoted "the driving energies of the world but rather a blank and empty face . . . or changeless extension" (86). The "historical momentum and sense of coherence" that Quinones attributes to past cultures thus became modernism's "point of departure" (33). To Georg Lukács, "[t]he denial of history, of development, and thus of perspective" represented for modern culture "the mark of true insight into the nature of reality" (34).

The historical values that had once meant reassurance thus no longer seemed applicable in a far different and complex world, since the linear time associated with those values conferred a repetitious, enervating, and meaningless quality upon existence. The modernist response was to disrupt the ideological associations of linear time, returning to, as D. H. Lawrence remarked, an appreciation for "the pagan manner of thought" (*Apocalypse* 97). Arguing that "[o]ur idea of time as a continuity in an eternal, straight line has crippled our consciousness cruelly," Lawrence warned that "we have to drop our own manner of on-and-on-and-on, from a start to a finish, and allow the mind to move in cycles, or to flit here and there over a cluster of images" (97–98). The widespread appeal of ahistoric myth for modernists can be attributed in part to this desire to rupture the bonds of history, rejecting linear time in favor of the cyclical time embraced by ancient civilizations.

Building on Immanuel Kant's repudiation of objective time (Kern 11) as well as Henri Bergson's postulation of time as duration—the notion that time within an individual consciousness represents an incessant flow rather than a series of distinct sequential moments—modernists valued the personal experience of temporality. "The thrust of the age," as Stephen Kern observes in *The Culture of Time and Space*, thus "was to affirm the reality of private time against that of a single public time, and to define its nature as heterogeneous, fluid, reversible" (34). Indeed, Martin Heidegger pointed to, as Françoise Dastur observes, individuals' "very peculiar relation to time, since only on their basis can the nature of time be deciphered"; therefore, "[h]uman beings are not *in* time as are things of nature, but . . . *are* time" (3).[2]

Orlando offers a particularly pertinent reference to the individual perception of time that modernists were endeavoring to explore:

> An hour, once it lodges in the queer element of the human spirit, may be stretched to fifty or a hundred times its clock length; on the other hand, an hour may be accurately represented on the timepiece of the mind by one second. This extraordinary discrepancy between time on the clock and time in the mind is less known than it should be. (98)

The internal "stream of thought" (1:224) that modernist writers attempted to capture stems from this individualized form of temporal perception, influenced by William James's 1890 conception of subjective time in which past, present, and future merge to become "sensibly continuous" and "without breach, crack, or division" (237). The modernist fascination with the nature of memory, grounded in Bergsonian and Jamesian thought, is simply another aspect of the privileging of subjective over objective time.

The assault on the tyranny of public or linear time appears throughout the modernist canon. James Joyce's *Ulysses*, for instance, translates the consciousness of a single day into an elaborate series of reflections and associations that persistently undermine a reader's sense of linear time. Marcel Proust's complex protagonist of *Remembrance of Things Past* continually ponders the workings of memory and the subjective perception of temporal movement. The dreamy narrative of *To the Lighthouse* is interrupted by a brief but distinctive chapter with the suggestive title, "Time Passes." Characters' personal experiences of time in *Mrs. Dalloway* are punctuated by the ominous chiming of Big Ben to foreground, as Paul Ricoeur remarks, "the subtle variations between the time of consciousness and chronological time" (107), through which, as Meyerhoff puts it, "Mrs. Dalloway's whole day constitutes a specious present" (*Time and Literature* 39). Orlando exists for three centuries, significantly entering the nineteenth as a clock tolls in the background and a "huge blackness" rolls over London (225). In *The Return of the Soldier,* Rebecca West characterizes the time of history and civilization as irrecuperably bleak, precarious, and fragmented, unable to provide a sense of continuity across generations. Gudrun muses in *Women and Love* that "she had no father, no mother, no anterior connections" as she repudiates "[t]hat old shadow world, the actuality of the past" (400). Vita Sackville-West follows her female protagonist's movement from a husband's world dominated by linear time to a feminized realm of subjective time in *All Passion Spent*, unequivocally validating the latter over the former.

All of the temporal concerns raised by modernist writers were anticipated in the *fin de siècle* novels about the New Woman. The reverence for history in H. Rider Haggard's *She,* for example, suffered early attacks in the fiction of Thomas Hardy and Mona Caird, while the narrative experimentation of Olive Schreiner's *The Story of an African Farm*, along with a similar play with form that occasionally appears in other novels we have investigated, presages modernist manipulations of the genre. The gender anxieties that these texts articulated in their treatment of time subsequently surface as well in the novels of modernist women writers. One could argue, as does Marianne DeKoven in an essay on "gendered doubleness" in modernist fiction, that a schism marked the oeuvre; "female modernism," DeKoven explains, represents "a separate, previously buried or discredited tradition (or anti-tradition)" in sharp contrast to "high canonical male modernism" (19)—a distinction, I contend, in part attributable to different interpretations of the workings of time.

Novels about the New Woman, then, pointed the way to the modernist perception of time. They were the pioneering texts that helped to focus attention on time's multifarious effects on human consciousness and, in particular, the intricate interrelationships between time and gender. In demonstrating the myriad connections between the Victorian construction of time and the predominant perceptions of gender roles, New Woman narratives contribute substantively to our understanding of the nineteenth-century female's place in society and the subtle means by which that position was naturalized. It is time, then, to recognize the critical significance of this particular component of the New Woman novel, for it identifies temporality as one of the most complex and intriguing aspects of the Woman Question that so obsessed the nineteenth century.

Notes

Chapter 1
Introduction:
Victorian Temporality and the New Woman

1. Jerome Buckley, for instance, comments in *The Triumph of Time* that "[t]he Victorians, at least as their verse and prose reveal them, were preoccupied almost obsessively with time and all the devices that measure time's flight" (1–2). Also see Robin Gilmour's *The Victorian Period* for discussions of the Victorian preoccupation with time.

2. For helpful background on the New Woman, see, for example, Ann Ardis, Karl Beckson, Sally Ledger, Teresa Mangum (*Married, Middlebrow, and Militant*), Lyn Pykett *(The "Improper" Feminine* and *Engendering Fictions*), Jane Eldridge Miller, and Carolyn Christensen Nelson. I use the term "New Woman" broadly in regard to fiction, including both texts that praise or condemn this figure.

3. Also see, for example, Ledger's *The New Woman* (chapter 1), Pykett's *Engendering Fictions* (chapter 2), and Lucy Bland (chapters 2 and 4) for other discussions of the evolutionary aspects of the Woman Question.

4. The figure comes from Ardis (4).

5. As Ledger clarifies, "The New Woman as a category was by no means stable" (10); instead, "[t]he New Woman as a concept was, from its inception, riddled with contradictions" (16).

6. Here and subsequently, I draw my discussions of Victorian conceptions of temporality from numerous sources, both primary and secondary. Among the most useful secondary texts are Buckley's *The Triumph of Time*, Gilmour's *The Victorian Period,* and essays collected in J.T. Fraser's *The Voices of Time*. For background on mid-Victorian temporality, helpful materials include David S. Landes's *Revolution in Time,* Lawrence Wright's

Clockwork Man, and Peter Bowler's *The Invention of Progress*. For the late-Victorian period, pertinent sources include the essays in *The Study of Time* (Fraser et al.) and *The Voices of Time*, as well as Stephen Kern's *The Culture of Time and Space 1880-1918*. For general background on time in the Victorian and other periods, see Francis C. Haber's *The Age of the World*, C.A. Patrides's *Aspects of Time,* and the essay collections noted above.

7. See A. Bowdoin Van Riper's *Men among the Mammoths: Victorian Science and the Discovery of Human Prehistory*, for a discussion of Victorian perceptions on geology and archaeology.

8. See Richard Good's *Victorian Clocks* for descriptions and pictures of the many varieties.

9. Landes cites statistics on watch production to illustrate the claim that "[w]atches became that much more necessary to everyday life" (287) in the nineteenth century. Annual world output, Landes notes, rose from 350,000 to 400,000 watches in the late 1700s to 2.5 million watches 75 years later.

10. Buckley considers the Victorian "sense of history" as "central to the intellectual life of the nineteenth century" (12–13). Gilmour sees "in almost every area of Victorian intellectual life . . . a preoccupation with ancestry and descent, with tracing the genealogy of the present in the past, and with discovering or creating links to a formative history" (25). Similarly, Stephen Toulmin and June Goodfield designate the 1800s as "the Century of History" (232), while Raymond Chapman remarks on the period's "new respect for the value of history" (17) and its "idealisation of the past" (12).

11. Bland makes a similar point in discussing the relationship between science and religion, noting that "on the whole, most evolutionists were not wanting to oppose theology" (70).

12. Haber notes that Christianity also contains "an element of symbolic regeneration," but "it is not the determining characteristic of the Christian view of time" (12).

13. As V.A. Kolve remarks in a study of medieval drama that carries important implications here, the notion of eternity presupposes "timelessness, not infinite time" and "involves a release into a different and unimaginable dimension of experience"; when "[s]et against eternity," Kolve comments in reference to biblical writings, "all historical time is but a brief moment, a thousand years as one day" (117). Invoking Erich Auerbach's model of linear "horizontal" time and a "vertical" time that characterizes "a figural relationship between events," Kolve observes that important historical moments carry significance because of their relationship to God—who is "outside time"—rather than the horizontal relationships between them (119). As Kolve explains, "Human time is the artifact of God," which "is shaped by Him and expresses His truth"; although "[t]ime concerns us

because we are alive in it" as well as our realization that "God's plan for man's redemption can be worked out only in its terms," Christianity nevertheless presupposes "man's real business is eternity" (122).

14. For background on theories of history, see G. J. Whitrow as well as Hans Meyerhoff, Lewis Mumford, Patrides, and Bowler.

15. To Bowler, the concept of progress gained adherents in the Victorian period "because it offered the hope that current changes might be part of a meaningful historical pattern" and provide "the sense of order that Victorians craved" (3).

16. Victorian essayists even identified a culturally induced difference in the very perception of time by men and women (see chapter 5). That distinction prevailed into the twentieth century. A 1904 article in *Science*, published by the American Association for the Advancement of Science, related the results of an experiment that measured the sexes' differing subjective assessments of the passage of time. "In sum," the article reported, "the excess of general inaccuracy in the estimation of the given periods of time on the part of women . . . is no less marked than their tendency to overestimation" (MacDougal 708). A 1905 study claimed to corroborate these results (844).

17. Susan Morgan offers a very different interpretation of the gender implications of history. Morgan argues that "an idea of feminization is at the center of nineteenth-century fiction's ideas of historical process" (12), suggesting that in some fiction, "living in time, in history, is understood as a matter of becoming feminized" (13). Although I find Morgan's argument intriguing and agree in some respects, I take an opposite approach to the gendering of history in that I see history as being strongly masculinized in Victorian fiction.

18. Watches and clocks themselves tended to be associated with men. Landes, for instance, remarks that "[t]he British . . . were not strong on watches for women" (281). An 1842 pamphlet written by the creator of Big Ben characterized the British watch as serviceable but unfashionable to "the young man who studies appearance" (qtd. in Landes 281). The clocks that dominated the British household, as Lawrence Wright comments, were firmly under control of the "[p]aterfamilias [who] alone was authorised to touch the consecrated object" (151).

19. The germ of this gendered view may be the title of Francis Bacon's seventeenth-century treatise "Temporis Partus Masculus," or "The Masculine Birth of Time."

20. Anne McClintock contends that Victorians spatialized time to illustrate differences among groups. "Within this trope," she argues, "the agency of women, the colonized, and the industrial working class are disavowed and projected onto anachronistic space"; they are identified with the "prehistoric, atavistic, and irrational, inherently out of place in the historical time of modernity" (40).

Chapter 2
Buttressing the Binary:
Temporal Dichotomies in *She*

1. Written "at white heat" in six weeks, *She* was "a great and immediate success," Haggard says in his autobiography (*Days* 1:245). Selling thirty thousand copies in the first months after its publication (Cohen 232), *She* was designated in *Sixty Years of Best Sellers* as one of the Victorian texts whose sales reached one million copies (233). Although the novel was devoured by an appreciative public, Victorian reviewers were mixed in their reactions to it. The *Athenaeum*, for instance, deemed *She* a less successful effort than Haggard's *King Solomon's Mines*; *She* is "certainly fascinating," the reviewer noted, "but the treatment is lamentably unequal" to the earlier text (93). The *Pall Mall Gazette* commented that *She* "certainly falls short of excellence," and "[a]t times we are inclined to think it very cheap work" (5). Despite its "energy and intensity of imagination" and a "conception ... so powerful," the *Gazette* said, "we rebel with a sense of injury against the many defects of execution." *Blackwood's*, though remarking that "Haggard has not proved as yet that he has anything that can be called imagination at all," did allow that "invention he has of the most robust kind" (303). Enthusiastic reviews also appeared, however. In the *Academy* Haggard's friend, Andrew Lang, noted that "the more impossible it gets, the better ... Mr. Haggard does it," and the journal applauded Haggard's "astonishing imagination, and a certain *vraisemblance*, which makes the most impossible adventures appear true" to a sympathetic reader (36). The *Spectator* called *She* a "vivid and brilliantly told story" with a "spirited" plot (78).

2. The notion that She represents female essence has received much attention from critics. Sandra Gilbert and Susan Gubar, for instance, argue that She is "an ontological Old Woman" who "brings to the surface everyman's worry about *all* women" (7). In a related vein, Nina Auerbach sees She displaying "the awakened powers of the old, adored woman" (37), while Rebecca Stott categorizes She as a femme fatale. Anne McClintock remarks upon a "well-nigh pathological anxiety about female generative authority" found in Haggard's fiction (235). David Bunn maintains that Ayesha is the "eternal feminine" who is a metaphor for Africa since she "embodies the irrational" (20). Even Freud, as several critics have pointed out, saw She as the avatar of "the eternal feminine" (453).

3. See Patrick Brantlinger, Wendy Katz, and Laura Chrisman, for example, for discussions of *She* as imperialist fiction. In regard to the New Woman connections in *She*, which are my explicit concern, Gilbert and Gubar identify She as a "woman with monstrous powers" who is "in certain ways an entirely New Woman" (6). In a separate discussion, Gilbert notes that the New Woman "vividly suggested an ultimate triumph of otherness" and "would tend to evoke all the other subversive aspirations that were ... being voiced throughout the

British Empire" (*Coordinates* 133). Auerbach similarly asserts that *She* conveyed anxieties about "national and domestic reality" including "the learned and crusading 'new woman'" (37). Ann Ardis remarks that *She*, although appearing several years before the New Woman debate reached its height, "anticipates all the questions to be asked of the New Woman" (140).

4. In a "Suggested Prologue" for a dramatization of *She*, published in *Longman's Magazine*, Haggard foregrounded the centrality of time to *She* through numerous temporal references. Ayesha makes such pronouncements as "[a]ll Time is mine," "I am undying, and there lies the token of my doom," and "I have sown in the grave of Time" (494–95). *She*'s reviewers, however, tended to focus on the novel's moral overtones rather than its temporal undertones. The *Fortnightly Review*, for instance, sniffed at the notion that "there [is] anything delicately marvellous in the central conception of a woman two thousand years old, whose conduct" is "least objectionable" when that of "a commonplace coquette" ("The Fall of Fiction" 330). *Blackwood's*, like the *Academy*, viewed She as an "enchantress" (303). The *Saturday Review* dismissed her as a more forceful version of women "limited to a merely human term of years" (44).

5. Barri J. Gold offers an intriguing interpretation of this patriarchal lineage. In describing the "patriarchal parthenogenesis" of the frame narrative, an "insistent and repetitive removal of mother figures" that provides "a narrative of fathers giving birth to sons," and the "emphatically patrilineal" Vincey family, Gold argues that "traces of female progenitors . . . inevitably surface. In spite of their marginalization, the exceptional presence of these women always threatens the closure of the male genealogy" (306–8). In *Rider Haggard*, Norman Etherington makes the useful observation that "[t]he only member of the family ignored in Haggard's fiction is mother" (89).

6. See, for example, discussions by Chrisman and Etherington, as well as Gilbert and Gubar. The latter two critics additionally address *She*'s "alternative history," along with the text's "illusion of historicity" (10) and the "self-reflexive historicity with which Haggard presents his tale" (11). These critics, along with Bruce Mazlish and Stott, for instance, have also pointed to the scholarly paraphernalia that Haggard employs to emphasize authenticity. Gilbert and Gubar, for example, comment on the novel's "parodic scholarship" (11). My specific interest is the gendered polarization of history and ahistoricity.

7. The Cambridge association is important for two reasons. First, the fact that Cambridge added a separate history tripos to its curriculum attests to the increasing importance that the subject represented in the *fin de siècle*. Second, the fascination with Hellenism in classical scholarship reminds a reader of the homoerotic component of Greek culture with its emphasis on male community and female marginalization.

8. In his annotated version of *She*, Etherington notes that Haggard

rewrote descriptions of the potsherd to correspond to the fake one and revised a reference to one of the translations that was "a little free but quite accurate" to "accurate and elegant" as a result of Andrew Lang's assistance in compiling the translation (214).

9. The reference to Irish histories also offers a gender link. As S. J. Connolly's encyclopedia of Irish history suggests, the nineteenth century saw a movement from "supposed histories" of Ireland "that were in fact justifications of English conquest and colonization" to "serious antiquarian and historical work" by both nationalist and unionist historians, with the latter's ideas often appropriated by the former to promote Irish causes (243). In the parody, though, attributing an Irish history to "Lady Wilde" conjures an image of an aristocratic female dilettante lacking any rigorous training that qualifies her for the historiographic task. A female's connection to history thus is viewed not as admirable but absurd.

10. Evelyn Hinz offers an interesting application of Eliade's theories to *She*. Her 1972 reading, however, does not deal with gender. Instead, Hinz argues that the novel offers "an archetypal premise—that history repeats itself" to conclude that "progress is decline, that 'history' is the fall" (417). The voyage to Kôr thus represents a "basic mythological movement—the return to the beginning" (420). Although I certainly agree that *She* is distinguishing between linear and cyclical notions of history, I see a reverse valuation in which linear history is judged superior to a cyclical model.

11. Although *She* is set in central Africa, Said's theory is applicable because Ayesha is of Arabian origin. Indeed, the "Anglo-French-American experience of the Arabs and Islam . . . for almost a thousand years together stood for the Orient" (17). Orientalism is particularly appropriate for a discussion of Haggard's novel since the field "increased enormously in prestige" during the period (43). Other critics, such as Stott and Gilbert and Gubar, have likewise found Orientalism useful in their analyses of *She*.

12. Haggard was fascinated by Egypt and its classic civilization, claiming an understanding of Egyptians "from Menes down to the Ptolemaic period" (*Days* 1:255). Feeling "at home" with "the 'old' Egyptians" (255), Haggard considered Egypt his "greatest recreation to study" (2:158). In a 1907 number of the *Bookman*, he identified Breasted's *Ancient Egyptian Records* as the book that "interested me more than any other" (162). He also wrote a series of articles on his visits to the country. His close friend, Andrew Lang, penned an 1886 article on "Egyptian Divine Myths," a possible influence on Haggard.

13. In drawing a similar distinction between the Amahagger and Egyptians, Chrisman makes the important point that an equation of the two would "preclude any exploration of what it is that should make imperial discourse so bivalent in its desires and fears about racial otherness" (44). Orientalism, Chrisman comments, is "a divided and flexible construct" in the text, "not a monolith of otherness" (45–46).

14. Two editions of *She* in particular provide helpful biblical references: Etherington's *The Annotated She* and the Oxford World Classics version.

15. In his discussion of literary and pictorial representations, Bram Dijkstra observes that serpentine images were the most commonly used to depict women in the late century (305), building on the familiar Lamia myth (309). To *fin de siècle* males, Lamia was "perfectly representative of the New Woman who, in their eyes, was seeking to arrogate to herself male privileges, refused the duties of motherhood, and was intent upon destroying the heavenly harmony of feminine subordination in the family" (309).

16. See James Kissane's 1962 article for a discussion of Victorian mythology. Noting an eclectic mix of mythological theories in the period, Kissane credits George Grote's 1846 *History of Greece* with being the strongest influence on perceptions of myth, quoting Grote's remark that it is "a special product of the imagination and feelings, radically distinct from both history and philosophy" (8). Also see Kissane for insights into the views of Ruskin and Pater.

17. Stott comments, for example, that She's death scene reproduces the Victorian theory of recapitulation, which held that an organism reenacted predecessors' development but passed beyond the final stage of lower specimens (115). Gilbert and Gubar consider She's death as both a devolution and a reassertion of patriarchal law through "unholy intercourse with the phallic 'pillar of Life'" (19). Other critics, such as Etherington and Alan Sandison, have also remarked on the evolutionary aspects of *She*.

18. The passage also stresses deterioration and desiccation, which offers an intriguing link to textuality. She's skin turns "dirty brown and yellow" in contrast to its former unblemished whiteness; and her "withered" skin resembles an old parchment. These adjectives, along with earlier references to her face being "graven" and "stamp[ed]" with age, more importantly suggest that Ayesha has been converted into a text that can be marked and contained. Parodic attention to the transformation scene attests that some readers, at least, caught this connection. In Andrew Lang's *He*, the mummified central character resembles a bunch of rags suitable for a "paper-mill" (86); in *Punch* (31 Mar. 1888), She becomes "a dirty buff" color resembling a "withered parchment, or the cover of a Whig Quarterly" (148–49). As a text, all of these references suggest, She is transformed from an unmanageable and mysterious force that acts upon others to an inert and readable surface that instead can be controlled through inscription or erasure.

19. Although Ayesha's maternal activities are restricted to her disinterested eugenic experimentation, she nevertheless serves as an emblem of the primal mother. The Victorian ideology of female "nature" physiologically and emotionally linked Woman with maternity, deemed to be a necessary and integral component of female subjectivity. As critics have remarked, descriptions of terrain and She's dwelling place carry strong maternal connotations as well as sexual inferences.

20. Other critics have likewise seen this connection. Stott argues, for instance, that *She* represents "a journey inside a female body" (95), while Bunn sees the "landscape becom[ing] increasingly feminized and eroticized" (19). Showalter offers a variation on this interpretation, asserting that the landscape is masculine as well as feminine since the Englishmen enter Kôr through "rear cave entrances into the 'bowels of a great mountain'" (86). I suggest that the *She* reference brings to mind the *OED* definition of "bowel" as the "interior of anything," its "heart"—or Kôr.

21. I follow several critics in describing She as a maternal figure. Morton N. Cohen, for instance, describes She as the "archetypal Great Mother" (110), Etherington considers her as "a mother in disguise" (*Rider Haggard* 89), and Showalter identifies Ayesha as the "Ur-mother" (85).

22. Even though mosquitoes had not yet been identified as the vector for malaria at the time Haggard was writing, swamps were considered to harbor the disease.

23. *Ayesha* has received only occasional attention from modern critics. Neither did the novel garner much contemporary critical reaction, relegated to a paragraph or two in the *Dial*, the *Bookman*, and *Punch*.

24. Ayesha is resurrected yet again in Haggard's 1921 *She and Allan*, in which intrepid explorer Allan Quatermain reminisces about his encounter with She after perusing *She*. In this version, Ayesha is termed "She-who-commands" and demonstrates her characteristic traits in the 1887 novel. Heavily veiled and clothed in white, "she breathed out power"—a power "not quite human" (175). Again She is emblematic of female essence, as she is described by one observer as "not one woman, but all women" (176); more tellingly, Quatermain equates her womanhood with a perverse divinity, remarking upon her being "half divine (though, I think, rather wicked or at any rate unmoral in her way) and yet all woman" (xi). Other similarities to the 1887 novel include a frame narrative that stresses the "exactness" and factual basis of the story (viii); Ayesha's antiquated Arabic, which Quatermain finds as baffling as Holly did (177); a penetrating gaze that makes Quatermain feel as if she "were looking, through me as though she would discover my very soul" (189); and her serpentine hissing that turns Quatermain's "blood cold" (217).

25. A similar distinction between female subject positions—idealized submission versus unnerving power—is drawn even more obviously in the 1887 *Allan Quatermain* by contrasting two sister queens. One sister, the blonde White Queen, is described in terms of her "sweet face," "tender majesty," and "loving-kindness" (145), resembling "an angel out of heaven" (192) who exhibits the "nature of loving woman" (266); and she frequently addresses her husband as "lord." The Lady of the Night, however, plots (twice) to murder her sister and unleashes a devastating civil war—even leading the battle charge. As in *Ayesha*, the "good" version of womanhood ultimately prevails.

Chapter 3
Trapping the Female in Time:
History and Aesthetics in *Tess of the d'Urbervilles*

1. Hardy's verse reveals an obsession over the workings of time. See, for example, "The Clock-Winder," "The Clock of the Years," "The Absolute Explains," "So, Time," and "The History of an Hour."

2. In noting the pronounced interest in time and the various material ways in which it is manifested in *Jude the Obscure*, Janet H. Freeman argues that the "conjunction of space and time . . . is a first principle in the logic" of the novel ("Highways" 165).

3. Some critics, however, have identified New Woman traits in *Tess*. Penny Boumelha, disputing the notion that *Tess* preceded New Woman fiction, comments that "novels dealing with sex and the New Woman were already no longer a novelty" and points to Tess as offering a "new element of polemic" (119). Ann Ardis contends that "[t]he fact that Tess' wedding-night confession falls into the white space between chapters" underscores that "the only place for the New Woman in *Tess* will be that reserved for her as 'a pure woman'" (75). Gail Cunningham, although asserting that *Tess* precedes "the New Woman of popular fiction," claims that Tess "at various points expresses views which would command the admiration of these later heroines" (80). Along similar lines, Gillian Beer considers Tess as "a possible form for the 'new' woman—both survivor and intelligent forerunner" (257).

4. See, for example, Jane Adamson's essay, which explores the "shaping" and "re-shaping" of time in the text (21); Terence Wright's "Space, Time, and Paradox," which analyzes history—particularly in relation to Tess's personal history—in both temporal and spatial terms; and Simon Trezise's "Places in Time," which incorporates Mikhail Bakhtin's notion of the "chronotype" to show the relationship of the Wessex landscape to time.

5. In a related vein, Michael Ragussis argues that "Tess's body is almost literally a vehicle for the working out of the family history" (142), "a body in the service of a name, the family name" (136).

6. Tess O'Toole also notes that women are not part of the chronicle, which addresses "battles fought and services rendered to the government rather than an account of the domestic or private sphere associated with women" (106). O'Toole further remarks that "Tess's maternal family history is generically distinct from her paternal one: it is associated with ballads and bawdy tales rather than with chronicles and legends," a point with which I firmly agree.

7. The explanations are based on the Penguin edition's gloss of these references.

8. G. Glen Wickens offers the useful observation that Parson Tringham's tracing of the d'Urberville line exemplifies "the Victorian emphasis on history and the origin of things" (100).

9. Also see O'Toole for a similar discussion of the female's relationship to history (especially 104–13) as well as to orality (86). O'Toole presents a detailed exploration of the significance of family history in Hardy's fiction. She notes, for example, that "the female axis of the family ... suggest[s] a juxtaposition of woman and history as belonging to antithetical spheres" (107) and that a woman is "the vehicle for the working out of a family history from which she is in large measure excluded" (106).

10. Shirley Stave sees a similar connection between women and paganism but stresses the sexual rather than historical implications that I address. Heathenism, she argues, "empowers" women by "allow[ing] for the articulation of their sexuality," in contrast with Christianity's efforts to regulate erotic behavior (107).

11. Stave views Sue's relationship to paganism from the opposite perspective, considering Sue as "Hardy's bearer of culture within the text" (134). Citing Sue's widespread reading and fondness for music and art, "the determiners of 'culture'" (134), Stave claims that Sue evidences a "dissociation from the Pagan" except in intellectual terms (141).

12. Boumelha likewise argues that, despite the similarity of the cousins' histories, Sue becomes "the instrument of Jude's tragedy, rather than the subject of her own" (148). While Boumelha characterizes the effect as providing "a man's picture of a woman," I suggest that the marginalization of Sue's history in favor of Jude's offers further evidence of the masculinist construction of history that Hardy presents in his texts.

13. The Darwinian implications of *Tess* have been explored in detail by a number of critics, such as Laura Otis, Peter Morton, and Kevin Padian, and could occupy an entire chapter themselves. Though not treating *Tess* specifically, George Levine asserts that Hardy followed late-century scientists in questioning the reliability of observation as a source for knowledge, arguing that Hardy both valued and undercut ocular authority. Gillian Beer also points to the Darwinian time scales at work in Hardy's fiction as well as his interest in late-century writings on human descent.

14. Although often pressed to convert his novels into dramatic form, Hardy was reluctant to do so. In his 1892 essay "Why I Don't Write Plays," Hardy justifies his position in commenting that "the novel affords scope for getting nearer to the heart and meaning of things than does the play" (139). Hardy did agree to pen a stage version of *Tess* after receiving much encouragement from actresses—among them Ellen Terry and Sarah Bernhardt—and other theatrical personages, but the play was not performed in England until thirty years after it was written (although an unauthorized version based on the novel was staged in 1900). Across the Atlantic, playwright Lorimar Stoddard dramatized Hardy's novel—completing the project in five days—for the American stage, where it appeared in 1897. See Marguerite Roberts's *Tess in the Theatre* and Keith Wilson's *Thomas Hardy on Stage* for these and other detailed discussions on Hardy's views and responses to requests for theatrical versions of his novels

as well as performance histories.

15. O'Toole also addresses this point, observing that "[f]or women, history necessarily means sexual history" (104). Helena Michie comments that Tess is "a text to be read, interpreted, and edited" (112). Noting that "Tess' bodily fate is already inscribed," Michie remarks that "Tess' body is less that of an individual than the temporal manifestation of a historical force." Also see Jules David Law's essay on the relationship between "the gendered body" and history in *Tess*.

16. Early titles for the novel highlight its concern with both temporal oppression and female essence: "Too Late, Beloved" and "The Body and Soul of Sue," the original name for Tess.

17. Michie argues that Jocelyn's sculptures represent "a form of sexual repression, a 'translation' of desire" into art (111). His affection for women, Michie asserts, "is the love of women as they are reproduced," as when "[h]e realizes his love for the first Avice only after she dies and he studies an old photograph of her" (112). I suggest that Jocelyn's works disturbingly demonstrate the parallel perspectives of the masculinist aesthetic vision and the cultural conception of female essence.

18. See Book Two, chapters five through seven, for these and similar descriptions.

19. Critical commentary has explored the aesthetic implications of the novel. For example, Lyn Pykett touches on the point in noting that the three Avices "remain framed . . . by the aesthetic codes by which they are represented," which Pykett characterizes as "the dominant aesthetic codes governing the representation of the female body" ("Ruinous Bodies" 165). John Kucich comments that the novel shows "how tenuous the canon of artistic honesty is" (216). Patricia Ingham reads the novel as conveying "the idea that moulding women to a preconceived artistic ideal does not work" (102). She sees the novel "reflect[ing] on what such art [as Jocelyn's] does with women"; the novel reveals that art's "attempted appropriation . . . inevitably fails" (100). Michael Ryan argues that the text is "a mockery of aestheticism" and an assault on contemporary views (173), while George Wotton similarly contends that the novel provides "a fiercely satirical view of the idealizing vision" (140).

20. See Miller's *Fiction and Repetition* for the complete quote (152).

21. See Sheila Berger's *Thomas Hardy and Visual Structures* for a detailed discussion of framing devices in Hardy's fiction.

22. Also see Wotton for an analysis of the "essential nature" of Hardy's female characters, especially chapter 9. Wotton argues that "Hardy's writing puts the ideological construction of 'Woman' into contradiction by showing that the perception of women's 'essential nature' is always conditioned upon who is doing the seeing" (122).

23. Margaret R. Higonnet's contention that Hardy highlights "features that he could encode as feminine," such as Tess's "mobile peony mouth" (204), reinforces my point, as does Pykett's assertion that Tess is initially included

among a group whose "physical attributes" are "non-differentiating" ("Ruinous Bodies" 158).

24. Freeman makes a similar point in arguing that "it is fatal for her [Tess] to be seen, and to be seen is to be taken, possessed" ("Ways" 322).

25. The most telling example of the sun's masculinization comes in this statement: "The sun . . . had a curious sentient, personal look, demanding the masculine pronoun for its adequate expression" (136).

26. I agree in this regard with Joan Grundy's assessment of landscape paintings in which figures are inserted: "however 'typical,'" such a scene "almost inevitably appears to have a story to tell" (33). Grundy helpfully identifies a "cross-fertilisation" between Victorian novels and paintings through their common desire to "tell stories" (30).

27. Jean Jacques Lecercle identifies the nonhistorical form of time at work in the novel somewhat differently than I do, as "the time of folklore and myth, the cyclical time of repetition" (12).

28. Critics have commented extensively upon the shaping of Tess's subjectivity by observers. Terry Eagleton, for instance, notes that "Tess' subjective sense of herself as 'a pulsing life'" is informed by an ongoing "awareness of her own externality for others" ("Thomas Hardy" 160). James Kincaid similarly asserts that Tess represents an "empty shape" that conforms to others' desire, "ready to be filled in and then longed for" (13), while Kaja Silverman remarks that Tess lacks an "integral visual consistency" and instead "must be painted, imprinted, and patterned in order to be seen" (9). Wotton sees in Tess "the most dramatic image of the way Hardy's women are harried, harassed and in Tess's case hunted by the masculine gaze," through which each male character "treats her according to his vision of her" (131). Otis, arguing that in observing the female body one projects a particular reading onto that somatic text, points to Annie Escuret's contention that Tess is always reduced to a body upon which male desire is mapped (16). Dianne Fallon Sadoff expands on the visual implications by exploring both the textual and filmic gazes directed on Tess. Rebecca Stott considers Tess as "a resistant site for the myriad discourses which are inscribed upon her," since the "proliferation of signs and readings" enable her to elude and delay signification (185), yet Stott points to Tess's "inevitable appropriation" (194).

29. Joseph Allen Boone interprets this scene as "paradise regained" for Angel that enables him to enjoy an "unsullied, feminine ideal" (111). Boone's reading reinforces my ongoing argument that a presumption of female essence informs the novel.

30. Terence Wright sees "a transcendent defeatism in [Tess's] nature which looks for suspension of time and a proscribing of space" and notes, for instance, Tess's desire "that she and Clare could court forever" (46).

31. Silverman remarks that the Edenic scene "project[s] Tess and Angel into a time and place outside history," when "[h]istory has not yet begun" (18). I would suggest that time itself did not begin until after the Fall.

32. See Rosemarie Morgan and Laura Claridge for readings of the passage as a parodic treatment of the Edenic story.

33. Hardy's fascination with Stonehenge was conveyed in an 1899 interview about a proposal to sell the famous structure. Living within "a bicycle ride" of Stonehenge, the interviewer remarks, Hardy "made special visits" to it "to get his lights for the chapter" in *Tess* (196). Hardy characterized the relic "as a page of history" that "must remain the wonder of Salisbury Plain, and of England" (197).

34. Although I agree with Stott that Stonehenge "evokes a heathen, pagan past before history, before record and figuration" (194–95), I would qualify that remark to note that Stonehenge also represents the beginnings of history.

Chapter 4
Reinterpreting Evolutionary Development:
Feminine Psychology in *The Beth Book* and *The Heavenly Twins*

1. As Cynthia Eagle Russett points out, Darwin's *Descent* "became the source book for a generation and more of research in evolutionary psychology" (40).

2. Interest in psychology itself dates back at least to John Locke's seventeenth-century treatise on human understanding, but my concern here is psychology's particular emergence as a Darwinian scientific discipline in the late nineteenth century.

3. Robin Gilmour credits Spencer as the "first to offer a fully evolutionary psychology"—the notion that "the mind is formed in the process of adjusting to its environment, and cannot be studied apart, . . . inherit[ing] through the nervous system the legacy of its predecessors' adaptations" (139). Gilmour adds, however, that such assumptions were derived "speculatively, without any practical demonstration."

4. As described by L. S. Jagyna, the most influential school of thought in *fin de siècle* psychology held that human cognition stemmed from the same mechanisms that determined the mental processes of the lower animals (109–10). Even the most sophisticated intellectual products derived from "the most simple neural phenomenon," viewed as the "basic unit from which all the higher manifestations of mind developed" (111). For general background on Victorian psychology, see Jagyna's essay, as well as J. C. Flugel's *A Hundred Years of Psychology,* Gardner Murphy's *Historical Introduction to Modern Psychology,* and William R. Woodward and Mitchell G. Ash's *The Problematic Science: Psychology in Nineteenth-Century Thought.*

5. The hold of scientific discourse on the public imagination is evidenced, Alan P. Barr observes, by the host of popular publications that "bristled with the current scientific essays" and public scientific talks that "became a popular art and a powerful form of education" (25). As Barr stresses, "[i]t was not just closet geologists and naturalists manqué who discussed Lyell and Darwin."

6. Lyn Pykett has also commented on Grand's view of the female in *The "Improper" Feminine* as more highly developed than the male, since males are "closer to brute nature" (155). Maleficent male characters "are portrayed as not only physically diseased, but also as merely appetitive creatures." Terry Lovell makes a similar point in noting that Grand saw women's presumed "moral superiority" as an evolutionary advancement and "the fate of 'the race'" as being dependent on women (126).

7. Another source of Grand's evolutionary knowledge presumably was her husband, David McFall, a physician. According to Grand's biographer, Gillian Kersley: "Like a leach she sucked from him any and every medical detail and fact, 'collecting material for which she had no use at the moment, and storing it without design'" (35). As a medical man, McFall certainly would have been familiar with Darwinian theory.

8. In this respect, Grand resembled other late-century feminists who offered dramatically different interpretations of Darwinian theory than did mainstream evolutionists. As Lucy Bland remarks, "Darwin's theory was so multivalent that it allowed feminists to make readings in stark contrast to the dominant readings of the day," refiguring women as the ones "who would lead humanity forward to [a] new and glorious age" (85). Also see Pykett's *The "Improper" Feminine* (chapter 16).

9. See, for example, *The Modern Man and Maid* (1898), which contends that the perfection of humanity depends on improvement of the marital relationship; and "The New Aspect of the Woman Question" (1894), which argues that resolution of this ongoing Victorian concern would lead to stronger men and women.

10. As David Rubinstein explains, though "[p]rejudice masquerading as science was no longer unchallenged by the end of the century," such opinions "retained the hold over lay and much scientific opinion" (3). He adds, "The belief that women were less capable of rational and original thought than men was too firmly rooted in a male-dominated society to submit to easy destruction." Also see Joan Burstyn's "Education and Sex" and Kate Flint's *The Woman Reader* (chapter 4) for helpful discussions of late-Victorian perceptions of the sexes' mental abilities.

11. See Carol A. Senf's introduction to the 1992 edition of *The Heavenly Twins* and Magnum's *Married, Middlebrow, and Militant* for details on the novel's publication history. Information on readership for *The Beth Book* is scanty at best. Terry Lovell helpfully remarks, though, that the novel "was less well received" than *The Heavenly Twins*, yet nevertheless a "success" (123). One marker of *The Beth Book*'s popularity is that it was published not only in London, but also in New York and Toronto in 1897, according to listings in Joan Huddleston's bibliography of Grand's texts. The two novels that I discuss were part of a trilogy including the 1888 *Ideala*.

12. See Peter J. Bowler's *The Invention of Progress* for a discussion of the progressionist aspects of Darwinism.

13. Victorian reviewers, who generally criticized *The Beth Book*, were particularly unimpressed by its focus on childhood experiences and other lengthy discussions of Beth's interests. Observing that "Sarah Grand is getting a very heavy hand" (743), the *Athenaeum* opined that Beth "occasionally does and says amusing things as a child," but "even those things are spoilt by her precocious air of setting the world to rights by them"; as a result, Beth "becomes a perfectly insupportable bag of fads and views without a spark of humanity" (744). Commenting that "[i]n the whole range of English fiction there never was a heroine who was described at greater length or in a greater variety of situations," the *Spectator* sniffed that "[w]e are even told why she disliked catsup" and "initiated (much against our will) into the mysteries of her toilet" (691). In the 1899 *Novel-Reader's Handbook*, William Roberton complained that *The Beth Book* is "dreadfully long" and lacked an "exciting story" (148), and he quoted the *Spectator* review as justification for having "never attempted the study of Mrs. Grand's 'woman of genius'" (149). On a more positive note, the *Dial* said that "the story of Beth's childhood is told with no little insight and charm," even though the reviewer lamented that "it is difficult to state just what purpose" underlay the novel (78).

14. See Pykett, *The "Improper" Feminine*, for a discussion of Beth as a "Wordsworthian infant" and "a late nineteenth-century version of the Kristevan semiotic" (178–80).

15. In its valorization of nature, *The Beth Book* seems to invoke Romanticist—particularly Wordsworthian—notions of the artist-genius who derives inspiration and imaginative power from the outdoors. The key difference between the two perspectives is that the canonical Romantic poets based their philosophy on a specifically male observer, whose perceptions of nature carried important gender implications. I agree in this respect with Anne K. Mellor's theorization of the particularly masculine valence in Romanticism developed in her *Romanticism and Gender*.

16. Women's undeniable literary accomplishments, evidenced by the prominence of female authors, could be readily dismissed by casting women, as anthropologist J. McGrigor Allan did, as "diligent workers" in "the lighter departments of literature" (ccvii), while "man reigns supreme" in literature's "highest realms" (ccx).

17. For other critical perspectives on Beth's mimicry, see Mangum (*Married*), Ruth Smalley, and John Kucich.

18. Critics have offered interesting discussions of the importance of oratory in the novel. Mangum, for instance, discusses oratory's transgressive aspects—noting that "Beth as a fictional female orator represented the New Woman in one of her most threatening guises" (*Married* 186). Smalley focuses on the protagonist's acquisition of a specifically female voice. Pykett asserts that Beth's oratory "bear[s] an interesting resemblance to Hélène Cixous's descriptions of the privileging of the voice in feminine writing" (*The "Improper" Feminine* 185).

19. Indeed, an 1897 essay on "Women at Oxford and Cambridge" decried "the insidious process of gradual assimilation of girls' education to boys' which is going on around us" (551).

20. See Mangum (*Married*, chapter 5) for a discussion of Beth's version of a feminist aesthetic. Also see Talia Schaffer and Kathy Alexis Psomiades, *Women and British Aestheticism*, on late-century aestheticism, the female aesthete, and the New Woman.

21. One Victorian reviewer denied that Beth could even be considered a genius. The *Bookman* asserted that "[t]he 'Woman of Genius' portion of the title may be ignored," since "[n]o woman of genius is presented" (106). "By genius is probably meant persistent energy," the reviewer condescendingly noted.

22. Max Nordau's late-century *Degeneration*, though directing its venomous assaults on the aesthetes, could also be read as a criticism of women in general as well as the New Woman. As Pykett remarks, "In effect, Nordau describes a civilization which is in the process of becoming unhealthily feminized" and "many of the characteristics which Nordau attributes to the degenerate are those which . . . were attributed to modern woman" (*Engendering Fictions* 30). As Linda Dowling has noted, New Women and aesthetes were frequently grouped together by contemporary observers, since both were viewed as "a profound threat to established culture" ("The Decadent" 435). Nordau's book vilified "degenerate" geniuses, for "[t]hey corrupt and delude" in exercising a "baneful" influence (24). The "sane genius" (23) is presumably male in Nordau's opinion, for he neglects any discussion of female geniuses. The fact that Nordau dedicated *Degeneration* to Lombroso further suggests a gendered view of genius.

23. J. S. Mill's 1869 *Subjection of Women* lost much of its influence when Darwin's *Descent of Man* appeared in 1871, according to Flavia Alaya's study of nineteenth-century perceptions of genius. By then, Alaya observes, "it became clear that the floodtide of scientific persuasion about sex roles was well on its way to quenching any new feminist brushfires *The Subjection* might have started" (265). Alaya notes that "male genius was synonymous with British civilization"; Mill's argument "did not have the strength" to counter attempts "to identify power with 'genius' and both with the Anglo-Saxon male character" (268).

24. See, for example, Kucich, Mangum (*Married*), and Penny Boumelha ("The Woman of Genius") for intriguing views of genius in *The Beth Book*.

25. Comte argued strenuously about the moral superiority of women and their importance in contributing to the positivist goal of "social regeneration" (173). Like Grand, Comte had an essentialist view of women, in his case attributing to them such qualities as a strong capacity for love, social responsibility, feeling, affection, and goodness. Grand, however, would have parted company with Comte's contention that women were intellectually inferior to men. "In all kinds of force," Comte asserted, "whether physical, intellectual, or practical, it is certain that Man surpasses Woman,

in accordance with the general law prevailing throughout the animal kingdom" (169).

26. Critics have commented briefly on the evolutionary elements of *The Heavenly Twins,* but the subject has not been explored in depth. Gerd Bjorhovde identifies the novel as "a psychological study of the effects of heredity, environment, and repression on character" (90), noting also the text's general concern with personality development as evidenced by the titling of individual sections. Lovell observes that "Grand was heavily influenced by the doctrine of evolution as it had been applied to social development" (126).

27. Victorian reviewers generally applauded the novel's treatment of its main characters. Although qualifying its praise, the *Spectator* remarked that "with, perhaps, one or two exceptions," *The Heavenly Twins* characters "are really made to live" (395). The *Nation,* one of several U.S. publications that reviewed Grand's books, noted that *The Heavenly Twins'* "dominant motive," identified as "the elevation of man's moral status" to the level of woman's, is "zealously, even thrillingly, dealt with in the story of Evadne" (374). The *Academy* agreed, characterizing Evadne as "a high-minded girl" whose life provides "the main interest for author and readers" (368), as did the *Athenaeum,* which commended Grand for "surmount[ing] a great difficulty with success" in relating Evadne's experiences (342). The *Pall Mall Gazette,* however, found Evadne "a very slow and none too well-bred young woman" (3). Reviewers tended to ignore Edith's story, but they were particularly enthralled with the exploits of Angelica and her twin. To the *Athenaeum,* for example, the twins "are among the most delightful and amusing children in fiction" (342); to *Punch,* "their diversions delighted" its reviewer "hugely," a sentiment shared by the public, which has "taken lovingly to the Twins" (93); and to *Shafts,* the twins "are a unique and incomparable creation" of which "the reader never tires" (268). The *Pall Mall Gazette,* though, dismissed the twins as "rather amusing youngsters, and that is all" (3).

28. John Neubauer argues that adolescence "came of age" during the period (6), which he attributes to the culmination of "long-term changes in social institutions and habits, . . . the growth of science and technology, and the reorganization of family structures" (7). Neubauer especially credits the educational institutions for the emergence of an "adolescent subculture" (71), a point that John Springhall likewise stresses in viewing adolescence as an "unintended byproduct of the cloistering of so many middle and upper-class youths in boarding schools" (25). Population figures quoted by Springhall attest to the strong presence of Victorian adolescents: citing an 1881 census of England and Wales, Springhall reports that more than half of the population was under age twenty-four, with some 46 percent of that figure under age twenty (38). In likewise contending that adolescence was "first 'discovered' in the nineteenth century," Carol Dyhouse dates the

"proliferation of discussion and writing about 'youth'" from the final decade (115).

29. See Magnum (*Married*, chapter 4) and Kate Flint (chapter 2) on Evadne's reading practices.

30. As Bland observes in a discussion of Victorian views of sexual selection, many late-century feminists thought that "the human evolutionary process was moving from natural selection to conscious, moral selection," and "the women's movement was part of this 'inevitable movement forward'" (84).

31. See Elaine Showalter's "Syphilis, Sexuality, and the Fiction of the Fin de Siècle" for a discussion of the literary implications of syphilis in late-century texts.

32. See Carolyn Christensen Nelson on the novel's stance toward women kept in ignorance (chapter 2).

33. See Bland for a discussion of women as "sexual selectors" (83–84).

34. See, for example, Charlotte Goodman's "The Lost Brother, The Twin: Women Novelists and the Male-Female Double Bildungsroman," which Mangum cites in a discussion of the strategy at work in *The Heavenly Twins*. Mangum argues that in "comparing the development of a male child and a child who shared exactly the same environment, opportunities, and advantages, Grand demonstrated the ways children were conditioned to accept gender roles" (*Feminist Fiction* 159–60).

35. Galton did address sexual differences, however, in remarking that they "begin to assert themselves even in the nursery, where all the children are treated alike" (*Inquiries* 39). He pointed specifically to the female's "capricious and coy" attributes, which represented "a heritage of the sex, together with a cohort of allied weaknesses and petty deceits." Romanes noted a general difficulty in distinguishing between nature and nurture, but in the case of the sexes, "no such difficulty obtains" (665).

36. See, for instance, Mangum's discussion of the "ironic reversal of the twins' characters and names" ("Sex" 74ff).

37. As William James described female development, at age twenty a woman's "character is, in fact, finished in its essentials," while a man's "character is still gelatinous" and maturing to a greater degree (2:369).

38. Bjorhovde likewise reads this behavior as indicating a "father-child relationship," characterizing Angelica as "the naughty child" who acts "in exactly the same way that a child would try to attract attention" (111).

Chapter 5
Controlling Women's Time: Regulatory Days and Historical Determinism in *The Daughters of Danaus*

1. Caird "was for a while probably the best-known and certainly the most decried feminist in England," observes Margaret Morganroth Gullette (494).

Unfortunately, only limited biographical information is available on Caird, despite her prominence in the nineteenth century. Biographical data compiled by Gullette and contributors to literary encyclopedias offer some clues about Caird's life. Born in 1854, Caird was married at age twenty-three to James Alexander Caird, a Scot of prominent family who was eight years her senior. She bore her only child, a son, seven years later, and began writing on marriage at about the same time. Married for forty years until her husband's death, Caird traveled frequently from Scotland to England, developing a circle of literary and artistic acquaintances in London that included Olive Schreiner. Caird died in 1932.

2. In a memoir, Fiona Macleod (William Sharp) attests to the controversy that Caird's writings on marriage generated, commenting that her work "met with acute hostility" accompanied by "much misunderstanding and unmerited abuse" (226). In a similar vein, Katharine Tynan asserts in her memoir that Caird "was one of the sensations of that year, having set on foot the *Daily Telegraph* discussion . . . 'Is Marriage a Failure?'" (341).

3. Caird published her first novel, *Lady Hetty*, anonymously in 1875, which was followed soon thereafter by two more novels—*Whom Nature Leadeth* (1883), appearing pseudonymously, and *One that Wins* (1887). The more successful *The Wing of Azrael* appeared in 1889, and Caird's signature text, *The Daughters of Danaus*, five years later. A prolific writer in both the 1880s and 1890s, Caird also produced a short story collection, *A Romance of the Moors* (1891); the marriage novels *Beyond the Pale* (1897) and *The Pathway of the Gods* (1898); the essay collection, *The Morality of Marriage* (1897); and the antivivisectionist *A Sentimental View of Vivisection* (1895). She continued writing over subsequent decades, stopping only a year before her death in 1932. After the turn of the century she published two other antivisectionist texts, *The Inquisition of Science* (1903) and *The Stones of Sacrifice* (1915); a travel book, *Romantic Cities of Provence* (1906); and a mystical novel, *The Great Wave* (1931).

Biographical sources remark on the wide audiences of her novels, particularly *The Daughters of Danaus*. *The Feminist Companion to Literature in English* identifies *The Daughters of Danaus* as the "best known" of Caird's novels (170), a point reiterated in other accounts of her work. *The Daughters of Danaus* apparently was ignored by contemporary critics, for no reviews appeared in such mainstream journals as the *Atheneaum, Bookman,* or *Academy*. The only review available comes in the feminist *Shafts*, which treats the novel sympathetically. In quoting Hadria's despair that "[i]nstead of *doing* a thing, she had to be perpetually struggling for the chance to do it," the *Shafts* reviewer asserted that the sentiment "reveals the whole tragedy and pathos of a woman's life" (23). Even obituaries give scant details about Caird, concerned more with funeral arrangements and relatives than her work.

4. See Pykett (*The "Improper" Feminine*), however, for a discussion of

the temporal demands on Hadria (181–83).

5. Also see Pykett (*The "Improper" Feminine*) for a discussion of Smith's essay (181). Pykett additionally addresses the demands on a woman's time cited by Caird and other writers ("Portraits," 143-44; *The "Improper" Feminine*, 181–83), as does Margaret Diane Stetz.

6. For a general treatment of advice manuals, see Kate Flint (chapter 5).

7. Mrs. Warren's text was "typical" of one approach found in the "amazing number of authorities on household management," notes Patricia Branca (13). The text, with sales of thirty-six thousand copies in the initial year of publication, depicted the "inexperienced wife" as a "congenital idiot who was presumably anxious to have her mistakes corrected."

8. See George Pickering's *Creative Malady* (165–77) for details on Nightingale's illness.

9. See Laurie Langbauer for a discussion of the "everyday," which she designates as "a crucial category, because its consolidations and deconstructions touch directly on the subject's relation to ideology and culture" (23).

10. In one pertinent reference, for instance, Mill comments that "the wife is the actual bond-servant of her husband: no less so, as far as legal obligation goes, than slaves commonly so called" (32).

11. In an interview, Caird credited Mill as "the first to help me to bring ... thoughts and feelings [about equal rights for women] into form" (421).

12. Caird argues the same idea in her 1888 "Marriage" essay, criticizing "the careless use of the words 'human nature,' and especially 'woman's nature'" (186):

> History will show us, if anything will, that human nature has an apparently limitless adaptability, and that therefore no conclusion can be built upon special manifestations which may at any time be developed. Such development must be referred to certain conditions, and not be mistaken for the eternal law of being. (186)

13. See Ledger (chapter 1) on evolutionary discourses in the novel.

14. Pykett associates the Gothic aspect of Viola's home with its sinister west wing, "both a gothic domain and a region of silence and shadows suggesting ghosts, death, and a history of violence against women" ("The Cause" 134).

15. Though available biographical information does not mention a familiarity with Nietzsche's work, the parallels between the two writers' assessments of history are startling.

16. See Laura Otis's essay for a detailed discussion of organic memory.

17. I offer here a different interpretation than Ann Ardis's reading of the closure as "not merely dysphoric" but "euphorically dysphoric" (72). Ardis argues that the ending "cannot be read as Viola's punishment for committing both adultery and murder" but "an indictment of the entire social system."

I see the closure as wholly negative, indicating that Viola is entirely defeated by the power of the past to shape the present.

Chapter 6
Dissolving the Boundaries: Temporal Subversion in *The Story of an African Farm*

1. In the 1887 essay "About Fiction," Haggard laments the scarcity of novels that "have excited . . . profound interest," noting that within the past five years only *My Trivial Life and Misfortunes* and *African Farm* qualified for that distinction (180).

2. Despite—or because of—its assaults upon the status quo, *African Farm* was a successful book. Nancy L. Paxton comments that the novel was among the first post-Eliot feminist texts accorded positive reactions from both critics and the public (566). Contemporary critical response tended to be laudatory as to Schreiner's vision but disappointed in her technical prowess. The *Fortnightly Review* complained in 1883 that the novel revealed "[t]he hand of the beginner . . . betrayed by a number of faults of proportion and perspective," but it also praised the novel's "refreshing temerity," "original" characters, "fresh" style, and story "of fascinating interest" (882). Similarly, the *Athenaeum* in 1891 said *African Farm* "is a work of genius—immature in parts, and unequal as a whole, certainly, but a novel which has brought something new into literature" (46). However, in comparing the novel to the Brontës' writings, as did several other reviewers, Virginia Woolf claimed in 1925 that *African Farm* "has the limitations of those egotistical masterpieces without a full measure of their strength" (103).

3. Poised on the cusp of canonicity, *African Farm* has garnered increasing critical attention, particularly that attuned to narrative issues. Devoting a chapter of *Writing Beyond the Ending* to Schreiner's novel, Rachel Blau DuPlessis, for example, argues that *African Farm* critiques and signals "the 'end'" of the three prevailing narratives of Christian teleology, *Bildungs* or quest, and romance plots (21). Similarly, Joseph Allen Boone designates *African Farm* as "[o]ne of the most experimentally as well as thematically 'daring'" of the New Woman novels (131). Cherry Clayton comments that "[t]he chief subversion in the novel is of conventional plot, a series of actions which enact a determined evolution, a causal sequence related to linear development in time"; "linear absolutes," she adds, "belong to the conventionally male world of authority and action" (*Woman's Rose* 54). Gerd Bjorhovde observes of the text that "[i]n a way it can hardly be said to be a novel at all" (46). Gerald Monsman, interrogating the novel's resistance to closure, views "chronological and scenic disruptions . . . [as] frustrat[ing] any attempt to fix a unilinear sequence of events" ("Patterns" 265) in this "experimentally open-ended" novel (253). The narrative, Monsman says, "is an invisible or perpetually deferred whole" and the story's "meaning

lies in its substitutions, in the perpetual turning back upon themselves of its discontinuous, nomadic images" ("The Idea" 250).

4. Other critics have also commented on the significance of the watch. Joyce Avrech Berkman, for example, remarks that "[t]he primary image to evoke the terror of God's judgment for Schreiner is the watch or clock"; for Waldo, "the clock was a fearsome symbol of time passing, of the final heartbeat, of death and eternal damnation" (48). Anne McClintock, observing that "[t]he clock is a repeated motif in Schreiner's tales," adds, "For Schreiner, the clock is a grotesque fetish of Victorian industrial progress: mechanical, mundane, deadly" (278). In a 1988 essay, Monsman notes a correlation between a watch and a "male time" that is "set in counterpoint to the organic rhythms of nature and female fluidity" and "epitomizes a constrained, patriarchal version of nature and divinity"; he relates the moon to the female, characterizing it as "the matriarchal spirit of free-ranging, nonrational forces and a source of timeless feminine power" ("Olive Schreiner" 587–88). In a 1991 essay, Monsman further comments on a "parallel . . . between the punishing patriarchal God and the forgiving and maternal moon" ("Olive Schreiner" 12). Monsman also offers an interesting interpretation of the significance of the moon and watch in his 1985 *Texas Studies in Literature and Language* article, maintaining, for instance, that "moon time is female time" (253). In various writings on *African Farm*, critics develop their discussions of these images in other veins than my reading, but they assess several of the issues I explore from both similar and different perspectives.

5. Sandra Gilbert and Susan Gubar make the intriguing point that the remote karoo functions "as a liminal zone in which characters freed from the normative restraints of Western civilization can act out their desires" (63). The karoo thus can be seen as a site promoting the fluidity of gender positions that I see at work in the novel.

6. See George P. Landow's *Victorian Types, Victorian Shadows* for a discussion of the typology of Christ and the antichrist.

7. Kristeva perhaps inadvertently alludes to that ambiguity in her explanation of monumental temporality, noting that it is reminiscent of both Kronos—a male mythological figure—and the resurrectional myths that characterize "all religious beliefs" and "perpetuate the vestige" of "a maternal cult" (17).

8. As Gilbert and Gubar point out, Bonaparte Blenkins "signifies the entry of history into the tale," since the novel's sole date refers to his arrival at the farm (54).

9. Berkman similarly observes that Schreiner rejected conventional Christian views (43) and, in *African Farm*, "carefully and graphically [depicts] a Christian's loss of faith" (46).

10. As Marianne Hirsch remarks, Peter Brooks limits his explanation of "'female plot' to a footnote," which he characterizes as "'a resistance and what we might call an "endurance": a waiting (and suffering) until the woman's desire can be a permitted response to the expression of a man's desire'" (165). In a

related vein, Sally Robinson notes in a discussion of multiplicity in female texts that Cixous "argues that teleology excludes both female desire and language, that the 'feminine' cannot be expressed within closed structures" (114).

11. "Allegories," McCracken comments in his analysis of *African Farm*, "are a form of *écriture féminine* [in] engaging with and attempting to put into question systems of thought that exclude women's experience" (236).

12. Patrick Fairbairn, an eminent Victorian authority on scriptural typology, wrote that allegorical interpretation is to be applied only "[w]hen the scriptural narrative is actually held to have had no foundation in fact, to be a mere mythos or fabulous representation, devised for the sole purpose of exhibiting the mysteries of divine truth"; or if the narrative "in its immediate representation" is "incapable of any adequate or satisfactory sense" (16). See Landow for a helpful discussion of Fairbairn, allegory, and biblical reading, especially pp. 51–54.

13. Symons writes of a discussion with Schreiner that illuminates her perception of *African Farm*: "one can express humanity, not merely this man or that, so that a whole story can be concentrated into a tiny allegory, as she feels the *African Farm* is" (Cronwright-Schreiner 185).

14. As Berkman observes, Schreiner's concept of progress mixed predominant Victorian views with her own iconoclastic opinions. To Schreiner, progress was measured by "the degree to which patterns of domination had diminished" to promote "global unity" (74). Furthermore, Berkman comments, Schreiner "faulted Social Darwinism for its rationale in defending race, gender, and class inequality," recognizing "in its logic the interconnectedness of all three modes of domination" (77).

15. According to a chronology developed by S. C. Cronwright-Schreiner from letters and biographical material, Schreiner began *From Man to Man* in 1873. She continued working on additions and revisions until 1918, two years before her death. The unfinished novel was first published in 1927, the same year that *Undine* appeared in print.

16. Berkman points out that Schreiner lived during a period in which "an array of compelling ideologies of progress influenced popular thought," including positivism, Darwinism, socialism, and Hegelian thought (74). Berkman also notes that "Schreiner saw much that disturbed her," which "spurred her to develop an alternative concept of progress, a unique blend of prevalent theories with her original research and interpretation."

17. Among critics considering *African Farm* a realist text is Bjorhovde, who argues that Schreiner sought a "'truer' and more realistic kind of writing" rather than follow the artifice and constrictions of Victorian literature (50). Schreiner, Bjorhovde asserts, had "chosen to side with the 'new realists' rather than with the 'romancers.'" Both Bjorhovde and Ann Ardis consider 1885 as the start of the debate over the "new realism," following William C. Frierson in his 1928 *PMLA* article on the subject. Ardis points to *African Farm*'s preface as evidence that Schreiner is criticizing "classic realism" in the novel (64), a contention with which I firmly agree. Louise Green sees Schreiner's narrative approach as "a

contestation of the structures of identity implicit in realist representation" (21). Berkman comments that Schreiner "blended romantic and realistic literary styles" (195).

18. See the *New Review*'s 1890 forum on realism for Hardy's and Linton's views, and the 1885 *Literature at Nurse or Circulating Morals* for Moore's opinions. Also pertinent to the debate is Edmund Gosse's 1893 *Questions at Issue*, which expresses reservations about realism's future while noting its useful contributions. Though "the novel of experiment has had its day," he writes, "[i]t would be difficult, I think, for any one but a realistic novelist to overrate the good that realism in fiction has done" (152).

19. The approach here is reminiscent of Dickensian novels that foreground the influence of sensory experience on a subject's development. In the second chapter of *David Copperfield*, the adult character recalls "[t]he first objects that assume a distinct presence before me, as I look far back into the blank of my infancy" (24). The narrator proceeds in this chapter to describe his earliest memories through a child's sensory impressions. In the opening chapter of *Great Expectations*, Pip describes "[m]y first most vivid and broad impression of the identity of things" as he recollects the elements associated with "a memorable raw afternoon" in a churchyard (35).

20. See Green for a different reading of the mirror's significance in *African Farm*. Green argues that Lyndall "seems to be at once captured by the mirror and at the same time empowered by it to constitute a self outside of the identities prescribed for her" (30).

21. Berkman interprets this story as revealing Schreiner's denial of "the maleness of God," a point that she sees reiterated in another story, "In a Ruined Chapel" (55). Berkman devotes a chapter of her book on Schreiner to an interesting discussion of androgyny.

22. Schreiner described her belief in immortality in an 1892 letter. "I cannot conceive of either birth or death, as anything but simple changes in the endless existence," adding that "[n]either birth nor death are [*sic*] final to me" (Rive 213).

23. As Monsman similarly observes, the narrative "is simply a fragment of a larger context of incident, one story behind another like the layers of a lily bulb" ("Patterns" 265).

Afterword
Pointing the Way to Modernist Time

1. Also see Jane Eldridge Miller's *Rebel Women* for a discussion of New Women and Edwardian fiction.

2. As Dastur explains in a discussion of Heidegger's *Being and Time*, "[t]he question of Being and the question of time . . . do not represent two separate themes" but "a *single* question, that of the Temporality of Being" (9). In

Heidegger's model, time serves as "the true principle of individuation" (5). For Heidegger, "*ordinary* time is not related to primordial time, as the objective time of nature is to the subjective time of the soul; the virtue of the Heideggerian problematic, instead, is that it negates the very subject-object distinction" (xxx).

Works Cited

Primary Sources

Adam, Juliette. "Woman's Place in Modern Life." *Fortnightly Review* 57 (1892): 522–29.

Albert, Prince. *The Principal Speeches and Addresses.* London: John Murray, 1862.

Alfred, Lord Tennyson. "Songs from 'The Princess.'" *Poetry of the Victorian Period.* 3rd ed. Eds. Jerome Hamilton Buckley and George Benjamin Woods. n.p.: HarperCollins, 1965.

Allan, J. McGrigor. "On the Real Differences in the Minds of Men and Women." *Journal of the Anthropological Society of London* 7 (1869): cxcv–ccxix.

Allen, Grant. "Plain Words on the Woman Question." *Fortnightly Review* 52 (1889): 448–58.

———. "Woman's Place in Nature." *Forum* 7 (1889): 258–63.

Anderson, Elizabeth Garrett. "Sex in Mind and Education: A Reply." *Fortnightly Review* 21 (1874): 582–94.

The Antiquity of Man (reviews). *Saturday Review* 7 Mar. 1863: 311–12.

———. *Westminster Review* 79 (1863): 517–51.

Arling, Nat. "What is the Role of the 'New Woman?'" *Westminster Review* 150 (1898): 576–87.

Arnold, Matthew. "Dover Beach." *Poetry of the Victorian Period.* 3rd ed. Eds. Jerome Hamilton Buckley and George Benjamin Woods. n.p.: HarperCollins, 1965.

Ayesha (reviews). *Bookman* 29 (1905): 88.

———. *Dial* 1 Jan. 1906: 20.

———. *Punch* 18 Oct. 1905: 288.

Bergson, Henri. *Time and Free Will.* 1888. Trans. F. L. Pogson. London: George Allen and Unwin, 1910.

The Beth Book (reviews). *Athenaeum.* 27 Nov. 1897: 743–44.

———. *Bookman* 8 (1897): 106.

———. *Dial* 1 Feb. 1898: 78.

———. *Spectator* 13 Nov. 1897: 691–92.

Blackwell, Antoinette Brown. *The Sexes Throughout Nature.* New York: G. P. Putnam's Sons, 1875.

"The Book of 1906 Which Has Interested Me Most." *Bookman* 32 (1907): 162.

Bulley, A. Amy. "The Political Evolution of Women." *Westminster Review* 134 (1890): 1–8.

Burnham, William H. "The Study of Adolescence." *Pedagogical Seminary* 1 (1891): 174–95.

Caird, Mona. *The Daughters of Danaus.* 1894. New York: Feminist Press, 1989.

———. "The Emancipation of the Family, Part I." *North American Review* 150 (1890): 692–705.

———. "The Emancipation of the Family, Part II." *North American Review* 151 (1890): 22–37.

———. "The Future of the Home." Reprint in *Turn of the Century Women* 2.2 (1985): 3–9.

———. Interview. *Women's Penny Paper* 28 Jun. 1890: 421–22.

———. "Marriage." *Westminster Review* 130 (1888): 186–201.

———. *The Morality of Marriage and Other Essays on the Status and Destiny of Woman*. London: George Redway, 1897.

———. "Phases of Human Development I." *Westminster Review* 141 (1894): 37–51.

———. "Phases of Human Development II." *Westminster Review* 141 (1894): 162–79.

———. *The Wing of Azrael*. London: Trubner, 1889.

Campbell, Harry. *Differences in the Nervous Organisation of Man and Woman: Physiological and Pathological*. London: H. K. Lewis, 1891.

Carlyle, Thomas. "On History." *The Works of Thomas Carlyle*. Vol. 27. London: Chapman and Hall, 1899.

———. *Sartor Resartus*. 1834. Garden City: Doubleday, 1937.

———. "Shooting Niagara: and After?" 1867. *Scottish and Other Miscellanies*. London: E. P. Dutton, 1915.

Carroll, Lewis. *Alice's Adventures in Wonderland*. 1865. London: Puffin, 1962.

Comte, Auguste. *System of Positive Polity: First Volume*. (1851). New York: Burt Franklin, n.d.

[Craik, Dinah M.] *A Woman's Thoughts About Women*. New York: Rudd and Carleton, 1858.

Darwin, Charles. *The Descent of Man and Selection in Relation to Sex*. New York: Hurst, n.d.

———. *The Origin of Species*. 1859. New York: Penguin, 1958.

The Daughters of Danaus (review). *Shafts* 3 (1895): 23–24.

Delauney, G. "Equality and Inequality in Sex." *Popular Science Monthly* 20 (1881–82): 184–92.

De Morgan, John. *He*. 1887. *They: Three Parodies of H. Rider Haggard's* She. Eds. Reginald and Douglas Menville. New York: Arno, 1978.

"Devereux, Roy." *The Ascent of Woman*. Boston: Roberts Brothers, 1896.

Dickens, Charles. *David Copperfield*. 1850. New York: Signet, 1980.

———. *Great Expectations*. 1860. London: Penguin, 1985.

"The Doom of 'She.'" *Punch* 31 Mar. 1888: 148–49.

Ellis, Havelock. 1890. *The New Spirit*. London: Walter Scott, n.d.

———. *Women and Marriage: Or, Evolution in Sex*. London: William Reeves, 1888.

Engels, Friedrich. "Socialism: Utopian and Scientific" *Social and Political Philosophy: Readings from Plato to Gandhi*. Eds. John Somerville and Ronald E. Santoni. Garden City: Anchor, 1963.

Fairbairn, Patrick. *The Typology of Scripture. Vol. 1: Patriarchal Period*. Philadelphia: Daniels and Smith, 1852.

"The Fall of Fiction." *Fortnightly Review* 50 (1888): 324–36.

Forrest, G. F. *Misfits: A Book of Parodies*. Oxford: Frank Harvey, 1905.

Freud, Sigmund. *The Interpretation of Dreams*. Trans. James Strachey. New York: Basic Books, 1955.

Froude, James Anthony. *Short Studies on Great Subjects*. New York: Scribner's, 1897.

Galton, Francis. *Hereditary Genius: An Inquiry into Its Laws and Consequences*. 1869. London: Macmillan, 1914.

———. *Inquiries into Human Faculty and Its Development*. 1883. London: J. M. Dent and Sons, 1973.

Gamble, Eliza Burt. *The Evolution of Woman: An Inquiry into the Dogma of Her Inferiority to Man*. New York: G. P. Putnam's Sons, 1894.

Gaskell, Catherine Milnes. "Women of To-day." *Nineeenth Century* 26 (1889): 776–84.

Geddes, Patrick, and J. Arthur Thomson. *The Evolution of Sex*. New York: Charles Scribner's Sons, 1889.

Gosse, Edmund. "The Decay of Literary Taste." *North American Review* 161 (1895): 109–18.

Grand, Sarah. *The Beth Book.* 1897. New York: Dial, 1980.

———. *The Heavenly Twins.* 1893. Ann Arbor: U of Michigan P, 1992.

———. "The Modern Girl." *North American Review* 158 (1894): 706–14.

———. *The Modern Man and Maid.* New York: Crowell, 1898.

———. "The New Aspect of the Woman Question." *North American Review* 158 (1894): 270–76.

Grote, George. "Grecian Legends and Early History." *The Minor Works of George Grote.* Alexander Bain. New York: Burt Franklin, 1974.

———. *A History of Greece.* Vol. 1. London: John Murray, 1888.

"A Haggard Annual." *Punch* 5 Dec. 1889: n.pag.

Haggard, H. Rider. "About Fiction." *Contemporary Review* 51 (1887): 172–80.

———. *Allan Quatermain.* 1887. Oxford: Oxford UP, 1995.

———. *Ayesha: The Return of "She."* 1904. New York: Dover, 1978.

———. *Cleopatra.* 1889. *The Favorite Novels of H. Rider Haggard.* New York: Blue Ribbon, 1928.

———. *The Days of My Life.* Ed. C. J. Longman. 2 vols. London: Longmans, Green. 1926.

———. *Elissa; or The Doom of Zimbabwe.* 1895. London: Longmans, 1900.

———. *She.* 1887. Oxford: Oxford UP, 1991.

———. *She and Allan.* New York: Longmans, Green, 1921.

———. "Suggested Prologue to a Dramatised Version of 'She.'" *Longman's* 2 (1888): 492–97.

Hardy, Thomas. "Candour in English Fiction III." *New Review* 2 (1890): 15–17.

———. *The Collected Letters of Thomas Hardy*. Eds. Richard Little Purdy and Michael Millgate. Vol. 1. Oxford: Clarendon P, 1978.

———. *Collected Poems*. New York: Macmillan, 1925.

———. *Jude the Obscure*. 1896. London: Penguin, 1978.

———. *A Laodicean*. 1881. New York: Harper, 1905.

———. *The Mayor of Casterbridge*. 1886. London: Penguin, 1978.

———. *A Pair of Blue Eyes*. 1873. London: Penguin, 1986.

———. "The Profitable Reading of Fiction." *The Selected Writings of Thomas Hardy*. Ed. Irving Howe. Greenwich: Fawcett, 1966.

———. "Shall Stonehenge Go?" *Thomas Hardy's Personal Writings*. Ed. Harold Orel. New York: St. Martin's, 1990.

———. *Tess of the D'Urbervilles*. 1891. London: Penguin, 1978.

———. *Tess of the D'Urbervilles: A Tragedy in Five Acts. Tess in the Theatre*. Ed. Marguerite Roberts. Toronto: U of Toronto P, 1950.

———. *The Well-Beloved*. 1897. Oxford: Oxford UP, 1986.

———. "Why I Don't Write Plays." *Thomas Hardy's Personal Writings*. Ed. Harold Orel. New York: St. Martin's, 1990.

———. *The Woodlanders*. 1887. London: Penguin, 1981.

Harper, Charles G. *Revolted Woman: Past, Present, and to Come*. London: Elkin Mathews, 1894.

Harrison, Frederic. "The Emancipation of Women." *Fortnightly Review* 56 (1891): 437–52.

Harvey, H. E. "The Voice of Woman." *Westminster Review* 145 (1896): 193–96.

The Heavenly Twins (reviews). *Academy* 29 Apr. 1893: 368.

———. *Athenaeum* 18 Mar. 1893: 342.

———. *Nation* 16 Nov. 1893: 374–75.

———. *Pall Mall Gazette* 3 Apr. 1893: 3.

———. *Punch* 24 Feb. 1894: 93.

———. *Shafts* 25 Feb. 1893: 268.

———. *Spectator* 25 Mar. 1893: 395.

"Hee! Hee!" *Punch* 26 Feb. 1887: 100–01.

Hegel, G. W. F. *The Philosophy of History*. Trans. J. Sibree. New York: Dover, 1956.

Hewitt, Emma Churchman. "The 'New Woman' in Her Relation to the 'New Man.'" *Westminster Review* 147 (1897): 335–37.

Hogarth, Janet E. "Literary Degenerates." *Fortnightly Review* 57 n.s. (1895): 586–92.

Huxley, T. H. *Evolution and Ethics and Other Essays*. 1894. New York: Greenwood, 1968.

James, William. *The Principles of Psychology*. 1890. 2 vols. New York: Dover, 1950.

Jamieson, Herbert. "The Modern Woman." *Westminster Review* 152 (1899): 571–76.

Lancaster, E. G. "Psychology and Pedagogy of Adolescence." *Pedagogical Seminary* 5 (1897–98): 61–128.

Lankester, E. Ray. "Degeneration: A Chapter in Darwinism." 1880. *1900: A Fin-de-Siècle Reader*. Eds. Mike Jay and Michael Neve. London: Penguin, 1999.

Lang, Andrew. *He*. 1887. *They: Three Parodies of H. Rider Haggard's She*. Eds. R. Reginald and Douglas Menville. New York: Arno, 1978.

———. "Egyptian Divine Myths." *Nineteenth Century* 20 (1886): 423–40.

Lawrence, D. H. *Apocalypse*. London: Martin Secker, 1932.

———. *Women in Love*. New York: Viking, 1960.

Linton, Eliza Lynn. "Candour in English Fiction II." *New Review* 2 (1890): 10–14.

———. "The Partisans of the Wild Women." *Nineteenth Century* 31 (1892): 455–64.

———. "The Wild Women as Social Insurgents." *Nineteenth Century* 30 (1891): 596–605.

Loftie, Mrs. *Social Twitters*. London: Macmillan, 1879.

Lombroso, Cesare. *The Man of Genius*. London: Walter Scott, 1891.

Macaulay, Thomas Babington. *History of England*. Vol. 1. New York: John Wurtele Lovell, 1856.

———. "Sir James Mackintosh." *Critical, Historical, and Miscellaneous Essays and Poems*. Vol. 2. New York: American, 1880.

MacDougal, Robert. "Sex Differences in the Sense of Time." *Science*. 29 Apr. 1904: 707–8.

"Macleod, Fiona." *A Memoir*. Vol. 1. New York: Duffield, 1912.

"Manly Women." *Saturday Review* 22 Jun. 1889: 756–57.

Martineau, Harriet. *Autobiography*. Boston: Houghton, Osgood, 1879.

Marx, Karl. *Capital*. 1867. Ed. C. J. Arthur. London: Lawrence & Wishart, 1992.

———. *A Contribution to the Critique of Political Economy*. Trans. N. I. Stone. *Social and Political Philosophy: Readings from Plato to Gandhi*. Eds. John Somerville and Ronald E. Santoni. Garden City: Anchor, 1963.

Maudsley, Henry. "Sex in Mind and in Education." *Fortnightly Review* 21 (1874): 466–83.

Mill, Hugh Robert. "Time Standards of Europe." *Nature* 23 Jun. 1892: 174–76.

Mill, John Stuart. *The Subjection of Women*. 1869. Indianapolis: Hackett, 1988.

Moore, George. *Literature at Nurse or Circulating Morals*. London: Vizetelly, 1885.

Nietzsche, Friedrich. *Untimely Meditations*. Trans. R. J. Hollingdale. Cambridge: Cambridge UP, 1983.

Nightingale, Florence. *Cassandra*. 1852. New York: Feminist Press, 1979.

———. *Cassandra and Other Selections from Suggestions for Thought*. Ed. Mary Poovey. New York: New York UP, 1993.

Nordau, Max. *Degeneration*. New York: Howard Fertig, 1968.

"Official Catalogue of the Great Exhibition." *Edinburgh Review* 94 (1851): 557–98.

Oliphant, Margaret. "The Anti-Marriage League." *Blackwood's* 159 (1896): 135–49.

Ouida. "The New Woman." *North American Review* 158 (1894): 610–19.

Pater, Walter. *Greek Studies*. 1895. London: MacMillan, 1910.

———. *The Renaissance*. 1893. Berkeley: U of California P, 1980.

Pearson, Karl. *The Ethic of Freethought*. 2nd ed. London: Adam and Charles Black, 1901.

Pike, Luke Owen. "Woman and Political Power." *Popular Science Monthly* 1 (1872): 82–94.

"The President's Address." *British Medical Journal* 14 Aug. 1886: 338–39.

Richardson, Benjamin Ward. "Woman's Work in Creation." *Longman's* 8 (1886): 604–19.

Ritchie, David G. *Darwinism and Politics*. London: Swan Sonnenschein, 1889.

Roberton, William. *The Novel-Reader's Handbook: A Brief Guide to Recent Novels and Novelists*. Birmingham: Holland, 1899.

Romanes, George J. "Mental Differences Between Men and Women." *Nineteenth Century* 21 (1887): 654–72.

Ruskin, John. *The Queen of the Air.* 1869. Chicago: Geo. M. Hill, n.d.

Schott, C. A. "Standard Railroad Time." *Nature* 15 Nov. 1883: 70.

Schreiner, Olive. *Dreams.* Boston: Little, Brown, 1922.

———. *From Man to Man.* 1927. Chicago: Cassandra, 1977.

———. *Olive Schreiner Letters.* Vol. 1. Ed. Richard Rive. Oxford: Oxford UP, 1988.

———. *The Story of an African Farm.* 1883. New York: Penguin, 1971.

———. *Undine.* New York: Harper and Brothers, 1928.

———. *Woman and Labor.* New York: Frederick A. Stokes Co., 1911.

She (reviews). *Academy* 15 Jan. 1887: 35–36.

———. *Blackwood's* 141 (1887): 302–05.

———. *Murray's* 1 (1887): 287.

———. *Pall Mall Gazette* 4 Jan. 1887: 5.

———. *Saturday Review* 8 Jan. 1887: 44.

———. *Spectator* 15 Jan. 1887: 78–79.

Smith, Alys W. Pearsall. "A Reply from the Daughters II." *Nineteenth Century* 35 (1894): 443–50.

Spencer, Herbert. *The Principles of Psychology.* 1855. Vol. 1. New York: D. Appleton, 1897.

———. *The Principles of Sociology.* 1876. Vol. 1. New York: D. Appleton, 1896.

———. "Progress: Its Law and Cause." *Essay: Scientific, Political, and Speculative.* Vol. 1. New York: D. Appleton, 1896.

———. "Psychology of the Sexes." *Popular Science Monthly* 4 (1873–74): 30–38.

The Story of an African Farm (review). *Fortnightly Review* 40 (1883):882.

Stutfield, Hugh E. M. "The Psychology of Feminism." *Blackwood's* 161 (1897): 104–17.

———. "Tommyrotics." *Blackwoods* 157 (1895): 833–45.

Sykes, A. G. P. "The Evolution of the Sex." *Westminster Review* 143 (1895): 396–400.

[Symons, Arthur]. *Athenaeum* 10 Jan. 1891: 46.

Symons, Arthur. "The Painting of the Nineteenth Century." *Strangeness and Beauty: An Anthology of Aesthetic Criticism.* Eds. Eric Warner and Graham Hough. Vol. 2. Cambridge: Cambridge UP, 1983.

———. "The World as Ballet." *Strangeness and Beauty: An Anthology of Aesthetic Criticism.* Eds. Eric Warner and Graham Hough. Vol. 2. Cambridge: Cambridge UP, 1983.

Tynan, Katharine. *Twenty-five Years: Reminiscences.* New York: Devin-Adair, 1913.

"Universal or World Time." *Nature* 1 Apr. 1886: 521–23.

Warren, Mrs. *How I Managed My House on 200 Pounds a Year.* London: Houlston and Wright, 1864.

Webb, Beatrice. *My Apprenticeship.* London: Longmans Green, 1926.

Webster, Augusta. *A Housewife's Opinions.* London: Macmillan, 1879.

"What Woman is Fitted For." *Gender and Science: Late Nineteenth-Century Debates on the Female Mind and Body.* Ed. Katharina Rowold. Bristol: Thoemmes, 1996.

Wilde, Oscar. "The English Renaissance in Art." *Strangeness and Beauty: An Anthology of Aesthetic Criticism.* Eds. Eric Warner and Graham Hough. Vol. 2. Cambridge: Cambridge UP, 1983.

———. *The Picture of Dorian Gray.* 1891. London: Penguin, 1985.

"Women at Oxford and Cambridge." *Quarterly Review* 186 (1897): 529–51.

Woolf, Virginia. "Olive Schreiner." *New Republic* 18 Mar. 1928: 103.

———. *Orlando.* 1928. New York: Harcourt Brace Jovanovich, 1956.

———. *A Room of One's Own.* 1929. San Diego: Harcourt Brace Jovanovich, 1981.

Yerkes, Robert M. and F. M. Urban. "Sex Differences in the Estimation of Time." *Science* 22 Dec. 1905: 843–44.

Secondary Sources

Adamson, Jane. "*Tess,* Time, and Its Shapings." *Critical Review* 26 (1984): 18–36.

Alaya, Flavia. "Victorian Science and the 'Genius' of Woman." *Journal of the History of Ideas* 38 (1977): 261–80.

Altick, Richard D. *Victorian People and Ideas.* New York: Norton, 1973.

Ardis, Ann L. *New Women, New Novels: Feminism and Early Modernism.* New Brunswick: Rutgers UP, 1990.

Auerbach, Nina. *Woman and the Demon.* Cambridge: Harvard UP, 1982.

Barr, Alan P. "Evolutionary Science and the Woman Question." *Victorian Literature and Culture* 20 (1992): 25–54.

Barthes, Roland. *S/Z.* 1970. Trans. Richard Miller. New York: Hill and Wang, 1974.

Beckson, Karl. *London in the 1890s: A Cultural History.* New York: Norton, 1992.

Beer, Gillian. *Darwin's Plots.* London: Ark, 1985.

Berger, Sheila. *Thomas Hardy and Visual Structures.* New York: New York UP, 1990.

Berkman, Joyce Avrech. *The Healing Imagination of Olive Schreiner: Beyond South African Colonialism.* Amherst: U of Massachusetts P, 1989.

Berman, Art. *Preface to Modernism*. Urbana: U of Illinois P, 1994.

Bjorhovde, Gerd. *Rebellious Structures: Women Writers and the Crisis of the Novel 1880–1900*. Oslo: Norwegian UP, 1987.

Blain, Virginia, Patricia Clements, and Isobel Grundy, eds. *The Feminist Companion to Literature in English*. New Haven: Yale UP, 1990.

Bland, Lucy. *Banishing the Beast: Sexuality and the Early Feminists*. New York: New York, 1995.

Boone, Joseph Allen. *Tradition Counter Tradition: Love and the Form of Fiction*. Chicago: U of Chicago P, 1987.

Boumelha, Penny. *Thomas Hardy and Women: Sexual Ideology and Narrative Form*. Madison: U of Wisconsin P, 1985.

———. "The Woman of Genius and the Woman of Grub Street: Figures of the Female Writer in British *Fin de Siècle* Fiction." *ELT* 40 (1997): 164–80.

Bowler, Peter J. *The Invention of Progress: The Victorians and the Past*. Oxford: Basil Blackwell, 1989.

Branca, Patricia. *Silent Sisterhood: Middle–Class Women in the Victorian Home*. London: Croom Heim, 1975.

Brandon, S. G. F. *Time and Mankind*. London: Hutchinson, 1951.

Brantlinger, Patrick. *Rule of Darkness: British Literature and Imperialism, 1830–1914*. Ithaca: Cornell UP, 1988.

Brooks, Peter. *Reading for the Plot: Design and Intention in Narrative*. New York: Random House, 1984.

Buckley, Jerome Hamilton. *The Triumph of Time*. Cambridge: Harvard UP, 1966.

Bunn, David. "Embodying Africa: Woman and Romance in Colonial Fiction." *English in Africa* 15.1 (1988): 1–28.

Burstyn, Joan N. "Education and Sex: The Medical Case Against Higher Education for Women in England, 1870–1900." *Proceedings of the American Philosophical Society* 117.2 (1973): 79–89.

Burton, Antoniette. *Burdens of History: British Feminists, Indian Women, and Imperial Culture, 1865–1915.* Chapel Hill: U of North Carolina P, 1994.

Bury, J. B. *The Idea of Progress: An Inquiry into its Origin and Growth.* New York: Macmillan, 1932.

Butler, Judith. *Gender Trouble: Feminism and the Subversion of Identity.* New York: Routledge, 1990.

———. "Performative Acts and Gender Constitution: An Essay in Phenomenology and Feminist Theory." *Performing Feminisms: Feminist Critical Theory and Theatre.* Ed. Sue-Ellen Case. Baltimore: Johns Hopkins UP, 1990.

Chamberlin, J. Edward. "Images of Degeneration: Turnings and Transformations." *Degeneration: The Dark Side of Progress.* Eds. J. Edward Chamberlin and Sander L. Gilman. New York: Columbia UP, 1985.

Chapman, Raymond. *The Sense of the Past in Victorian Literature.* London: Croom Helm, 1986.

Chrisman, Laura. "The Imperial Unconscious? Representations of Imperial Discourse." *Critical Quarterly* 32.3 (1990): 38–58.

Cixous, Hélène. "Castration or Decapitation?" Trans. Annette Kuhn. *Signs* 7 (1981): 41–55.

———. "The Laugh of the Medusa." Trans. Keith Cohen and Paula Cohen. *Signs* 1 (1976): 875–93.

———. "Sorties." *The Newly Born Woman.* Cixous and Catherine Clément. Trans. Betsy Wing. Minneapolis: U of Minnesota P, 1986.

Claridge, Laura. "Tess: A Less than Pure Woman Ambivalently Presented." *Texas Studies in Literature and Language* 28 (1986): 324–38.

Clayton, Cherry. "Olive Schreiner: Paradoxical Pioneer." *Women and Writing in South Africa.* Ed. Cherry Clayton. Marshalltown: Heinemann, 1989.

———. Introduction. *Olive Schreiner: The Woman's Rose.* Cape Town: Ad. Donker, 1986.

Clayton, Jay. "Narrative and Theories of Desire." *Critical Inquiry* 16.1 (1989): 33–53.

Cohen, Morton N. *Rider Haggard: His Life and Works.* New York: Walker, 1960.

Connolly, S. J. *The Oxford Companion to Irish History.* Oxford: Oxford UP, 1998.

Coward, Rosalind. *Patriarchal Precedents: Sexuality and Social Relations.* London: Routledge and Kegan Paul, 1983.

Cronwright-Schreiner, S. C. *The Life of Olive Schreiner.* London: T. Fisher Unwin Ltd., 1924.

Crosby, Christina. *Victorians and "The Woman Question."* New York: Routledge, 1991.

Cunningham, Gail. *The New Woman and the Victorian Novel.* New York: Barnes and Noble, 1978.

Dastur, Françoise. *Heidegger and the Question of Time.* Trans. François Raffoul and David Pettigrew. Atlantic Highlands: Humanities Press International, 1998.

DeKoven, Marianne. "Gendered Doubleness and the 'Origins' of Modernist Form." *Tulsa Studies in Women's Literature* 8.1 (1989): 19–42.

Deleuze, Gilles. *Proust and Signs.* Trans. Richard Howard. New York: George Braziller, 1972.

Dijkstra, Bram. *Idols of Perversity: Fantasies of Feminine Evil in Fin-de-Siècle Culture.* New York: Oxford UP, 1986.

Dowling, Linda. "The Decadent and the New Woman in the 1890s." *Nineteenth-Century Fiction* 33 (1979): 434–53.

———. *Language and Decadence in the Victorian Fin de Siècle.* Princeton: Princeton UP, 1986.

DuPlessis, Rachel Blau. *Writing Beyond the Ending: Narrative Strategies of Twentieth Century Women Writers.* Bloomington: Indiana UP, 1985.

Dürr, Walter. "Rhythm in Music: A Formal Scaffolding of Time." *The Voices of Time.* Ed. J. T. Fraser. 2nd ed. Amherst: U of Massachusetts P, 1981.

Dyhouse, Carol. *Girls Growing Up in Late Victorian and Edwardian England.*

London: Routledge and Kegan Paul, 1981.

Eagleton, Terry. *The Ideology of the Aesthetic.* Oxford: Basil Blackwell, 1990.

———. "Thomas Hardy: Nature as Language." *Critical Quarterly* 13 (1971): 155–62.

Eksteins, Modris. "History and Degeneration: of Birds and Cages." *Degeneration: The Dark Side of Progress.* Eds. J. Edward Chamberlin and Sander L. Gilman. New York: Columbia UP, 1985.

Eliade, Mircea. *The Myth of the Eternal Return.* Trans. Willard R. Trask. London: Routledge and Kegan Paul, 1955.

Etherington, Norman. *The Annotated She.* Bloomington: Indiana UP, 1991.

———. *Rider Haggard.* Boston: Twayne, 1984.

Fabian, Johannes. *Time and the Other: How Anthropology Makes Its Object.* New York: Columbia UP, 1983.

Fee, Elizabeth. "The Sexual Politics of Victorian Social Anthropology." *Feminist Studies* 1.3–4 (1973): 23–39.

Flint, Kate. *The Woman Reader: 1837–1914.* Oxford: Clarendon, 1993.

Flugel, J. C. *A Hundred Years of Psychology: 1833–1933.* New York: Macmillan, 1934.

Foucault, Michel. *Discipline and Punish.* Trans. Alan Sheridan. New York: Vintage, 1977.

Frankle, Barbara Stein. "The Genteel Family: High-Victorian Conceptions of Domesticity and Good Behavior." Diss. U of Wisconsin, 1969.

Fraser, J. T., ed. *The Voices of Time.* 2nd ed. Amherst: U of Massachusetts P, 1981.

Fraser, J. T., F. C. Haber, and G. H. Muller, eds. *The Study of Time.* Berlin: Springer-Verlag, 1972.

Freeman, Janet H. "Highways and Cornfields: Space and Time in the Narration of *Jude the Obscure.*" *Colby Quarterly* 27 (1991): 161–73.

———. "Ways of Looking at Tess." *Studies in Philology* 79 (1982): 311–23.

Frierson, William C. "The English Controversy over Realism in Fiction 1885–1895." *PMLA* 43 (1928): 533–50.

Frye, Northrup. *Anatomy of Criticism*. Princeton: Princeton UP, 1957.

Gilbert, Sandra. "Rider Haggard's Heart of Darkness." *Coordinates: Placing Science Fiction and Fantasy*. Eds. George E. Slusser, Eric S. Rabkin, and Robert Scholes. Carbondale: Southern Illinois UP, 1983.

Gilbert, Sandra, and Susan Gubar. *No Man's Land: The Place of the Woman Writer in the Twentieth Century*. Vol. 2: *Sexchanges*. New Haven: Yale UP, 1989.

Gilmour, Robin. *The Victorian Period: The Intellectual and Cultural Context of English Literature 1830–1890*. London: Longman, 1993.

Gold, Barri J. "Embracing the Corpse: Discursive Recycling in H. Rider Haggard's *She*." *ELT* 38 (1995): 305–27.

Good, Richard. *Victorian Clocks*. London: British Museum P, 1996.

Gorman, Frank H., Jr. *The Ideology of Ritual: Space, Time and Status in the Priestly Theology*. Sheffield: JSOT, 1990.

Green, Louise. "The Unhealed Wound: Olive Schreiner's Expressive Art." *Pretexts* 6 (1997): 21–34.

Grundy, Joan. *Hardy and the Sister Arts*. New York: Harper, 1979.

Gullette, Margaret Morganroth. Afterward. *The Daughters of Danaus*. New York: Feminist Press, 1989.

Haber, Francis C. *The Age of the World: Moses to Darwin*. Baltimore: Johns Hopkins P, 1959.

Hardy, Florence Emily. *The Life of Thomas Hardy*. Hamden: Archon, 1970.

Higonnet, Margaret R. "Fictions of Feminine Voice: Antiphony and Silence in Hardy's *Tess of the D'Urbervilles*." *Out of Bounds: Male Writers and Gender(ed) Criticism*. Eds. Laura Claridge and Elizabeth Langland. Amherst: U of Massachusetts P, 1990.

Hinz, Evelyn. "Rider Haggard's *She*: An Archetypal 'History of Adventure.'" *Studies in the Novel* 4 (1972): 416–31.

Hirsch, Marianne. "Ideology, Form, and 'Allerleirauh': Reflections on *Reading for the Plot*." *Children's Literature* 14: 163–68.

Homans, Margaret. *Women Writers and Poetic Identity*. Princeton: Princeton UP, 1980.

hooks, bell. *Black Looks: Race and Representation*. Boston: South End, 1992.

Huddleston, Joan. *Sarah Grand: A Bibliography*. Queensland: U of Queensland, 1979.

Ingham, Patricia. *Thomas Hardy*. Atlantic Highlands: Humanities Press International, 1990.

Irigaray, Luce. *The Irigaray Reader*. Ed. Margaret Whitford. Oxford: Blackwell, 1991.

———. *Je, Tu, Nous: Toward a Culture of Difference*. Trans. Alison Martin. New York: Routledge, 1993.

———. *This Sex Which Is Not One*. Trans. Catherine Porter and Carolyn Burke. Ithaca: Cornell UP, 1985.

Jackson, Rosemary. *Fantasy: The Literature of Subversion*. Methuen: London, 1981.

Jagyna, L. S. "The Physiology of Mind, the Unity of Nature, and the Moral Order in Victorian Thought." *British Journal for the History of Science* 14 (1981): 110–32.

JanMohamed, Abdul R. "The Economy of Manichean Allegory: The Function of Racial Difference in Colonialist Literature." *Critical Inquiry* 12.1 (1985): 59–87.

Jardine, Alice. "Introduction to Julia Kristeva's 'Women's Time.'" *Signs* 7 (1981): 5–12.

Katz, Wendy R. *Rider Haggard and the Fiction of Empire*. Cambridge: Cambridge UP, 1987.

Kern, Stephen. *The Culture of Time and Space 1880–1918*. Cambridge:

Harvard UP, 1983.

Kersley, Gillian. *Darling Madame: Sarah Grand and Devoted Friend.* London: Virago, 1983.

Kilgour, Maggie. *From Communion to Cannibalism: An Anatomy of Metaphors of Incorporation.* Princeton: Princeton UP, 1990.

Kincaid, James. "'You Did Not Come': Absence, Death and Eroticism in *Tess.*" *Sex and Death in Victorian Literature.* Ed. Regina Barreca. Bloomington: Indiana UP, 1990.

Kissane, James. "Victorian Mythology." *Victorian Studies* 6 (1962): 5–28.

Kolve, V. A. *The Play Called Corpus Christi.* Stanford: Stanford UP, 1966.

Kranidis, Rita S. *Subversive Discourse: The Cultural Production of Late Victorian Feminist Novels.* New York: St. Martin's, 1995.

Kristeva, Julia. "About Chinese Women." *The Kristeva Reader.* Ed. Toril Moi. New York: Columbia UP, 1986.

———. *Powers of Horror.* Trans. Leon S. Roudiez. New York: Columbia UP, 1982.

———. "Women's Time." Trans. Alice Jardine and Harry Blake. *Signs* 7 (1981): 13–35.

Kucich, John. *The Power of Lies: Transgression in Victorian Fiction.* Ithaca: Cornell UP, 1994.

Landes, David S. *Revolution in Time: Clocks and the Making of the Modern World.* Cambridge: Harvard UP, 1983.

Landow, George P. *Victorian Types, Victorian Shadows: Biblical Typology in Victorian Literature, Art, and Thought.* Boston: Routledge and Kegan Paul, 1980.

Langbauer, Laurie. *Novels of Everyday Life: The Series in English Fiction, 1850–1930.* Ithaca: Cornell UP, 1999.

Law, Jules David. "Sleeping Figures: Hardy, History, and the Gendered Body." *ELH* 65 (1998): 223-57.

Lecercle, Jean Jacques. "The Violence of Style in *Tess.*" *Alternative Hardy.* Ed. Lance St. John Butler. Houndsmill, Basingstoke: Macmillan, 1989.

Ledger, Sally. *The New Woman: Fiction and Feminism at the Fin de Siècle.* Manchester: Manchester UP, 1997.

Levine, George. *Darwin and the Novelists: Patterns of Science in Victorian Fiction.* Cambridge: Harvard UP, 1988.

Lovell, Terry. *Consuming Fiction.* London: Verso, 1987.

Lukács, Georg. *Realism in Our Time: Literature and the Class Struggle.* Trans. John and Necke Mander. New York: Harper and Row, 1964.

Mangum, Teresa. "Feminist Fiction and Fictional Feminism: Sarah Grand and the New Woman Novel." Diss. U of Illinois, 1990.

———. *Married, Middlebrow, and Militant: Sarah Grand and the New Woman Novel.* Ann Arbor: U of Michigan P, 1998.

———. "Sex, Siblings, and the Fin De Siecle" *The Significance of Sibling Relationships in Literature.* Eds. JoAnna Stephens Mink and Janet Doubler Ward. Bowling Green: Popular, 1992.

Mazlish, Bruce. "A Triptych: Freud's *The Interpretation of Dreams*, Rider Haggard's *She,* and Bulwer-Lytton's *The Coming Race.*" *Comparative Studies in Society and History* 35 (1993): 726–45.

McClintock, Anne. *Imperial Leather: Race, Gender and Sexuality in the Colonial Contest.* New York: Routledge, 1995.

McCracken, Scott. "Stages of Sand and Blood: the Performance of Gendered Subjectivity in Olive Schreiner's Colonial Allegories." *Women's Writing* 3 (1996): 231–42.

Mellor, Anne K. *Romanticism & Gender.* New York: Routledge, 1993.

Meyerhoff, Hans. *The Philosophy of History in Our Time.* Garden City: Doubleday, 1959.

———. *Time in Literature.* Berkeley: U of California P, 1968.

Michie, Helena. *The Flesh Made Word: Female Figures and Women's Bodies.* New York: Oxford UP, 1987.

Miller, J. Hillis. *Fiction and Repetition*. Cambridge: Harvard UP, 1982.

———. *Thomas Hardy: Distance and Desire*. Cambridge: Harvard UP, 1970.

Miller, Jane Eldridge. *Rebel Women: Feminism, Modernism and the Edwardian Novel*. London: Virago, 1994.

Moi, Toril. *Sexual/Textual Politics: Feminist Literary Theory*. London: Routledge, 1985.

Monsman, Gerald. "The Idea of 'Story' in Olive Schreiner's *Story of an African Farm*." *Texas Studies in Literature and Language* 27 (1985): 249–69.

———. "Olive Schreiner." *International Literature in English: Essays on the Major Writers*. Ed. Robert L. Ross. New York: Garland, 1991.

———. "Olive Schreiner: Literature and the Politics of Power." *Texas Studies in Literature and Language* 30 (1988): 583–610.

———. "Patterns of Narration and Characterization in Schreiner's *The Story of an African Farm*." *ELT* 28 (1985): 253–70.

Morgan, Rosemarie. *Women and Sexuality in the Novels of Thomas Hardy*. London: Routledge, 1988.

Morgan, Susan. *Sisters in Time: Imagining Gender in Nineteenth-Century British Fiction*. Oxford: Oxford UP, 1989.

Morton, Peter. "*Tess of the D'Urbervilles:* A Neo-Darwinian Reading." *Southern Review* 7 (1974): 38–50.

Mosedale, Susan Sleeth. "Science Corrupted: Victorian Biologists Consider 'The Woman Question.'" *Journal of the History of Biology* 11: 1–55.

Mumford, Lewis. *Technics and Civilization*. New York: Harcourt, Brace, 1934.

Murphy, Gardner. *Historical Introduction to Modern Psychology*. New York: Harcourt, Brace, 1949.

Nelson, Carolyn Christensen. *British Women Fiction Writers of the 1890s*. New York: Twayne, 1996.

Neubauer, John. *The Fin-de-Siècle Culture of Adolescence*. New Haven: Yale UP, 1992.

Osborne, L. Mackenzie. "The 'Chronological Frontier' in Thomas Hardy's Novels." *Studies in the Novel* 4 (1972): 543–55.

Otis, Laura. "Organic Memory: History, Bodies and Texts in *Tess of the D'Urbervilles*." *Nineteenth Century Studies* 8 (1994): 1–22.

O'Toole, Tess. *Genealogy and Fiction in Hardy: Family Lineage and Narrative Lines*. New York: St. Martin's, 1997.

Padian, Kevin. "'A Daughter of the Soil': Themes of Deep Time and Evolution in Thomas Hardy's *Tess of the D'Urbervilles*." *Thomas Hardy Journal* 13.3 (1997): 65–81.

Patrides, C. A., ed. Introduction. *Aspects of Time*. Manchester: Manchester UP, 1976.

Paxton, Nancy L. "*The Story of an African Farm* and the Dynamics of Woman-to-Woman Influence." *Texas Studies in Literature and Language* 30 (1988): 562–82.

Pickering, George. *Creative Malady*. New York: Oxford UP, 1974.

Pratt, Annis. *Archetypal Patterns in Women's Fiction*. Bloomington: Indiana UP, 1981.

Psomiades, Kathy Alexis. *Beauty's Body: Femininity and Representation in British Aestheticism*. Stanford: Stanford UP, 1997.

Pykett, Lyn. "The Cause of Women and the Course of Fiction: The Case of Mona Caird." *Gender Roles and Sexuality in Victorian Literature*. Ed. Christopher Parker. Brookfield, Vt.: Scolar, 1995.

———. *Engendering Fictions: The English Novel in the Early Twentieth Century*. London: Edward Arnold, 1995.

———. *The "Improper" Feminine: The Women's Sensation Novel and the New Woman Writing*. London: Routledge, 1992.

———. "Portraits of the Artist as a Young Woman: Representations of the Female Artist in the New Woman Fiction of the 1890s." *Victorian Women Writers and the Woman Question*. Ed. Nicola Diane Thompson. Cambridge: Cambridge UP, 1999.

———. "Ruinous Bodies: Women and Sexuality in Hardy's Late Fiction." *Critical Survey* 5 (1993): 157–66.

Quinones, Ricardo J. *Mapping Literary Modernism: Time and Development.* Princeton: Princeton UP, 1985.

Ragussis, Michael. *Acts of Naming: The Family Plot in Fiction.* New York: Oxford UP, 1986.

Ricoeur, Paul. *Time and Narrative.* Vol. 2. Trans. Kathleen McLaughlin and David Pellauer. Chicago: U of Chicago P, 1985.

Roberts, Marguerite. *Tess in the Theatre.* Toronto: U of Toronto P, 1950.

Robinson, Sally. "The 'Anti-Logos Weapon': Multiplicity in Women's Texts." *Contemporary Literature* 29.1 (1988): 105–24.

Rubinstein, David. *Before the Suffragettes: Women's Emancipation in the 1890s.* New York: St. Martin's, 1986.

Russell, J. L. "Time in Christian Thought." *The Voices of Time.* Ed. J. T. Fraser. 2nd ed. Amherst: U of Massachusetts P, 1981.

Russett, Cynthia Eagle. *Sexual Science: The Victorian Construction of Womanhood.* Cambridge: Harvard UP, 1989.

Ryan, Michael. "One Name of Many Shapes: *The Well-Beloved.*" *Critical Approaches to the Fiction of Thomas Hardy.* Ed. Dale Kramer. New York: Barnes and Noble, 1979.

Sadoff, Dianne Fallon. "Looking at Tess: The Female Figure in Two Narrative Media." *The Sense of Sex: Feminist Perspectives on Hardy.* Ed. Margaret R. Higonnet. Urbana: U of Illinois P, 1993.

Said, Edward W. *Orientalism.* New York: Vintage, 1979.

Sandison, Alan. *The Wheel of Empire.* New York: St. Martin's, 1967.

Schaffer, Talia, and Kathy Alexis Psomiades, eds. *Women and British Aestheticism.* Charlottesville: UP of Virginia, 1999.

Schivelbusch, Wolfgang. *The Railway Journey: The Industrialization of Time and Space in the 19th Century.* Berkeley: U of California P, 1986.

Sedgwick, Eve Kosofsky. *The Coherence of Gothic Conventions*. New York: Methuen, 1986.

Senf, Carol. Introduction. *The Heavenly Twins*. Ann Arbor: U of Michigan P, 1992.

Shiach, Morag. *Hélène Cixous: A Politics of Writing*. London: Routledge, 1991.

Showalter, Elaine. *Sexual Anarchy: Gender and Culture at the Fin de Siècle*. New York: Viking, 1990.

———. "Syphilis, Sexuality, and the Fiction of the Fin de Siècle." *Sex, Politics, and Science in the Nineteenth Century Novel*. Ed. Ruth Yeazell. Baltimore: Johns Hopkins UP, 1986.

Siegel, Sandra. "Literature and Degeneration: The Representation of 'Decadence.'" *Degeneration: The Dark Side of Progress*. Eds. J. Edward Chamberlain and Sander Gilman. New York: Columbia UP, 1985.

Silverman, Kaja. "History, Figuration and Female Subjectivity in *Tess of the D'Urbervilles*." *Novel* 18.3 (1984): 5–28.

Smalley, Ruth Ann. "A Widening Consciousness: Women Novelists and Autobiographical Fiction in Victorian Britain." Diss. U of Iowa, 1992.

Springhall, John. *Coming of Age: Adolescence in Britain 1860–1960*. Dublin: Gill and Macmillan, 1986.

Stave, Shirley A. *The Decline of the Goddess: Nature, Culture, and Women in Thomas Hardy's Fiction*. Westport: Greenwood, 1995.

Stetz, Margaret Diane. "*New Grub Street* and the Woman Writer of the 1890s." *Transforming Genres: New Approaches to British Fiction of the 1890s*. Eds. Nikki Lee Manos and Meri-Jane Rochelson. New York: St. Martin's, 1994.

Stewart, Garrett. *Death Sentences: Styles of Dying in British Fiction*. Cambridge: Harvard UP, 1984.

Stott, Rebecca. *The Fabrication of the Late-Victorian Femme Fatale: The Kiss of Death*. Houndmill, Basingstoke: Macmillan, 1992.

Toulmin, Stephen and June Goodfield. *The Discovery of Time*. New York: Harper and Row, 1965.

Trezise, Simon. "Places in Time: Discovering the Chronotope in *Tess of the D'Urbervilles*." *Critical Survey* 5 (1993): 136–42.

Van Riper, A. Bowdoin. *Men Among the Mammoths: Victorian Science and the Discovery of Human Prehistory*. Chicago: U of Chicago P, 1993.

Whitrow, G. J. "Reflections on the History of the Concept of Time." *The Study of Time*. Eds. J. T. Fraser, F. C. Haber, and G. H. Muller. Berlin: Springer-Verlag, 1972.

Wickens, G. Glen. "Victorian Theories of Language and *Tess of the d'Urbervilles*." *Mosaic* 19 (1986): 99–115.

Wilson, Keith. *Thomas Hardy on Stage*. New York: St. Martin's, 1995.

Winnett, Susan. "Coming Unstrung: Women, Men, Narrative, and Principles of Pleasure." *PMLA* 109 (1990): 505–18.

Woodward, William R. and Mitchell G. Ash, eds. *The Problematic Science: Psychology in Nineteenth-Century Thought*. New York: Praeger, 1982.

Wotton, George. *Thomas Hardy: Towards a Materialist Criticism*. Totowa: Barnes and Noble, 1985.

Wright, Lawrence. *Clockwork Man*. London: Elek, 1968.

Wright, Terence. "Space, Time and Paradox: The Sense of History in Hardy's Last Novels." *Essays and Studies* 44 (1991): 41–52.

Index

Adam, Juliette, 9
Adamson, Jane, 241n. 4
Adolescence, 114, 132–33, 137–38
Alaya, Flavia, 248n. 23
Albert, Prince, 20
Allan, J. McGrigor, 122, 247n. 16
Allegory, 36, 167–68, 207–10, 212
Allen, Grant, 6, 122, 129
Altick, Richard D., 12, 19
Anderson, Elizabeth Garrett, 7
Anthropology, 25, 55–56, 57
Archaeology, 11, 166
Ardis, Ann, 227, 233nn. 2, 4, 237n., 3 , 241n. 3, 252n. 17, 255n. 17
Aristotle, 17, 37, 163
Arling, Nat, 9, 10
Arnold, Matthew, 187
Arnold, Thomas, 15
Art, and gender, 89, 91–105, 209–10, 217–18; and ideology, 153
Ash, Mitchell G., 245n. 4
Auerbach, Erich, 234n. 13
Auerbach, Nina, 236n. 2, 237n. 3
Augustine, 17

Bachofen, J. J., 25, 57

Bacon, Francis, 235n. 19
Barr, Alan P., 245n. 5
Barthes, Roland, 208, 209
Beautiful, the, 50, 134
Beckson, Karl, 233n. 2
Beer, Gillian, 241n. 3, 242n. 13
Berger, Sheila, 243n. 21
Bergson, Henri, 185–86, 229
Berkman, Joyce Avrech, 254nn. 4, 9, 255nn. 14, 16, 256n. 21
Berman, Art, 181–82
Bildungsroman, 115, 116, 119, 137, 150
Bjorhovde, Gerd, 227, 249n. 26, 250n. 38, 253n. 3, 255n. 17
Blackwell, Antoinette Brown, 112, 131
Bland, Lucy, 233n. 3, 234n. 11, 246n. 8, 250nn. 30, 33
Boone, Joseph Allen, 244n. 29, 253n. 3
Boumelha, Penny, 241n. 3, 242n. 12, 248n. 24
Bowler, Peter, 15, 19, 21, 234n. 6, 235nn. 14, 15, 246n. 12
Branca, Patricia, 157, 252n. 7
Brandon, S. G. F., 21
Brantlinger, Patrick, 236n. 3
Brooks, Peter, 207, 254n. 10
Buckle, H. T., 16
Buckley, Jerome, 233nn. 1, 6, 234n., 10
Bulley, A. Amy, 9
Bunn, David, 236n. 2, 240n. 20
Burnham, William H., 138
Burstyn, Joan, 246n. 10
Burton, Antoinette, 29
Bury, J. B., 16
Butler, Judith, 125, 126, 127, 132
Butler, Samuel, 185

Caird, Mona, 2, 8, 10, 157, 163, 164, 177–79, 181, 184, 231; *The Daughters of Danaus,* 29, 151–54, 158, 159–82, 188; *The Wing of Azrael,* 182–88
Campbell, Harry, 111–12, 117, 119, 121, 122, 124, 126, 133
Carlyle, Thomas, 14, 15, 16, 19
Chamberlin, J. Edward, 23
Chapman, Raymond, 19, 234n. 10
Childhood, development in, 114–25, 127, 137, 139, 146, 216–17
Chrisman, Laura, 236n. 3, 237n. 6, 238n. 13
Christianity, as anti-evolutionary, 144–46; and creationism, 10–11, 15; and evolution, 16–17, 21; and history, 16–18; influence of, 22; vs. paganism, 17–18, 24–25, 47–53, 66–68, 75–77; and patriarchy, 24, 49, 138, 139, 144–45, 196–203, 206, 208, 214–15. *See also* History, as secularized religion
Cixous, Hélène, 27, 127, 207, 224, 247n. 18, 255n. 10; on bisexuality, 221, 222; on history, 38, 46, 75, 81, 177, 188
Claridge, Laura, 245n. 32
Clarke, Edward, 129
Clayton, Cherry, 210, 253n. 3
Clayton, Jay, 207
Clocks, 71–72; history of, 14, 22; as images, 149, 162–63, 173–74, 175, 180, 183, 196, 197–99, 220, 230
Closure, 64, 107, 176–77, 187–88, 224–25

Cohen, Morton, 240n. 21
Comte, Auguste, 20, 135, 211, 248–49n. 25
Conduct books, 157–58, 159
Connolly, S. J., 238n. 9
Coward, Rosalind, 25
Craik, Dinah Mulock, 151, 155–56
Crosby, Christina, 24–25
Cross-dressing, 147–49, 222
Cunningham, Gail, 153, 241n. 3

Darwin, Charles, 15, 21–22, 109–14, 118, 122, 133, 245n. 5; *The Descent of Man and Selection in Relation to Sex,* 25–26, 56, 109, 133, 245n. 1, 248n. 23; and environment, 137, 138; *On the Origin of Species,* 11–12, 21–22, 109, 114
Dastur, Françoise, 229, 256–57n. 2
Degeneration, 22–23, 44, 78–81, 145, 175
DeKoven, Marianne, 231
Delauney, G., 133
Deleuze, Gilles, 209
De Morgan, John, 40, 64–65
Derrida, Jacques, 206
"Devereux, Roy," 112–13, 123, 150
Development, reversal of, 58–60, 222–24
Devolution. *See* Evolution
Dickens, Charles, 256n. 19
Dijkstra, Bram, 239n. 15
Dowling, Linda, 172, 248n. 22
DuPlessis, Rachel Blau, 54, 190, 192, 207, 224, 253n. 3
Dürr, Walter, 170–71, 172
Dyhouse, Carol, 138, 166, 249–50n. 28

Eagleton, Terry, 91, 244n. 28
Education, and biology, 113–14, 127–33, 139–41; female, 6–7, 129–32, 141, 179–80
Eksteins, Modris, 15, 23
Eliade, Mircea, 18, 42
Ellis, Havelock, 5, 141, 157
Emerson, Ralph Waldo, 159
Engels, Friedrich, 20
Escuret, Annie, 244n. 28
Etherington, Norman, 237nn. 5, 6, 8, 237–38n. 8, 239nn. 14, 17, 240n. 21
Eugenics, 45–46
Evolution, and civilizations, 19, 22, 44–45, 56, 210–11; vs. devolution, 22–23, 55–57, 62, 78–81; and the family, 131; and race, 116, 117, 119, 210; and women, 6, 8–9, 25–26, 55–57, 109–19, 121–22, 126, 127, 129, 133, 135–41, 143–47, 150, 178–79
Evolutionary psychology, defined, 110–14. *See also* Evolution, women and

Fabian, Johannes, 21, 28, 44
Fairbairn, Patrick, 255n. 12
Fee, Elizabeth, 25, 55
FitzGerald, Edward, 183
Flint, Kate, 246n. 10, 250n. 29, 252n. 6
Flugel, J. C., 245n. 4
Forrest, G. F., 40
Foucault, Michel, 157
Frankle, Barbara Stein, 157
Fraser, J. T., 233–34n. 6
Freeman, Janet H., 241n. 2, 244n. 24
Freud, Sigmund, 236n. 2

Frierson, William C., 255n. 17
Froude, James, 15
Frye, Northrop, 33–34

Galton, Francis, 134, 146, 250n. 35
Gamble, Eliza Burt, 113, 118, 126, 136
Gaskell, Catherine Milnes, 156
Geddes, Patrick, 110, 111
Genius, 115, 118, 119, 133–36, 155, 158, 161
Geology, 11–12, 16
Gilbert, Sandra, 58–59, 236n. 2, 236–37n. 3, 237n. 6, 238n. 11, 239n. 17, 254nn. 5, 8
Gilmour, Robin, 14, 19, 233n. 1, 234n. 10, 245n. 3
Gold, Barri J., 237n. 5
Good, Richard, 234n. 8
Goodfield, June, 234n. 10
Goodman, Charlotte, 250n. 34
Gosse, Edmund, 8, 256n. 18
Gothic, 53, 54–55, 182
Grand, Sarah, 2, 8–10, 26, 28–29, 111, 113, 114, 153; *The Beth Book*, 29, 110, 113, 114–36, 137, 139–40, 141, 150; *The Heavenly Twins*, 28–29, 110, 113, 114, 129, 137–50, 162–63, 178–79
Great Exhibition, 14, 20
Green, Louise, 255–56n. 17, 256n. 20
Grote, George, 16, 53, 239n. 16
Grundy, Joan, 244n. 26
Gubar, Susan, 58–59, 236nn. 2, 3, 237n. 6, 238n. 11, 239n. 17, 254nn. 5, 8
Gullette, Margaret Morganroth, 250–51n. 1

Haber, Francis C., 17, 18, 234nn. 6, 12
Haggard, H. Rider, 2, 24, 28, 189, 253n. 1; *Allan Quatermain*, 240n. 25; *Ayesha*, 65–69; *Cleopatra*, 47–48; *Elissa*, 52–53; *She*, 29, 31–69, 177, 189, 231; *She and Allan*, 240n. 24
Hall, G. Stanley, 138
Hardy, Thomas, 2, 24, 28, 212, 231, 256n. 18; *Jude the Obscure*, 72, 76–78, 79–80, 97; *A Laodicean*, 72, 78, 79–80; *The Mayor of Casterbridge*, 72, 97; *A Pair of Blue Eyes*, 72, 96; *Tess of the d'Urbervilles*, 29, 71–107, 169, 177, 182; *The Well-Beloved*, 72, 93–96; *The Woodlanders*, 72, 96–97
Harper, Charles G., 5, 6
Harrison, Frederic, 4–5, 20
Harvey, H. E., 9
Hegel, G. W. F., 15, 20, 47
Heidegger, Martin, 229, 256–57n. 2
Hering, Ewald, 185
Hewitt, Emma Churchman, 9
Higonnet, Margaret R., 243n. 23
Hinz, Evelyn, 238n. 10
Hirsch, Marianne, 254n. 10
History, vs. ahistoricity, 24–25, 34, 41–48, 74–78, 81; and authenticity, 34–36, 39, 66; and the female body, 74, 82–85, 89–90; and repetition, 85–86, 177–78, 180, 183–88; as secularized religion, 15–19; unhealthiness of, 22, 180–82, 184; Victorian valuation of, 15–16. *See also* Progress

Hogarth, Janet E., 8, 134
Homans, Margaret, 46
hooks, bell, 56
Huddleston, Joan, 246n. 11
Huxley, T. H., 23

Imperialism, 19, 32
Ingham, Patricia, 243n. 19
Intuition, vs. reasoning, 121–22, 124
Irigaray, Luce, 27, 104, 124, 174; on history, 56; on the mother, 58, 59

Jackson, Rosemary, 55
Jagyna, L. S., 245n. 4
James, William, 117, 118, 121, 185, 230, 250n. 37
Jamieson, Herbert, 9
JanMohamed, Abdul R., 32–33
Jardine, Alice, 26

Kant, Immanuel, 229
Katz, Wendy R., 34, 236n. 3
Kern, Stephen, 229, 234n. 6
Kersley, Gillian, 246n. 7
Kilgour, Maggie, 56
Kincaid, James, 244n. 28
Kissane, James, 239n. 16
Kolve, V. A., 234–35n. 13
Kranidis, Rita, 153
Kristeva, Julia, 103, 126–27, 152–53, 190, 254n. 7; on abjection, 58; on language, 60, 171, 192–93; "Women's Time," 4, 26–27, 91, 192, 204–5, 207
Kucich, John, 243n. 19, 247n. 17
Künstlerroman, 158
Langbauer, Laurie, 252n. 9
Lancaster, E. G., 138

Landes, David S., 13–14, 233n. 6, 234n. 9, 235n. 18
Landow, George P., 254n. 6, 255n. 12
Lang, Andrew, 39–40, 42, 46–47, 236n. 1, 238nn. 8, 12, 239n. 18
Language, acquisition of, 119–20, 124–25, 127–28, 214–15; and the body, 115, 125, 126–27; and dance, 172; and development, 119–28, 214, 223–24; and linearity, 192–94, 218; and the mother, 59–60; music as, 171–72; oral vs. written, 75–76, 115, 122–23, 127, 136, 140
Lankester, E. Ray, 23
Law, Jules David, 243n. 15
Lawrence, D. H., 229
Lecercle, Jean Jacques, 244n. 27
Ledger, Sally, 233nn. 2, 3, 5, 252n. 13
Lessing, Gotthold, 170
Levine, George, 21, 242n. 13
Linton, Eliza Lynn, 5, 212, 256n. 18
Loftie, Mrs., 159
Lombroso, Cesare, 133, 248n. 22
Lovell, Terry, 246nn. 6, 11, 249n. 26
Lukács, Georg, 229
Lyell, Charles, 11, 12, 16, 245n. 5

Macaulay, Thomas Babington, 16, 19–21, 78–79
"Macleod, Fiona," 251n. 2
Mangum, Teresa, 233n. 2, 246n. 11, 247nn. 17, 18, 248nn. 20, 24, 250nn. 29, 34, 36
Marriage, 7–9, 145–46, 149, 152, 154, 161–65, 183–84

Martineau, Harriet, 155, 158
Marx, Karl, 20–21, 157
Maternity. *See* Motherhood
Matriarchy, 25, 55–56
Maudsley, Henry, 7, 119, 129, 141
Mazlish, Bruce, 237n. 6
McClintock, Anne, 28, 235n. 20, 236n. 2, 254n. 4
McCracken, Scott, 207, 255n. 11
Mellor, Anne K., 247n. 15
Meyerhoff, Hans, 15, 228, 230, 235n. 14
Michie, Helena, 243nn. 15, 17
Mill, John Stuart, 8, 20, 112, 161, 163, 248n. 23, 252nn. 10, 11
Miller, Jane Eldridge, 233n. 2, 256n. 1
Miller, J. Hillis, 87, 243n. 20
Mimicry, 124–27
Modernism, 2, 181–82, 227–31
Modernity, 28, 42–43
Moi, Toril, 33, 127
Monsman, Gerald, 253–54n. 3, 254n. 4, 256n. 23
Moore, George, 212, 256n. 18
Moore, William Withers, 129–30
Morgan, Rosemarie, 245n. 32
Morgan, Susan, 235n. 17
Morris, William, 50
Morton, Peter, 242n. 13
Mosedale, Susan Sleeth, 111
Motherhood, 9–10, 37, 45–47, 52, 58–60, 67, 68, 134, 163–64, 219–20; and contamination, 59–60; critique of, 9–10, 152, 163–64; and duties, 6–7, 112, 129–31, 170
Mumford, Lewis, 14, 235n. 14
Murphy, Gardner, 245n. 4
Myth, 53–54, 90–91, 229

Narrative, and desire, 207; linear, 190, 206–8, 210, 211–12, 213, 224–25
Nature, and gender, 46–48, 63, 65, 119–21, 134–35, 192, 201–2
Nelson, Carolyn Christensen, 233n. 2, 250n. 32
Neubauer, John, 137, 249n. 28
New Man, 222, 225
New Woman, and class, 10, 28–29, 72–73; debate over, 3–10, 31–32; and evolution, 57, 111, 135–36, 143–44, 150; and race, 28–29
Nietzsche, Friedrich, 22, 26, 180–82, 184, 187, 229, 252n. 15
Nightingale, Florence, 151, 154, 155, 158, 160–61
Nordau, Max, 23, 248n. 22

Oliphant, Margaret, 7–8
Organic memory, 185
Orientalism, 44–45, 56
Originality, and women, 124, 126
Otis, Laura, 242n. 13, 244n. 28, 252n. 16
O'Toole, Tess, 241n. 6, 242n. 9, 243n. 15
Ouida, 5, 6

Padian, Kevin, 242n. 13
Parodies, 39–41, 42, 46–47, 64–65
Pater, Walter, 53, 92, 153
Patrides, C. A., 234n. 6, 235n. 14
Paxton, Nancy L., 253n. 2
Pearson, Karl, 6, 7
Pickering, George, 252n. 8
Pike, Luke Owen, 122
Plato, 17
Pratt, Annis, 170

Progress, 80, 122; critique of, 20–21, 177, 181, 210–12; vs. stasis, 44, 85; Victorian conceptions of, 19–23. *Also see* Degeneration
Proust, Marcel, 96
Psomiades, Kathy Alexis, 91, 248n. 20
Pykett, Lyn, 227, 233nn. 2, 3, 243n. 19, 243–44n. 23, 246nn. 6, 8, 247nn. 14, 18, 248nn. 22, 251–52n. 4, 252nn. 5, 14

Quest romance, 31, 32, 33–34
Quinones, Ricardo J., 228, 229

Race, and gender, 32–33, 56, 116, 117, 119
Ragussis, Michael, 241n. 5
Realism, 190, 212–13
Reproduction. *See* Motherhood
Richardson, Benjamin Ward, 130
Ricoeur, Paul, 230
Ritchie, David G., 112, 144
Roberton, William, 247n. 13
Roberts, Marguerite, 242–43n. 14
Robinson, Sally, 255n. 10
Romanes, George, 7, 117, 124, 250n. 35
Rubinstein, David, 246n. 10
Ruskin, John, 53, 79
Russett, Cynthia Eagle, 111, 245n. 1
Ryan, Michael, 243n. 19

Sadoff, Dianne Fallon, 244n. 28
Said, Edward, 44, 238n. 11
Sandison, Alan, 239n. 17
Schaffer, Talia, 248n. 20
Schreiner, Olive, 2, 3, 24, 29, 253n. 1; *From Man to Man*, 210–12,

220, 221; short stories of, 220–21; *The Story of an African Farm*, 29–30, 176, 189–210, 212–25, 231; *Undine*, 197–99, 220, 221; *Woman and Labor*, 3, 216–17, 222
Sedgwick, Eve Kosofsky, 54–55
Senf, Carol A., 246n. 11
Sexuality, female, 8, 50–51, 65, 73, 84–85, 174–75, 207
Showalter, Elaine, 240nn. 20, 21, 250n. 31
Silverman, Kaja, 98–99, 244nn. 28, 31
Smalley, Ruth, 247nn. 17, 18
Smith, Alys W. Pearsall, 156
Socialism, 20–21
Spencer, Herbert, 20, 111, 117, 124, 129, 131, 133, 245n. 3
Springhall, John, 138, 249n. 28
Stave, Shirley, 242nn. 10, 11
Stetz, Margaret Diane, 252n. 5
Stewart, Garrett, 223–24
Stott, Rebecca, 236n. 2, 237n. 6, 238n. 11, 239n. 17, 240n. 20, 244n. 28, 245n. 34
Stutfield, Hugh E. M., 8, 122
Sublime, the, 50, 134
Swinburne, Algernon Charles, 50, 77
Sykes, A. G. P., 3
Symons, Arthur, 172, 210, 255n. 13
Syphilis, 145

Thomson, J. Arthur, 110, 111
Time, demands on women's, 151, 152, 154–62, 164–66, 172–74; gendered, summarized, 23–30, 32; and immortality, 49, 51, 53–55, 63, 67; natural order of, defined, 3–4, 15–30; cyclical, theories of, 17–19, 26–27; linear, theories of, 17–19, 26; Victorian engrossment in, 10–14. *See also* Christianity; Evolution; History; Progress
Toulmin, Stephen, 234n. 10
Trains, 12–14, 72, 166, 168–70, 176
Trezise, Simon, 241n. 4
Tynan, Katharine, 251n. 2

Ussher, Bishop, 10

Van Riper, A. Bowdoin, 234n. 7
Vico, G. B., 18

Warren, Mrs., 158, 252n. 7
Watches, history of, 13, 14; as images, 63, 72, 166–68, 191, 196–97, 200
Watts, George, 210
Webb, Beatrice, 154–55, 158, 165
Webster, Augusta, 155
Whitrow, G. J., 18, 235n. 14
Wickens, G. Glen, 241n. 8
Wilde, Oscar, 92
Wilson, Keith, 242–43n. 14
Winnett, Susan, 207
Woman Question, 3, 32, 111
Woodward, William R., 245n. 4
Woolf, Virginia, 154, 253n. 2
Wotton, George, 243nn. 19, 22, 244n. 28
Wright, Lawrence, 14, 233–34n. 6, 235n. 18
Wright, Terence, 241n. 4, 244n. 30